PRO TOOLS® 10

ADVANCED POST PRODUCTION TECHNIQUES

Joel Krantz

Course Technology PTR

A part of Cengage Learning

COURSE TECHNOLOGY
CENGAGE Learning®

Australia, Brazil, Japan, Korea, Mexico, Singapore, Spain, United Kingdom, United States

COURSE TECHNOLOGY
CENGAGE Learning®

Pro Tools® 10
Advanced Post Production Techniques
Joel Krantz

Publisher and General Manager,
Course Technology PTR:
Stacy L. Hiquet

Associate Director of Marketing:
Sarah Panella

Manager of Editorial Services:
Heather Talbot

Senior Marketing Manager:
Mark Hughes

Acquisitions Editor:
Orren Merton

Project Editors:
Cathleen Small and Kate Shoup

Technical Reviewer:
Justin Fraser

Copy Editor:
Kezia Endsley

Interior Layout:
Shawn Morningstar

Cover Designer:
Mike Tanamachi

DVD-ROM Producer:
Brandon Penticuff

Indexer:
Claudia Self

Proofreader:
Caroline Roop

For product information and technology assistance, contact us at
Cengage Learning Customer & Sales Support, 1-800-354-9706

For permission to use material from this text or product,
submit all requests online at **cengage.com/permissions**
Further permissions questions can be emailed to
permissionrequest@cengage.com

Pro Tools is a registered trademark of Avid Technology Inc.
All other trademarks are the property of their respective owners.

All images © Cengage Learning unless otherwise noted.

Library of Congress Control Number: 2012930787

ISBN-13: 978-1-133-78886-7

ISBN-10: 1-133-78886-6

Course Technology, a part of Cengage Learning
20 Channel Center Street
Boston, MA 02210
USA

Cengage Learning is a leading provider of customized learning solutions with office locations around the globe, including Singapore, the United Kingdom, Australia, Mexico, Brazil, and Japan. Locate your local office at:
international.cengage.com/region

Cengage Learning products are represented in Canada by Nelson Education, Ltd.

For your lifelong learning solutions, visit **courseptr.com.**

Visit our corporate Web site at **cengage.com.**

This book includes material that was developed in part by the Avid Technical Publications department and the Avid Training department.

Printed in the
United States of America
1 2 3 4 5 6 7 14 13 12

This book is dedicated to aspiring and professional sound editors, recording engineers, mixers, audio enthusiasts, and anyone else who loves working with post production sound and Pro Tools.

Acknowledgments

The author would like to acknowledge the following individuals from Avid/Digidesign (current and former), who have provided critical assistance, input, information, and material for this book and its many editions over the years: Simon Sherbourne, Tom Dambly, Eric Kuehnl, Tim Mynett, Andy Cook, Mark Altin, Andy Hagerman, Joe Kay, Jim Metzendorf, Bobby Lombardi, Jordan Glasgow, Curt Raymond, Rich Holmes, Scott Church, Jon Connolly, Ozzie Sutherland, Christopher Woodland, Toby Dunn, Shane Ross, Doug Tissier, Pete Richert, Danny Caccavo, Stan Cotey, Gannon Kashiwa, Scott Wood, Tom Graham, Greg Robles, Mark Jeffery, Paul Foeckler, Rachelle McKenzie, Tim Carroll, Wendy Abowd, and Dave Lebolt.

Special Thanks

Agent MX-Zero exercise materials used for this book provided courtesy of Tom Graham and Avid Technology, Inc. For more information on the making of the film, check out the producer/co-writers blog at http://community.avid.com/blogs/avid/archive/tags/Thomas+Graham/default.aspx.

Schweppes exercise materials courtesy of Directorz|Jeff Bednarz/Director|Editorial: CharlieUniformTango—Jack Waldrip/Editor.

Rob Campbell, for co-authoring portions of this book and the *310M Advanced Music Production Techniques* book, as well as providing editorial comment and advice.

Frank Cook, for offering development editorial advice, templates, and always a voice of reason.

Justin Fraser, for offering extremely thorough and useful editorial comments, which really helped to make the book the best that it could be.

Felix Lau, for helping to prepare and verify the exercise material for this book.

Nate Thomas (my mentor and friend), and the rest of the faculty and staff in the Department of Cinema and Television Arts at California State University, Northridge.

Extra-Special Thanks

Michele Krantz (my wife and best friend) and my daughters (Natalie and Samantha) for putting up with my long hours and time away from the family as I completed this book.

Kudos and extra-special thanks to all Avid Learning Partners and Certified Instructors, who have tirelessly worked with us to help shape this program and who have generously provided their valuable feedback for our courseware.

About the Author

The courseware for this book was developed by **Joel Krantz**, with contributions from numerous Avid staff and independent contractors. The book is published through an ongoing partnership between Cengage Learning and Avid Technology, Inc.

Joel has a diverse background in both music and post production sound. Joel began his career studying Music Education at Susquehanna University (Selinsgrove, PA), where he graduated with a Bachelor of Music degree in 1985. He completed a Master of Music degree in 1998 at New York University, where he studied music composition and music technology. While a student at NYU, Joel began working for Digidesign (now Avid Technology, Inc.) in 1992 as a product specialist and training instructor. Joel began teaching the first company Pro Tools training classes to end users (along with his West Coast counterpart, Shane Ross) shortly after joining Digidesign. The success of these early classes became the template for the current training classes that are offered today.

After leaving Digidesign in 1998, Joel relocated to the Los Angeles area to pursue a career in post production sound. His recent film sound credits include *Déjà vu*, *Sojourn*, and a documentary film, *War of the Gods*, which was recently screened at the 2011 El Sawy International Film Festival in Cairo, Egypt. In addition to working in film sound, Joel has also edited and mixed television promos for Fox Television and DirecTV. Joel is an active member of the Audio Engineering Society (AES), Broadcast Education Association (BEA), Society of Motion Picture & Television Engineers (SMPTE), and the University Film & Video Association (UFVA).

Joel currently serves as a full-time Film Production faculty member in the Department of Cinema and Television Arts at California State University, Northridge. In addition, Joel continues to work as a freelance audio editor and mixer, and teaches as an Avid Certified Expert Instructor at Video Symphony (Burbank, CA). He also continues to consult for Avid as an author, a lecturer, and an Avid Master Instructor, teaching end user Pro Tools instructor certification classes.

Although teaching is his passion, Joel continues to keep himself busy with freelance film and video projects, consulting, publishing, and spending time with his wife Michele, daughters Natalie and Samantha, and chocolate Labrador Retriever, Hershey.

Contents

Exercise 1
Pro Tools HD Hardware Configuration   43

Lesson 2
Troubleshooting a Pro Tools System   47

Exercise 2
Troubleshooting a Pro Tools System 91

Lesson 3
Synchronizing Pro Tools with Linear Video 95

Exercise 3
Synchronizing Pro Tools with Linear Video   137

Lesson 4
Tactile Control of Pro Tools   147

Exercise 4
Tactile Control of Pro Tools   175

Lesson 5
Post Production Recording Techniques   181

Exercise 5
Recording and Editing Foley   193

Lesson 6
Editing Workflows   201

Exercise 6
Sound Effects Design Using Plug-ins   231

Lesson 7
Pro Tools HD/HDX Mixing Concepts   239

Exercise 7
Mixer Experiments   275

Lesson 8
Advanced Mixing Techniques   297

Exercise 8
Advanced Mixing and Routing   345

Lesson 9
Mixing Using Satellite Link   351

Exercise 9
Mixing Using Satellite Link   367

Lesson 10
Advanced Layback   375

Exercise 10
Advanced Layback Options   407

Appendix A
Pro Tools HD-Series Audio Interface Calibration   419

Appendix B
Synchronization Concepts   423

Appendix C
Avid ISIS and Pro Tools Workflows   437

Appendix D
Video Tape Duplication Instructions   451

Appendix E
Answers to Review Questions   455

Index   469

Introduction

Welcome to *Pro Tools 10 Advanced Post Production Techniques* and the Avid Learning Series. Whether you are interested in self study or would like to pursue formal certification through an Avid Learning Partner, this book in the Avid Learning Series provides key information toward attaining the highest level of Avid Pro Tools certification: Expert Certification for Post Production. This book builds on the information provided in the *210P Pro Tools Post Production Techniques* book, providing advanced configuration, troubleshooting, recording, editing, signal routing, and mixing tips, techniques, and workflows for working with post production sound. To complete this course, readers can enroll with an Avid Learning Partner to take the Avid Pro Tools Expert Certification exam for post production (after completing all lower-level certification exams).

The material in this book covers advanced audio post production techniques and workflow principles you need to complete an advanced Pro Tools post production project, from initial setup and configuration of a Pro Tools HD system, through editing, with final mixdown and output. After completing and mastering the material in this final book in the Avid Learning Series, you will be prepared to embark on a career in professional post production sound using Pro Tools.

Using the DVD

The DVD-ROM included with this book contains media files for the exercises that appear at the end of each lesson.

If you purchased an ebook version of this book, you may download the DVD contents from www.courseptr.com/downloads. Please note that you will be redirected to the Cengage Learning site.

Exercise Media

The Exercise Media folder on the DVD provides all the required audio, video, and related media files for the 10 exercises in this book. The exercise session files are all saved as Pro Tools template files (.ptxt), so when opening each exercise file, you will be prompted to save the session to an appropriate storage location. The Completed Exercises folder provides session files of each completed exercise for reference.

Tip: For best playback results, you should copy all the exercise media files to a local hard drive prior to using them.

About the Video Files

With the exception of the linear video lessons and exercises in this book (Lessons and Exercises 3 and 10), which provide an option to use standard definition NTSC or PAL QuickTime video, all the other video files used in the exercises are provided in a high-definition 23.976FPS QuickTime format (1,280×720), referenced to HD 720p–23.976. Although the provided HD video material can also be used with either an NTSC or PAL video reference, this is not an officially recommended or supported Avid workflow.

Prerequisites

This book has been written for use by individual self-learners or students enrolled in the PT310P course at an Avid Learning Partner (ALP). The PT310P course is the fifth course in a series designed to prepare candidates for Pro Tools Expert Certification in Post Production. As such, this book assumes the reader has a thorough understanding of all the concepts covered in the following lower-level courses and books:

- Pro Tools 101: Introduction to Pro Tools

- Pro Tools 110: Pro Tools Production I

- Pro Tools 201: Pro Tools Production II

- Pro Tools 210P: Pro Tools Post Production Techniques

Tip: Readers who have not completed the lower-level courses or obtained equivalent professional experience should seek out an Avid Learning Partner and complete the necessary study to ensure their understanding of the background material required for this book.

System Requirements

The exercises included in this book require access to a system configuration suitable to run Pro Tools HD 10.*x* software using DSP-accelerated PCIe hardware with an Avid SYNC Peripheral, Avid PRE (or other PRE-compatible microphone preamp), a MIDI or USB keyboard, and a single-port (or multi-port) MIDI interface. A professional standard definition (or HD) videotape recorder supporting (RS-422) 9-pin Machine Control is highly recommended (but not required). To verify the most recent system requirements, visit www.avid.com/US/products/Pro-Tools-Software/support.

Becoming Avid Certified

Avid certification is a tangible, industry-recognized credential that can help you advance your career and provide measurable benefits to your employer. When you're Avid certified, you not only help to accelerate and validate your professional development, but you can also improve your productivity and project success.

Avid offers programs supporting certification in dedicated focus areas, including Media Composer, Sibelius, Pro Tools, Worksurface Operation, and Live Sound.

To become certified in Pro Tools, you must enroll in a program at an Avid Learning Partner, where you can complete additional Pro Tools coursework if needed and take your certification exam. For information about how to locate an Avid Learning Partner, please visit www.avid.com/training.

Pro Tools Certification

Avid offers three levels of Pro Tools certification:

- Pro Tools User
- Pro Tools Operator
- Pro Tools Expert

The 100-, 200-, and 300-level Pro Tools courses are designed to prepare candidates for each of these certification levels, respectively.

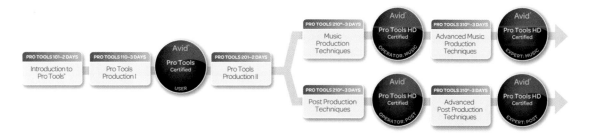

User Certification

User certification prepares individuals to operate a Pro Tools system in an independent production environment.

Courses/books associated with User certification include:

- Pro Tools 101: Introduction to Pro Tools 10
- Pro Tools 110: Pro Tools Production I

These core courses can be complemented with Pro Tools 130, Pro Tools for Game Audio.

Operator Certification

Operator certification prepares engineers and editors to competently operate a Pro Tools system in a professional environment. Candidates can specialize in music production, post production, or both.

Courses/books associated with Operator certification include:

- Pro Tools 201: Pro Tools Production II
- Pro Tools 210M: Music Production Techniques
- Pro Tools 210P: Post Production Techniques

Control surface certification options and a live sound certification option are also available at the Operator level.

Expert Certification

The Expert curriculum offers professionals the highest level of proficiency with individual or networked Pro Tools systems operating in a professional, fast-paced environment. Candidates can specialize in music production, post production, and/or ICON worksurface techniques.

Courses associated with Expert certification include:

- Pro Tools 310M: Advanced Music Production Techniques
- Pro Tools 310P: Advanced Post Production Techniques
- Pro Tools 310I: Advanced ICON Techniques

Pro Tools HD Hardware Configuration

This lesson explains the configuration, features, components, and benefits of Avid's hardware-based DSP-accelerated Pro Tools systems—Pro Tools|HDX and Pro Tools|HD. These systems start with the same Pro Tools software you've learned in other courses, but add purpose-built PCIe expansion cards and audio interfaces (HD I/O, MADI I/O, and HD OMNI) to meet the needs of professional engineers and producers. By adding dedicated processing power and predictable signal routing, Pro Tools|HDX and Pro Tools|HD provide a reliable and scalable system for any professional audio production environment.

Media Used: None

Duration: 90 minutes

GOALS

- Set up and identify the components and connections in a Pro Tools HD hardware system

- Verify system compatibility

- Configure Avid hardware peripherals

- Optimize and configure the settings for a Pro Tools system

- Understand the need and uses for non-administrator (standard) accounts

- Understand Pro Tools session file interchange

Many options and settings affect the reliability of your hardware-based Pro Tools environment. A properly installed and maintained Pro Tools system will provide many hours of trouble-free operation. This lesson discusses the proper way to install and configure a hardware-based Pro Tools system for post production, helping you to avoid costly downtime and allowing your system to operate at peak efficiency.

Setting Up a Pro Tools HD System

When using a Pro Tools HD system, there are a variety of hardware configurations and options that can be used. This section will discuss the supported Pro Tools HD hardware options that are available.

Pro Tools HD/HDX System Basics

As you've learned in earlier courses, Avid offers three types of Pro Tools systems: Pro Tools software systems for personal music and desktop post production, Pro Tools|HD Native systems for medium budget production and post production facilities, and Pro Tools|HDX and Pro Tools|HD systems for the ultimate in professional audio production. Pro Tools|HDX and Pro Tools|HD hardware systems are far more powerful than typical host-based systems; however, the systems are also more complex and can include a variety of interconnected components and interfaces.

Pro Tools HD Terminology

Throughout this course book, we use the term *Pro Tools* to refer to the standard Pro Tools software running on any supported hardware configuration. We use the term *Pro Tools HD* to refer to Pro Tools HD software running on a supported system. When referring to previous-generation Pro Tools HD PCIe hardware (such as HD Core and HD Accel PCIe cards), the phrase *Pro Tools|HD hardware* is used. When referring to the newest generation of (non-Native) Pro Tools HD PCIe hardware, the phrase *Pro Tools|HDX hardware* is used. Finally, when referring collectively to all Pro Tools HD PCIe hardware (Pro Tools|HD, Pro Tools|HDX, and Pro Tools|HD Native), the phrase *Pro Tools HD PCIe hardware* will be used.

Pro Tools 10 Systems Comparison

Pro Tools software (excluding Pro Tools HD) is sold separately from the hardware, allowing you to run it on a wide range of digital audio hardware platforms including Avid, M-Audio, Core Audio, ASIO, Pro Tools|HD Native, Pro Tools|HD, and Pro Tools|HDX.

Note: Only Pro Tools|HDX, Pro Tools|HD, and Pro Tools|HD Native hardware support
Pro Tools HD software.

Table 1.1 compares the features of the different Pro Tools platforms, allowing you
to judge which platform will work best for a given project.

Components of Pro Tools HD PCIe Hardware Systems

In order to achieve greater power and flexibility, Pro Tools|HDX and Pro Tools|HD
PCIe hardware require various core components. Optional components are available to expand the capabilities of the system as needed.

Basic System Components

Although the various configurations of Pro Tools|HDX and Pro Tools|HD systems
have different input and output capacities, track counts, and plug-in and mixer
processing, all systems must include the following basic system components: the
computer, the Pro Tools software, and one or more storage volumes.

- **Computer.** All Pro Tools systems require a qualified Mac or Windows computer for basic operation. The computer houses the Pro Tools HD PCIe
  hardware (cards), runs the Pro Tools software, and carries out related host
  processing tasks, such as running Native (host-based) plug-ins and virtual
  instruments.

- **Pro Tools Software.** Pro Tools Software handles the display, recording, playback, editing, and mixing of audio and MIDI data, controls audio interfaces
  and synchronization peripherals, manages digital signal processing and software plug-in controls, routes system inputs and outputs, and controls operation of the hard drives.

- **Storage Volumes.** All Pro Tools systems require at least one or more Avid-
  compatible storage volumes, in addition to the storage device used to boot
  your system. (The actual number of volumes required depends on the track
  count of the system, as well as the Disk Cache setting.) Although the Pro
  Tools software will be installed on the boot or system drive, recording to and
  playing back audio and video from this drive is not recommended. Additional
  networked or local storage volumes should be connected and dedicated to
  the recording and playback of audio and video. For the best performance,
  separate storage volumes for both audio and video playback/record are highly
  recommended.

Table 1.1 Pro Tools 10 Features Comparison Chart

Capabilities	Pro Tools Software	Pro Tools Software with Complete Production Toolkit	Pro Tools HD Software with HDINative Hardware	Pro Tools HD Software with Pro Tools|HD Hardware	Pro Tools HD Software with Pro Tools|HDX Hardware
Maximum number of voices (at 44.1/48kHz)	96 mono or stereo	256	256	192	256/HDX card (768 maximum)
Total number of voiceable tracks (at 44.1/48kHz)	128	768	768	768	768
Maximum number of Auxiliary Input tracks	128	512	512	512	512
Maximum number of Master Fader tracks	64	64	64	64	64
Total I/O channels	Up to 32	Up to 32	Up to 64	Up to 160	Up to 192
Maximum sample rates	Up to 192kHz	Up to 192kHz	Up to 192kHz	Up to 192kHz	Up to 192kHz
Maximum Automatic Delay Compensation (at 44.1/48kHz)	16,383 samples	16,383 samples	16,383 samples	4095 samples	16,383 samples
Maximum internal mix buses	256	256	256	256	256

Pro Tools HD PCIe Hardware Components

The Pro Tools HD software is compatible with a number of different Pro Tools HD PCIe cards, which are discussed here:

- **Pro Tools|HD Native PCIe Card.** The Pro Tools|HD Native Core card, shown in Figure 1.1, is the main card of a Pro Tools|HD Native hardware system. The Pro Tools|HD Native Core card provides up to 256 tracks of recording or playback, with a maximum of 768 total tracks in a session. The Pro Tools|HD Native Core card also provides 64 channels of I/O to the system, supporting a total of four HD-series audio interfaces. Unlike Pro Tools|HD DSP-based hardware systems, Pro Tools|HD Native hardware systems are not expandable, supporting only a single Pro Tools|HD Native Core card in the system. Also, since the Pro Tools|HD Native card has no built-in DSP processing for plug-ins, it relies entirely on the host for plug-in processing power.

Figure 1.1
Pro Tools|HD Native Core card.

**In the Avid
Learning Series**
For more information about Pro Tools|HD Native hardware systems, consult the Pro Tools 200-level course books or visit www.avid.com/protools.

- **Pro Tools|HDX PCIe Card.** The HDX PCIe card, shown in Figure 1.2, is the newest generation of DSP-accelerated Pro Tools hardware, and is the main card of an HDX-based system. You must have at least one HDX PCIe card installed in an Avid-qualified computer or expansion chassis, although you can add more HDX PCIe cards for expanded track counts, expanded I/O, and increased DSP processing power (at the time of print, up to a maximum of three). Each HDX PCIe card installed in the system provides up to 256 simultaneous record/play tracks (at 44.1/48kHz), with up to 768 tracks maximum in a three-card system. The HDX card supports up to 32-bit, 192kHz Pro Tools sessions. In addition, each HDX card provides two DigiLink mini ports for connecting up to four HD audio interfaces, providing up to 64 channels of I/O per card, with a three-card system supporting a maximum of 192 channels of I/O. Each HDX card includes 18 DSP chips that have double the processing power of previous generation Accel DSP chips, so adding multiple HDX cards to a single system greatly expands the total available DSP processing power of the system.

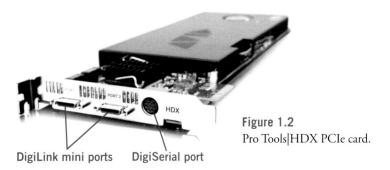

DigiLink mini ports   DigiSerial port

Figure 1.2
Pro Tools|HDX PCIe card.

Caution: You cannot combine Pro Tools|HDX PCIe cards with Pro Tools|HD Core/Accel PCIe cards in the same system. The newer generation HDX PCIe cards can only be combined with other cards of the same type.

■ **Pro Tools|HD Core Card.** The previous generation HD Core card is the base card of a Pro Tools|HD DSP-accelerated system. The Pro Tools|HD Core card, shown in Figure 1.3, provides up to 96 simultaneous tracks of audio recording or playback (at 44.1/48kHz). The HD Core card also provides 32 channels of I/O to the system, supporting up to two HD-series audio interfaces.

Figure 1.3
Pro Tools|HD PCIe Core card.

Note: A single Pro Tools|HD Core card can be installed in a system with up to six additional HD Accel cards. Pro Tools|HDX PCIe cards are not compatible with any other Pro Tools|HD PCIe cards.

■ **Pro Tools|HD Accel Card.** Previous generation Pro Tools|HD hardware systems with HD Core cards installed can use one or more HD Accel cards to expand the capacity and power of the system. Like HDX PCIe cards, these cards can expand the number of simultaneous record/play tracks (up to 192 tracks maximum at 44.1/48kHz), allow additional I/O (up to 160 channels), and expand the available DSP processing power. Up to six HD Accel cards can be installed in a single Pro Tools|HD hardware system (in addition to the HD Core card), for a total of seven cards in a supported expansion chassis. HD Accel cards provide support for DSP-based plug-ins and have more powerful DSP chips than the older generation HD Process cards, although they are not as powerful as the newer generation HDX PCIe cards. (See Figure 1.4.)

Figure 1.4
HD Accel PCIe card.

Caution: Pro Tools|HD hardware supports only TDM DSP plug-ins, and does not
         support AAX DSP plug-ins. Likewise, Pro Tools|HDX hardware supports
         only AAX DSP plug-ins, and does not support TDM DSP plug-ins.

Pro Tools HD Audio Interfaces

As mentioned in the previous section, a Pro Tools HD system's I/O can be expanded with additional HD-series audio interfaces.

■ **HD Audio Interfaces.** All Pro Tools HD hardware systems require at least one rack-mountable HD-series audio interface that handles analog-to-digital and digital-to-analog conversion of input and output signals. The audio interface allows you to connect Pro Tools to the rest of your studio. The HD-series audio interfaces currently available include the HD I/O (shown in Figure 1.5), HD MADI, and HD OMNI. The HD I/O interface comes in three configurations:

  ● 8 analog in × 8 analog out × 8 digital in/out

  ● 16 analog in × 16 analog out

  ● 16 digital in × 16 digital out

Figure 1.5
Pro Tools HD I/O interface.

Pro Tools|HD Hardware Future Support

Previous generation HD Core/Accel PCIe and HD-series interfaces such as the 192 I/O and 96 I/O are currently supported in Pro Tools 10 and are still commonly used. In future software releases beyond Pro Tools 10, previous generation Pro Tools|HD hardware may still work, but it will not be officially tested or supported by Avid.

Multiple audio interfaces can be added to all Pro Tools HD systems to increase the number of I/O channels available. For example, with a three card HDX system, you can have 12 HD I/Os connected for 192 channels of input/output, or three MADI I/Os for 192 channels of MADI.

Note: On all Pro Tools HD hardware systems, only a single **HD OMNI** interface can be used, with or without additional HD audio interfaces.

In the Avid Learning Series   For a review of the available Pro Tools HD-series audio interfaces, please consult the Pro Tools 201 course book or visit www.avid.com/protools.

Optional Pro Tools HD Hardware Components

In addition to the Pro Tools HD PCIe hardware components and HD-series audio interface options mentioned in the previous sections, you can also add the following optional hardware components to any HD hardware system.

■ **PRE.** The Avid PRE is an eight-channel preamp designed specifically for the Pro Tools HD environment. PRE accepts microphone, line, and direct instrument (DI) level inputs on all eight channels and can be placed anywhere in the studio. Furthermore, the PRE can be remote controlled through MIDI using settings stored and recalled with sessions.

Tip: Configuration and usage of the Avid PRE is discussed later in this lesson and in Lesson 5.

■ **SYNC HD.** SYNC HD and the older SYNC I/O are common multi-purpose synchronization peripherals for synchronizing Pro Tools HD hardware systems to a variety of devices. SYNC HD supports both standard definition (SD) and high definition (HD) video reference, making it ideal for Pro Tools HD system installations in modern post production facilities. While SYNC HD supports all major industry-standard clock sources and timecode formats, the previous generation SYNC I/O only supports SD reference rates.

Tip: Configuration and usage of the SYNC HD with linear video is discussed in Lesson 3.

Benefits of Pro Tools DSP-Accelerated Hardware Systems

Pro Tools HD systems using DSP-accelerated PCIe cards offer a significant performance advantage over both standard Pro Tools software systems and Pro Tools|HD Native systems, including expandability to incorporate up to 192 channels of I/O; optional expansion cards for real-time audio processing on dedicated DSP chips; and incredible low latency control—all of which give Pro Tools HDX hardware the ability to handle the largest post production tasks.

Pro Tools|HDX hardware systems utilize Avid's dedicated DSP hardware and custom Field Programmable Gate Array (FPGA) technology to carry out real-time signal routing, mixing, and processing of multiple audio signals. The FPGA technology of Pro Tools|HDX hardware provides ultra low audio latency and greatly expands the audio throughput and signal routing capabilities of the system.

 Lesson 7 provides more detailed information about Pro Tools|HD and HDX hardware signal routing and the DSP-based processing power in the Pro Tools HD mixer.

The power of a Pro Tools HD system comes from a combination of Pro Tools HD software and the Pro Tools HD PCIe hardware components. As previously discussed, the capabilities of a Pro Tools|HDX hardware system can be increased by installing additional HDX PCIe cards. Because Pro Tools|HDX hardware systems can utilize the DSP-based processing power on the HDX cards in addition to the Native (host-based) processing power of the computer, they are the most powerful Pro Tools systems ever built.

System Compatibility Information

Ensuring rock solid reliability and stability with your Pro Tools system starts with making sure you are using Avid tested and approved hardware and software. The components of a Pro Tools HD system, such as the computer, hard drives, and a range of hardware and software options, are subject to compatibility requirements, which reflect configurations of Avid products and third-party products that have been tested and qualified by Avid.

For the latest compatibility information, visit the Avid website at www.avid.com or from within the Pro Tools 10 software, choose Help > Avid Knowledgebase. Support information can be found under the Support & Services link on the Avid website. The Avid support section is arranged by Avid product family (for example Pro Tools, Media Composer, Euphonix, and Pinnacle).

Tip: You can access additional help options from within the Pro Tools 10 software by choosing Help > Avid Audio Forums and Help > Customer Assist.

Pro Tools|HD/HDX Hardware Installation

Every Pro Tools expert should be comfortable installing Pro Tools hardware and software. For Pro Tools operators early in their career, this level of technical skill will open the door to many opportunities. For experienced engineers and mixers, being able to maintain and troubleshoot a system is also essential to keep sessions running smoothly.

To install the hardware for a Pro Tools|HDX system:

1. Install the HDX PCIe cards into your computer before installing Pro Tools software. HDX PCIe cards require power beyond what the PCIe bus can deliver. A custom power cable (included) is used to connect HDX PCIe cards to the optional power connector on the motherboard in your Mac or to a hard drive power source in your PC. For systems with more than one HDX PCIe card, each card will require a connection to the power source utilizing the single power cable. (See Figure 1.6.)

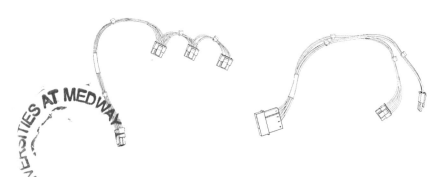

Figure 1.6
HDX PCIe card Mac power cable (left) and PC power cable (right).

2. If you are using multiple HDX cards, the cards must be interconnected using an HDX TDM cable. The cable can be installed only one way, so look for the IN and OUT ports on each card as well as the connector. (See Figure 1.7.)

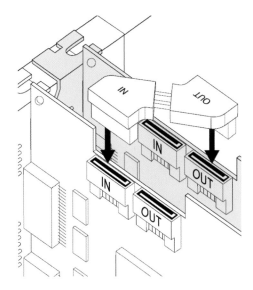

Figure 1.7
Connecting two HDX PCIe cards with an HDX TDM cable.

3. Once the cards are installed, connect the HD-series audio interface(s) using the DigiLink cable(s) included with each HD-series audio interface. If you are using multiple audio interfaces or a SYNC HD, also connect the Loop Sync cables at this point. (See Figure 1.8.)

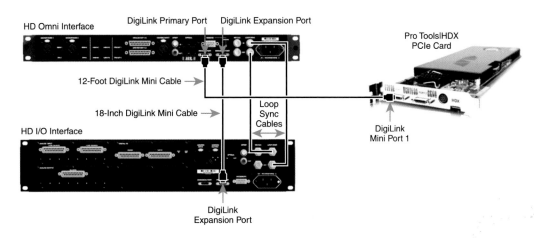

Figure 1.8
Connecting HD-series interfaces with DigiLink and Loop Sync cables.

Tip: You can find details on how to install, connect, and configure the components of a Pro Tools HD PCIe hardware system in the Pro Tools|HDX, HD, and HD Native Quick Start Guides.

Tip: On Mac systems only, an Avid-approved Blackmagic Design PCIe video card can be installed along with Pro Tools HD PCIe hardware in any available slot after all Pro Tools HD PCIe cards have been installed.

Pro Tools HD Post System Configuration

The system diagram in Figure 1.9 shows a configuration for a full-featured post production system with Pro Tools|HDX PCIe hardware, peripherals, and Avid Mojo SDI video subsystem. Connections between the components of the system are also shown in schematic form.

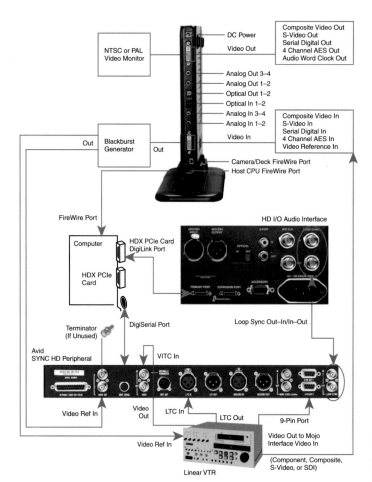

Figure 1.9

Avid Mojo SDI and Pro Tools|HDX post production system.

Tip: Connecting the LTC Out from the VTR to the SYNC Peripheral LTC In is not
required if Serial Timecode is enabled as the positional reference in the
Session Setup window.

Tip: The Video Ref ports are non-terminated loop-through connections. If the
Video Ref Out port is not used, you must terminate it using the included
75-ohm BNC terminator.

Tip: In addition to Avid Mojo SDI, Pro Tools 10 also supports the Blackmagic
DeckLink Extreme and Intensity Pro video cards on Mac systems. For a
complete list of Pro Tools supported video cards, go to www.avid.com.

Tip: If using a Blackmagic Design PCIe video card with Pro Tools, it is recommended that you connect the Video Reference clock out from the SYNC HD
to the Video Reference in on the Blackmagic Design card, so that Pro Tools
and the video card are using the same video clock reference.

Configuring Avid Peripherals

When using Pro Tools HD PCIe hardware, there are a number of optional Avid
hardware peripherals that can be connected to the system, providing additional features and functionality. These peripherals must be set up and configured properly
before you attempt to use them with your system.

SYNC HD and Tri-Level Sync

SYNC HD provides input for system clock reference using either standard definition (SD) video reference or high definition (HD) video reference (Tri-Level
sync), connected to the Sync HD's Video Ref connector. Because there is only one
available Video Ref (In) connector (the other is used for optional loop-through to
another device), only one video clock reference can be connected at a time (either
SD Video Reference or HD Video Reference).

Note: The original SYNC I/O does not support HD sync (Tri-Level sync) and does
not offer an upgrade path. You must have a SYNC HD for this option to be
available in the Clock Reference menu.

To set the clock reference to an HD video reference signal:

1. In Pro Tools, choose SETUP > SESSION.

2. In the **SYNC SETUP** section of the Session Setup window, choose VIDEO REFERENCE (HD) from the CLOCK REFERENCE pop-up menu, as shown in Figure 1.10.

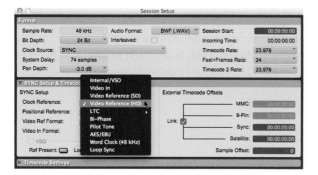

Figure 1.10
Clock Reference options in the Session Setup window.

3. Choose the video reference rate from the VIDEO REF FORMAT pop-up menu. When the clock reference is set to VIDEO REFERENCE (HD), the video reference rates shown in Figure 1.11 are available in the VIDEO IN FORMAT pop-up menu.

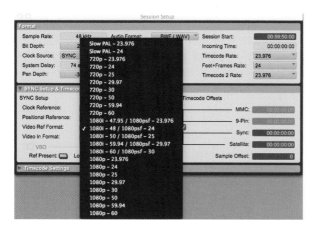

Figure 1.11
Video reference rate options when the clock reference is set to Video Reference HD.

Matching HD Reference Rate Settings

When working in Tri-Level sync environments, whether using an HD video tape recorder or non-linear HD media (QuickTime HD or Avid DNxHD), you should set your Tri-Level sync source to the same rate you are using. For example, when using a Sony HDCAM SR deck at 1080P with a frame rate of 23.976FPS, Pro

Tools should be set for Video Ref Format = 1080p – 23.976. Similarly, when using a QuickTime HD 1080i file with a frame rate of 23.976FPS, the sync generator and Pro Tools should be set for 1080i – 47.95/1080psf – 23.976.

For more information about HD video and digital television standards, visit the Advanced Television Systems Committee's website at http://www.atsc.org.

PRE

PRE (shown in Figure 1.12 and Figure 1.13) is an eight-channel remote controllable microphone preamplifier designed by Avid. Although PRE is designed to be integrated into Pro Tools systems, it can also be utilized as a standalone mic preamp. PRE and other third-party PRE-compatible microphone preamps are ideally suited to working with Pro Tools, because they can be controlled from within the Pro Tools application and from an Avid worksurface. Additionally, any mic preamp settings are stored with the session and can be recalled with the session.

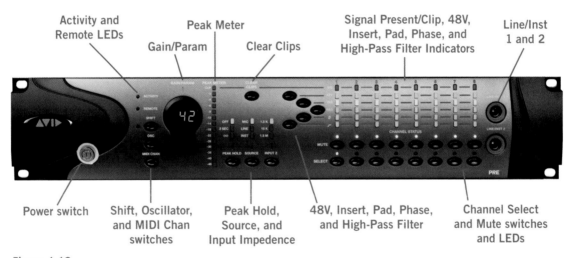

Figure 1.12
PRE front panel.

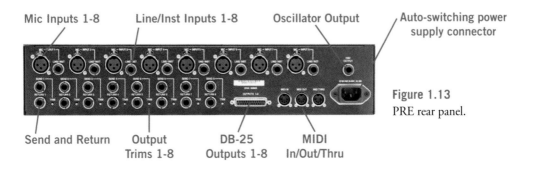

Figure 1.13
PRE rear panel.

Tip: Although this section details the connection and configuration of an Avid **PRE** for use with Pro Tools, other third-party **PRE**-compatible microphones preamps would be configured in a similar way.

Connecting to Pro Tools

There are four steps in setting up PRE to be controlled by Pro Tools:

1. Make audio and MIDI connections to PRE.

2. Configure the MIDI settings.

3. Declare PRE in the Peripherals dialog box.

4. Map PRE outputs to an audio interface's inputs within the I/O Setup dialog box.

Each step is discussed in more detail in the following sections.

Making Audio Connections

To use PRE as a preamp in a Pro Tools system, the PRE's DB25 audio output must be physically connected to analog inputs on an audio interface (such as an HD I/O) in your Pro Tools system or through a patchbay that is then connected to Pro Tools inputs (see Figure 1.14). The PRE does not have any A/D converters and is an analog-only device.

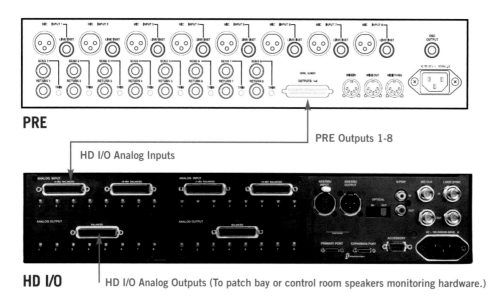

Figure 1.14
Avid PRE outputs connected to an HD I/O interface's inputs.

If the audio interface that the PRE is connected to has more than eight analog inputs (like an HD I/O with an extra analog input card), be sure to note which inputs are being connected to the PRE. Pro Tools uses the input channel association to understand which mic pre channel to control. This routing association between the PRE output and audio interface input is made through the mic-preamps page of the I/O Setup dialog box.

Using PRE with D-Command or D-Control

After connecting a PRE to an HD-series audio interface, the interface outputs are then connected to the main inputs on the XMON interface, allowing control room monitoring using the D-Command/D-Control.

 PRE control using the Pro Tools software is covered later in this book.

Making MIDI Connections

Remote control commands are sent to PRE over a standard MIDI connection. To facilitate this communication, the Pro Tools computer requires a compatible MIDI interface.

Connecting a Single PRE

When connecting a single Avid PRE, the unit can be connected to any available MIDI IN and OUT ports on your MIDI Interface.

To connect a PRE to a MIDI interface:

1. Make sure that a MIDI interface is connected and configured.

 Refer to the MIDI interface's reference guide for information on how to connect and configure the interface.

2. Connect a MIDI cable between the MIDI OUT port on your PRE and a MIDI IN port on your MIDI interface.

3. Connect a MIDI cable between the MIDI IN port on your PRE and a MIDI OUT port on your MIDI interface.

Connecting Multiple PREs

Up to nine PREs can be accessed by Pro Tools. When connecting multiple PREs, each PRE can be connected to a separate MIDI IN/OUT port on a multi-port MIDI interface. In this configuration, when using separate dedicated MIDI ports for each PRE, MIDI channel number assignments can be the same or different. As an alternative, when only a single MIDI IN/OUT port is available, multiple PREs can be daisy-chained through a single shared MIDI IN/OUT port, in which case, each PRE must be assigned a unique MIDI channel number.

To daisy-chain multiple PREs using a single shared MIDI port:

1. Connect a MIDI interface MIDI OUT port to the first PRE's MIDI IN.

2. Connect the first PRE's MIDI OUT to the second PRE's MIDI IN. Repeat for each additional PRE that needs to be connected to the system.

3. Connect the last PRE's MIDI OUT to a MIDI IN port on your MIDI interface.

Configuring MIDI

If you are using multiple PREs, set each unit to a unique MIDI channel number. Keep in mind that if multiple PRE units are set to the same MIDI channel daisy-chained through one single shared MIDI IN/OUT port, they will not be able to receive messages to change their controls and settings independently. In other words, changing a setting on one unit will change that setting on all units set to the same MIDI channel.

Setting the PRE MIDI Channel

To set global receive/transmit MIDI channel on PRE:

1. Power on PRE.

2. On the PRE front panel, press **MIDI Chan**. The LED should be lit; if not, press and release again. The Gain/Param display will display the current MIDI channel (1–16).

3. Turn the **Gain/Param** control to change the MIDI channel. Turning the **Gain/Param** control will step through MIDI channel numbers. The channel will be set once you stop moving the control; you do not need to press an **Enter** key to set the channel.

4. Press **MIDI Chan** to exit MIDI Channel mode.

5. Repeat the previous steps for any additional PREs. Once completed, you must configure the PRE in AMS (Mac) or MSS (Windows).

Configuring PRE in the MIDI Studio

Next you will launch and configure the MIDI Studio for your PRE.

To configure AMS (Mac) or MSS (Windows) from within Pro Tools:

1. Choose **SETUP > MIDI > MIDI STUDIO**. AMS or MSS will launch, as appropriate for your system (Mac or Windows, respectively).

2. Add a new device. For convenience, you can choose **DIGIDESIGN** for the **MANUFACTURER** and **PRE** for the **MODEL** when specifying the properties for the new device. On a Mac, this will insert a picture of the PRE in the device page. If you have multiple PREs (as shown in Figure 1.15), be sure to give each a unique name so you can distinguish between them later.

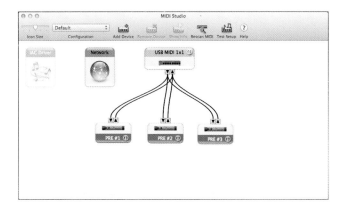

Figure 1.15
Multiple PREs in AMS using a single shared MIDI port.

3. Create your studio setup.

   - **In AMS (Mac).** Draw cable connections between the device icons so that the AMS graphical display accurately represents your actual MIDI connections.

   - **In MSS (Windows).** Select each PRE in turn and choose the port they are connected to (this will be the same for each PRE). Choose which Send and Receive channels the PRE is operating on (this will be different for each PRE). Figure 1.16 shows the MIDI Studio Setup window.

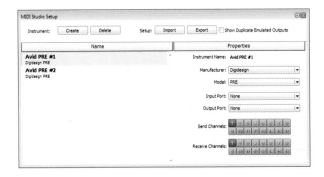

Figure 1.16
Configuring PRE in
MIDI Studio Setup.

Declaring PRE for Pro Tools Software

After PRE is configured in AMS/MSS, it needs to be declared in the Pro Tools
Peripherals dialog box before it can be mapped in the I/O Setup dialog box.

To declare PRE as a peripheral in Pro Tools:

1. Choose SETUP > PERIPHERALS.

2. Click on the MIC PREAMPS tab. The Mic Preamps tab is shown in Figure 1.17.

3. Choose PRE from the TYPE pop-up menu.

4. From the RECEIVE FROM pop-up menu, choose PRE's source port and a
   MIDI channel (derived from the AMS/MSS MIDI setup) to receive data.

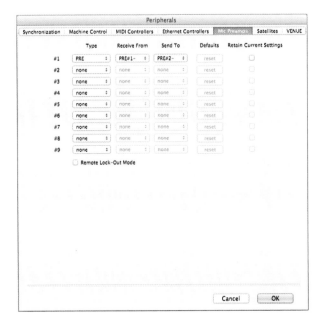

Figure 1.17
Peripherals dialog box:
Mic Preamps tab.

5. From the **SEND TO** pop-up menu, choose a destination port (this will be the same device that you chose in the previous step), and a MIDI channel to transmit data.

6. Repeat steps 3–5 for any additional PREs.

7. Click **OK**.

Additional Options in the Peripherals Dialog Box

In addition to declaring PRE in the Peripherals dialog box, you can also set the following options:

- **Reset.** Press Reset to return PRE parameters to their defaults. Resetting takes place immediately; you do not need to press OK to reset parameters.

- **Retain Current Settings.** If this setting is enabled and you open a session, the PRE settings will not be changed. However, if you save the session, any PRE settings that were in the session will now be overwritten with the current session. Also, if you create a new session with Retain Current Settings enabled, the new session will inherit the PRE settings.

- **Remote Lock-Out Mode.** Select Remote Lock-Out Mode to disable front panel controls from being used to control PRE. Lock-Out mode does not occur until you click OK to close the Peripherals dialog box.

Tip: PRE can be taken out of Remote Lock-Out mode by unchecking the Remote Lock-Out Mode box in the Pro Tools Peripherals dialog box or by powering PRE off and then back on.

Global Preferences for PRE

All front panel settings are stored in the Pro Tools session, but a number of other settings are stored in the Pro Tools system's global preferences. It is important to note which settings these are, as they may change when the session is moved to a different Pro Tools system.

The following settings are stored in the global preferences:

- Number of PREs declared

- Lockout state

- Retain Current Setting state

- Online/Offline status

- Output assignments

Mapping PRE Outputs to an Audio Interface in I/O Setup

PRE outputs must manually be mapped to the HD-series interface inputs before
their audio and remote controls will be available within Pro Tools.

To map PRE output to the HD-series interfaces input:

1. Choose SETUP > I/O SETUP.

2. Click the MIC PREAMPS tab (shown in Figure 1.18).

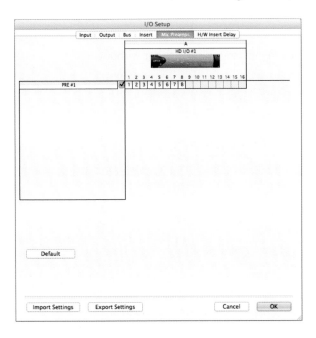

Figure 1.18
I/O Setup: Mic Preamps tab.

3. Click on the box directly under the interface inputs that are connected to
   the PRE.

4. Repeat for each of the PRE paths that are connected to the Pro Tools system.

Mic preamp paths can be:

■ Renamed, for easier identification after changing or renaming audio interfaces.

■ Remapped to different input destinations.

■ Deactivated (or reactivated) to manage unavailable or unused I/O resources.

Mic preamp paths cannot be:

■ Deleted.

■ Exported or imported with an I/O setup.

If you have multiple PRE units in the I/O setup, the order in which PRE paths appear follows the order in which they were assigned in the Mic Preamps tab of the Peripherals dialog box.

Using PRE in Standalone Mode

PRE can be used as a standalone mic/line/instrument preamplifier, either without Pro Tools or with Pro Tools when a MIDI connection is not available for remote control. At power up, PRE units in standalone mode default to the settings they had when last powered down.

Connecting Audio Sources and Adjusting PRE Parameters

Most PRE parameters can be changed using the front panel switches, from the Pro Tools software, or using an approved Avid worksurface. In the following sections, all PRE channel parameters are controlled using the front panel switches.

Tip: Controlling a PRE from the Pro Tools software is covered in Lesson 5.

To edit channel controls:

1. Press the **SELECT** switch for the channel you want to edit. You can select multiple channels for simultaneous editing by holding **SHIFT** while selecting channels.

2. Press a channel control switch to change its current setting. For example, if the 48V LED is off, pressing **48V** will enable phantom power for all the selected channels.

Connecting Microphones

To connect a microphone as an audio source:

1. Press the **CHANNEL SELECT** switch for the mic input you will be using.

2. Change the input source to **MIC**, by pressing **SOURCE** one or more times.

3. Make sure the gain is turned down, especially if the monitors are turned up.

4. Verify that 48V phantom power is disabled. Press **48V**, so that the LED is off.

5. Plug a microphone directly into the Mic input on the back of the PRE. These inputs accept XLR connections.

6. If your microphone requires phantom power, press **48V**.

7. Turn the **GAIN/PARAM** control to raise the gain. Use the Peak Meter to determine the proper level.

Connecting Line Level and Instrument Level Sources

To connect a line/instrument level audio source:

1. Press the **CHANNEL SELECT** switch for the Line/Inst Input you will be using.

2. Change the Input source to **LINE** or **INST**, by pressing **SOURCE** one or more times.

3. Plug a line level source (such as a DVD player), or a DI source (such as a guitar) into a Line/Inst Input on the front or back of PRE. These inputs accept balanced/unbalanced TRS connectors.

4. Turn the **GAIN/PARAM** control to raise the gain. Use the Peak Meter to determine the proper level.

Adjusting Input Gain

To set the input gain on a channel:

1. If the Gain/Param display currently shows a MIDI channel, press **MIDI**. The display should now show an input gain level.

2. Press the **SELECT** switch for the channel you want to adjust.

3. Rotate the **GAIN/PARAM** control to adjust the input gain.

Audio Interface Calibration

The installation and connection of audio interfaces is considered to be part of the basic Pro Tools HD system installation (covered earlier in this lesson). However, included here is a section on how and why to calibrate the input and output levels of your interfaces.

I/O Calibration Example

Pro Tools 201 discussed the importance of selecting the correct input operating levels when connecting analog signals from external devices. For example, the HD I/O's analog inputs (and outputs) can be switched in the Hardware Setup dialog box between +4dBu, and –10dBV. However, within these general operating standards, the HD I/O's input and output levels can be trimmed up or down by several decibels. There are three reasons you might do this:

- To ensure the operating levels are equal on all channels.

- To match the interface's input and output levels to the optimum working levels and headroom of external equipment.

- To conform to particular industry or regional standards.

Tip: Only the HD I/O and the previous generation 192 I/O audio interfaces support reference level calibration on both input and output. The HD OMNI interface supports only speaker/monitor output calibration. All other HD-series audio interfaces have fixed calibrations that cannot be altered.

Some Notes about Calibration

Traditionally, the operating levels of different pieces of analog equipment (such as a recorder and mixing desk) are adjusted so that their nominal 0VU levels match. Ideally, they will have the same amount of headroom, so signals from one device cannot clip the circuitry on the other. The situation is less clear with digital equipment like Pro Tools, which effectively has no headroom in the sense used for analog equipment.

The maximum signal level that Pro Tools can encode is given the designation 0 decibels, Full Scale (dBFS), and there is no headroom above this. Anything louder than 0dBFS is clipped. Trim controls on the HD I/O interface allow you to adjust the voltage that represents the 0dBFS point, allowing you to calibrate the operating levels of Pro Tools with external analog equipment.

The most common industry standards for calibration are 0VU (referenced to either +4dBu nominal or +6dBu peak) calibrated to –18dBFS), –20dBFS, or –22dBFS. After choosing a calibration reference level, you will need to calibrate the analog inputs and outputs of your audio interfaces. After calibration is complete, you can choose analog input or output reference levels of either +4dBU or –10dBV in the Hardware Setup window (shown in Figure 1.19).

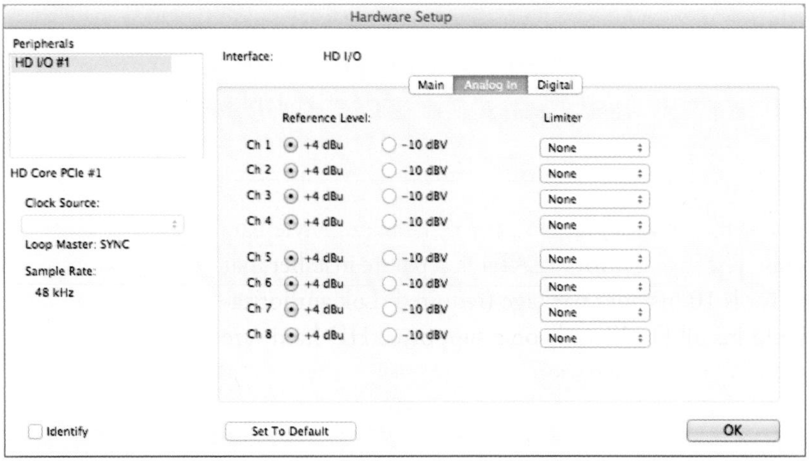

Figure 1.19
Hardware Setup,
Analog In page.

Tip: HD I/O interfaces are factory calibrated so that their +4dBu inputs are set for 20dB headroom above +4dBu/0VU.

 For more information about calibration and step-by-step directions for calibrating an HD audio interface, refer to Appendix A, "Pro Tools HD-Series Audio Interface Calibration."

Verifying Installation of Additional Pro Tools Software Options

When installing Pro Tools HD software, the Pro Tools installer provides an additional software option called the Avid Video Engine, which supports Avid video record/playback using Avid Mojo or Mojo SDI. To verify if the Avid Video Engine is installed, look for a folder called Video Engine installed in the following directory:

- **Windows.** C:\ (or other System Boot Drive)\Program Files\Avid\Pro Tools \DAE\Video Engine

- **Mac.** System Boot Drive/Library/Application Support/Avid/Video Engine

In addition to the Avid Video Engine install option, you can also enable and use the Satellite Link option and Machine Control if you purchased the corresponding iLok authorizations. These two options do not require any additional software installation. Instead, they can be enabled in the software only if a valid iLok authorization is found.

Later in this book, you will learn about Machine Control and using Satellite Link Option for mixing.

The HEAT software option is available for Pro Tools HD DSP-based hardware systems only. HEAT, which stands for Harmonically Enhanced Algorithm Technology, is an add-on installed in the *Plug-Ins* folder of your system. After installation, HEAT is enabled in the *Options* menu, allowing you to apply analog-style harmonic distortion to your mixes. The installer for HEAT is a separate installer that is included as part of the Pro Tools 10 installer package (required iLok authorization sold separately). You should install HEAT only on a supported HD hardware system containing a valid HEAT iLok authorization.

 Using HEAT is beyond the scope of this book. For more information about HEAT, consult the "HEAT Option Guide" in the Pro Tools Documentation

On the Web folder or visit www.avid.com. (Click the Support & Services link.)

Windows 7 System Optimization

There are a number of steps that Avid suggests you take to optimize your computer system for use with Pro Tools. Some of these steps are listed in the following sections, but the full steps required to make these adjustments (plus some optional optimizations) can be found in the Mac and Windows 7 optimization guides in the Avid Knowledge Base.

Windows 7 Required Optimizations

In order to ensure that your Pro Tools HD software runs without problems, the following optimizations are required.

Tip: After changing Windows system settings, you will need to restart your computer.

Optimize Hard Disk Performance

This optimization allows your hard drive to work more efficiently when recording and playing back audio files, and can sometimes resolve DAE Error –9073.

To optimize hard disk performance:

1. Open the START menu and choose COMPUTER.

2. Right-click on the **C:** drive.

3. Choose PROPERTIES.

4. Uncheck COMPRESS THIS DRIVE TO SAVE SPACE.

5. Uncheck ALLOW FILES ON THIS DRIVE TO HAVE CONTENTS INDEXED.

6. Click APPLY and then click OK.

Disable User Account Control (UAC)

Turning off UAC can help with the "Session must be on an audio record volume" error and various issues with launching Pro Tools.

To turn off user account control:

1. Choose START > CONTROL PANEL.

2. Click USER ACCOUNTS AND FAMILY SAFETY.

3. Click USER ACCOUNTS.

4. Click on CHANGE USER ACCOUNT CONTROL SETTINGS.

5. Set the slider to NEVER NOTIFY.

6. Click OK.

7. Restart the computer.

Configuring System Standby and Power Management

When using Pro Tools, the Windows System Standby power scheme must be set to *Always On*. This prevents long record passes from stopping due to system resources powering down.

To configure Windows power management:

1. Choose START > CONTROL PANEL.

2. Click POWER OPTIONS, as shown in Figure 1.20.

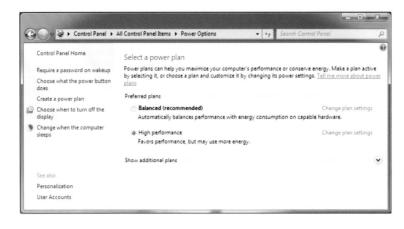

Figure 1.20
Windows 7 Control Panel
Power Options.

3. In the PREFERRED PLANS section, select HIGH PERFORMANCE.

4. Click CHANGE PLAN SETTINGS.

5. Click CHANGE ADVANCED POWER SETTINGS.

6. In the POWER OPTIONS dialog box, choose HARD DISK > TURN OFF HARD DISK AFTER.

7. Click the SETTING option.

8. Select the value in the SETTING (MINUTES) field and press BACKSPACE on your computer keyboard or scroll the value to NEVER.

9. Click OK. The hard disk setting will change to Never and the Power Options dialog box will close.

10. In the Edit Plan Settings window, click SAVE CHANGES and close the window.

Note: Pro Tools automatically switches to the "High Performance" power management configuration on launch. Windows reverts to previously selected power management settings (if different) when exiting Pro Tools. Consequently, when optimizing the power management settings for Pro Tools, you should only optimize using the High Performance configuration.

Install Latest Device Drivers (Pro Tools 9 and 10 Only)

It is always important to install the latest drivers available for your audio interface to ensure maximum compatibility with Pro Tools.

- If you have an Avid/Digidesign interface, visit http://www.avid.com/drivers to download the latest drivers that are compatible with Pro Tools 10.

- For third-party interfaces, visit the manufacturer's website to download the latest drivers available for your audio interface.

Windows 7 Recommended Optimizations

Pro Tools can also be affected by other software and hardware drivers installed on your computer. For best possible performance, it is recommended (but not required) that you do the following:

- Avoid running any unneeded programs at the same time as Pro Tools.

- Turn off any software utilities that run in the background, such as Windows Messenger, calendars, and disk maintenance programs.

- Turn off any non-essential USB devices while running Pro Tools.

Windows 7 Optional Optimizations

The following system optimizations may help Pro Tools perform better on some systems, although they are not required. It is recommended that you try these optimizations only when necessary, as they may disable or adversely affect the functionality of other programs on your system.

Windows 7 optional optimizations include:

- Adjust processor scheduling
- Disable screen savers
- Adjust display performance
- Disable USB power management (USB interfaces only)

Disable System Startup Items

The fewer items in use by your computer, the more resources are available for Pro Tools. Some startup applications may be consuming unnecessary CPU resources, and can be turned off.

If you disable any of the following startup items, do so carefully:

- Portable media serial number (required for some applications that utilize a copy protection key)
- The Plug-and-Play service
- Event log
- Cryptographic services
- Startup items

To disable system startup items:

1. From the START menu, type **msconfig** in START SEARCH and press ENTER to open the System Configuration Utility.

2. Under the GENERAL tab, choose SELECTIVE STARTUP.

3. Deselect LOAD STARTUP ITEMS and click OK.

4. Click RESTART to restart the computer.

5. After restarting, the computer displays a System Configuration message. Check to see if Pro Tools performance has increased before you deselect the Don't Show This Message Again option. If performance has not changed, run msconfig and return your computer Startup Selection back to Normal Startup—Load All Device Drives and Services. Alternatively, try disabling startup items and non-essential processes individually.

Mac OS System Optimization

To ensure optimum performance with Pro Tools, configure your computer first. Before configuring your computer, make sure you are logged in as an Administrator for the account where you want to install Pro Tools. For details on Administrator privileges in Mac OS X, see your Apple OS X documentation.

There are a number of default system settings and keyboard shortcuts for Mac OS that cause conflicts and diminished system performance. Change these settings before using Pro Tools.

Turning Off Software Update

Do not use the Mac OS X automatic software update feature, as it may upgrade your system to a version of Mac OS that has not yet been qualified for Pro Tools.

 For details on qualified versions of Mac OS, see the latest compatibility information at www.avid.com.

On the Web

To turn off the Mac software update feature:

1. Choose SYSTEM PREFERENCES from the APPLE menu.

2. Click SOFTWARE UPDATE.

3. Click the SCHEDULED CHECK tab.

4. Deselect CHECK FOR UPDATES.

5. When you are done, close the window to quit System Preferences.

Turning Off Energy Saver

Using Energy Saver's default settings can have a negative impact on Pro Tools performance.

To turn off the Energy Saver feature:

1. Choose SYSTEM PREFERENCES from the APPLE menu.

2. Click ENERGY SAVER.

3. Set the COMPUTER SLEEP setting to NEVER.

4. Set the DISPLAY SLEEP setting to NEVER.

5. Deselect the PUT THE HARD DISK(S) TO SLEEP WHEN POSSIBLE option.

6. When you are done, close the window to quit System Preferences.

Disabling or Reassigning Keyboard Shortcuts

To have the full complement of Pro Tools keyboard shortcuts, you need to disable or reassign conflicting Mac OS X keyboard shortcuts in the Apple system preferences.

Tip: For a complete list of Pro Tools keyboard shortcuts, consult the *Keyboard Shortcuts Guide*, which can be accessed from within Pro Tools by choosing *Help > Keyboard Shortcuts*.

Mac OS X 10.7 (Lion)

To disable or reassign Mac keyboard shortcuts used by Pro Tools Mac OS X 10.7 (Lion):

1. From the APPLE menu, choose SYSTEM PREFERENCES.

2. Click KEYBOARD.

3. Click the KEYBOARD SHORTCUTS tab to display the Keyboard Shortcuts page, shown in Figure 1.21.

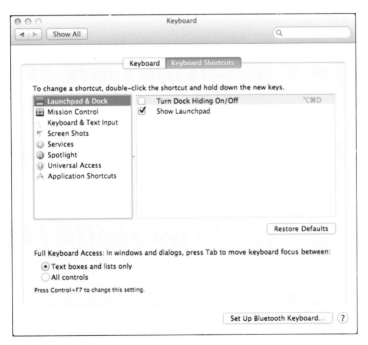

Figure 1.21
Mac OS X 10.7 (Lion) Keyboard Shortcuts page in System Preferences.

4. You can disable or reassign Mac keyboard shortcuts that conflict with Pro Tools keyboard shortcuts. The following list includes several common Mac keyboard shortcuts that, depending on the make and model of your Mac, may also be used by Pro Tools.

- Under Launchpad & Dock
  - Turn Dock Hiding On/Off

- Under Mission Control
  - Mission Control
  - Application Windows
  - Show Desktop
  - Show Dashboard
  - Mission Control > Move Left a Space
  - Mission Control > Move Right a Space
  - Mission Control > Switch to Desktop

- Keyboard & Text Input
  - Move Focus to the Window Drawer

- Under Services
  - Send File to Bluetooth Device
  - Search with Google
  - Spotlight
  - Search Man Pages in Terminal

- Under Spotlight
  - Show Spotlight Search Field
  - Show Spotlight Window

- Under Universal Access
  - Zoom
  - Contrast

- Under Application Shortcuts
  - Show Help Menu

Mac OS X 10.6 (Snow Leopard)

To disable or reassign Mac keyboard shortcuts used by Pro Tools Mac OS X 10.6 (Snow Leopard):

1. From the APPLE menu, choose SYSTEM PREFERENCES.

2. Click KEYBOARD.

3. Click the KEYBOARD SHORTCUTS tab to display the Keyboard Shortcuts page, shown in Figure 1.22.

Figure 1.22
Mac OS X 10.6 (Snow Leopard) Keyboard Shortcuts page in System Preferences.

4. You can disable or reassign Mac keyboard shortcuts that conflict with Pro Tools keyboard shortcuts. The following list includes several common Mac keyboard shortcuts that are also used by Pro Tools.

   - Under Dashboard & Dock
     - Turn Dock Hiding On/Off
     - Dashboard

   - Under Exposé and Spaces
     - All Windows
     - Application Windows
     - Desktop

- Under Keyboard & Text Input
  - Move Focus to the Window Drawer

- Under Spotlight
  - Show Spotlight Search Field
  - Show Spotlight Window

- Under Application Shortcuts
  - Show Help Menu

Disabling Spotlight Indexing

The Mac OS Spotlight feature automatically indexes files and folders on local hard drives in the background. In most cases, this is not a concern for normal Pro Tools operation. However, if Spotlight starts indexing drives while recording in a Pro Tools session with high track counts for an extended period of time, it can adversely affect Pro Tools system performance, although the Disk Cache setting in Pro Tools may eliminate most conflicts with Spotlight. You may want to disable Spotlight indexing for all local drives before using Pro Tools for big recording projects.

To disable Spotlight indexing:

1. Choose APPLE > SYSTEM PREFERENCES > SPOTLIGHT.

2. In the Spotlight window, click the PRIVACY tab.

3. To prevent indexing of a drive, drag its icon from the desktop into the list.

Enabling Journaling for Audio Drives

To yield higher performance from audio drives, enable journaling. This is normally done when initializing a drive with Disk Utility and choosing the format option, Mac OS Extended (Journaled). However, if the drive is already initialized, you can enable journaling using the following process.

To enable journaling on an existing drive:

1. Launch the Disk Utility application, located in System Drive/ Applications/Utilities.

2. Select the volume in the left column of the Disk Utility window.

3. Choose FILE > ENABLE JOURNALING or press COMMAND+J.

Non-Administrator (Standard) Accounts

Pro Tools supports both administrator and non-administrator (standard) accounts for Windows and Mac OS systems. This may be useful in facilities or educational institutions where multiple Pro Tools users share workstations. Different engineers or students can work extensively with Pro Tools, while being restricted from installing software, or accessing protected hard disk and server locations.

Implications of Non-Administrator (Standard) Accounts

Pro Tools requires Administrator access for installation. Other considerations apply for Preference settings and disk access.

Pro Tools Preferences

Pro Tools creates individual preference settings files for each user account on the system. Therefore, whenever users log in and launch Pro Tools, they will find Pro Tools preferences configured the same way as when they last logged in. User preferences are stored in the following locations:

- **Windows.** Documents and Settings\\<username>\\Application Data\\Avid

- **Mac.** Users/<username>/Library/Preferences

Disk Access and Work Locations

Standard account users are only allowed to save Pro Tools sessions and audio/video files within their own Home directories. This is quite restrictive, as it limits users to working on the system drive. The system administrator should grant Read/Write access to the required external media drives and (on Mac volumes) enable the Ignore Ownership on This Volume setting for normal Pro Tools operation.

Caution: Some third-party software plug-ins, video file formats, and other software options used with Pro Tools might not function properly when run with a non-administrator (standard) account. For further information on possible software incompatibilities with non-administrator (standard) accounts, contact the software developer directly.

Configuring a Non-Administrator (Standard) Account for Pro Tools Users

Note that no special steps are required to configure user accounts to use Pro Tools on Windows computers. During installation of Pro Tools, the installer automatically creates a user group called Pro Tools Users and adds Everyone to the group.

All non-administrator user accounts will have access to Pro Tools, with the limitations outlined above.

To configure a standard user account on Mac OS:

1. Log in to Mac OS using an Administrator account.

2. Under the APPLE menu, choose SYSTEM PREFERENCES and the select ACCOUNTS (Mac OS 10.6) or USERS & GROUPS (Mac OS 10.7).

3. Click the PLUS (**+**) button to create a new account (shown in Figure 1.23).

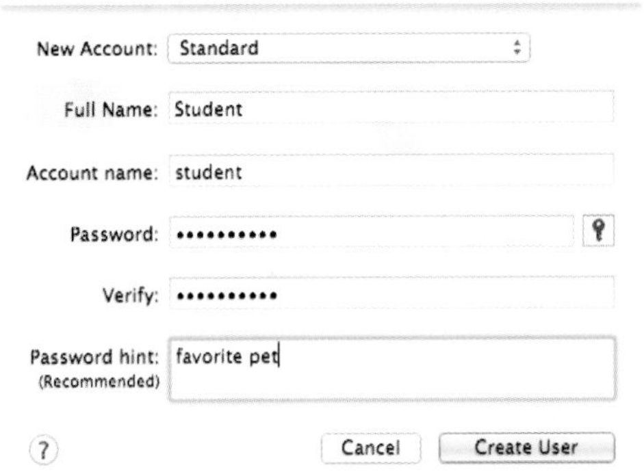

Figure 1.23
Creating a new Standard account using Mac OS 10.7 (Lion).

4. In the New Account window, choose STANDARD from the pop-up menu, enter the account info, and then click CREATE USER. A new account appears in the account column.

Pro Tools Session File Interchange

When exchanging Pro Tools sessions between different Pro Tools systems using different hardware and software versions, there are a number of potential pitfalls when opening sessions created on other systems. Pro Tools session files can generally be opened by newer software versions, but not older software versions. To convert a Pro Tools session file to an older format, you must use the *Save Copy In* command from the *File* menu, and choose the appropriate software version. The following is a listing of the most current Pro Tools session file formats:

■ **Pro Tools 10.** Sessions ending with the file extension .ptx

■ **Pro Tools 7.0 through Pro Tools 9.0.5.** Sessions ending with the file extension .ptf

■ **Pro Tools 5.1 through Pro Tools 6.9.** Sessions ending with the extension .pts

Session Compatibility Between Pro Tools HD and Pro Tools

Although sessions created using Pro Tools 10.0 can be opened on Pro Tools HD 10.0, and likewise sessions created on Pro Tools HD 10.0 can be opened on Pro Tools 10, there are a number of limitations.

Opening Pro Tools HD Sessions in Pro Tools

A Pro Tools HD session can be opened with Pro Tools, but certain session components open differently or not at all.

When opening a Pro Tools HD 10.0 session in Pro Tools 10.0, the following occurs:

- Any tracks beyond the first 128 are made inactive.

- Any Instrument tracks beyond 64 are made inactive.

- Any Auxiliary Input tracks beyond 128 are made inactive.

- DSP plug-ins with Native equivalents are converted; those without equivalents are made inactive. (Native plug-ins remain Native plug-ins while running on the host system. If the session is reopened on a Pro Tools HD DSP-accelerated system, the plug-ins will revert back to DSPs plug-ins.)

- Multichannel surround tracks are removed from the session.

- Unavailable input and output paths are made inactive.

- HEAT (if enabled) is deactivated. When re-opened on a HD system, settings are retained, but HEAT must be re-enabled.

Groups:

- Mix groups keep only Main Volume information.

- Mix/Edit groups keep only Main Volume and Automation Mode information.

- Automation overflow information for grouped controls is preserved.

- Group behavior of Solos, Mutes, Send Levels, and Send Mutes is preserved.

- Solo Mode and Solo Latch settings are dropped.

Video:

- Only the main Video track is displayed.

- Only the first QuickTime movie in the session is displayed or played back.

- If the session contains QuickTime movies in the Clip List but no Video track, the session opens with a new Video track containing the first QuickTime movie from the Clip List.

- The Timeline displays and plays back only the video playlist that was last active. Alternate video playlists are not available.

Sharing Sessions Created on Different Pro Tools Software Versions

Pro Tools makes it easy to share sessions between different software versions of a particular Pro Tools system.

Pro Tools 10.0 sessions cannot be opened with lower versions of Pro Tools. To save a Pro Tools 10.0 session so it is compatible with a lower version of Pro Tools, use the *File > Save Copy In* command to select the appropriate session format.

Saving Pro Tools 10.0 Sessions to Pro Tools 7–Pro Tools 9 Format

To save a Pro Tools 10.0 session so it is compatible with Pro Tools version 7.x through 9.x, use the *File > Save Copy In* command to choose the Pro Tools 7–Pro Tools 9 Session format.

When saving a Pro Tools 10.0 session to Pro Tools 7–Pro Tools 9 Session format, the following occurs:

- Any audio tracks beyond 256 are made inactive.

- Clip gain settings are dropped. If you want to apply any clip gain settings for the session copy, you must manually render clip gain settings first.

- Fades will be rendered when the session is opened in a lower version of Pro Tools.

- Sessions with mixed bit depths must convert all files to the same bit depth and file format.

- Sessions with files that have a bit depth of 32-bit floating point must be converted to 24-bit or 16-bit.

- For sessions with RF64 files larger than 4GB, these files will be unavailable to lower versions of Pro Tools. (You will manually need to consolidate these files to less than 4GB so that the audio can be available to lower software versions of Pro Tools.)

Opening Pro Tools 9.0 Sessions with Pro Tools 8.5, 8.1, and 8.0

A Pro Tools 9.0 session can be opened with Pro Tools 8.5, 8.1, and 8.0 but certain session components open differently or are removed completely.

Note: When opening a Pro Tools 9.0 session with Pro Tools 8.5, 8.1, or 8.0, you are warned that you are opening a session that was created with a newer version of Pro Tools and that not all session components will be available.

When opening a Pro Tools 9.0 session with Pro Tools 8.5 or 8.1, the following occurs:

- Any audio tracks beyond 256 are made inactive.

- Any internal mix buses beyond 128 are made inactive.

- The stereo pan depth reverts to –2.5dB for the stereo mixer. The pan depth for surround mixer remains at –3.0dB at center.

If the session is opened in Pro Tools 8.0, in addition to the above, the following also occurs:

- Output bus assignments are removed.

- HEAT (if present) is removed.

Review/Discussion Questions

1. What is the maximum number of simultaneous audio tracks that can play back on a Pro Tools|HDX system with two HDX PCIe cards?

2. How many simultaneous audio tracks can play back on Pro Tools 10 software with Complete Production Toolkit installed?

3. What is the maximum number of HD-series audio interfaces that can be connected to a single Pro Tools|HDX PCIe card?

4. How many microphone inputs are available on an Avid PRE?

5. What benefits does a Pro Tools|HDX system have over a Pro Tools|HD Native system?

6. What is the name of the cable that is used to connect two Pro Tools|HDX PCIe cards together inside the computer?

7. What is audio interface calibration and which HD-series interfaces support calibration?

8. When is it necessary to install the Avid Video Engine?

9. List at least two system software settings on either a Mac or Windows system that should be changed or disabled when installing a Pro Tools HD system.

10. Why do some facilities prefer to run Pro Tools using a non-administrator (standard) account?

11. How would you convert a Pro Tools 10.1 session, so that it could be opened on a Pro Tools system running version 9.0.5 software?

12. What is the file extension on both a Pro Tools 9 and a Pro Tools 10 session file?

Pro Tools HD Hardware Configuration

In this exercise, you will recommend all of the Pro Tools hardware and software that will be needed to satisfy the precise needs of a busy audio post production facility.

Media Used:

None

Duration:

20 minutes

GOALS

- Recommend and list Pro Tools–related hardware and software required to fulfill two specific scenarios

Getting Started

You are working at a busy audio post production facility that needs to purchase two new Pro Tools systems for different tasks. Pro Tools System #1 will be used for mixing larger film and television projects on a dub stage, and Pro Tools System #2 will be used for recording orchestral music on a scoring stage. You are the main Pro Tools audio engineer at your facility, so you have been given the task of researching and recommending the necessary equipment that should be purchased to suit the separate needs for each separate Pro Tools system.

You have been told not to recommend unnecessary hardware/software and that both of the new Pro Tools systems need to be Apple Macintosh-based systems (including two separate computer displays) with a minimum of 16GB RAM. The separate requirements for each system are as follows.

Pro Tools System #1: Film/TV dub stage mixing system:

- Play back up to 500 simultaneous tracks of audio at 44.1kHz or 48kHz (16- or 24-bit)

- Provide 2TB of video storage and 4TB of audio storage (internal SATA)

- Mix stereo and surround sound projects (up to 7.1 surround)

- Provide up to 64 separate channels of AES/EBU Digital I/O

- Display and use timecode frame rates (23.976, 24, 25, and 29.97FPS)

- Display and use 35mm Feet+Frames

- Sync to and generate LTC (Longitudinal Timecode)

- Sync to VITC and be able to generate a timecode window burn

- Sync to both Bi-Level and Tri-Level sync

- Play back SD/HD QuickTime video and display on an HDTV monitor using HDMI

- Have the option to sync using 9-Pin Machine Control and Satellite Link

- Mix using an Avid worksurface with at least 32 faders and surround joysticks

- Apply AudioSuite, Native, and DSP-based plug-ins to sessions

- Open and save Pro Tools session versions 7.0 through 10.x

Pro Tools System #2: Orchestral scoring stage system:

- Play back up to 192 simultaneous tracks of audio at 44.1kHz or 48kHz (16- or 24-bit)

- Provide 2TB of video storage and 4TB of audio storage (internal SATA)

- Record up to 64 separate channels of analog audio using Pro Tools–controlled mic preamps

- Provide up to 64 channels of analog input/output

- Display and use timecode frame rates (23.976, 24, 25, and 29.97FPS)

- Display and use 35mm Feet+Frames

- Sync to and generate LTC (Longitudinal Timecode)

- Sync to VITC and be able to generate a timecode window burn

- Sync to both Bi-Level and Tri-Level sync

- Play back SD/HD QuickTime video and display on an HDTV monitor using HDMI

- Record using an Avid worksurface with at least 32 faders

- Apply AudioSuite, Native, and DSP-based plug-ins to sessions

- Open and save Pro Tools session versions 7.0 through 10.x

Create Your Own Customized Equipment List

Based on the audio post production facility's requirements, develop your own list of Pro Tools hardware/software that will fulfill all of the needs of the facility for each separate system and enter it on a separate piece of paper.

Tip: You can look back at this lesson and use the Internet to research the options that are available.

Pro Tools System #1: Film/TV Dub Stage Mixing System

Tip: It is not necessary to include in your list third-party Pro Tools plug-ins, audio speakers, cables, and other smaller accessories.

Apple computer hardware and peripherals (including required OS):

Avid Pro Tools hardware and peripherals:

Avid Pro Tools software options:

Third-party hardware peripherals:

Pro Tools System #2: Orchestral Scoring Stage System

Tip: It is not necessary to include in your list third-party Pro Tools plug-ins, audio speakers, cables, and other smaller accessories.

Apple computer hardware and peripherals (including required OS):

Avid Pro Tools hardware and peripherals:

Avid Pro Tools software options:

Third-party hardware peripherals:

Troubleshooting a Pro Tools System

This lesson discusses the proper troubleshooting of a Pro Tools HD-series system with Avid video hardware.

Media Used: None

Duration: 120 minutes

GOALS

- Troubleshoot a Pro Tools system
- Update the firmware for Avid hardware
- Configure Pro Tools Record/Playback settings
- Update I/O settings
- Configure audio and video pull options

Introduction

When working under the tight deadlines and demands of a busy post production facility, it is necessary to keep your Pro Tools system (including its audio and video hardware) working in peak operating condition. This lesson shows you many of the useful ways to troubleshoot your Pro Tools system, so that you can minimize or avoid any delays that keep you from completing your project.

Avid Knowledge Base

The Avid Knowledge Base is an online database containing thousands of entries that cover common issues, such as DAE errors, and their solutions. Knowledge Base also contains general technical information about Pro Tools and Avid hardware. The most up-to-date version of this database is available on the Avid website.

To use Knowledge Base:

1. From within Pro Tools, choose HELP > PRO TOOLS KNOWLEDGE BASE, or from your web browser, go to www.avid.com, click the SUPPORT & SERVICES link, and then in the right sidebar (under PRO TOOLS SUPPORT), click KNOWLEDGE BASE.

2. In Knowledge Base, enter keywords into the SEARCH field and then click SEARCH.

3. In the REFINE RESULTS column, you can refine the search results as desired. See Figure 2.1.

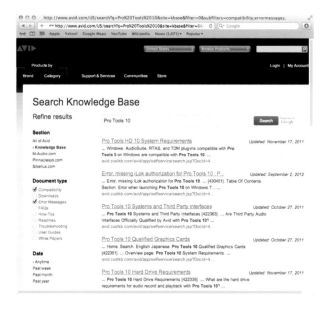

Figure 2.1

Search Avid Knowledge Base: Refine Results.

4. Click the text of any of the search results to see the full Knowledge Base entry, as shown in Figure 2.2.

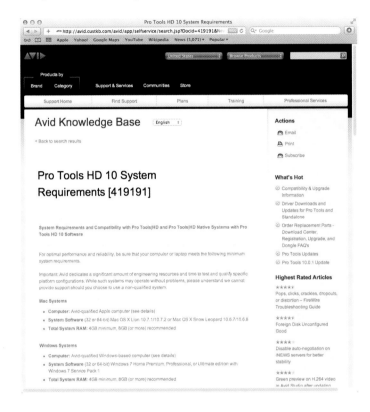

Figure 2.2
Avid Knowledge Base search result details.

Here are some hints to help with your searches:

■ Do not use full phrases such as "Which records in the Knowledge Base describe 9073 errors?" Use only the words or numbers you want to search for, such as "DAE 9073."

■ Do not use punctuation marks or special characters.

■ Every record that contains all the words entered in the search field will be returned (the text search is an AND search). All fields in the database are searched. For example, searching for "–36 error ATTO" finds this text: "DAE error –36 is thrown when initiating or during playback with the drive connected to an ATTO card."

■ The order of the search text does not matter. Searching for "6042 error" will find "error 6042."

- Knowledge Base searches are not case sensitive. Searching for "dae" will find "DAE."

- Knowledge Base does not currently support Boolean search modifiers such as +, –, or quotation marks. All text entered will be part of the search.

Tip: **You can access additional help options from within Pro Tools by choosing Help > Avid Audio Forums and Help > Customer Assist.**

Using DigiTest to Identify Hardware Problems

DigiTest is a useful diagnostic tool for troubleshooting and updating firmware for Pro Tools HD-series hardware systems. You can also use DigiTest to verify a system after you have changed or added hardware to it.

The DigiTest application is automatically installed as part of the Pro Tools 10 Installer in the Pro Tools Utilities folder, located on your system hard drive. See Figure 2.3.

Figure 2.3
DigiTest utility icon.

Running DigiTest

Run the DigiTest diagnostic application to identify Pro Tools|HD cards and verify that they are correctly installed and working properly.

Caution: **Before you run DigiTest, lower the volume of your monitoring system and all output devices. Additionally, be sure to remove your headphones. Very loud digital noise may be emitted during the test.**

To run DigiTest:

1. From the **PRO TOOLS UTILITIES** folder, double-click the **DIGITEST** application program.

   DigiTest opens and lists the supported cards it finds in your system, in their corresponding slot location. If you have a large number of cards and connected interfaces, it may take a while for the main DigiTest screen to appear, as the application scans the cards and interfaces connected to the system.

2. In the **TESTS** tab of the DigiTest window, shown in Figure 2.4, verify that all cards you want to test are checked and then click **RUN**.

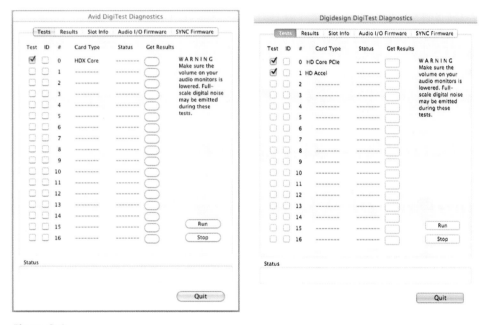

Figure 2.4
DigiTest main window using Pro Tools|HDX hardware (left) and Pro Tools|HD hardware (right).

Note: An HD-series audio interface must be connected to the first port on the first HDX PCIe card. With previous generation HD Core PCIe hardware, an HD audio interface should be connected to the HD Core card. In addition to being connected, the HD audio interface must be powered on in order for the test to run properly, since the audio interface supplies the system clock used for testing.

- DigiTest begins by checking the arrangement of your cards.
- After checking card arrangement, DigiTest checks card functionality. The Status box for each tested card will indicate Passed or Failed.

Note: DigiTest only reports valid test results for slots containing Avid cards.

3. After the test is completed, do one of the following:
   - If all of the Avid cards pass, quit DigiTest and restart your computer.
   - If any cards fail, you can review test details by clicking the Results tab. Following review, you will need to quit DigiTest, power down your system, and reinstall your cards. Verify proper card seating and card interconnect cable connections.

4. When DigiTest has completed, restart your computer.

Tip: After running DigiTest, you must restart your computer. If you attempt to launch Pro Tools without restarting, Pro Tools will start to launch, but will eventually abort the launch and request that your restart your computer.

Updating Avid Firmware

Firmware is the operating software code embedded in a hardware device. Many Avid hardware peripherals (including all HDX cards, worksurfaces, video hardware, audio interfaces, and SYNC Peripherals) contain firmware that can be updated to fix bugs and add new functionality.

Note: Some third-party control surfaces may not have upgradable firmware. To find out if your third-party control surface requires a firmware update, contact the device manufacturer.

HDX Card Firmware

The latest generation DSP-accelerated HDX cards have upgradable firmware that can be updated once the cards are installed in a system. The firmware update code is included in the main Pro Tools software. When Pro Tools is launched, the firmware version is checked. If an update is available, you will be prompted to upgrade the firmware or cancel the upgrade. Once the firmware has been updated, Pro Tools will launch normally.

Caution: Early Apple Mac Pro computers ("Harpertown" models) encounter errors when performing Pro Tools HDX PCIe firmware updates. Attempting to update HDX firmware with a "Harpertown" Mac Pro will render the card unusable and should be avoided.

Control Surfaces and Worksurfaces

Each release of Pro Tools software includes the latest versions of firmware for Avid control surfaces and worksurfaces. With the exception of EUCON-enabled control and worksurfaces (which require a separate installation of software), this is part of the basic software package, and requires no extra installation. As soon as you declare a control surface or worksurface in the Ethernet Controllers tab of the Peripherals dialog box, Pro Tools will check whether the connected device has matching firmware. If not, a dialog box will appear informing you that new firmware needs uploading to the device. Follow the on-screen instructions, and your control surface/worksurface will be updated. In some instances, a new firmware file will be made available for download separately from a Pro Tools update. In this case, you can replace the file manually, and Pro Tools will prompt you to upload the firmware to the control surface/worksurface when you next launch. Controller files are located in the following locations:

■ **Mac:** [System Disk]/Applications/Avid/Pro Tools/Controllers/

■ **Windows:** [System Disk]\Program Files\Avid\Pro Tools\DAE\Controllers\

Note: Avid EUCON-enabled control surfaces and worksurfaces do not update their firmware through the Pro Tools software. Instead, their firmware is updated using the EuControl software application (for Artist Series), MC App (for MC Pro or System 5-MC), or eMix (for System 5 and its variants), which auto-launches when the computer is turned on. For more information about updating firmware for Avid EUCON-enabled hardware devices, consult the Pro Tools EUCON User Guide.

Updating SYNC Peripheral Firmware

As with control surfaces and worksurfaces, SYNC Peripheral firmware may be required for new versions of Pro Tools software. Pro Tools checks that the SYNC Peripheral's firmware is up to date at launch, or when you declare a SYNC Peripheral in the Synchronization tab of the Peripherals dialog box. If an update is required, you will be prompted, and should follow the onscreen instructions. See Figure 2.5.

The current version of SYNC firmware is "1.1.0" and needs to be updated to at least version "1.2.1" before it can be used. Please quit Pro Tools, launch the DigiTest utility, and click on the SYNC Firmware tab for instructions.

OK

Figure 2.5
SYNC HD firmware update warning.

Tip: When upgrading from Pro Tools version 9.x to Pro Tools 10.0 software, the Avid SYNC Peripheral will not require a firmware update.

When upgrading the firmware of a SYNC Peripheral, you will be asked to follow several steps, including power cycling the unit while holding down the Set button.

There are a couple of issues when updating SYNC Peripheral firmware:

SYNC Peripheral Not Connected to DigiSerial Port

The SYNC Peripheral must be connected to the DigiSerial port on either the HDX/HD Core PCIe card or to the PC COM-1 port (Windows only) for firmware updates.

Firmware Not Found

The latest version of SYNC Peripheral firmware is automatically installed in the Pro Tools Utilities folder when you install the Pro Tools HD software. If you have mistakenly deleted the SYNC Peripheral firmware software since the initial installation, the best course of action is to install it immediately, as this will stop the problem from recurring at a later date. If you don't have the Pro Tools 10 installer, you can download the firmware from www.avid.com.

To reinstall the SYNC Peripheral firmware file using the Pro Tools 10 installer:

1. Quit Pro Tools and run the installer.

2. In the **PACKAGE NAME** column, select only the **PRO TOOLS UTILITIES** option, as shown in Figure 2.6. This option will install the SYNC Peripheral firmware.

3. Follow the instructions to complete the install.

Although Pro Tools automatically prompts you to update firmware when required, it's also possible to initiate a firmware update manually. This can be a last resort to try to fix a SYNC Peripheral that is behaving incorrectly, when all other steps have not solved the issue.

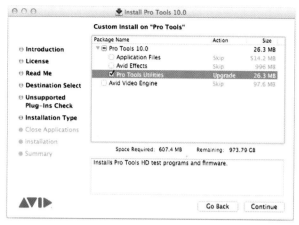

Figure 2.6
Custom Pro Tools 10 Install.

To reload the firmware on a SYNC Peripheral manually:

1. Launch the DIGITEST utility and then click the **SYNC FIRMWARE** tab.

2. If the SYNC Peripheral is connected to the **DIGISERIAL** port, choose the HDX or HD Core card from the menu.

Tip: On some Apple Macintosh computers using **HD Core/Accel** hardware, the Pro Tools|HD Accel card might be selected by default, requiring you to select the HD Core card in the menu before updating the SYNC Peripheral's firmware.

3. Choose the **SERIAL PORT** and **SYNC TYPE**, and then click **BEGIN UPDATE**, as shown in Figure 2.7.

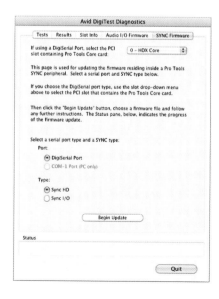

Figure 2.7
SYNC Firmware tab of the DigiTest utility.

Tip: Follow the onscreen instructions very closely, being careful to power-cycle your SYNC Peripheral exactly when instructed.

Avid Mojo SDI/Avid Mojo Firmware

When new updates of Pro Tools or Media Composer software are installed, it may be necessary to update the firmware in your Avid Mojo SDI or Avid Mojo video hardware to be compatible with your new software. When the software first launches, it checks to verify that the currently installed firmware of the Avid Mojo SDI or Avid Mojo hardware is the correct version. If required, the software automatically updates the firmware of your Avid video peripheral on launch. After completing a firmware update, you are required to power-cycle your Avid video hardware, and then re-launch the Pro Tools software. See Figure 2.8.

Figure 2.8
Avid video peripheral firmware update message.

Audio Interface Firmware

The firmware in Pro Tools HD-series audio interfaces can be updated using the DigiTest utility (see "Using DigiTest to Identify Hardware Problems" earlier in this lesson).

To update audio interface firmware from DigiTest:

1. Make sure the audio interfaces are connected and powered on.

2. Launch DigiTest.

3. Click the AUDIO I/O FIRMWARE tab, shown in Figure 2.9.

Figure 2.9
DigiTest Audio I/O Firmware tab.

4. In the **Displaying Information For Slot** menu, select the Pro Tools
   PCIe card that is connected to the HD-series audio interface you want
   to update. See Figure 2.10.

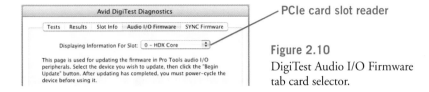

PCIe card slot reader

Figure 2.10
DigiTest Audio I/O Firmware
tab card selector.

Tip: On some Apple Macintosh computers using **HD Core/Accel** hardware, the Pro
ToolsIHD Accel card might be selected by default, requiring you to select the
HD Core card in the menu before updating audio interface firmware on the
first (primary) audio interface.

5. In the **Device Selection** section, choose between the first and second
   interface (primary or expansion) connected to the HD card. The type
   of interface will be displayed automatically in the Product section.
   See Figure 2.11.

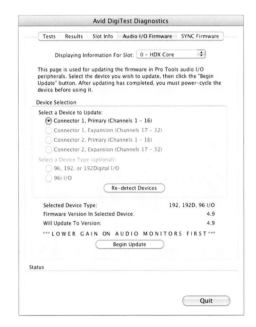

Figure 2.11
Audio I/O Firmware page in DigiTest.

6. Mute your speaker monitors.

7. Click **Begin Update**.

8. When the update is complete, quit DigiTest and restart the computer.

Deleting Pro Tools Settings Files

There are times when the settings files Pro Tools uses become unreadable or corrupted, causing the Pro Tools software to become unstable and behave erratically. After deleting these files and restarting your computer, Pro Tools creates new replacement files that return your Pro Tools system to normal operation.

Deleting settings files will cause the following:

- Pro Tools Preference options will be reset to the factory default settings.

- Ethernet and MIDI controllers will be disabled and must be re-enabled.

- Machine control will be disabled (if enabled).

- Options and Setup menu options will be reset to the factory default settings.

- Satellite Link Option will be disabled (if enabled).

Deleting Settings Files on Mac Systems

On Mac-based Pro Tools systems, all of the files that can be deleted are located in the same directory location.

To locate and delete the settings files:

1. Quit the Pro Tools application (if open).

2. Go to INTERNAL SYSTEM DRIVE/ADMINISTRATOR USERNAME/LIBRARY/ PREFERENCES.

Shortcut: The User Library folder is hidden by default with the Mac OS X 10.7 (Lion) release. In order to access the User Library folder from within the Finder, press Option and then select Library from the Go menu.

Note: On Mac OS X 10.7 (Lion), you can permanently show the User Library folder in the Finder by launching Terminal and typing chflags nohidden/Users/ <Username>/Library, followed by the Return key.

3. In the Preferences folder, Command-click to select each of the following files:

   - **com.digidesign.DigiTest.plist:** Stores the last position of the DigiTest window on the desktop.

   - **com.digidesign.ProTools.plist:** Stores the last position of various windows (Mix window, Edit window, which windows were visible, and so on) in the Pro Tools application.

- **DAE Prefs (folder):** This folder stores a log of which plug-ins are installed on the system and the active plug-in librarian menu choices (for example, the Root Settings Folder location).

- **DigiSetup.OSX:** This file stores the last run hardware state of the Pro Tools environment including how many DSP cards are installed, the last used sample rate, whether a SYNC HD is present and its last used settings, and so on.

- **Pro Tools Prefs:** Stores the current user's most recent preference settings that were set in the Pro Tools application.

4. Drag the selected files to the trash, or press **COMMAND+DELETE** to move the selected files to the trash. See Figure 2.12.

Figure 2.12
Mac OS X: Deleting Pro Tools preference files.

5. Empty the trash and restart your computer.

Tip: You must restart the computer after deleting the files listed above.

Deleting Settings Files on Windows Systems

Windows Pro Tools systems have two directories containing the Pro Tools settings files.

To locate and delete the DAE Prefs folder:

1. Quit the Pro Tools application (if open).

2. Choose **START MENU > COMPUTER > LOCAL DISK (C:)** (or correct System Hard Drive). Then click **SHOW THE CONTENTS OF THIS DRIVE** (if files aren't showing).

3. Navigate to **PROGRAM FILES > COMMON FILES > DIGIDESIGN > DAE**.

4. Right-click on the **DAE PREFS** folder and choose **DELETE**.

Note: Be sure you are deleting the DAE Prefs folder, and not the DAE folder. If you delete the DAE folder, you will need to reinstall Pro Tools and any third-party plug-ins you had installed.

To locate and delete the Pro Tools Preference file:

1. Go to START MENU > MY COMPUTER > LOCAL DISK (C:) (or correct System Hard Drive) > USERS > (your User file folder) > APPDATA > ROAMING > AVID > PRO TOOLS.

2. If the AppData folder is not visible, go to CONTROL PANEL > FOLDER OPTIONS > VIEW tab, and then enable SHOW HIDDEN FILES, FOLDERS, AND DRIVES. Click APPLY and OK.

3. Right-click the PRO TOOLS PREFS.PTP file and choose DELETE. See Figure 2.13.

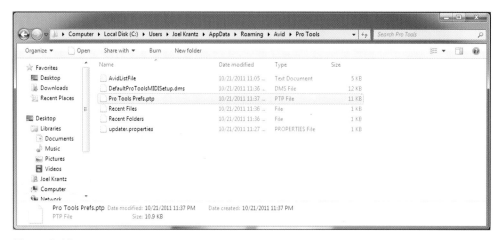

Figure 2.13
Windows: Deleting the Pro Tools Preferences file.

4. You can also delete the DIGITEST.EXE-(8-DIGITS).PF preference file located at the C:\WINDOWS/PREFETCH directory.

5. Empty the recycle bin and restart your computer.

Note: You must restart the computer after deleting the files listed above.

Deleting Database Files

Pro Tools creates a media database file for every hard drive connected to the system, including the system drive. If any of these database files become corrupt, it can cause unusual behavior such as system slowness or erratic behavior. If in doubt, these files can be deleted, and will be regenerated when Pro Tools is relaunched.

To delete media databases on Mac OS computers:

1. If Pro Tools is running, quit Pro Tools.

2. Go to [MAC SYSTEM DRIVE]/LIBRARY/APPLICATION SUPPORT/AVID/PRO TOOLS/DATABASES/UNICODE/VOLUMES.

3. Delete the entire contents of the VOLUMES folder.

Caution: Do *not* delete the whole Databases or Unicode folder, since this would cause all catalogs to be lost.

4. Relaunch Pro Tools. (Restarting the computer is not necessary.)

To delete media databases on Windows computers:

1. If Pro Tools is running, quit Pro Tools.

2. Go to C:\ PROGRAM FILES\AVID\PRO TOOLS\DATABASES\UNICODE\ VOLUMES.

3. Delete the entire contents of the VOLUMES folder.

Caution: Do *not* delete the whole Databases or Unicode folder, since this would cause all catalogs to be lost.

4. Relaunch Pro Tools. (Restarting the computer is not necessary.)

Note: In previous versions of Pro Tools, a software utility called the Tech Support Utility was included with the software, providing an easy way to delete Pro Tools database and settings files. At the time of print, no such utility was available for Pro Tools 10. Previous versions of the Tech Support Utility are not compatible with Pro Tools 10.

Understanding Voice Allocation

In order for an audio track to play back or record, the track must be assigned a *voice*. All Pro Tools systems have a maximum number of voices, depending on the hardware configuration. The number of voices supported by your system determines how many simultaneous audio tracks can play back or record. Separate from the voice count of a Pro Tools system, each system also has a maximum number of allowable audio tracks that it will support in a session, referred to as voiceable (or virtual) tracks.

For example, a Pro Tools|HDX system with one PCIe card provides 256 voices (simultaneous channels of audio playback and recording) at 48kHz, whereas a previous generation Pro Tools|HD 2 system provides up to 192 voices of audio playback and recording, at 48kHz. Despite the difference in voice count between the two hardware systems, both of these systems support 768 total voiceable (virtual) tracks in the session.

Track Priority and Voice Assignment

Pro Tools allows you to create many more audio tracks than available voices. Although all audio tracks in a session can record and play back audio, not all of them can be recorded to or played back simultaneously.

When the number of tracks in a session exceeds the number of available voices, the tracks with the lowest priority will not be heard. In these situations, Pro Tools assigns priority to tracks that compete for the available voices. Because there can be more audio tracks than available voices, Pro Tools provides multiple ways of adjusting the playback priority of audio tracks.

Note: Voice allocation works differently on Pro Tools|HDX systems and previous generation Pro Tools|HD systems.

Number of Voices (Pro Tools|HDX Systems Only)

Like the fixed voice count of Pro Tools software with Complete Production Toolkit and Pro Tools|HD Native hardware systems, Pro Tools|HDX hardware systems also have a fixed voice count of 256 voices when using a single card system. Pro Tools|HDX systems containing two or more cards allow you to expand the voice count, providing 256 voices per HDX PCIe card, with a maximum voice count of 768 total voices (with three HDX cards). For testing session compatibility and performance on systems with lower voice counts, expanded Pro Tools|HDX systems also allow you to set the Number of Voices setting in the Playback Engine dialog box at 256, 512, or 768 voices. Table 2.1 shows the voice count options that are available when using multi-card Pro Tools|HDX hardware systems.

Table 2.1   Pro Tools|HDX Voice Count Options

Number of HDX Cards	Max Voice Count	Playback Engine Voice Count Options
1	256	256 only
2	512	256 or 512
3 or more	768	256, 512, or 768

One major benefit of the Pro Tools|HDX hardware is that it does not use DSP chips for voices. Instead, each Pro Tools|HDX card has a dedicated FGPA chip, which provides 256 voices per card (as mentioned in Lesson 1, "Pro Tools HD Hardware Configuration"). See Figure 2.14. Since the HDX card's DSP chips are not used for voices, the track count of a session will have no impact on the DSP available for mixing or plug-in processing. This is one major benefit of the Pro Tools|HDX hardware over the previous generation Pro Tools|HD hardware, which shares the Pro Tools|HD card's DSP chips for both voices and DSP plug-ins and mixing.

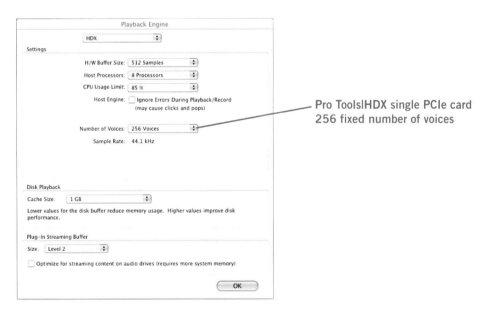

Pro Tools|HDX single PCIe card
256 fixed number of voices

Figure 2.14
Fixed voice assignments with a single Pro Tools|HDX PCIe card in the Playback Engine dialog box.

Number of Voices (Pro Tools|HD Systems Only)

In contrast to the high voice counts of Pro Tools|HDX systems, previous generation Pro Tools|HD systems have more limited voice counts, but provide more options for managing the voice counts of your session in the Playback Engine dialog box. The total voice count on a Pro Tools|HD system ranges from a minimum of 16 voices to a maximum of 96 voices for a single Pro Tools|HD PCIe card system, doubling to a maximum of 192 voices for a system containing two or more Pro Tools|HD PCIe cards (at 44.1kHz or 48kHz). See Figure 2.15.

Tip: When choosing the voice count for previous generation Pro Tools|HD DSP
      hardware, you should select the highest number of voices with the smallest
      number of DSP chips to meet your needs. Increase the number of chips
      (or decrease the number of voices) as needed to avoid PCI bus errors
      (DAE error -6042).

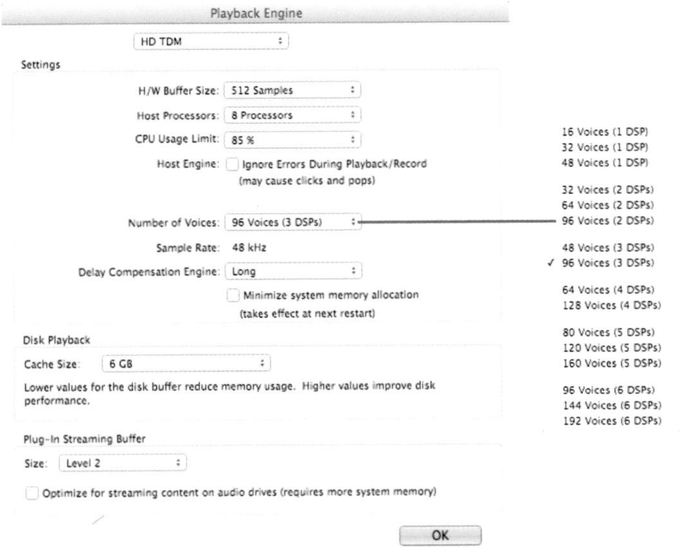

Figure 2.15
Pro Tools|HD hardware's selectable voice counts in the Playback Engine dialog box.

On Pro Tools HD-series hardware systems, once you choose a voice count, the DSP chips used for voices are 100% allocated when the session is opened and cannot be used for anything other than voice count. For example, if you set the Number of Voices to 192 voices (6 DSPs) for a session that will only be using 16 voices, you are essentially wasting hardware processing power that could be used for other processes, such as DSP plug-ins or mixing power.

Note: Unlike previous generation Pro Tools|HD PCIe hardware, Pro Tools|HDX
        hardware systems do not use DSP chips for allocating voices, so the
        maximum voice count is always available, and no DSP processing power
        is wasted on unused voices.

On both Pro Tools|HDX and Pro Tools|HD hardware systems, adding Native
plug-ins on Aux Inputs, Instruments tracks, and Master Faders requires
additional voices. However, using DSP plug-ins on Pro Tools|HDX and
Pro Tools|HD hardware will automatically place the plug-in on the PCIe
hardware's DSPs. For more information about how Native plug-in usage
affects voice count on Pro Tools|HDX and Pro Tools|HD hardware systems,
see Lesson 7, "Pro Tools HD/HDX Mixing Concepts."

Tip: At low and moderate sample rates on Pro Tools|HD PCIe hardware systems,
       you can also choose how many voices will be allocated to each DSP chip.
       This allows for voice load balancing in large sessions to alleviate possible
       system errors related to PCI bus timing conflicts.

Setting Voice Assignment

In Pro Tools, all new audio tracks are assigned (dyn) dynamic voicing by default.
Dynamic voicing simply means Pro Tools will allocate the first available voice to
track one, and continue to assign and increment through all of the available voices,
until the number of audio tracks in the session exceeds the total number of available voices. When the total number of audio tracks in the session exceeds the
available voice count, lower priority tracks will not play back or record. When
using dynamic voicing, Pro Tools automatically takes care of the voice management in the background, assigning voices not in use by other tracks.

Track priority, or "which track gets a voice," is determined by a track's position in
the session relative to other tracks. The topmost track in the Edit window (or the
leftmost track in the Mix window) gets the highest priority. When using previous
generation Pro Tools|HD hardware only, track voices can also be assigned to an
explicit voice number.

Note: With Pro Tools HD and Pro Tools software with Complete Production Toolkit,
        when recording using QuickPunch, TrackPunch, and DestructivePunch,
        additional voices are required. Also, on Pro Tools|HD and Pro Tools|HDX
        systems, the initial insert of a Native (host-based) plug-in on non-audio
        tracks uses additional voices.

Explicit Voice Assignment (Pro Tools|HD Systems Only)

When using a Pro Tools|HD system with a limited voice count, you can conserve voices by sharing them between multiple tracks. For instance, you may have two different final stereo music cues that do not play back in the exact same location in a film or television project. You might choose to place these music cues on separate tracks because, in addition to allowing different clip arrangements, they can then have different plug-in processing as well. Using the default dyn voice assignment, both tracks would utilize two voices each. However, when you assign each of the stereo music tracks to the same pair of voices, as long as there is no overlap between the clips on each track, all clips will play back in their entirety, sharing the same voice pair, thus conserving two voices for use elsewhere in the session. Conversely, if a clip overlap does occur between two or more audio tracks with the same explicit voice assignment, only the highest priority track will play during the overlap.

With Pro Tools|HD systems only, you can assign specific (or *explicit*) voices to multiple tracks, so that the same voices are shared by more than one track. This feature is called *voice borrowing*. For stereo and multichannel tracks, voices appear in pairs and multichannel groups. Voices already explicitly assigned to another track appear in bold in the Voice Selector's pop-up menu. The combination of playback/record tracks and shared voiced tracks comprises the total number of voiceable tracks on a Pro Tools|HD system.

Tip: With Pro Tools|HD, tracks assigned to a specific voice number take priority over dynamically allocated tracks and support voice borrowing.

Tip: Elastic Audio and Native plug-ins are not allowed on explicitly voiced tracks (Pro Tools|HD only). Use Dynamically Allocated Voicing (dyn) only for tracks using Elastic Audio or Native plug-ins.

Note: On Pro Tools|HDX systems, explicit voice assignments do not exist. Instead, voices are always dynamically allocated automatically by the Pro Tools software.

To set the voice assignment for an audio track:

1. Click the track's **Voice Selector** and choose either **Dyn** or **Off**, or select a **voice number** (Pro Tools|HD hardware only). See Figure 2.16.

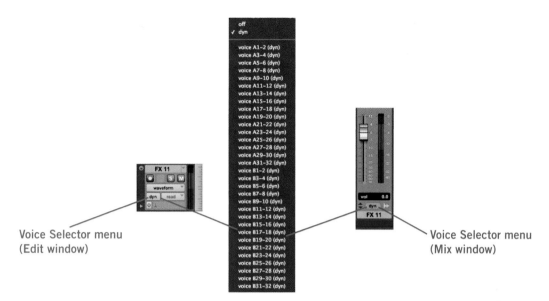

Figure 2.16
Pro Tools|HD Voice Selector menu.

In Figure 2.17, two stereo music tracks (MX_01 and MX_02) are assigned to (explicit) voices A7-8 (and share the same color for clips). In the empty areas of the MX_01 track, the audio clips on the MX_02 track will pop through and play back. This allows you to effectively utilize more tracks in your session than your maximum number of available voices. Notice, however, that where clips overlap on the MX_01 and MX_02 tracks, only the MX_01 track will play back. This is useful when you want to have an alternate take or different version displayed in the Edit window, but don't want the track to be audible.

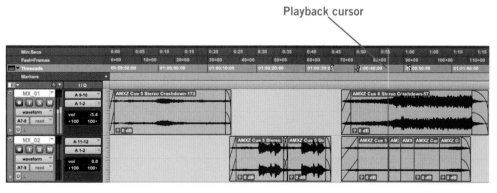

Figure 2.17
Only the MX_01 track is playing at the playback cursor.

Changing the Priority of Tracks

The lowest-numbered (highest priority) audio tracks that are active *and* have their voice assignment set to dyn (dynamic voicing) are the tracks that play back. (The total number of tracks that play back depends on the maximum number of voiced audio tracks allowed by your system.)

Tracks that are higher-numbered (lower priority) than those with a voice do not play back and you cannot record to them. Also, their default dyn voice assignments are colored dark blue to indicate there are insufficient voices available for track playback or recording.

Note: Tracks do not play back or record when they are inactive, when their voice assignment is set to off, or when all available voices are allocated to higher priority tracks in the session.

If you have more tracks in your session than available voices (which is unlikely when using Pro Tools|HDX hardware), or if you have more than one track assigned to the same voice (Pro Tools|HD hardware only), Pro Tools will allocate the available voices to tracks according to their priority. See Figure 2.18.

Figure 2.18
Audio tracks 257–260 will not play back or record because all available voices are allocated to higher priority tracks.

You can increase the priority of audio tracks in several ways:

■ In the Edit window, drag the track up above other tracks in the session.

■ In the Mix window, drag the track to the left of other tracks in the session.

■ In the Tracks List, drag the track name to a higher position in the list.

You can free the voice in use by a track in several ways:

■ Set the track's Voice selector to off.

■ Deactivate the track.

■ Remove *all* of the track's output and send assignments.

■ (Pro Tools|HD hardware systems only): If the Mute Frees Assigned Voice option is enabled in the Options menu, mute the track during playback.

Note: On Pro Tools|HD hardware systems only, enabling Mute Frees Assigned Voice
in the Options menu can cause a noticeable muting/soloing delay on audio
tracks, even with Extended Disk Cache enabled.

Deactivating Tracks

Audio tracks, Auxiliary Inputs, Master Faders, and Instrument tracks can be made
inactive. Deactivating a track will free any DSP and Native resources (plug-ins,
mixing) or voices used by the track. Tracks will automatically be made inactive if
a session is opened on a system with fewer available voices and DSP processing
power than the originating system.

Because voices are primarily used by audio tracks, deactivating other
types of tracks (Aux Inputs, Instrument tracks, and Master Faders) will not
usually free voices in your session, unless the track is using additional
voices as a result of Native plug-in usage. For more information about
how Native plug-in usage affects voice count on Pro Tools|HDX and Pro
Tools|HD systems, see Lesson 7.

To deactivate a track, do one of the following:

1. Right-click the track nameplate in the **MIX** or **EDIT** window and choose
   MAKE INACTIVE. See Figure 2.19.

Figure 2.19
Choosing Make Inactive in the right-click track menu.

2. Select the track and choose **TRACK > MAKE INACTIVE**. This is useful when
   you want to make a number of tracks inactive.

3. Control+Command-click (Mac) or Ctrl+Start-click (Windows) on the
   track type icon in the Mix window. No confirmation dialog box will
   appear for this action. See Figure 2.20.

Figure 2.20
Using modifier keys to deactivate a track.

4. Click on the track type icon in the **Mix** window and choose **Make Inactive**. Click again and choose **Make Active** to reactivate the track. This is useful when you want to make a single track inactive. See Figure 2.21.

Figure 2.21
Click on a track icon to make the track inactive.

Playback Engine Advanced Options

As you learned in previous Pro Tools courses, the Playback Engine dialog box contains multiple settings that directly affect your Pro Tools system's performance (see Figure 2.22). It is therefore useful to understand how these settings can be configured to correct playback or recording problems.

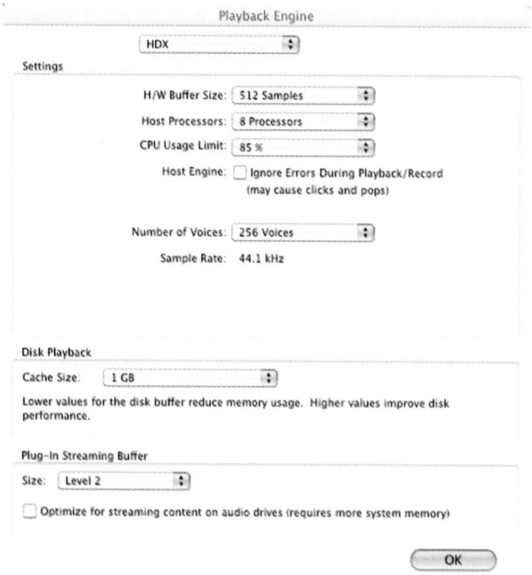

Figure 2.22
HDX PCIe card in the Playback Engine dialog box.

Optimizing Voice Count Settings (Pro Tools|HD Systems Only)

As you learned earlier in this lesson, voice count determines the maximum number of audio tracks (disk tracks) that can play back or record simultaneously.

The maximum number of voices you can use is limited by your Pro Tools hardware and the sample rate of the session.

Tip: Refer to the Pro Tools Reference guide for a detailed breakdown of voice
limits by hardware and sample rate.

If your session contains more audio tracks or Native plug-ins than the available
voices for your Pro Tools hardware allows, the error message shown in Figure 2.23
will appear.

There are more active audio or Native-
enabled tracks than available voices. As a
result, one or more audio or Native-enabled
tracks will not play.

OK

Figure 2.23
Insufficient voice allocation warning.

Since Pro Tools|HDX hardware systems have much higher track counts than pre-
vious generation Pro Tools|HD hardware, it is unlikely that you will receive insuf-
ficient voice allocation warnings when using a Pro Tools|HDX hardware system. If
you do receive insufficient voice allocation warnings on a Pro Tools|HDX system,
increasing the Number of Voices (if possible) in the Playback Engine dialog box
will resolve the problem. If the voice count cannot be increased in the Playback
Engine dialog box, the only remaining option that will resolve the problem is to
change the priority of tracks (as described in the previous section of this lesson).

When using previous generation Pro Tools|HD hardware, insufficient voice
allocations warnings are more common, but can be corrected by increasing the
current voice allocation in the Playback Engine dialog box. However, this also
increases the total DSP processing usage. Conversely, reducing the voice count on
Pro Tools|HD hardware for sessions with unnecessarily high settings frees up DSP
processing for other tasks. This is especially true on older HD systems containing
a single HD Core card (HD1), or a single Core card with one Accel card (HD2),
where available DSP chips are at a premium. Remember that DSP chips are used
for voices on Pro Tools|HD hardware, whereas Pro Tools|HD Native and HDX
use an FPGA for voices. When attempting to insert DSP plug-ins on a system that
has insufficient available DSP-based processing power, the DAE -7204 error message shown in Figure 2.24 will appear.

One or more plug-ins could not be made
active because there is not enough free DSP
(error #DAE error –7204 was encountered.).

OK

Figure 2.24
DAE error -7204 warning.

Reducing voice count will provide more available processing power for DSP plug-ins on Pro Tools|HD, but will also reduce PCI traffic for all Pro Tools|HDX and Pro Tools|HD hardware-based systems. This is useful in systems where there is a high level of PCI or FireWire activity caused by other resource-hungry devices being used with your Pro Tools HD cards (for example, Avid Mojo SDI or an Avid ISIS network).

Choosing Number of DSPs for a Given Voice Count (Pro Tools|HD Hardware Only)

When using Pro Tools|HD hardware only, the Number of Voices pop-up menu in the Playback Engine dialog box provides options to choose a number of combinations for voice counts and the number of DSPs used for voices. For example, you can choose to run 96 voices using two, three, or even six DSPs. The reason for this is to enable a Pro Tools Expert to optimize the way in which Pro Tools manages its data in different hardware configurations. Certain other PCIe cards in the computer may use the PCI bus in ways that interfere with Pro Tools, especially in large systems containing a PCIe video card or when an Avid ISIS network is used. When you assign high voice counts with fewer DSPs, PCI communication timing becomes more critical. In many situations, you should be able to use the most efficient voice count settings, that is, high voice count with low DSP usage. However, if Pro Tools reports the DAE error -6042 (PCI bus too busy), you can try raising the number of DSPs dedicated to voices.

To optimize the number of voices for the session:

■ Select the number of voices from the Playback Engine's **Number of Voices** pop-up menu, as shown in Figure 2.25.

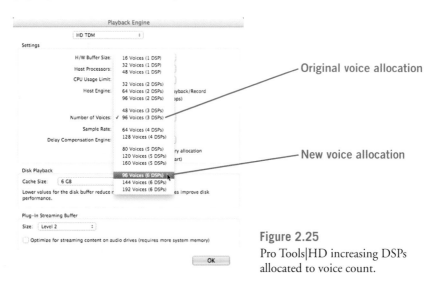

Figure 2.25
Pro Tools|HD increasing DSPs allocated to voice count.

Note: Pro Tools|HD Native and HDX hardware do not use DSPs for their fixed voice
counts. However, high track count sessions may lead to PCI traffic errors
when competing with other systems that share PCI bus bandwidth such as
the FireWire bus, Ethernet bus, and USB bus.

Disk Playback Cache Size
(Pro Tools HD and Complete Production Toolkit)

The Cache Size setting in the Playback Engine dialog box determines the amount
of memory DAE allocates to manage disk buffers, affecting audio playback and
elastic audio performance. In most cases, the default setting of Normal is an optimized cache size that works well for most sessions. This is the only option available
unless you are using Pro Tools HD software or Pro Tools software with Complete
Production Toolkit.

Pro Tools HD and Pro Tools software with Complete Production Toolkit lets you
load audio files used in Pro Tools sessions into RAM for cached playback. Pro Tools
prioritizes files closest to the current playhead location. This way, when you start
playback, those files are already cached for playback. This is especially useful when
working with shared media storage (such as with Avid Unity MediaNetwork and
ISIS shared storage systems), since it will improve system performance because it is
not streaming as much media directly from the network during real-time playback.

Note: Although Pro Tools 10 now supports the use of any type of local or networked storage, not all storage solutions will work well with Pro Tools.

To determine the maximum amount of RAM available for disk cache, Pro Tools
polls the computer for the amount of RAM installed and subtracts approximately
3GB with Mac systems or 4GB with Windows systems. (Note that Windows systems reserve more RAM for the system than Mac systems.) For example, if your
computer has 10GB of RAM installed, the total amount of RAM available for the
disk cache will be around 7GB (Mac) or 6GB (Windows).

To set the amount of RAM to be used by the disk cache:

1. Choose SETUP > PLAYBACK ENGINE.

2. From the CACHE SIZE selector, select the amount of RAM you want to
allocate to the Disk Cache and then click OK. See Figure 2.26.

Figure 2.26
Setting the Disk Playback Cache Size.

Cache Meters in the System Usage Window

Pro Tools HD and Complete Production Toolkit provide two additional meters in the System Usage window for monitoring Disk Cache: Disk Cache and Timeline Cached. These meters are present only if the Normal setting is changed to a fixed cache size in the Playback Engine dialog box.

Tip: To access the System Usage window in Pro Tools, choose Window > System Usage.

- **Disk Cache:** Indicates how much of the allocated disk cache is filled, as a percentage. For example, if the Cache Size in the Playback Engine is set to 1GB and a session uses 256MB of audio files, the Disk Cache meter reads 25%. If all of the audio in the session is cached (including files in the Clip List that are not on the timeline), the Disk Cache meter appears green.

- **Timeline Cached:** Displays the amount of audio in the session timeline cached in RAM. If the selected Cache Size in the Playback Engine is the same or greater than the amount of audio on the timeline, the Timeline Cache meter reads 100% and it appears green (indicating that all of the audio on the timeline is cached in RAM). This is useful for letting you know how much audio can still be added to the timeline and be cached in RAM.

If the total amount of audio in the timeline is more than the selected Cache Size in the Playback Engine, the Timeline Cached meter shows the percentage of audio on the timeline that is cached in RAM. For example, if the selected Cache Size in the Playback Engine is 256MB and the amount of audio on the timeline is 1GB, the Timeline Cached meter reads 25% and appears yellow. See Figure 2.27.

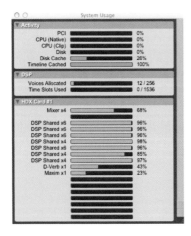

Figure 2.27
System Usage window showing Disk Cache and Timeline Cached meters with 6GB Cache Size setting.

Note: The Disk Cache and Timeline Cached meters are not available in the
System Usage meter when the disk playback cache size in the Playback
Engine dialog box is set to Normal.

Tip: You can use the cache meters in the System Usage window to determine
whether to assign more or less RAM to the disk cache for the current session.

The disk playback cache size defaults to Normal, which works well for smaller sessions. However, when session track counts exceed the maximum recommended number of tracks per hard disk (usually above 32–48 tracks), the DAE error -9073 (disk too slow) warning may appear. This warning indicates that the session's hard disk cannot provide the required data throughput rate necessary to play back or record all of the session's tracks. Increasing the disk playback cache size will correct the problem by allowing Pro Tools to cache audio to RAM. The table below summarizes the advantages and disadvantages of using higher and lower cache size settings, and can be used to correct playback or recording problems within your sessions.

Table 2.2 lists some general guidelines for allocating higher and lower Disk Cache settings in the Playback Engine dialog box.

Table 2.2   Disk Cache Settings Guidelines

Disk Cache Setting	Advantages	Disadvantages
Normal	Pro Tools dynamically allocates disk cache RAM automatically based on the number of tracks in the session.	Pro Tools does not buffer as much audio in RAM, so high track count sessions could cause disk playback errors. Also higher disk usage in the System Usage window.
User Selected Fixed RAM amount	More of the session's timeline audio is loaded into RAM, providing better performance in high track count sessions and sessions utilizing networked storage.	Utilizes more of the computer's total available system RAM.

Note: Video files are not cached with audio files when using Extended Disk Cache
and are always streamed from hard disk. This can cause the system to not
be as fast and responsive as one might expect, even when 100% of the
timeline is cached in RAM.

Monitoring DSP Resources (Pro Tools DSP-Accelerated Systems Only)

In the previous section of this lesson, you learned how the System Usage window is used to monitor the disk cache settings you configured in the Playback Engine dialog box. For Pro Tools|HDX and Pro Tools|HD systems, the System Usage window also provides DSP Usage gauges that help you monitor the DSP usage on your system. See Figure 2.28.

- **Voices Allocated**: Displays the total number of disk voices that can be allocated and the number of voices currently allocated. This includes all voices whether they are allocated explicitly or dynamically, as well as any voices used for routing Native plug-in processing.

- **Time Slots Used (Pro Tools|HD):** Time slots are similar to patch cables, with the DSP's inputs and outputs acting like the patch points on a patchbay. Pro Tools|HD uses time slots for passing signals between DSPs. The Time Slot gauge displays a total number of 512 time slots available and the number of time slots currently used.

- **Time Slots (Pro Tools|HDX)**: Pro Tools|HDX hardware uses time slots differently than Pro Tools|HD hardware. Pro Tools|HDX hardware uses "crossbars" to move data between DSP chips on the HDX card. When moving data between cards in a multiple card system, time slots are used as a dedicated multiplexed bus (via the HDX TDM cable) for intercard communication. Therefore, in a single HDX card system (or when a second or third HDX card is "idle"), no time slots will be used, and the System Usage Time Slots meter will display 0/1536.

- **DSP Usage**: For Pro Tools|HDX or Pro Tools|HD DSP hardware, this meter displays (in percent) how much of the system's DSP processing power is currently being used for mixing and DSP processing.

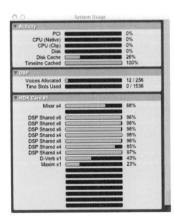
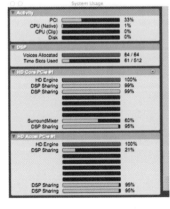

Figure 2.28

System Usage window using a single Pro Tools|HDX PCIe card (left) and Pro Tools|HD Core/Accel PCIe cards (right).

Monitoring Native Resources (Recap)

As you learned in previous Pro Tools 100-level and 200-level courses, the System Usage window also includes activity meters that indicate how much of your system's CPU processing power is being used to process Native audio plug-ins, process Elastic Audio, and write and play back automation and MIDI.

Very rarely does automation, MIDI, or non-DSP activity by itself cause DAE errors, although high track count sessions containing dense areas of automation can cause CPU overload and errors that are *not* the result of Native plug-in processing. Pro Tools provides separate meters allowing you to monitor the processing activity hitting the main processors.

To monitor the usage of Native resources during a Pro Tools session, choose Window > System Usage. As shown in Figure 2.29, you have the following options:

Figure 2.29
System Usage window activity meters.

- **CPU (Native)**: Displays the amount of CPU processing activity for host-based plug-in processing, as well as automation and MIDI playback.

- **CPU (Elastic)**: Displays the amount of processing activity for real-time Elastic Audio processing and clip gain.

- **Disk**: Displays the amount of hard disk processing activity.

As these meters approach their limits, host processing and recording or playback of audio, MIDI, and automation data can be affected. If CPU or PCI activity is high, a system error may occur. If disk activity is high, Pro Tools may play back some automation data late, with plug-in automation being most susceptible. This can happen during particularly dense periods of activity, such as while using the Bounce to Disk command.

To reduce CPU processing load in a session, do some of the following:

- Reduce the density of automation in places where it shows the most activity.

- Turn off meters in Sends view, if enabled (by deselecting Show Meters in Sends View in the Display Preferences page).

- Reduce the number of instances of Native plug-ins, or convert the Native plug-ins to DSP plug-ins.

- Reduce the overall amount of Elastic Audio real-time processing by switching to rendered processing.

Advanced Pro Tools I/O Setup

In the Pro Tools 110 and Pro Tools 201 courses, you learned how the I/O Setup window can be used to configure and manage the various interface and bus path assignments in your sessions. This section discusses how to exchange sessions between Pro Tools HD software-based systems that do not have identical audio interfaces.

Remapping

When a session is opened on a system with different I/O, session paths are reassigned to the currently available hardware when possible.

For example, a session that was recorded using a Pro Tools|HD-series hardware system and a single 192 I/O audio interface and a single 96 I/O interface would include 32 output paths spread across the two 16-channel interfaces. If that session were taken to a different Pro Tools HD system, for example, an HD I/O-based system, the first 16 outputs would be mapped to the HD I/O's available output channels, as shown in Figure 2.30.

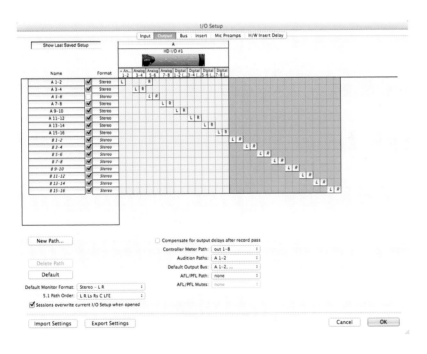

Figure 2.30
Output paths remapped on an HD I/O system.

Unavailable I/O is shown in dark gray. Any tracks assigned to unavailable output paths will have the output paths grayed out and inaudible. If the automatic remapping is not suitable to your session's requirements, you can manually shift paths to more appropriate I/O, and make unused paths inactive.

Show Last Saved Setup

When I/O remapping has occurred, the Show Last Saved Setup button appears in the top-left corner of the I/O Setup window. Clicking on this button displays the audio interfaces used in the original session, as shown in Figure 2.31. This temporary display lets you check the original I/O configuration for reference when re-configuring the session for your system, even if the session came from a different version of Pro Tools, or from a different Pro Tools hardware platform.

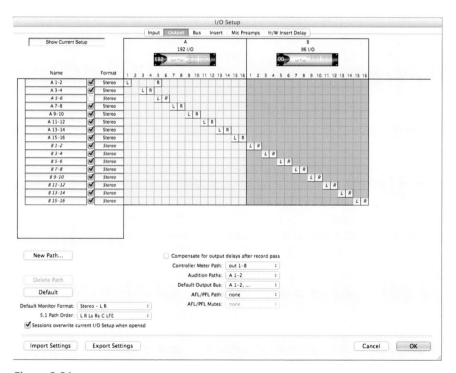

Figure 2.31
Show Last Saved I/O Setup.

Sessions Overwrite Current I/O Setup When Opened

The "Sessions overwrite current I/O Setup when opened" option (first introduced in Pro Tools 8.1) was added to the I/O Setup dialog box, in order to solve session interchange issues (such as maintaining studio settings on different Pro Tools systems) and to provide better overall workflows for session interchange. This setting determines whether the current input, output, insert, mic preamps, and hardware insert delay settings configured on your system will be overwritten by any of the I/O settings stored within a session, when opened. Since different Pro Tools systems often use different channel outputs for speakers, disabling this checkbox will allow you to replace the original settings, mappings, and input/output assignments saved with the session with your own studio's default settings, mappings, and input/output assignments. See Figure 2.32.

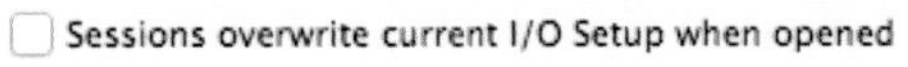

☐ Sessions overwrite current I/O Setup when opened

Figure 2.32
Sessions overwrite current I/O Setup when opened option from I/O Setup (disabled).

In versions of Pro Tools earlier than Pro Tools 8.1, I/O settings are recalled from the Pro Tools session document, so studio settings corresponding to your hardware could potentially change each time a session is opened, resulting in a temporary loss of audio monitoring paths. In the most recent versions of Pro Tools, I/O settings such as Input, Output, Insert, Mic Preamps, and H/W Insert Delay can be recalled from the system, while buses are always saved and recalled with the session file. Since buses are specific to the mixer configuration in Pro Tools, you want to retain your bussing when you open a session on any system. The ability to apply your studio's system settings to any session you open, while maintaining the bussing configuration saved with the session, allows you to quickly and easily exchange sessions between many different Pro Tools systems.

■ **Sessions Overwrite Current I/O Setup When Opened (disabled by default)**: Disabling this setting is the recommended default setting when exchanging sessions with other Pro Tools systems running Pro Tools version 8.1 or higher. When this setting is disabled, Pro Tools recalls I/O assignments from the system (rather than the session), with all output bus paths of the session automatically remapping to the system output paths. Disabling this option allows you to overwrite the session's I/O settings and apply your preferred studio I/O assignments, names, and routings, allowing you to maintain your studio output monitoring path assignments for any sessions you open.

Tip: Enabling or disabling the Sessions Overwrite Current I/O Setup When Opened option in any page of the I/O Setup dialog box affects all of the other pages as well.

■ **Sessions Overwrite Current I/O Setup When Opened (enabled)**: Recommended for session compatibility with Pro Tools sessions earlier than Pro Tools 8.1. When enabled, Pro Tools recalls I/O assignments, names, and routings from the session file (rather than the system), with the output bus paths of the session remaining mapped to the output paths saved with the session. When enabled, any custom settings saved with the session that do not match your system may need to be reconfigured in the I/O Setup dialog box. Be aware that using this option uses the originating session's I/O Setup mappings, ignoring your default system I/O Setup mappings (inputs, outputs, buses, and so on).

Tip: Due to changes in the I/O Setup window bussing options first introduced in Pro Tools 8.1, it is recommended that you enable the Sessions Overwrite Current I/O Setup When Opened option for legacy Pro Tools session behavior and full compatibility with Pro Tools sessions created in software versions earlier than 8.1. When exchanging sessions with other Pro Tools systems running Pro Tools 8.1 or higher, this option should be disabled. This option is disabled by default.

Audio and Video Pull Options

When working with digital audio or video, there are three standards that are commonly used worldwide, as listed in Table 2.3.

Table 2.3   Common Audio and Video Standards

Standard	Frame Rate	Speed or Clock Reference
Film and HD cinema	24FPS	50Hz/60Hz
PAL	25FPS	50Hz
NTSC	29.97 and 23.976FPS	59.94Hz

Because of the different speed references that each of these standards use, it becomes necessary to change the speed of audio and video when converting between any of these standards. Failure to change clock speeds when converting audio and video originally referenced to one of these standards for a different standard will result in audio and video drifting out of sync.

In order to change the speed of the audio, Pro Tools varies the sample rate clock of the session's audio faster or slower (in real-time) using the Loop Sync Master peripheral's sample rate crystal (usually a SYNC HD or SYNC I/O). For example, when using a SYNC HD as the Loop Sync Master, if the session's nominal sample rate is 48,000Hz (samples/second), when the sample rate is pulled down 0.1%, the Loop Sync Master peripheral multiplies the original 48,000Hz sample rate × 0.999 = 47,952Hz (samples/sec). Likewise, if a session's nominal sample rate is 48,000Hz (samples/second), when the sample rate is pulled up 0.1%, the Loop Sync Master peripheral multiplies the original 48,000Hz sample rate × 1.01 = 48,480Hz (samples/sec). The same sample rate multiplication process occurs in the hardware when pulling up and down using other pull factor percentages.

Note: All versions of Pro Tools 10 software supports audio and video pulls without a SYNC HD, SYNC I/O, or HD-series audio interface, although it is not possible to pull the sample rate clock of third-party audio interfaces using Pro Tools.

Fortunately, Pro Tools does all of the mathematical calculations for the user, providing a simple and accurate way to convert audio and video from any reference to another, while maintaining accurate sync. This is accomplished using the Audio and Video Rate Pull Up/ Down menus in the Session Setup window. See Table 2.4.

Tip: Pull options for HD workflows are beyond the scope of this book.

Table 2.4   Common Audio and Video Pull Standards

Converting From	Converting To	Audio Pull Rate	Video Pull Rate
PAL Video (25FPS)	NTSC Video Broadcast (29.97FPS)	4.1% down	4.1% down
NTSC Video Broadcast (29.97FPS)	PAL Video (25FPS)	4.1% up	Not available
PAL Video (25FPS)	Film (24FPS)	4% down	4% down
Film (24FPS)	PAL Video (25FPS)	4% up	4% up
NTSC Video Broadcast (29.97FPS)	Film (24FPS)	0.1% Up	Not available
Film (24FPS)	NTSC Video Broadcast (29.97FPS)	0.1% down	0.1% down

Choosing a Pull Up/Down Rate

Using Pro Tools software with a SYNC HD (or SYNC I/O) peripheral allows you to change the speed of your audio and video to match the required film, NTSC, or PAL conversion (see Figure 2.33).

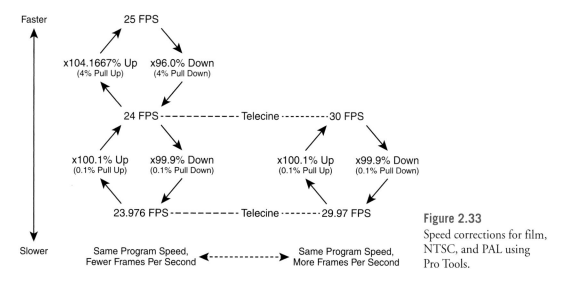

Figure 2.33
Speed corrections for film, NTSC, and PAL using Pro Tools.

The Pro Tools Audio and Video Rate Pull Up and Pull Down controls are located in the Session Setup window. See Figure 2.34.

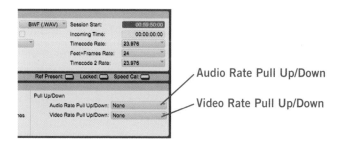

Figure 2.34
Pull Up/Down menus in the Session Setup window.

- ■ **Audio Rate Pull Up/Down:** Controls audio sample rate.

- ■ **Video Rate Pull Up/Down:** Controls video frame rate.

Note: QuickTime Video Pull options are currently limited to 0.1% Up/Down regardless of frame rate. Also, when using Avid video, no video pull options are available.

The choices available in these menus are determined by the session's Timecode Rate. Combinations can be applied by choosing from both menus.

Note: 4% pull factors are not available in 176.4kHz and 192kHz sessions.

Auto Match Pull Factors

Auto Match Pull Factors is available from the Timecode Rate menu in the Session Setup window (directly below the Incoming Time counter; see Figure 2.35). When Auto Match Pull Factors is enabled, Pro Tools adjusts audio and video playback rates as needed to match any changes to the current session's Timecode Rate.

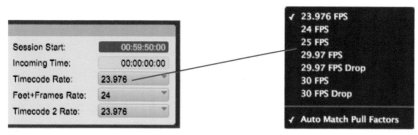

Figure 2.35
Frame Rate menu with Auto Match Pull Factors enabled.

Auto Match Pull Factors are always applied and calculated relative to the current pull setting and the session's Timecode Rate. When enabled, if the session Timecode Rate is changed in such a way that the video would have to be pulled by an unsupported amount, the video remains unaffected. This setting remains enabled once it is turned on (even after changing the Timecode Rate), is not enabled by default, and its state is stored with the session file.

To use Auto Match Pull Factors:

1. Set or verify the actual frame rate of the current (source) Pro Tools session.

2. Enable AUTO MATCH PULL FACTORS from the TIMECODE RATE menu.

3. Change the frame rate in the TIMECODE RATE menu to the new (destination) frame rate you want to convert the session to.

The Pull Up/Down rates will automatically change the audio playback rate (and the video playback rate if a supported pull is chosen) as needed to match the change to the current session Timecode Rate.

Note: Since video pulls are limited to 0.1% up or down when using QuickTime video, even with Auto Match Pull Factors enabled, video pulls will not follow audio pull settings when changing the Timecode Rate, unless the pull rate is 0.1% up or down. This essentially limits the use of video pulls to only workflow conversions between NTSC and film projects. Also, Avid video pulls are not currently supported at all in Pro Tools.

Example of Using Auto Match Pull Factors

When Auto Match Pull Factors is enabled, Pro Tools links audio and video pull factors when changing the session Timecode Rate. For example, assume a Pro Tools session containing QuickTime video is set to a Timecode Rate of 29.97FPS, the audio and video are both playing with no audio pulls, and Auto Match Pull Factors is enabled.

If you then change the session Timecode Rate to 24FPS, both the Audio and Video Rate Pull settings would change by +0.1% (the appropriate pull setting required by the change in Timecode Rate). In this example, the QuickTime video pull follows the audio pull, since QuickTime can be pulled up or down 0.1%.

Auto Match-enabled pull factors are applied to any existing Audio Rate Pull Up/Down. For example, if audio were already being pulled –0.1% down when you changed the session Timecode Rate from 29.97FPS to 24FPS, the Audio Rate Pull Up/Down menu would switch to None.

In one final example, assume a Pro Tools session containing PAL QuickTime video is set to a Timecode Rate of 25FPS, the audio and video are both playing with no audio pulls, and Auto Match Pull Factors is enabled.

If you then change the session Timecode Rate to 29.97FPS, only the Audio Pull settings would change to –4.1% down (the appropriate pull setting required by the change in Timecode Rate). In this example, since the QuickTime video does not support a –4.1% pull down, the QuickTime video pull will remain unchanged.

Video Rate Pull Up/Down

The Video Rate Pull Up/Down menu (located below the Audio Rate Pull Up/Down menu in the Session Setup window) allows you to change the frame rate of video playback independently from the audio pulls (if any). Video pull options are not available when using Avid video, and become available only in the Video Rate Pull Up/Down menu when using QuickTime video (any frame rate) and are limited to 0.1% pulls; see Figure 2.36.

Figure 2.36
Video Rate Pull Up/Down options.

Tip: Both Audio and Video pull rates are saved with the session.

What Is Pulled Up or Down?

The following sections describe how related Pro Tools features are affected by Pull Up and Down rates.

Timecode Ruler

Video Pull Up and Down does not affect the Timecode Ruler. Be sure to set the session Timecode Rate to the correct frame rate for your project. For example, when working with 23.976FPS video and pulling the video up by 0.1%, switch the session Frame Rate to 24FPS to keep the Timecode Ruler aligned.

Audio and Video Pull Problems

Since transferring audio between film, NTSC video, and PAL video projects requires exact pull settings, if these settings are set incorrectly, sync issues will result.

Also, sometimes double pull settings are performed in error, when projects received are not clearly labeled or designated as running at film, PAL, or NTSC speed. For example, if audio that originated from a film project is pulled down 0.1% in an Avid picture editing system before importing into an NTSC Pro Tools session, the audio should not be pulled down after import into the NTSC Pro Tools session. If, however, it was not made clear to the Pro Tools operator that the original film-referenced audio had already been pulled down to video speed, the Pro Tools operator might assume that the audio needs to be pulled down 0.1%. If this occurs, in reality two pull-downs (or a double pull) have occurred. This double pull-down will cause the audio to noticeably drift out of sync with the picture.

Errors like this do occur. To avoid such mistakes, if you are unsure of the correct speed of audio and video you receive, always verify with the originator of the files before configuring the pull settings in Pro Tools.

Typical Example Workflow Scenarios Using Audio Pulls

Now that you have an understanding of how and why audio and video pulls options are used in Pro Tools and how they are enabled, this final section of the lesson will present two different workflow example scenarios where specific audio pull options are necessary.

United States Documentary Film Project

A documentary film project is shot on film using 24FPS for the film and 24FPS for the production audio (using a field recorder capturing BWF/WAV files at 48kHz, 24-bit). During the Telecine process, the film is transferred to a Sony HDCAM video format using the 3:2 Pull Down method (for more information about 3:2 Pull Down, please consult Appendix A of this book). During the Telecine process, the film is slowed down slightly (0.1%) to match the speed difference between film and HD video. After the Telecine process, the HD video runs at 23.976FPS. The original 24FPS field recorder production audio is also slowed down 0.1% to match the picture. The picture and audio are then imported into a 23.976FPS Avid project and edited. When the picture and audio are ready for audio post production work in Pro Tools, the project's video and audio are exported to Pro Tools as a 23.976FPS AAF project. After the project is transferred into Pro Tools, the project remains a 23.976FPS project (running 0.1% slower than the original film). After all the audio elements are edited and mixed, the audio in the project must be returned to its original 24FPS speed, so that it can be properly synchronized with the final edited film print.

Tip: Most North American reality television shows and documentaries shot in HD are edited and mixed using 23.976FPS. Since 23.976FPS and 29.97FPS audio projects use the same speed reference in North American territories, no sample rate pull is required to convert the project's audio to SD (standard definition) NTSC video speed.

To change the session audio from 23.976FPS (HD video speed) to 24FPS (film speed):

1. Enable AUTO MATCH PULL FACTORS from the TIMECODE RATE menu.

2. Change the frame rate in the TIMECODE RATE menu from 23.976FPS to 24FPS (the new destination frame rate of your audio).

The Pull Up/Down rates will automatically change the audio pull to 0.1% Up (to match the proper film speed).

Note: Most film projects create print master audio stems in Pro Tools still refer-
       enced to HD or SD video speed, with the audio corrected to film speed during
       the final Dolby, DTS, SDDS, or DCP (Digital Cinema Package) encoding
       process. This makes unpulling the audio in Pro Tools unnecessary for most
       film projects.

European Feature Film Project

A feature film project is shot on 35mm film using 24FPS for the film camera and 24FPS for the production audio (using a field recorder capturing BWF/WAV files at 48kHz, 24-bit). The film is transferred without sound to PAL video format using the Telecine process (for more information about Telecine, please consult Appendix B of this book). During the Telecine process to PAL video, the film is sped up (4%) to match the speed and frame rate difference between film and PAL video. After the Telecine process, the video runs at 25FPS. The PAL video tape is then captured into a 24p PAL Avid Media Composer project, capturing the video tape at the PAL rate of 25FPS, capturing every picture frame. The Avid picture editing system stores two video fields as a single progressive frame, which is played back and edited at 24FPS. The field recorder audio is then imported into the Avid project at the original film rate and speed, syncing perfectly with the 24p project. When the picture and guide track audio are ready for audio post production work in Pro Tools, the project's audio is exported as a 24FPS AAF project with accom- panying 24FPS QuickTime video.

Using Pro Tools, a new BWF/WAV, 24-bit, 48kHz session is created, with a Timecode Rate of 24FPS (matching the original field recorder audio). In order to make sure that all alternate production audio takes are available for editing, all of the original field recorder audio is imported into the session using the original Timecode Rate of 24FPS with no audio pulls enabled.

Next, the 24FPS AAF Avid audio export and QuickTime video is imported into the Pro Tools session, with the session remaining at 24FPS. After all audio elements are edited and the final mix is completed, the audio in the session is printed to audio stems for final delivery to the post house making the final film print.

Note: Using this 24p PAL Avid workflow, there are no audio pulls necessary in
       Pro Tools, because the Avid Media Composer system performs a "reverse
       Telecine" with the PAL video media in order to create and export 24FPS
       media running at the same speed and frame rate as film.

Review/Discussion Questions

1. What is the name of the web-based search tool on Avid's website?

2. What is the DigiTest utility used for?

3. What is Avid hardware "firmware"?

4. How do you update an Avid D-Control ES's firmware?

5. How do you update an Avid SYNC HD's firmware?

6. Where are DigiBase index database files for volumes stored, and why is it sometimes necessary to delete them?

7. How many voices does a Pro Tools HDX system with two installed HDX cards have?

8. What are "explicit voices" and which Pro Tools systems support them?

9. What is the Disk Cache setting in the Playback Engine dialog box used for?

10. How can the Disk Cache setting be useful when playing back audio over a network?

11. How many time slots are available on Pro Tools|HD and Pro Tools|HDX DSP-accelerated hardware?

12. What does disabling the I/O Setup checkbox, "Sessions Overwrite Current I/O Setup When Opened" do?

13. What are audio and video pull options used for?

14. Which audio pull setting is needed to convert NTSC 29.97FPS audio to film speed?

15. Which audio pull setting is needed to convert PAL 25FPS audio to film speed?

Lesson 2 Keyboard Shortcuts

Shortcut	Description
Control+Command-click (Mac)/Ctrl+Start-click (Windows)	**Toggle a track active or inactive on Mix window track icon**

Troubleshooting a Pro Tools System

In this exercise, you will use the Avid Online Knowledge Base to find possible causes and solutions to several common errors. You will open a Pro Tools session with missing media and address other problems that must be corrected. After correcting the problems with the session, you will then export the session for other delivery formats using Audio Pull options in the Session Setup window.

Media Used:
310P Exercise 02.ptxt (Pro Tools session file)

Duration:
30 minutes

GOALS

- Use Avid Knowledge Base searches
- Delete Pro Tools settings files
- Enable Disk Cache in the Playback Engine dialog box
- Convert sessions using audio pulls for NTSC and PAL formats

Getting Started: Using Avid Knowledge Base

1. Assuming you have a computer with an Internet connection, use the Avid Online Knowledge Base to try to find possible causes and solutions to the following errors, when using Pro Tools 10.x (or higher):

Error	Possible Cause	Solution
Pro Tools failure to launch	_____	_____
DAE Error -36	_____	_____
DAE Error -9073	_____	_____

Tip: Feel free to write on a separate piece of paper instead of writing in your book.

Correcting Pro Tools System Performance Problems

Your Pro Tools system has been running somewhat sluggishly and searches in the Workspace browser take longer than normal. You know that deleting the Pro Tools preference and database files, forcing Pro Tools to refresh its settings files will solve the problem.

1. Delete only the Pro Tools preference and all database files (including Volume.dbb files).

2. After successfully deleting the settings files, restart your computer.

3. After your computer has restarted, launch the Pro Tools software.

Tip: The first time you launch Pro Tools after deleting the settings files, it is normal for Pro Tools to take slightly longer to launch.

Opening and Playing the Pro Tools Session

1. Open **310P EXERCISE 02.PTXT**, located on the book DVD at directory at **EXERCISE MEDIA/310P CLASS AUDIO FILES v10/310P EXERCISE 02** (or other location specified by the course instructor).

2. In the **SAVE NEW SESSION AS** dialog box, name the session as desired, saving into an appropriate location on a valid storage volume.

When the session opens, the following six tracks should appear (shown in Figure 2.37):

- Video (QuickTime video track)
- FX Stem (stereo audio track)
- DIA Stem (stereo audio track)
- Music Stem (stereo audio track)
- ST Mix Stem (stereo audio track)
- Main (stereo Master Fader)

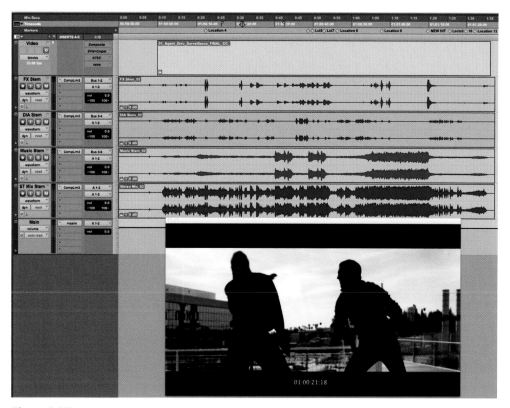

Figure 2.37
310P Exercise 2 session with all media.

3. In order to facilitate smoother playback and reduce the risk of audio playback errors, enable Extended Disk Cache by choosing **SETUP > PLAYBACK ENGINE**, and choosing the highest available setting from the **CACHE SIZE** menu. The example shown in Figure 2.38 is enabling a 7GB Cache Size. Your maximum setting may be different depending upon the amount of available RAM in your computer.

Figure 2.38
Choosing a Cache Size in the
Playback Engine dialog box.

Converting Sessions Using Audio Pulls

The current session is using a 23.976FPS HD QuickTime video file. The audio
for the session needs to be converted to the following formats:

- NTSC SD Video Standard

- PAL SD Video Standard

Tip: Enable Auto Match Pull Factors in the Timecode Rate menu of the Session
Setup window to make it easy to convert your session to the above listed
formats.

Note: For this exercise scenario, assume that the session's correctly pulled audio
with corresponding Timecode Rate is being converted in this exercise to
match an external linear video source that exists elsewhere.

1. Starting with your saved session in the previous section of this exercise, use
    FILE > SAVE AS and name the new session *Your Name* 310P Ex2 NTSC,
    saving it into an appropriate location on a valid storage volume.

2. If not already enabled, enable AUTO MATCH PULL FACTORS in the
    TIMECODE RATE menu of the SESSION SETUP window.

3. After saving the new session, change the TIMECODE RATE in the SESSION
    SETUP window from 23.976FPS to the NTSC Timecode Rate (29.97FPS).

Tip: When changing the original 23.976FPS Timecode Rate to 29.97FPS NTSC
video speed, the Audio Rate Pull Up/Down setting will not change, which is
correct for NTSC conversion. The Timecode Rate change to 29.97FPS will
make the session compatible with a NTSC linear video source.

4. Save the session when you have verified the proper TIMECODE RATE and
    AUDIO RATE PULL UP/DOWN settings for NTSC video.

5. Repeat Steps 1–4, saving the file with **PAL** replacing **NTSC** in the file name
    and converting the original 23.976FPS session to PAL SD video in Step 3.

6. When you have completed all of these steps, save and close your session.

Synchronizing Pro Tools with Linear Video

This lesson covers some of the common synchronization hardware and techniques used when using Pro Tools with linear video. Although non-linear video is much more commonly used today, you may still encounter projects that originate or finish on video tape, and thus require you to transfer audio and video between Pro Tools and a linear video deck.

Media Used: 310P Exercise 03.ptxt (NTSC, PAL, or HD) and 310P Exercise 03 Linear Video Tape (NTSC, PAL, or HD)

Duration: 120 minutes

Note: In order to complete this lesson and exercise, you will need to have access to a Pro Tools HD system, a professional video tape recorder supporting RS-422 (9-pin), and an Avid SYNC Peripheral. In addition, you will need to create a linear video tape containing the specific media required for this lesson/exercise. For instructions on creating the linear video tape for this lesson, see Appendix D, "Video Tape Duplication Instructions." If you do not have access to the above equipment, then you can skip this lesson and exercise.

GOALS

- Configure Pro Tools for synchronization with a linear video deck
- Prepare for online recording
- Configure and enable 9-pin serial machine control
- Use Machine Control shortcuts
- Use Spot mode with a linear video deck
- Use time stamps

Introduction

When using Pro Tools for post production, it is still common to synchronize Pro Tools to external timecode and clock sources, such as DAT machines, video decks, and analog or digital multi-tracks. In order to use these common post production machines in conjunction with Pro Tools, it is important to understand exactly how these devices connect to and interface with the Pro Tools hardware and the computer.

Understanding how to synchronize Pro Tools audio and video hardware peripherals and use them with external timecode devices is an important skill to acquire if you want to work in a post production facility, because many projects still originate and finish on these external timecode machines. This lesson covers configuring the Avid SYNC Peripherals and many of the techniques used to accurately synchronize Pro Tools to timecode from external video devices.

Configuring the Hardware and Software for Linear Video Sync

Pro Tools can automatically record or play back audio synchronized to an external timecode source (such as a VTR, DA-88, or timecode DAT machine). In order for Pro Tools HD-series hardware systems to synchronize to an external timecode source, they require an external timecode synchronization peripheral, such as an Avid SYNC HD (see Figure 3.1).

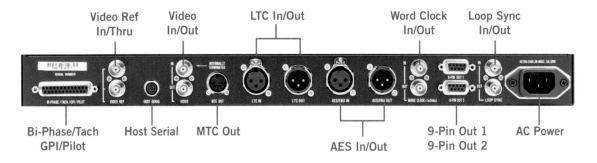

Figure 3.1
Avid SYNC HD rear panel connectors.

Tip: The SYNC HD and the SYNC I/O are referred to collectively as SYNC
       Peripherals for the remainder of this book.

Connecting the SYNC Peripheral (Recap)

When connecting a SYNC Peripheral for synchronization with a linear video deck, the following connections are necessary:

■ Host serial cable connecting the SYNC Peripheral to the Pro Tools|HDX, Pro Tools|HD, or Pro Tools|HD Native card's Host Serial connector (see Figure 3.2).

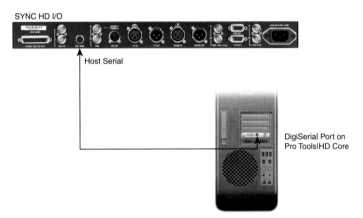

Figure 3.2
Host serial connections, SYNC HD to Pro Tools|HD.

■ Loop Sync Clock interconnecting all Pro Tool HD-series audio interfaces to the SYNC Peripheral using the Loop Sync In/Out connectors (see Figure 3.3).

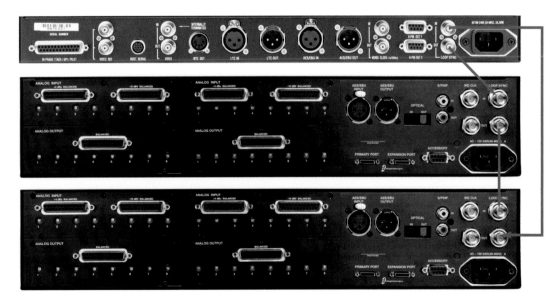

Figure 3.3
SYNC HD Loop Sync in an expanded Pro Tools HD system.

SYNC Peripheral Standalone Mode

A SYNC Peripheral can be used as a standalone synchronization converter, time-code generator, clock generator, and timecode character generator, although a SYNC Peripheral cannot generate Video Reference. The term "standalone" refers to a system utilizing a SYNC Peripheral that is not controlled from within the Pro Tools software. SYNC Peripherals are connected to timecode and clock signals as needed, and configured from the front panel.

Tip: Although all **SYNC Peripheral** settings can be accessed from the front panel in standalone mode, you also have the option of connecting the **SYNC Peripheral** to a serial port on the host CPU (using an approved USB-serial converter on Macintosh, or a COM port on Windows computers) allowing remote computer control of the device.

Connecting a Linear Video Source

When using a linear video deck in audio post production applications, to ensure that Pro Tools runs at the same speed as the video deck, they must both be resolved or referenced to a common clock sync signal. This is usually Bi-Level sync for standard definition video reference (also often referred to as video reference, black-burst, or house sync), or Tri-Level sync when using a high-definition video device.

 For more information about video reference, consult Appendix B of this book.

For SYNC Peripherals to resolve to house sync:

■ Connect the house video reference/blackburst signal to the SYNC Peripheral's Video Ref In port. This is a non-terminated loop-through connection. If the second Video Ref connector is not used, you must terminate it using the supplied 75-ohm precision terminator resistor.

For SYNC Peripherals to receive a signal from an NTSC/PAL video clock source or VITC positional reference input:

■ Connect the Composite Out video signal to the SYNC Peripheral Video In port.

Note: The Video In connector on the **SYNC Peripheral** only supports composite video. Also, termination of the Video Out port is not required as the Video In port is internally terminated.

Connecting Longitudinal Timecode (LTC)

When synchronizing Pro Tools with a linear timecode source (such as a video deck), longitudinal timecode (LTC) is commonly used, providing precise timecode location data, so that Pro Tools can align the playback or record position with the linear timecode device. SYNC Peripherals provide LTC input and output connectors.

To input LTC to a SYNC Peripheral:

- Connect the LTC signal from your machine, synchronizer, or other source to the SYNC Peripheral LTC In port.

Tip: The separate LTC track on most professional video tape recorders is commonly referred to as the address track.

To output LTC from a SYNC Peripheral:

1. Connect the LTC Out from the SYNC Peripheral to your external device.

Summary of Pro Tools SYNC Peripheral Connections

To synchronize Pro Tools to an external video deck using video reference and LTC/VITC, the following primary SYNC Peripheral connections are recommended:

- Host serial connected from SYNC Peripheral to Pro Tools|HDX, Pro Tools|HD, or Pro Tools HD|Native card.

- Clock to Pro Tools HD audio interfaces and SYNC Peripheral via Loop Sync In/Out.

- Video reference (or Tri-Level sync) signal to the SYNC Peripheral's Video Ref In port.

- LTC Out of the Linear Video Deck to LTC In of the SYNC Peripheral.

- Composite Video Out of the Linear Video Deck to Video In of the SYNC Peripheral (for optional VITC).

Enabling the SYNC Peripheral (Recap)

After you have confirmed that all of the necessary SYNC Peripheral hardware connections have been made, and all hardware devices and peripherals are powered on, you are ready to configure the Pro Tools software for synchronization with the linear video device.

In the Avid Learning Series

For a review of the SYNC Peripheral settings in the Synchronization tab of the Peripherals dialog box, and the available Loop Sync Clock Options in the Session Setup window, consult the PT210P book.

Clock Versus Positional Reference

In order for Pro Tools to accurately synchronize to another device, they must have two reference types in common. First, they must both have a common clock (or speed) reference. A post production clock reference (such as video reference, Tri-Level sync, or word clock) tells both sync devices (such as Pro Tools and a video deck) how fast to go. Without a common speed reference, even if Pro Tools and a video deck start out playing in perfect sync, over time the devices will drift out of sync.

Second, both sync devices must have a common positional reference (or address). The positional reference (usually timecode) tells both sync devices where to locate to prior to beginning synchronized playback or record. Usually one device generates a positional reference for the other to follow, which ensures that both devices locate to the same synchronized starting point. Without a positional reference to follow, even if Pro Tools and a video deck are playing/recording at exactly the same speed, they will never achieve accurate sync, because they will not start in sync to begin with.

With identical clock and positional references shared between all devices, accurate sync will be achieved, even over long periods of time. When all sync devices are playing back or recording using the same common clock and positional references, the system is referred to as a *resolved* system. It is highly recommended that once common speed and address references for a project are chosen, you maintain these references throughout all stages of the project to prevent any sync discrepancies.

SYNC Peripheral as the Clock Reference

The selected clock source device determines your choices for clock reference. When the SYNC Peripheral is the clock source, it is the loop master. Clock and Positional Reference selectors become active in the SYNC Setup area of the Session Setup window, as shown in Figure 3.4.

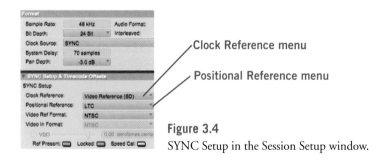

Clock Reference menu

Positional Reference menu

Figure 3.4
SYNC Setup in the Session Setup window.

When the SYNC Peripheral is not the selected clock source device, the Clock Reference menu in the SYNC Setup area switches to Loop Sync. Conversely, when the SYNC Peripheral is the selected clock source device, clock reference choices become available, including Internal/VSO, Video In, Video Reference, LTC, Bi-Phase, Pilot Tone, AES/EBU, and Word Clock.

To choose a SYNC Peripheral clock reference:

1. From within the Session Setup window, select a SYNC Peripheral clock choice from the Clock Reference menu. Most post projects will use either Video Reference (SD) or Video Reference (HD). See Figure 3.5.

Figure 3.5
SYNC Setup Clock Reference menu.

Valid and Invalid Clock Sources

When you choose a clock source that is valid and a consistent speed for your hardware to clock to, the Locked and Speed Cal indicators will be lit solid in the Session Setup window, as shown in Figure 3.6.

Tip: The Locked and Speed Cal indicators can also be displayed in the Edit and Transport windows if the Synchronization display option is enabled.

Figure 3.6
The Locked and Speed Cal indicators lit in Session Setup.

If you choose a clock source that is currently invalid or unavailable, you will see the Locked indicator blinking and the Speed Cal indicator unlit. This can happen when the current Video Format setting (PAL/NTSC) is different from the video reference signal, for example. You will also receive the warning shown in Figure 3.7.

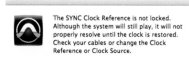

The SYNC Clock Reference is not locked. Although the system will still play, it will not properly resolve until the clock is restored. Check your cables or change the Clock Reference or Clock Source.

OK

Figure 3.7
Hardware clock sync warning.

In addition to the Locked and Speed Cal indicators, there is also a Ref Present indicator in the Session Setup window. This light is lit solid green when your SYNC Peripheral is receiving a valid video reference signal.

Tip: **Ref Present indicator can also be displayed in the Edit and Transport windows if the Synchronization display option is enabled.**

Positional Reference

Whereas the clock reference provides constant control over the speed of Pro Tools playback/recording, positional reference provides time address information (time-code) for the SYNC Peripheral timecode reader and generator. In other words, it tells Pro Tools where to locate to before beginning playback or recording. A common positional reference used for Pro Tools music production is longitudinal time-code (LTC), while post production uses both longitudinal timecode (LTC) and vertical interval timecode (VITC).

To select positional reference from within Pro Tools, choose a setting from the Positional Reference pop-up menu, as shown in Figure 3.8.

Figure 3.8
Positional Reference pop-up menu in the Session Setup window.

Using Auto LTC/VITC

If your SYNC Peripheral is receiving both LTC and VITC, you can select Auto LTC/VITC. When using Auto LTC/VITC, the SYNC Peripheral switches automatically between reading LTC and VITC, depending on which one is delivering the best timecode signal. Under most circumstances, using the transport at normal playback speeds and faster will use LTC, while using the transport at slower speeds (such as crawling and scrubbing) will use VITC. When Auto LTC/VITC is enabled, it is indicated on the front panel of the SYNC Peripheral by the LTC and VITC positional reference LEDs (both will be lit), and a decimal point between the minutes and seconds fields of the timecode display.

Because VITC can only be read at play speeds and slower (including when paused/parked), and LTC can only be read at play speeds and higher (including shuttle speeds), using the Auto LTC/VITC feature provides the best of both VITC and LTC reading, without having to manually switch settings.

 For more information about positional references, refer to Appendix B in this book.

Setting Frame Rates (Recap)

While using Pro Tools with a SYNC Peripheral, the frame rate and video format follow the session frame rate and video format settings. These settings are set in the Session Setup window. Before syncing your Pro Tools session with external linear devices, it is necessary to properly set the frame rates for the session. Pro Tools allows you to separately (and independently) choose a timecode rate and a feet+frames rate from within the Session Setup window. This is useful, because it provides the flexibility to reference points within a Pro Tools session using both timecode and feet+frames. This is important, as film projects are frequently transferred to video and the videotape then contains both a timecode and a feet+frames window burn.

Timecode Rate

This menu allows you to set the timecode rate for the current session.

To set the timecode rate:

1. If the Session Setup window is not open, do one of the following:

    • Choose SETUP > SESSION.

    • Press COMMAND+2 (Mac) or CTRL+ 2 (Windows) on the numeric keypad.

2. From the Timecode Rate pop-up menu, choose the desired frame rate for your project, as shown in Figure 3.9.

    • **23.976FPS**: Used for HD video projects.

    • **24FPS**: International film standard and also used for some HD video projects.

- **25FPS**: PAL standard definition audio/video format typically used for video projects (generally used in Europe, Africa, Asia, Australia, and some parts of South America).

- **29.97FPS**: NTSC Nondrop frame standard definition audio/video format typically used for film projects that are converted to NTSC (generally used in North and Central America, and some parts of Asia and South America).

- **29.97FPS Drop**: NTSC drop frame standard definition audio/video format typically used for television NTSC broadcast (generally used in North and Central America, and some parts of Asia and South America).

- **30FPS**: Music applications (non-video) and some film referenced audio.

- **30FPS Drop**: This less common frame rate is sometimes used for NTSC television programs that are shot on film.

Note: When Auto Match Pull Factors is enabled, Pro Tools adjusts audio playback rates as needed to match any changes to the current session's timecode rate.

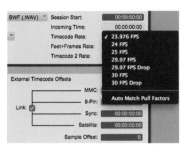

Figure 3.9
Timecode Rate menu options.

Secondary Timecode Ruler

The Timecode 2 pop-up menu allows you to set the frame rate for a secondary timecode ruler that references video frame rate in the timeline that is different from the session's timecode rate. Although you cannot select the Timecode 2 Ruler as the Main Timescale, you can edit with a 50FPS grid (for example) by setting the Main Timescale to Timecode at 25FPS, and then setting the grid resolution to ½ frame. The Timecode 2 Rate ruler is useful when using SD video in the Pro Tools timeline that may reference an HD video master using a different timecode frame rate.

Note: Changing the Timecode 2 Rate setting does not affect the settings of an Avid SYNC Peripheral.

Feet+Frames Rate

This menu allows you to set the feet+frames rate for the current session. Pro Tools users who work with audio post projects for film and have extensive experience working with 35mm film frequently use feet+frames.

Tip: When setting the feet+frames rate, Pro Tools only supports using 35mm feet+frames numbers.

To set the feet+frames rate:

1. From the Feet+Frames Rate pop-up menu, shown in Figure 3.10, choose from the following standard frame rates:

    ● 23.976FPS

    ● 24FPS

    ● 25FPS

Figure 3.10
Feet+Frames Rate menu options.

Video Ref Format

When working with video in Pro Tools, there are a variety of different supported standard definition (SD) and high definition (HD) formats that can be selected. It is important to choose the video reference format in Pro Tools that matches the actual format of your linear or non-linear video source.

SD Video Reference

After choosing a frame rate and Video Reference (SD) as your Clock Reference, you must choose the proper video format (either NTSC or PAL) from the Video Ref Format menu (see Figure 3.11). If the session already contains video, the Video Ref Format will be set automatically.

Figure 3.11
Video Ref Format menu (SD video).

HD Video Reference

When the Clock Reference is set to Video Reference (HD), HD video reference rates become available in the Video Ref Format menu, as shown in Figure 3.12. You can choose the HD format that matches your project.

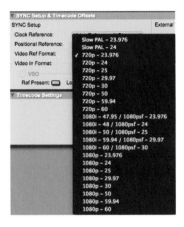

Figure 3.12
Video Ref Format menu (HD video).

Caution: You must have an Avid SYNC HD in order to choose HD Reference Rates in the Session Setup window. The previous-generation Avid SYNC I/O does not support HD video reference rates (Tri-Level sync).

On the Web   An in-depth discussion of HD video standards is beyond the scope of this book. For more information about HD video standards, go to www.moviola.com/book/export/html/274 or www.atsc.org.

Setting the Session Start Time (Recap)

After choosing the desired frame rate, you will also need to set or verify the session start time. Pro Tools allows you to set the session start time from within the Session Setup window, using any timecode number from hour 00 through hour 23.

To set the session start time, shown in Figure 3.13, you simply enter the session start time you want by highlighting the Session Start field, typing a new number, and pressing Return.

Figure 3.13
Session Start timecode from the Session Setup window.

Session Start Post Production Standards

Most professional post projects use a Session Start timecode number of 01:00:00:00 (or later), avoiding the default Session Start timecode number of 00:00:00:00, because if using a session start of 00:00:00:00, there are no negative timecode numbers that can be used for a linear video deck to use for pre-roll and cueing prior to the Session Start. Also, many film projects use the Session Start timecode number as a way of identifying the reel number for the film (i.e., Hour 01=Reel 1, Hour 02=Reel 2, etc.). Finally, avoiding a Session Start of 00:00:00:00 allows you to insert color bars, audio reference levels, and other sync tones one to two minutes earlier than the start of your session. For all of these reasons, you should avoid using 00:00:00:00 session starts, although it is acceptable to have sessions starting one to two minutes earlier than timecode number 01:00:00:00.

Tip: You can capture and copy the current timecode being received to the Session Start display by highlighting the display and pressing the Equals key (Mac) or Asterisk key (Windows) on the numeric keypad, followed by the Return key to confirm your entry.

Changing the Session Start Time

When changing the Session Start timecode number to an earlier number, the dialog box shown in Figure 3.14 appears.

Figure 3.14
Session Start Timecode Positions dialog box.

You must select one of the following options from this dialog box:

■ **Maintain timecode**: Choose this option to insert more time at the start of your session. This is helpful when you have clips in your session that have already been placed at specific timecode numbers that must not change.

■ **Maintain relative position**: Choose this option to apply a global offset to all clips placed in your session. All clips will remain in the same position relative to the start of the session and to each other.

This dialog box will not appear if there are no active clips or automation breakpoints placed on any tracks.

When changing the Session Start timecode number to a later number, the dialog box shown in Figure 3.15 appears.

Figure 3.15
Session Start Timecode Offset dialog box.

This dialog box warns you that since clips cannot exist earlier than the session start time, all clips will be offset to the new session start time.

Preparing for Online Recording

Before you are ready to begin online (timecode synchronized) recording, it is important to verify the Online Options preferences. To verify your online recording preferences, choose Setup > Preferences > Operation Page (see Figure 3.16). The following Online Options appear:

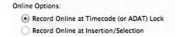

Figure 3.16
Online Record Options in the Operation page of preferences.

■ **Record Online at Timecode (or ADAT) Lock**: Choosing this option makes Pro Tools start recording on any tracks that are record-enabled as soon as the timecode is received, ignoring the position of the cursor or any selection that you might have made.

■ **Record Online at Insertion/Selection**: This option is often used to insert recorded audio that occurs at specific timecode numbers, while leaving all other previously recorded audio unchanged. Choosing this option makes Pro Tools record online only at the insertion cursor. If you make a selection, online recording only occurs between the start and end times of the selection, even if timecode is received prior to the selection start. If timecode is received later than the selection start, the error message shown in Figure 3.17 will appear.

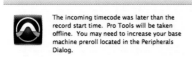

Figure 3.17
Online Record error message.

Digital Transfers and Sync

When recording audio into Pro Tools while slaving to timecode and using any of the audio interface's digital connectors, the Pro Tools system clock slaves to the incoming digital playback source's sample rate clock. It is therefore recommended to resolve Pro Tools and the digital playback source to a common system clock, such as video reference.

Verifying System Sync

After you have verified all of your SYNC Peripheral connections and Pro Tools software settings, you can check to make sure that your video deck is syncing properly with Pro Tools.

To verify sync between your video deck and Pro Tools:

1. Place Pro Tools online and then press **PLAY** on your video deck.

2. Timecode is fed into your SYNC Peripheral and Pro Tools will chase the timecode after it is up to speed.

3. If your video deck has a jog shuttle wheel, when you scrub the video, Pro Tools should read VITC when scrubbing, crawling, or paused, and LTC when at normal playback speed.

9-Pin (RS-422) Control of Pro Tools

Pro Tools can control the transport and track record-arming functions of an external machine (such as a video tape recorder) remotely using the Machine Control option (for Pro Tools HD hardware systems). This software option provides control of external machines, even if they are not physically located in the same room as the Pro Tools operator.

What Is RS-422?

The RS-422 standard (also known as 9-pin or Sony 9-pin due to its common 9-pin connector found on many professional audio and video devices) is a balanced four wire technical specification that was originally developed as a telecommunications standard for binary serial communications between two devices (such as a computer and a printer). Over the years, its usage has been expanded to allow software programs such as Pro Tools HD to control RS-422–compliant devices such as video tape recorders, multi-track tape machines, DAT machines, and other compatible linear and non-linear devices.

RS-422 is an updated version of the original unbalanced serial protocol known as RS-232, allowing much longer distances between connected devices. The RS-422 standard specification states which signaling voltages must be used, what connectors are to be used, and what pins on those connectors are to be used for each function, and recommends maximum distances over which the technology can be reliably used (currently up to 4,000 feet/1,219 meters). Pro Tools (RS-422) Machine Control allows the Pro Tools HD software to remotely control transport functions (such as play, record, stop, pause, rewind, fast forward, and eject) as well as remote record track arming functions of another RS-422 compliant device.

For more information on the RS-422 standard, visit either the Electronic Industries Alliance at www.ecaus.org or the Telecommunications Industry Association at www.tiaonline.org.

Tip: Machine Control is an optional software iLok licensed product for Pro Tools HD software that must be purchased separately.

Configuring 9-Pin Machine Control (Deck Control)

A SYNC Peripheral provides two 9-pin machine ports that support direct 9-pin connection for Machine Control-enabled Pro Tools HD hardware systems. Both ports can be connected simultaneously. In this configuration, Machine Control and a SYNC Peripheral provide all connections required for deck control including remote track arming, serial control, and other Machine Control features. In addition to the SYNC Peripheral 9-pin ports, you can also use the ports listed in Table 3.1.

Table 3.1   Machine Control Supported Connections

Connection Type	Mac	Windows
COM1 Port	N/A	Yes
COM2 Port	N/A	Yes
Keyspan USA28X USB-Serial Converter	Yes	No
SYNC 9-Pin Out 1	Yes	Yes
SYNC 9-Pin Out 2	Yes	Yes

To connect a machine for Machine Control serial mode, connect a 9-pin cable for each machine to one of the available supported ports listed in Table 3.1. With the Pro Tools Machine Control option enabled, Pro Tools can directly control the transport functions of one machine at a time. This requires a 9-pin serial cable to control the machine, which is supplied with the Machine Control option, in addition to the host serial cable discussed earlier in this lesson. When purchasing the Machine Control option, you must specify whether you are using a Mac or Windows computer, since the cables/adapters supplied with the boxed product are different for each operating system. Assuming that your synchronization peripheral and external machine are connected, configured properly, powered on, and in remote mode, you are ready to enable Machine Control.

To enable Machine Control:

1. Set your machine-controllable VTR to **REMOTE** or **EXTERNAL** mode to receive the 9-pin control commands from Pro Tools.

2. Choose **SETUP > PERIPHERALS**, and click the **MACHINE CONTROL** tab. The options shown in Figure 3.18 appear.

Figure 3.18
Machine Control tab in the Peripherals dialog box.

3. In the **9-PIN MACHINE CONTROL (DECK CONTROL)** section, click the **ENABLE** box to enable 9-pin serial machine control, as shown in Figure 3.19.

Figure 3.19
9-Pin Machine Control enabled in the Peripherals dialog box.

4. From the **PORT** pop-up menu, choose the serial port that you will be using for Machine Control. Supported ports include **KEYSPAN USB-SERIAL ADAPTER** ports (Mac), **COM1** or **COM2** (Windows), or when using a SYNC Peripheral, both Mac and Windows systems will be able to access either of the two **9-PIN OUT** ports for Machine Control. (In Figure 3.20, the **SYNC 9-PIN OUT 1** port is selected.)

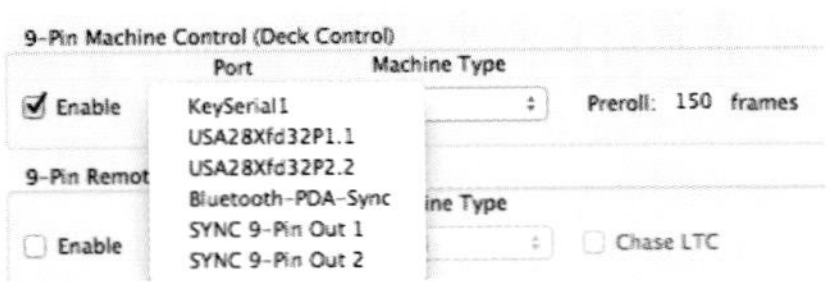

Figure 3.20
9-pin Machine Control port menu options (Mac).

Note: When using either the COM1 or COM2 port for 9-pin Machine Control on a Windows system, an approved RS-232 to RS-422 converter (such as the Rosetta Stone model 2/8 or 2/9) is recommended, although it may not be required for shorter cable runs.

5. From the **MACHINE TYPE** pop-up menu, choose the machine type you will be using. (This example uses a Sony SRW-5000 HDCAM-SR video recorder, as shown in Figure 3.21.)

Figure 3.21
Sony SRW-5000 HDCAM-SR video tape recorder enabled for machine control.

- **Preroll:** This option sets the amount of pre-roll before Pro Tools locks to the incoming timecode. Pro Tools defaults to 150 frames (approximately five seconds), which is usually sufficient. Choosing a shorter pre-roll time decreases the amount of audio heard prior to the insertion cursor, but might cause Pro Tools to lock to the incoming timecode late. Enter a new number if desired.

6. Click **OK** to close the window.

7. If you're using an Avid SYNC Peripheral with video reference as the clock reference, in the **SESSION SETUP** window, you can select **SERIAL TIMECODE** from the **POSITIONAL REFERENCE** pop-up menu. Enabling **SERIAL TIMECODE** as the **POSITIONAL REFERENCE** will allow faster timecode lock-up times between Pro Tools and the machine it is controlling.

8. When all of the settings have been configured, close the **SESSION SETUP** window. You are now ready to begin using Machine Control.

Using Pro Tools 9-Pin Serial Machine Control

Now that all of your hardware connections and software settings have been made, you are ready to begin using Machine Control.

Online and Offline Operation

To trigger Pro Tools playback or recording from an external source, you must put Pro Tools online.

There are several ways to put Pro Tools online:

■ Click the Online button in the Transport window or on an Avid worksurface (see Figure 3.22).

■ Press Command+J (Mac) or Ctrl+J (Windows).

■ Press Option+space bar (Mac) or Alt+space bar (Windows).

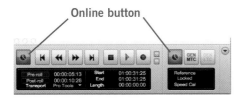

Figure 3.22
Online button enabled in the Transport window.

For online recording, make sure your record source is routed correctly to the Pro Tools hardware and the appropriate tracks are record-enabled.

Shortcut: To enable/disable Pro Tools online record, press Command+Option+space bar (Mac), Ctrl+Alt+space bar (Windows), or Online+Record on an Avid worksurface.

Note: Pro Tools requires approximately three seconds of pre-roll before online recording or playback begins.

Transport Controls

With Machine Control, the Pro Tools Transport becomes a multi-function controller.

To toggle the Pro Tools Transport Master between Pro Tools and the Machine (which places the machine's transport online), follow these steps:

1. From the MACHINE TRANSPORT pop-up menu (located in the TRANSPORT window as shown in Figure 3.23), choose ONLINE > MACHINE to enable its transport functions.

Machine Transport pop-up menu

Figure 3.23
Machine Transport pop-up menu.

Its name will have a check mark appended to it, indicating it is currently active, as shown in Figure 3.24.

Figure 3.24
Machine transport online (enabled).

2. In the same **MACHINE TRANSPORT** pop-up menu, choose **TRANSPORT** and one of the following options from the submenu:

- **Pro Tools**: Choose this option (shown in Figure 3.25) if you want Pro Tools to be the master transport, and the machine to follow Pro Tools selections. In this mode, the controls in the Transport window are focused on Pro Tools playback, recording, and so on. When Pro Tools is online and you begin playback or recording, the machine cues to Pro Tools, cueing to a pre-roll time before the current insertion time before rolling. The session locks to the machine's timecode.

Figure 3.25
Transport with Pro Tools enabled.

- **Machine**: Choose this option (shown in Figure 3.26) if you want the machine to act as the master transport, and Pro Tools to follow the machine. Only Play, Stop, Fast Forward, Rewind, and Record are active on the Transport window when the Machine option is enabled. In this mode, the controls in the Transport window are focused on the machine. When online, Pro Tools will slave to the machine. When offline, the Transport will only control the machine. When Pro Tools is slaved to the machine, the Pro Tools Transport can be used as a machine remote control or a system master control.

Figure 3.26
Transport with Machine enabled.

Shortcut: To toggle between Pro Tools and the Machine transports, press
Command+Backslash (Mac), Ctrl+Backslash (Windows), or Machine
Online on an Avid worksurface.

Machine Control Shortcuts

In addition to the standard Transport buttons, you can use the Machine Control
shortcut commands listed in Table 3.2 for playing and cueing.

Note: All commands listed in Table 3.2 require Transport = Machine to be enabled,
except for Toggle Transport Master.

Machine Control Error Messages

You might see the message shown in Figure 3.27 when you're trying to initialize
or use Machine Control.

Table 3.2   Machine Control Shortcuts

Command	Macintosh	Windows
Toggle Transport Master	Command+\	Ctrl+\
All Transport Buttons Off	Command+Period (.)	Ctrl+Period (.)
Rewind	Shift+Comma (,)	Shift+Comma (,)
Fast Forward	Shift+Period (.)	Shift+Period (.)
Shuttle Backward	Option+Comma (,)	Alt+Comma (,)
Shuttle Forward	Option+Period (.)	Alt+Period (.)
Cue to Selection Start	Command+Left Arrow	Ctrl+Left Arrow
Cue to Selection End	Command+Right Arrow	Ctrl+Right Arrow
Frame Bump Backward	Command+Option+Comma (,)	Ctrl+Alt+Comma (,)
Frame Bump Forward	Command+Option+Period (.)	Ctrl+Alt+Period (.)

Figure 3.27
Machine control enable error.

If you see this message, check the following:

- The 9-pin cable is connected to the video deck.

- The 9-pin cable is connected to the serial port you specified in the Machine Control section of the Peripherals dialog box.

- The video deck is turned on and set to Remote or External control.

Recording Slaved to an External Timecode Source

When your system is online and waiting to be triggered with Machine Control enabled, you are ready to record.

To record online using Pro Tools Machine Control:

1. Set your track input source.

2. Configure the HARDWARE SETUP.

3. Click the RECORD ENABLE button on the desired tracks in the Mix or Edit windows or on an Avid worksurface.

4. Put Pro Tools online.

5. Click the RECORD READY button in the TRANSPORT window or on an Avid worksurface.

6. Make an edit selection for the desired recording or, if stopping Pro Tools recording manually, locate the edit cursor to the desired record start location in the timeline.

7. Begin playback.

Pro Tools will automatically record audio synchronized to the timecode based on the session start time.

Synchronization Page Preferences

When using Machine Control, there are a number of Pro Tools Machine Control preference options that can be enabled from within the Synchronization tab of preferences. These options will be discussed in the following section of this lesson.

Machine Control

The Machine Control preference options are located in the Synchronization Preference tab, as shown in Figure 3.28. Five options are available that allow you to specify the Pro Tools aspects of Machine Control behavior.

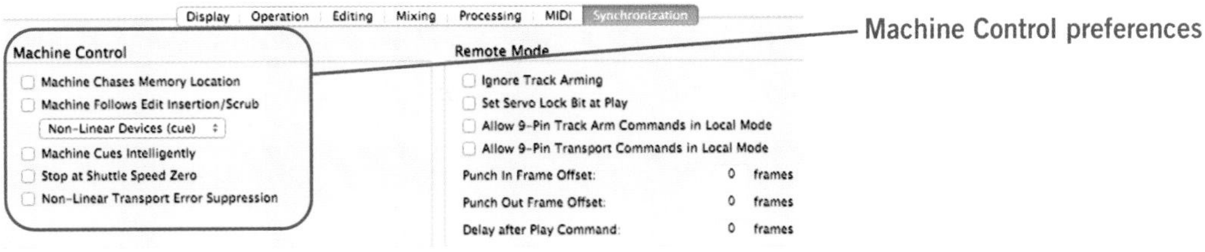

Figure 3.28
Pro Tools Machine Control preferences.

To access the Machine Control Preferences:

1. Choose SETUP > PREFERENCES, and then click the SYNCHRONIZATION tab.

2. The following MACHINE CONTROL PREFERENCES can be enabled/disabled:

   - **Machine Chases Memory Location**: With this option enabled, navigating to a specific location in a Pro Tools session with a Memory Location causes a connected transport to chase to that location.

   - **Machine Follows Edit Insertion/Scrub**: With this option enabled, navigating to a specific location in a Pro Tools session by moving the selection point or by scrubbing a track causes a connected transport to chase to that location.

   - **Machine Cues Intelligently**: With this option enabled, if you navigate to a cue point more than 10 seconds from the current location, Pro Tools will command a connected transport to shuttle to the desired location at full speed within 10 seconds of the cue point. Cueing will then slow to normal speed until the point is reached. This significantly speeds up tape cueing over long distances.

- **Stop at Shuttle Speed Zero**: With this option enabled, Pro Tools sends a Stop command when shuttle speed equals zero. Although most machines automatically stop when shuttle speed is equal to zero (in other words, whenever you stop shuttling), some machines require an explicit stop command to park correctly. Consult the manufacturer of your machine if you need to determine its shuttle stop capability.

- **Non-Linear Transport Error Suppression**: With this option enabled, Pro Tools will ignore any 9-pin errors received from non-linear audio and video devices.

Synchronization

The Synchronization preference options are also located in the Synchronization preference tab, as shown in Figure 3.29. There are three options that allow you to specify different aspects of Pro Tools sync delay and locking.

Figure 3.29
Synchronization preferences.

The following Synchronization preferences can be configured:

- **Minimum Sync Delay**: All external synchronization devices need a small amount of time to achieve synchronization lock. This amount varies for each device. You set the Pro Tools lock-up delay by entering a value for Minimum Sync Delay in the Synchronization preferences page. The lowest value available is 15 frames. Find the shortest possible lock-up time that your equipment can operate at consistently, and set this as the Minimum Sync Delay. When utilizing Avid Machine Control, enabling Serial Timecode as the Positional Reference in the Session Setup window will make machines lock up much faster. (Serial timecode requires both the Avid SYNC Peripheral and external devices to be locked to a house video reference.)

- **Delay Before Locking to Longitudinal Timecode/Delay Before Locking to Serial Timecode**: Both of these options allow you to enter a number of frames for Pro Tools to wait upon receiving incoming LTC or Serial Timecode, before attempting to lock to the incoming timecode signal. This delay gives a variable amount of frames for the LTC or Serial Timecode source to stabilize. This lets Pro Tools lock more accurately to any fluctuations that can occur when some linear LTC or Serial Timecode sources are first engaged. For example, a Sony SRW-5000 HDCAM linear video deck would need more time to lock with Pro Tools than a Doremi V1 non-linear video hard disk recorder.

Spot Mode in Post Production

Pro Tools Spot mode provides a convenient method for placing clips in sync with picture. This function can help you sync the beginning of a clip, the end of a clip, or any point within a clip, to a specific timecode location.

To spot a clip to a specific timecode start frame:

1. If the clip you want to spot is not already on a track, place the clip on the desired track.

2. Identify the timecode location where you want to trigger playback of your clip by pausing your video deck or digital video on that frame.

3. Right-click in the clip and choose **Spot**, as shown in Figure 3.30.

Figure 3.30
Spotting a clip using the right-click menu.

Tip: In Spot mode, you can also spot audio clips directly from any DigiBase browser to any audio track in your session by dragging and dropping the audio clip onto the desired track.

The Spot dialog box appears, as shown in Figure 3.31. The Spot dialog box always uses the last Time Scale chosen, although you can switch to any of the other available Time Scales at any time using the **Time Scale** pop-up menu.

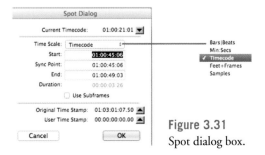

Figure 3.31
Spot dialog box.

Spot Mode Recap

1. Do one of the following:

   - If you want to sync using the start of the clip, press the **TAB** key on the keyboard until the **START** field becomes highlighted in the **SPOT** dialog box.

   - If you want to sync the end of the clip to a specified timecode number, rather than the start, press the **TAB** key to highlight the **END** field.

2. After the Start or End box is highlighted, do one of the following:

   - Type the desired **TIME SCALE** location (with no field separators).

   - Highlight a single field and type a new number. If you highlight a single field, you can choose from the following navigational tools:

     - Use the keyboard's **LEFT** or **RIGHT ARROW** key to select individual time fields to the left or right.

     - Use the **UP** or **DOWN ARROW** key to increment or decrement a field in single units.

     - To increase or decrease a single time field in increments larger than one, use the **PLUS** or **MINUS** key on the **NUMERIC** keypad. Enter a number and press the **RETURN** key to add or subtract the number to/from the currently selected field.

3. Enable the **USE SUBFRAMES** option if you want a resolution of 1/100th of a frame when using Timecode as the Time Scale.

4. After entering the desired numbers, click **OK**.

The clip will spot to the chosen Time Scale location. When the session is online, this clip will play back at the exact timecode number entered.

Shortcut: You can also Command+Right-click (Mac) or Ctrl+Right-click (Windows) on a clip to snap its start, sync point, or end to the selection start.

Current Time and the Timeline

As you edit sound for picture in Pro Tools, you spot and sync audio clips to the timeline rulers, located above the first track in your session. Once clips are properly edited and aligned to the timeline rulers in your session (see Figure 3.32), they will play back at their corresponding locations.

Figure 3.32
Common timeline ruler views used for post.

In addition to allowing you to enter timecode numbers manually and spot audio clips to the timeline of your session, the Spot dialog box also displays incoming timecode values received from external sources such as video tape recorders and players (see Figure 3.33). This incoming timecode (which is always displayed using the Timecode Time Scale) is displayed at the top of the Spot dialog box in the Current Timecode section. The Current Timecode display in the Spot dialog box is commonly used to capture the current timecode location from your external video source, and then copy it into the Start, Sync Point, or End fields. This feature allows you to quickly align audio clips (such as sound effects and music) to the linear picture and the timeline of your session, using the timecode from your video deck.

Figure 3.33
Capturing incoming timecode from a video deck in the Spot dialog box.

To align audio clips to the timeline of your session using the Current Timecode:

1. If the clip you want to spot is not already on a track, place the clip on the desired track.

2. Identify the timecode location where you want to trigger playback of your clip by pausing your video deck or digital video on that frame.

3. Right-click in the clip and choose **Spot**.

   The **Spot** dialog box appears (shown in Figure 3.34).

4. In the **Spot** mode dialog box, highlight the desired **Start** or **End** fields.

5. Click the **Current Timecode** (**Down** arrow) button, located at the top of the **Spot** dialog box, or press the Numeric Keypad **Equals** key to automatically enter a paused VTR's current timecode location into the highlighted **Start** or **End** box.

Figure 3.34
Spot dialog box.

6. Click **OK**.

The audio clip is aligned to the corresponding timecode number in the session's timeline ruler.

Tip: To accurately capture timecode from an external timecode source, use VITC or enable Serial Timecode as a Positional Reference in the Session Setup window.

Timecode and Feet+Frame Positions

The Spot dialog box allows you to work with any of the five time scales in the Time Scale pop-up menu. When Timecode or Feet+Frames is selected as the Main Time Scale, these time scales display time in the Spot dialog box, ruler views, and all other Pro Tools displays based on the timecode rate, feet+frames rate, and the session start time chosen in the Session Setup window. See Figure 3.35.

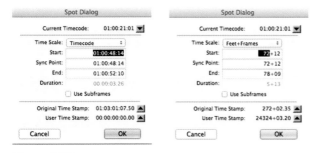

Figure 3.35
Spot dialog box with Timecode (left) and Feet+Frames (right).

Using Sync Points (Recap)

When working with non-linear video in the PT210P course, you learned that Pro Tools allows you to identify a specific point within a clip and spot or backtime that point to a timecode location (or other time scale value) using the Identify Sync Point command. This command is also used when working with linear video.

To spot or backtime a point within a clip to a timecode location:

1. Place your cursor at the desired sync location within a clip.

2. Choose **CLIP > IDENTIFY SYNC POINT**, or press **COMMAND+COMMA** (Mac) or **CTRL+COMMA** (Windows).

   A marker appears in the audio clip, indicating the location of the **SYNC POINT**, as shown in Figure 3.36.

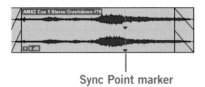

Figure 3.36
Clip containing a sync point marker.

Sync Point marker

Tip: You can scrub a sync point by using the Scrub tool or by changing the Selector tool into the Scrub tool by pressing the Control key (Mac) or Start key (Windows).

3. Identify the timecode location where you want to trigger playback of your clip by pausing your video deck on that frame and then right-clicking in the clip and choosing **SPOT**. The Spot dialog box will appear, as shown in Figure 3.37.

Figure 3.37
Sync Point field highlighted within the Spot dialog box.

When a **SYNC POINT** is present in the clip, the **SYNC POINT** field defaults to being highlighted in the Spot dialog box.

4. After the **SYNC POINT** field is highlighted, click the **CURRENT TIMECODE** (Down arrow) button at the top of the Spot dialog box or press the **EQUALS** key and then click **OK**.

   The sync point will spot to the chosen timecode location. When the session is online, this point in the clip will occur at the selected timecode location.

Tip: You can also align a clip's sync point to a timecode location by manually typing a timecode number into the Sync Point field of the Spot dialog box.

Tip: Only one sync point can be present within a single clip.

Table 3.3 provides a summary of the sync point shortcuts that are available when syncing a clip's sync point to either linear or non-linear video.

Table 3.3   Sync Point Shortcuts

Command	Macintosh	Windows
Identify sync point at the cursor location	Command+Comma (,)	Ctrl+Comma (,)
Remove sync point from a selected clip (Method 1)	Command+Comma (,)	Ctrl+Comma (,)
Remove sync point from a selected clip (Method 2)	Option-click on the sync point	Alt-click on the sync point
Align a clip's sync point to the selection start	Control+Shift-click	Start+Shift-click
Locate the cursor to the next sync point to the right	Tab (Tab to Transient off)	Tab (Tab to Transient off)
Locate the cursor to the next sync point to the left	Option+Tab (Tab to Transient off)	Ctrl+Tab (with Tab to Transient off)

You can also select the clips and spot them to the incoming timecode using the following Focus Key shortcuts:

- **Y:** Snaps the selected clip's start to the incoming timecode.
- **U:** Snaps the selected clip's sync point to the incoming timecode.
- **I:** Snaps the selected clip's end to the incoming timecode.

Automatically Spotting Clips

The Auto-Spot Clips option in Pro Tools simplifies the task of spotting clips even further. To use this feature reliably, you must use VITC or Serial Timecode.

To automatically spot a clip:

1. Identify the timecode location where you want to trigger playback of your clip by locating your video deck to the desired frame.

2. Choose **OPERATIONS > AUTO-SPOT CLIPS**, or press **OPTION+COMMAND+P** (Mac) or **ALT+CTRL+P** (Windows).

3. Do one of the following:

    ● In **Spot** mode, click the desired clip on the track with the **Grabber** tool, or in any other edit mode, **Right-click** the clip and select **Spot**.

    ● In **Spot** mode, drag the desired clip from the Clip List and drop it onto the desired track.

The clip will be automatically spotted to the current timecode location, bypassing the Spot dialog box.

Tip: You can also auto-spot a clip based on a sync point (if one is present).

Trimming a Clip with Spot Mode

If you want to edit the length of a clip to a specific timecode number, you can do so by trimming while in Spot mode.

To trim a clip using Spot mode:

1. Enable **Spot** mode.

2. Enable the (Standard) **Trim** tool (or any other Trim tool option).

3. Click the clip's head or tail with the **Trim** tool. The Spot dialog box appears, as shown in Figure 3.38.

Figure 3.38
Spot dialog box with Trim to Start options (left) and Trim to End options (right).

4. When you click the **Trim** tool in the first half of the clip, only the trim to **Start** and **Duration** options are available in the **Spot** dialog box. Click in the second half of the clip with the **Trim** tool to enter a trim to **End** or **Duration** trim value.

5. Enter a timecode number specifying exactly where you want to have the clip's beginning or end trimmed to, by using any of the previously discussed entry methods. Then click **OK**. The clip is trimmed to the exact timecode location you specify.

Automatically Spotting in Trim Mode

The automatic spot feature also works with Trim mode when using VITC or Serial Timecode.

To automatically trim clips:

1. Locate and pause your timecode source at the ending or starting frame you want to trim to.

2. Choose **OPTIONS > AUTO-SPOT CLIPS**.

3. Enable the **TRIM** tool.

4. In **SPOT** mode, click the head or tail of the clip (as desired). The clip is automatically trimmed to the frame you indicated.

Caution: Right-clicking and selecting Spot does not work with this trim process and will instead move the clip.

Locking Clips Recap

After completing your editing for a post production project, it is a good idea to "lock" clips (audio, MIDI, or video) or clip groups to a specific timecode location to keep them from being moved inadvertently out of sync with the picture. You may also want to protect them from any accidental editing. In the Pro Tools 210P course, you learned about the two clip-locking options that are available in Pro Tools: Time Lock/Unlock and Edit Lock/Unlock. See Figure 3.39.

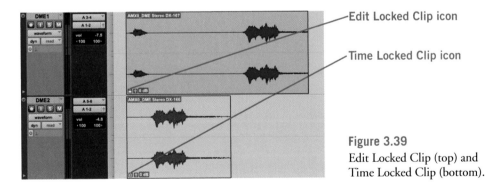

Edit Locked Clip icon

Time Locked Clip icon

Figure 3.39
Edit Locked Clip (top) and
Time Locked Clip (bottom).

- **Edit Lock/Unlock**: This command locks clips so that they cannot be edited (such as cutting, deleting, separating, or trimming) or moved to a different timecode location without a warning. Copied Edit Locked clips can be pasted to any track or time location, but the copy will also be Edit Locked at the new timecode location.

Shortcut: **Press Command+L (Mac) or Control+L (Windows) to Edit Lock/Unlock selected clips.**

■ **Time Lock/Unlock**: This command locks clips to a particular timecode location in a track, so that they cannot be moved accidentally. Time Locked clips cannot be moved in time. However, they can be edited in ways that do not change the clip's sync to a different timecode location (such as separating, trimming, AudioSuite processing, or even moving the clip to another track at the same time location). When separating a Time Locked clip, any new clips will also be locked to their timecode locations as well.

Shortcut: **Press Control+Option+L (Mac) or Start+Alt+L (Windows) to Time Lock/ Unlock selected clips.**

In the Avid Learning Series

For a complete review of Edit Locking and Time Locking clips, consult the PT210P (Pro Tools Post Production Techniques) book.

Working with Time Stamps

Time stamping allows Pro Tools to remember the original timecode (or other time scale) for each sample of audio that was recorded online (or synchronized to timecode). This feature is always enabled, and the original time stamping written into the audio file can never be erased. In addition to the original time stamp, Pro Tools also allows you to save an alternate time stamp known as the *user* time stamp. You can modify or change this time stamp at any time. You can also recall both the original time stamp and the user time stamp at any time, so that you can re-sync clips to their original or user-defined timecode locations.

Overwriting a User Time Stamp

Overwriting a user time stamp allows you to select a clip (or clips) and define or redefine a user time stamp that you can recall at any time. As you just learned, Pro Tools stores an original time stamp and a user time stamp with each clip, but you can alter only the user time stamp. This additional user time stamp is especially useful in a post production situation for storing, for example, a destination time stamp for a clip, while still retaining the original (source) time stamp.

Caution: **Original time stamps cannot be changed or overwritten.**

To write or overwrite a user time stamp:

1. In the Clip List, select the clip (or clips) to which you want to save user time stamps.

2. Do one of the following:

   • Choose CLIP LIST > TIME STAMP.

   • Press Command+Shift+M (Mac) or Ctrl+Shift+M (Windows).

   • Right-click directly on the clip(s) and choose TIME STAMP, as shown in Figure 3.40.

Figure 3.40
Clip List right-click menu.

The User Time Stamp dialog box appears, as shown in Figure 3.41.

Figure 3.41
User Time Stamp dialog box.

3. Enter a new timecode number using one of the following three methods:

   • Enter the numbers manually from the keyboard using the ARROW keys to highlight the desired field.

   • Click the CURRENT TIMECODE (UP ARROW) button to capture the incoming timecode address and enter it into the USER TIME STAMP field.

   • Click the CURRENT SELECTION (UP ARROW) button to enter the current edit selection's starting timecode number into the USER TIME STAMP field.

4. Click **OK** when finished.

Tip: If you select several clips before selecting the Time Stamp command, Pro Tools will allow you to create time stamps in batch mode. In this mode, Pro Tools will present a dialog box for each clip in succession, allowing you to quickly enter a new timecode number for each clip.

Generating a Timecode Window Burn

Avid SYNC Peripherals offer timecode character generation (also known as a timecode window burn or dubbing). This superimposes onto a video signal a small area called a window dub (or window burn, or timecode window) that displays timecode in the format: Hours:Minutes:Seconds:Frames. See Figure 3.42.

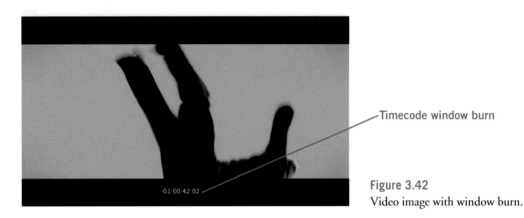

Timecode window burn

01:00:42:02

Figure 3.42
Video image with window burn.

A window dub provides a visual cue to your location in a project and can be helpful when spotting clips to video frames in Pro Tools, especially if your only timecode reference from tape is LTC. The SYNC Peripheral's character generator obtains its timecode address from the chosen positional reference.

Window Dub Requirements

Avid SYNC Peripherals can only burn a window dub onto an existing video signal. This means that at least one video "source" signal (from a VTR, non-linear editing system, or other video device) must be present at the Avid SYNC Peripheral's Video In connector.

There are two window dub scenarios that you might encounter, each of which requires different connections and settings in Pro Tools.

Scenario 1: Linear Video Deck with Address Track LTC Timecode

Avid SYNC Peripheral configured with the following settings (as shown in Figure 3.43):

- Clock Reference: Video Reference (SD) or Video Reference (HD)
- Positional Reference: LTC (not Auto LTC/VITC or Serial Time Code)
- Gen LTC (Generate Longitudinal Timecode): Disabled (in Transport window)

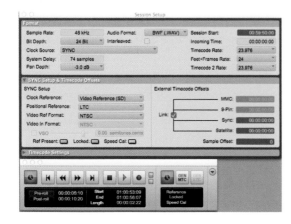

Figure 3.43
Session Setup window settings when creating
a window dub for a linear video source with LTC.

- Video Deck LTC Out connected to the Avid SYNC Peripheral LTC In

- Source video deck Composite Video Out connected to the Avid SYNC Peripheral Video In

- Avid SYNC Peripheral Video Out connected to the input of either a video recording device or a video monitor

- Pro Tools Transport Online

Note: The session's Timecode Rate setting in the Session Setup window must match the frame rate of your video deck (or other device).

Scenario 2: Non-linear Avid or QuickTime Video Source in Pro Tools Playing Back Through an Avid Video Peripheral or Other Supported Video Hardware

Avid SYNC Peripheral configured with the following settings (as shown in Figure 3.44):

- Clock Reference: Video Reference (SD) or Video Reference (HD)

- Positional Reference: Generate

- Gen LTC (Generate Longitudinal Time Code): Enabled (in the Transport window)

- Source video device Composite Video Out connected to the Avid SYNC Peripheral Video In

- Avid SYNC Peripheral Video Out connected to the input of either a video recording device or a video monitor

- Pro Tools Transport Offline (Gen LTC enabled)

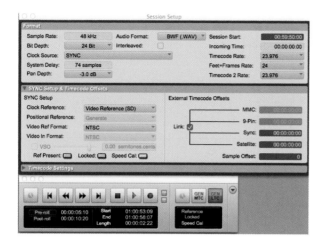

Figure 3.44
Session Setup window settings when creating a window dub for a non-linear video source with LTC.

Note: When using this workflow, the timecode window burn will not update when moving or nudging the insertion cursor from within Pro Tools. Instead, the window burn will only update during normal playback.

Hardware Configuration Diagram

Figure 3.45 shows the required connections for using an Avid SYNC Peripheral to overlay a timecode window burn onto a video source. You must verify that these connections have been made before enabling the software settings from within Pro Tools.

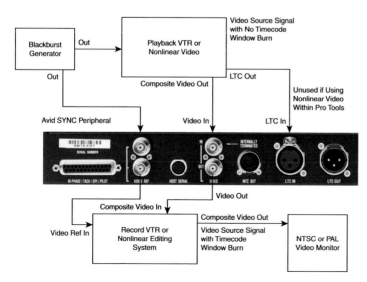

Figure 3.45
Connections for generating a timecode window burn using an Avid SYNC Peripheral.

To burn a window dub onto a video signal from Pro Tools:

1. Choose SETUP > PERIPHERALS and click the SYNCHRONIZATION tab.

2. Enable SYNC SETUP to make the Window Dub controls available.

3. Click ENABLE DUB WINDOW as shown in Figure 3.46.

Figure 3.46
Enabling a timecode dub window using SYNC setup from within Pro Tools.

4. Configure any of the following window burn appearance settings:

- **Size**: Sets the relative size of the window dub (small or large).

- **Vertical Position**: Sets the vertical position of the window dub, relative to the bottom of the video picture. The choices range from 10% From Bottom to 50% From Bottom, in 10% increments.

Caution: 10% from Bottom vertical position is outside the standard safe title area, which means it might not be visible on some video monitors. Also, although not possible when using an Avid SYNC Peripheral, timecode window burns positioned at the top of the video image might be one frame out of sync on some video monitors.

- **Horizontal Position**: Sets the window dub's relative horizontal position within the video picture. The choices include Extreme Left, Left, Center, Right, and Extreme Right.

Caution: The Extreme horizontal positions are outside the standard safe title area, which means they might not be visible on some video monitors.

- **Color**: Sets the color of the timecode numbers in the window dub, and the color of the window dub's background. The choices include White on Black Bkgnd, Black on White Bkgnd, White on Video Bkgnd, and Black on Video Bkgnd. (Video Bkgnd means that the window dub's background is transparent, so that the timecode numbers are displayed directly on top of the video signal, without a contrasting background box.) The default setting is White on Black Bkgnd.

5. After configuring the dub window settings, click **OK** to close the Peripherals dialog box.

When you start playback in Pro Tools, a window dub with timecode will be overlaid onto your video input signal, and passed out through the Video Out connector on the Avid SYNC Peripheral.

Tip: In addition to using an Avid SYNC Peripheral to generate a timecode window burn, you can also use a third-party software utility (such as Gallery Software's Virtual VTR or Digital Salade's Toki TC) to generate and save a timecode window burn into a QuickTime video file.

Review/Discussion Questions

1. What is the name of the connector on the SYNC HD that is used to distribute a common clock to multiple HD-series audio interfaces?

2. What is the name of the connector on the SYNC HD that is used to connect blackburst or house sync?

3. What is the difference between clock reference and positional reference?

4. What does the acronym LTC stand for and how is LTC used by Pro Tools?

5. What does the acronym VITC stand for and how is VITC used by Pro Tools?

6. How is the positional reference auto LTC/VITC useful?

7. List the most commonly used timecode frame rates for each of the following: PAL, NTSC, and Film.

8. When changing the Session Start time, what happens to existing audio in your session when you choose the Maintain Relative Position option?

9. What is the name of the technical standard protocol that is used by 9-pin serial Machine Control?

10. Name a keyboard shortcut (Mac or Windows) that can be used to put Pro Tools online.

11. List two causes for a Machine Control communication error in Pro Tools.

12. What is the Auto-Spot Clips option used for in Pro Tools?

13. How are edit-locked clips different from time-locked clips?

14. What are time stamps and how are they useful?

15. What is a timecode window burn and how is it useful in audio post-production?

Lesson 3 Keyboard Shortcuts

Shortcut	Description
Command+2 (numeric keypad) (Mac)/ Ctrl+2 (numeric keypad) (Windows)	Show Session Setup window
Command+J or Option+space bar (Mac)/ Ctrl+J or Alt+space bar (Windows)	Toggle Pro Tools Online
Command+\ (Mac)/Ctrl+\ (Windows)	Toggle Transport Master
Command+Period (.) (Mac)/ Ctrl+Period (.) (Windows)	All Transport Buttons Off
Shift+Comma (Mac and Windows)	Rewind
Shift+Period (.) (Mac and Windows)	Fast Forward
Option+Comma (,) (Mac)/Alt+Comma (,) (Windows)	Shuttle Backward
Option+Period (.) (Mac)/Alt+Period (.) (Windows)	Shuttle Forward
Command+Left Arrow (Mac)/Ctrl+Left Arrow (Windows)	Cue to Selection Start
Command+Right Arrow (Mac)/ Ctrl+Right Arrow (Windows)	Cue to Selection End
Command+Option+Comma (,) (Mac)/ Ctrl+Alt+Comma (,) (Windows)	Frame Bump Backward
Command+Option+Period (.) (Mac)/ Ctrl+Alt+Period (.) (Windows)	Frame Bump Forward
F3 (Mac and Windows)	Enable Spot mode
= (numeric keypad) (Mac and Windows)	Capture Incoming Timecode
Command+Comma (,) (Mac)/Ctrl+Comma (,) (Windows)	Identify sync point at the cursor location
Command+Comma (,) (Mac)/Ctrl+Comma (,) (Windows)	Remove sync point from a selected clip (Method 1)
Option-click on the sync point (Mac)/ Alt-click on the sync point (Windows)	Remove sync point from a selected clip (Method 2)
Control+Shift-click (Mac)/Start+Shift-click (Windows)	Align a clip's sync point to the selection start

Lesson 3 Keyboard Shortcuts

Shortcut	Description
Tab (Tab to Transient off) (Mac and Windows)	Locate the cursor to the next sync point to the right
Option+Tab (Tab to Transient off) (Mac)/ Ctrl+Tab (Tab to Transient off) (Windows)	Locate the cursor to the next sync point to the left
Y (Focus key) (Mac and Windows)	Snaps the selected clip's start to the incoming timecode
U (Focus key) (Mac and Windows)	Snaps the selected clip's sync point to the incoming timecode
I (Focus key) (Mac and Windows)	Snaps the selected clip's end to the incoming timecode
Option+Command+P (Mac)/Ctrl+Alt+P (Windows)	Auto-Spot Clip Enable (Mac)/Disable
= (numeric keypad) (Mac and Windows)	Capture Incoming Timecode
Command+L (Mac)/Ctrl+L (Windows)	Edit Lock/Unlock Clip
Control+Option+L (Mac)/Start+Alt+L (Windows)	Time Lock/Unlock Clip
Command+Shift+M (Mac)/Ctrl+Shift+M (Windows)	Time Stamp Clip

Synchronizing Pro Tools with Linear Video

In this exercise, you will configure and synchronize a Pro Tools HD system with a professional linear video deck using RS-422 (9-pin) Machine Control, using the *Agent MX Zero* movie trailer.

Media Used:

310P Exercise O3.ptx (Pro Tools session file) and 310P Exercise 3 videotape

Duration:

20 minutes

Note: This exercise requires a Pro Tools HD system, Avid SYNC Peripheral, Video Sync Generator (SD or HD), professional (SD or HD) video deck supporting 9-pin Machine Control, and the Machine Control option for Pro Tools. If you do not have all of these required items, you will not be able to complete this exercise.

GOALS

- Configure Pro Tools for synchronization with a linear video device
- Enable and use Machine Control
- Record audio into Pro Tools using Machine Control
- Use time stamps

Note: If you are using this book in an instructor-led class at an Avid Learning Partner, your instructor may choose to assign students to work on this exercise individually, in groups, or complete the exercise as an instructor-led class exercise, depending on the availability of equipment at your Avid Learning Partner facility.

Getting Started

1. Open **310P EXERCISE 03**.PTXT, located on the book DVD directory at **EXERCISE MEDIA/310P CLASS AUDIO FILES V10/310P EXERCISE 03** (or other location specified by the course instructor).

2. In the **SAVE NEW SESSION AS** dialog box, name the session as desired, saving into an appropriate location on a valid storage volume.

   The session will open with four pre-loaded stereo audio tracks, as shown in Figure 3.47.

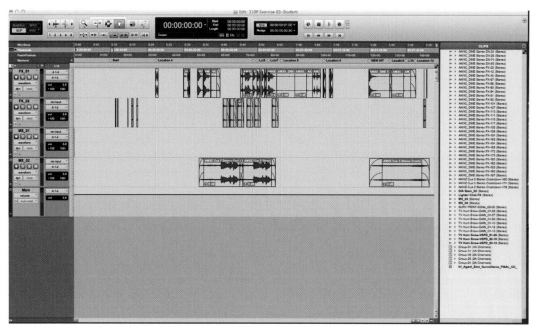

Figure 3.47
Exercise 3 starting view in the Edit window.

The session now contains two sets of stereo sound effects and music tracks, but no dialogue tracks. You will be synchronizing Pro Tools to the video deck, and then loading the missing dialogue for the scene into the session from a linear video tape.

Verifying the Synchronization Peripheral Settings

1. Choose SETUP > PERIPHERALS, and then click the SYNCHRONIZATION tab, as shown in Figure 3.48.

2. Verify that ENABLE SYNC HD (or ENABLE SYNC PERIPHERAL) is checked and then click OK.

Figure 3.48
Synchronization tab of the Peripherals dialog box.

Enabling Machine Control

1. From the front panel of the VTR, power on the machine (if it's not already on) and then place the machine into remote (or external) mode.

2. Insert the 310P Exercise 3 videotape into your video machine.

3. Choose SETUP > PERIPHERALS and click the MACHINE CONTROL tab, as shown in Figure 3.49.

4. Enable 9-PIN MACHINE CONTROL (DECK CONTROL) and choose the port (SYNC 9-PIN OUT 1 or other port that your VTR is connected to).

Tip: Make sure you select the proper port in the previous step so that it matches your machine's 9-pin connection.

5. Choose the MACHINE TYPE and click OK.

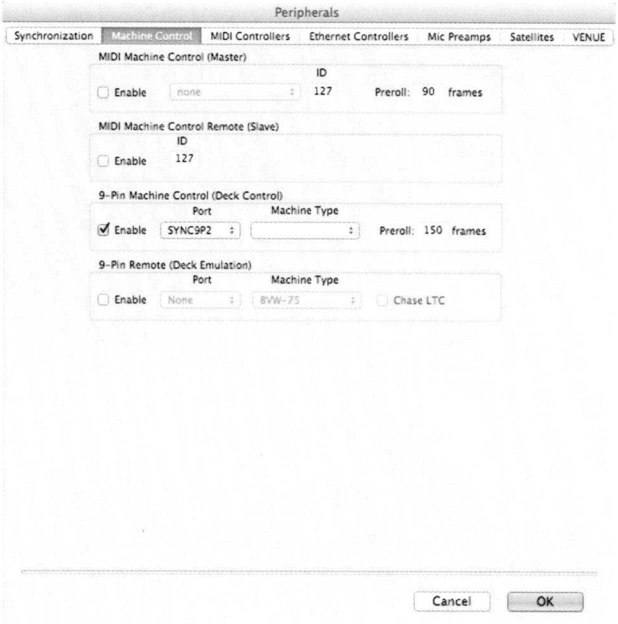

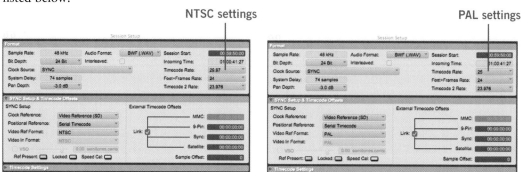

Figure 3.49
Machine Control tab of the Peripherals dialog box.

Configuring the Session Setup Window Settings

1. Open the SESSION SETUP window by choosing WINDOWS > SESSION SETUP.

Shortcut: Press Command+2 (Mac) or Ctrl+2 (Windows) on the numeric keypad to open the Session Setup window.

2. Configure the Session Setup window settings as shown in Figure 3.50 and listed below:

Figure 3.50
Session Setup settings: NTSC (left) and PAL (right).

- **Session Start (timecode):** 00:59:50:00

Caution: You must press Return or Enter after keying in a new Session Start time. After numeric entry, the warning Unable to Maintain Original Timecode Location will appear. Click OK to continue.

- **Timecode Rate**: 29.97FPS (NTSC), 25FPS (PAL), or 23.976FPS (if using an HD video deck)

- **Feet+Frames Rate**: 24FPS

- **Clock Reference**: Video Reference (SD) (or HD if using an HD video deck)

- **Video Ref Format**: NTSC, PAL, or 720p – 23.976 (if using an HD video deck)

- **Positional Reference**: Serial Timecode

Tip: Enabling Serial Timecode as the Positional Reference will allow faster lock-up times.

3. After all settings are configured correctly, close the **SESSION SETUP** window.

Getting Ready to Record Dialogue Audio

After you have verified that all session settings are correct and that Machine Control has been enabled, you are now ready to prepare an audio track for synchronized dialogue recording from the linear tape.

1. Create one new stereo audio track.

Shortcut: Press Command+Shift+N (Mac) or Ctrl+Shift+N (Windows) to open the New Tracks dialog box from the keyboard.

2. Drag the new stereo audio track to the top of the **EDIT** window and rename the audio track **DIA_01**. The Edit window should now look something like Figure 3.51.

3. Record-enable the **DIA_01** track.

4. Set the **DIA_01** track inputs to analog audio interface inputs A 1-2 (or other inputs connected to the output of your video deck), which should be connected to the video tape recorder (VTR) outputs 1-2. Figure 3.52 is using audio interface inputs A 1-2 (stereo).

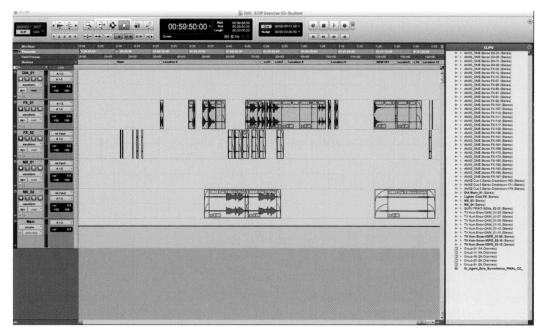

Figure 3.51
DIA_01 audio track record-enabled in the Edit window.

Figure 3.52
Dialog_01 track inputs set to inputs A 1-2.

Recording Audio Using Pro Tools Machine Control

1. In the **TRANSPORT** window, press the **ONLINE** button (it should start blinking). See Figure 3.53.

Shortcut: Press Command+J (Mac) or Ctrl+J (Windows) to put Pro Tools online.

Figure 3.53
Transport window Online enabled.

2. In the TRANSPORT window, enable TRANSPORT = PRO TOOLS, to make Pro Tools the master transport controlling the video deck.

Shortcut: **Press Command+Backslash (Mac) or Ctrl+Backslash (Windows) to toggle between Pro Tools and the Machine transports.**

3. Verify that the Online option in the OPERATION page of Preferences is set to RECORD ONLINE AT INSERTION/SELECTION, as shown in Figure 3.54.

Figure 3.54
Online Options in the Operation page of Preferences.

4. With TIMELINE/EDIT SELECTION LINK enabled, place the insertion cursor at the start of the session (00:59:50:00), and then play the videotape, verifying that record input signals are being received from the source.

5. Once you have verified your input signal source, you are ready to record. Again place the insertion cursor at the start of the session (00:59:50:00).

6. Place the Pro Tools TRANSPORT in online record mode (both the RECORD and ONLINE buttons should be blinking). See Figure 3.55.

Figure 3.55
Transport window with Online Record enabled.

Shortcut: **You can enable online record by pressing Option+Command+space bar (Mac) or Ctrl+Alt+space bar (Windows).**

7. Start playback to begin online recording.

8. When you reach the end of the *Agent MX Zero* movie trailer (approximate timecode number 01:01:30:00), stop online recording.

9. Disable the RECORD button on the DIA_01 track.

10. Rename the clip you just recorded DIA STEM_01 as shown in Figure 3.56.

Figure 3.56
Name the Clip dialog box.

11. Edit-lock the audio clip on the **DIA_01** track.

Shortcut: Press Command+L (Mac) or Ctrl+L (Windows) to edit-lock the audio clip.

Your session should now look similar to Figure 3.57.

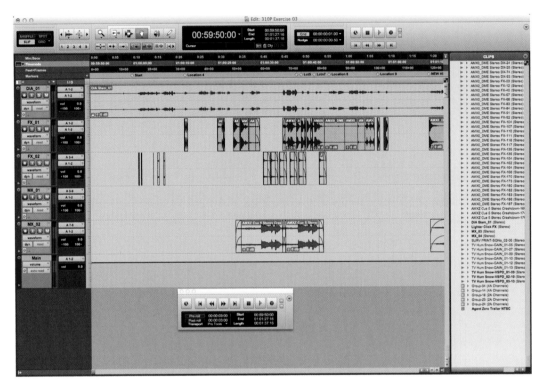

Figure 3.57
Agent MX Zero trailer session with recorded dialogue.

12. Before going on to the Using Time Stamps section of this exercise, practice using the Machine Control keyboard shortcuts shown in Table 3.5, until you feel comfortable using all of them.

Tip: All of the Machine Control shortcuts listed in Table 3.5 require Transport = Machine, except Toggle Transport Master.

Table 3.5   Machine Control Shortcuts

Command	Macintosh	Windows
Toggle Transport Master	Command+\	Ctrl+\
Rewind	Shift+Comma (,)	Shift+Comma (,)
Fast Forward	Shift+Period (.)	Shift+Period (.)
Shuttle Backward	Option+Comma (,)	Alt+Comma (,)
Shuttle Forward	Option+Period (.)	Alt+Period (.)
Cue to Selection Start	Command+Left Arrow	Ctrl+Left Arrow
Cue to Selection End	Command+Right Arrow	Ctrl+Right Arrow
Frame Bump Backward	Command+Option+Comma (,)	Ctrl+Alt+Comma (,)
Frame Bump Forward	Command+Option+Period (.)	Ctrl+Alt+Period (.)

Using Time Stamps

In the final part of this exercise, you will spot the MX_03 and MX_04 clips using an embedded time stamp. This time stamp was written into the file by the composer's engineer to speed up the spotting process in Pro Tools.

1. Using **Spot** mode, drag the **MX_03** audio clip from the Clip List to any location on the **MX_01** track.

2. Near the bottom of the **Spot** mode dialog box, click the **Up Arrow** button (located to the right of the **Original Time Stamp** number), to automatically enter the **Original Time Stamp** number in the **Start** field. See Figure 3.58.

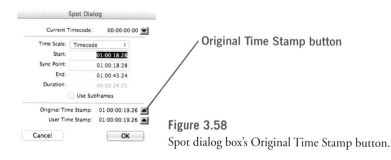

Original Time Stamp button

Figure 3.58
Spot dialog box's Original Time Stamp button.

3. After the number is entered, click **OK**. The **MX_03** audio clip is placed at the corresponding timecode number. Since the **MX_03** audio clip was pre-edited, after placing it at its **ORIGINAL TIME STAMP**, it should be in perfect sync with the picture.

4. Using **SPOT** mode, drag the **MX_04** audio clip from the Clip List to any location on the **MX_01** track.

5. Near the bottom of the **SPOT** mode dialog box, click the **UP ARROW** button (located to the right of the **ORIGINAL TIME STAMP** number), to automatically enter the **ORIGINAL TIME STAMP** number in the **START** field.

6. After the number is entered, click **OK**. The **MX_04** audio clip is placed at the corresponding timecode number. Since the **MX_04** audio clip was pre-edited, after placing it at its **ORIGINAL TIME STAMP**, it should be in perfect sync with the picture.

7. Save the session.

Your completed session should now look something like Figure 3.59.

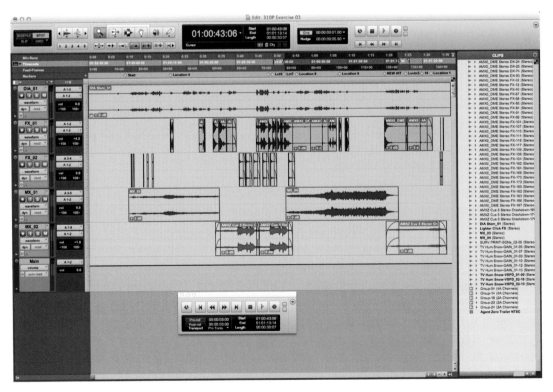

Figure 3.59
Completed *Agent MX Zero* trailer session with all dialogue, music, and sound effects.

Tactile Control of Pro Tools

This lesson describes how a standard alphanumeric keyboard can be used to greatly increase the speed with which you use Pro Tools.

Media Used: None

Duration: 45 minutes

GOALS

- Understand the theory and application of modifier keys
- Understand Keyboard Focus shortcuts and use them in practice
- Understand and control the Keyboard Focus mode
- Understand the usefulness of different numeric keypad modes

Introduction

Using a keyboard to access the functions you use regularly increases both speed and precision. As you become more familiar with Pro Tools (and dedicated to implementing these shortcuts into your workflow), you will start to develop "strings" of key combinations that will allow you to "touch-type" routine tasks. Just like standard typing, becoming efficient at controlling Pro Tools with a alphanumeric keyboard requires time and practice. In this lesson, you'll explore seldom used keyboard commands, review the general theory behind modifiers, and learn focus key functions you may have not known even existed in Pro Tools.

Parts of the Keyboard

There are four ways to access Pro Tools's functions on an alphanumeric keyboard containing a numeric keypad:

- Modifier keys
- Focus keys
- Function keys
- Numerical keypad

This lesson is divided into sections focused on each of these areas. Take time in each section to think about how to apply these shortcuts to your everyday workflows.

Computer Keyboard Recommendation

On both Macintosh and Windows systems, Pro Tools uses separate numeric shortcuts that utilize alpha numerals and numeric keypad numerals. In order to easily access both alphanumeric and numeric keypad shortcuts from within Pro Tools, it is recommended that you use a full-size extended keyboard that contains a numeric keypad. For laptop computers and computer keyboards that do not contain a numeric keypad, consult your computer's documentation for instructions that allow you to toggle your alphanumeric keyboard for numeric keypad shortcuts.

Modifier Keys

As you have encountered in lower-level Pro Tools books in the Avid Learning Series, many keyboard shortcuts in Pro Tools use *modifier keys*. By holding modifier keys while performing a key press or mouse action, you can access a variety of Pro Tools functions. Although keyboard modifiers are available on both Macintosh and Windows platforms, they have different names. Once you are familiar with which Macintosh and Windows modifier keys are equivalent, using keyboard shortcuts on either platform will be easier, regardless of the platform you started on.

Many common modifier and key combination listings are directly available through Pro Tools by clicking on the menu Help > Keyboard Commands. However, numerous key combinations do not have menu equivalents and some are contextual in nature.

Modifier Key and Menus

A basic use of modifier keys is to access menu functions. Most (but not all) menu functions that have a keyboard shortcut will have the key combination listed to the right of the function within the menu, as shown for the Edit menu in Figure 4.1.

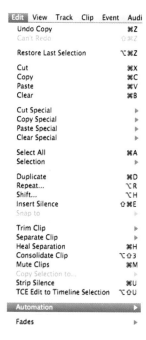

Figure 4.1

Keyboard combinations are shown to the right of menu functions.

Modifier Keys and Track Parameters

A number of functions are accessed by holding down modifier keys while clicking on track controls in the mixer or while changing track parameters. These functions can be:

- Modifiers that allow you to change a parameter across a number of tracks simultaneously
- Modifiers that change parameters on tracks containing the Edit cursor
- Modifiers that change the state or display of a parameter when clicked

Changing Parameters on Multiple Tracks Simultaneously

As you have encountered in previous courses, the Option key (Mac) or Alt key (Windows) is the root modifier for applying changes to all/multiple tracks at the same time. For example, Option/Alt-clicking on the Record Enable button on any audio track will attempt to place all audio tracks into Record Ready mode. The following is a list of parameters and track functions that behave in this way:

- Mute and Solo buttons
- Record Enable and TrackInput Monitor buttons
- Input and Output assignments
- Send assignments
- Voice assignments
- Plug-in/Insert assignments
- Automation modes
- Meter Clip (clearing)
- Volume/Peak/Delay display mode assignments
- Track height (Edit window)
- Track View display (Waveform, Pan, Automation, and so on, in the Edit window)
- Playlist pop-up selectors

To apply a parameter change to all tracks:

1. Option-click (Mac) or Alt-click (Windows) on the appropriate parameter control or pop-up selector on any track.

Tip: When using the Option/Alt modifier, only tracks of the same type will be affected. For example, holding Option/Alt while changing the output of a mono audio track will affect only mono audio tracks in the session.

To apply a parameter change to a selection of tracks:

1. Select all the tracks you want to be affected.

2. Option+Shift-click (Mac) or Alt+Shift-click (Windows) on the parameter control or pop-up selector on any of the selected tracks.

Changing Parameters on Tracks Containing the Edit Cursor

Pro Tools includes a collection of commands that allow you to toggle the Record Enable state, TrackInput Monitoring mode, and Mute and Solo status across all tracks containing the Edit cursor. These key commands act as toggles, meaning repeat presses switch between enabling and disabling the action.

To apply a track status change to all tracks containing the Edit cursor:

1. Place the Edit cursor within all tracks you want to change. A quick way to do this is to click and drag through the tracks with the Selector tool. To add the Edit cursor to non-adjacent tracks, Shift-click within the Edit playlist for each desired track. If LINK TRACK AND EDIT SELECTION is enabled, you can also simply select tracks to add them to the Edit selection.

2. Hold SHIFT and press the appropriate alpha key for the parameter to toggle. Each key is simply the first letter of the parameter, as listed in Table 4.1.

Figure 4.2 shows an example of using a track mute shortcut.

Table 4.1   Keyboard Shortcuts for Common Tasks

Keyboard Shortcut	Parameter Toggled on Tracks Containing Edit Cursor
Shift+R	Record Enable
Shift+I	TrackInput Monitoring mode
Shift+M	Track Mute
Shift+S	Track Solo

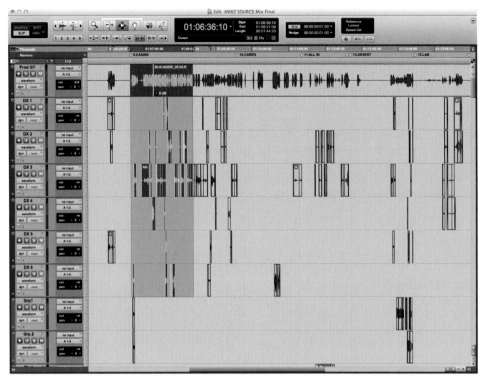

Figure 4.2
Tracks containing the Edit cursor muted using Shift+M shortcut.

Modifiers that Change a Parameter's State

Table 4.2 lists special functions accessed by clicking with a modifier key.

Mac	Windows	Parameter	Behavior
Command	Ctrl	Record Arm	Initiate Record Safe mode
Command	Ctrl	Solo	Solo Safe
Command	Ctrl	Plug-ins in Inserts view	Bypass Toggle
Command	Ctrl	Sends in Assignment or Single Send view	Send Mute Toggle
Command	Ctrl	Mix window Track data display	Toggle volume/peak/delay display

Table 4.2   Changing Parameter States

Table 4.2 Changing Parameter States (*continued*)

Mac	Windows	Parameter	Behavior
Command	Ctrl	Volume, Pan, Plug-in parameter, Send level, Automation playlist	Fine resolution mouse control
Command	Ctrl	Send assignment pop-up selector	Switch to Single Send view, or between Send Assignment views (depending on current state)
Option	Alt	Volume, Pan, Plug-in parameter, Send level	Set parameter to the default setting
Option+Command	Ctrl+Alt	Input/output assignments, Send assignments, Interface input and output assignments in I/O setup	Cascade paths (selects ascending I/O assignments for all tracks starting with the track you change). Add Shift to affect selected tracks only.

Focus Keys

The Keyboard Focus system in Pro Tools assigns a vast array of functions to the main alphanumeric section of your keyboard. Each of these functions can be accessed with a single keypress; you don't need to hold down a modifier key. The keyboard can be focused on one of several areas of the Pro Tools user interface. Each focus mode maps the keys to a different set of functions.

Pro Tools provides three Keyboard Focus modes:

- **Commands Focus:** Provides single-key shortcuts from the alphanumeric keyboard for editing, navigation, and playback. This is the mode used much of the time in Pro Tools.

- **Clips List Focus:** Allows clips and clip groups to be located and selected in the Clip List by typing the first few letters of a clip's name.

- **Groups List Focus:** Allows Edit and Mix groups to be enabled/disabled by typing a group's corresponding ID letter.

Assigning Keyboard Focus

You can set the Keyboard Focus mode using the mouse or using keyboard shortcuts. To set the Keyboard Focus mode with the mouse, you simply click the a–z button for the focus you want to enable. Figure 4.3 shows the three Keyboard Focus mode options that are available within the Edit window.

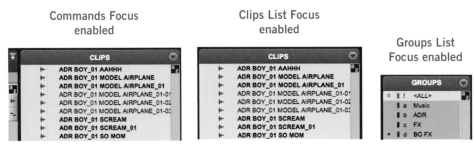

Figure 4.3
Keyboard Focus buttons.

To switch between the different Keyboard Focus modes using keyboard shortcuts, press Option+Command (Mac) or Ctrl+Alt (Windows) and numbers 1–3 on the alphanumeric keyboard.

Table 4.3 shows the shortcut for each focus button.

Table 4.3   Shortcuts for Changing Keyboard Focus

Mac	Windows	Behavior
Option+Command+1	Ctrl+Alt+1	Activates Commands Keyboard Focus mode
Option+Command+2	Ctrl+Alt+2	Activates Clips List Keyboard Focus mode
Option+Command+3	Ctrl+Alt+3	Activates Groups List Keyboard Focus mode

Note: You can enable only one Keyboard Focus mode at a time. Enabling a Keyboard Focus mode will disable the previously selected one.

Window Focus

Keyboard Focus mode shortcuts are always directed toward the active window in the software interface. The windows that support Keyboard Focus commands are the Edit window, Mix window, MIDI Editor windows, and the docked MIDI Editor window.

Not all Keyboard Focus modes are available in each window type:

- **Edit window:** All three modes are available.
- **Mix window:** Groups List Focus only.

- **MIDI Editor windows:** Commands Focus and Groups List Focus.
- **Docked MIDI Editor:** Commands Focus only.

Different Focus modes can be set in each open window. For example, the Edit window may have Clips List Focus selected at the same time that a MIDI Editor window has Commands Focus selected. However, only the active window (highlighted title bar) will respond to Focus shortcuts. To make a window active, click on it, or use a window selection shortcut—such as Command+= (Mac) or Ctrl+= (Windows)—to toggle between windows.

Edit Window Focus with the Docked MIDI Editor

When the docked MIDI Editor is present in the Edit window, two distinct areas in the Edit window can respond to Commands focus keys and toolbar shortcuts. These areas behave similarly to two separate windows, with only one active at any time for the purposes of Commands Focus and toolbar shortcuts. The active section is indicated by a yellow outline around its toolbar, as shown in Figure 4.4.

Docked MIDI Editor with yellow highlighted outline, indicating
it is the focused editor for key commands

Figure 4.4
Docked MIDI Editor focused for shortcuts and Commands focus keys.

Tip: If Groups List or Clips List Focus are selected in the Edit window, they will
remain active whether the docked MIDI Editor is focused or not.

Switching Focus Between the Docked MIDI Editor and the Main Edit Window

Clicking anywhere in the docked MIDI Editor will focus it for keyboard shortcuts; clicking elsewhere in the Edit window returns focus to the main area. There are also two keyboard shortcuts for switching focus, as shown in Table 4.4. These follow on from the main focus selection shortcuts from Table 4.3.

Table 4.4   Switching Focus Between Edit and MIDI Editor Windows

Mac	Windows	Behavior
Option+Command+1	Ctrl+Alt+1	Activates Commands Keyboard Focus mode
Option+Command+2	Ctrl+Alt+2	Activates the Clips List Keyboard Focus mode
Option+Command+3	Ctrl+Alt+3	Activates Groups List Keyboard Focus mode
Option+Command+4	Ctrl+Alt+4	Moves focus to the Edit window from the MIDI Editor
Option+Command+5	Ctrl+Alt+5	Moves focus to the MIDI Editor from the Edit window

Shortcuts That Follow the Edit Window Focus

The following shortcuts can be refocused to the docked MIDI Editor:

Commands Focus functions

- Most single-key functions described in the following section.

Tip: Some commands are only relevant to audio clips (such as fades) so they are not applicable in MIDI Editor views.

Toolbar functions

- Edit Tool selection
- Edit Mode selection
- Grid and Nudge Value selection

Navigation and View

- Zooming
- Paging (Page Up/Down, and so on)
- Track Heights (automation lanes only in MIDI Editor)

Commands Focus Mode Shortcuts

Commands Keyboard Focus mode enables all the single-key functions that are printed on custom Pro Tools keyboards (such as the built-in Pro Tools keyboard on a D-Control). See Figure 4.5. The Commands focus keys are color-coded into groups of keys with related functions, as follows:

- **Yellow:** Zoom, Display, and Numeric time-entry functions
- **Pink:** Edit functions

Note: The D, F, and G keys (used for fades) are colored purple on the Avid D-Control and some other custom keyboards.

- **Blue:** Transport and Locate functions
- **Green:** MIDI functions
- **Peach/Orange:** Tool or Mode selection
- **Red:** Record functions

Figure 4.5
Keyboard with color-coded shortcuts based on function.

Tip: With Commands Keyboard Focus mode disabled, you can still access the same set of functions by pressing Control (Mac) or Start (Windows) along with the associated alpha key.

Tip: The numeric keypad functions are determined by the Numeric Keypad Operation preference and are not affected by enabling/disabling Commands Keyboard Focus mode.

Zoom and Numeric Time Entry Functions

These yellow color-coded Commands focus keys allow single-key zooming and numeric time entry. The zoom and numeric entry functions are shown in Figure 4.6. Table 4.5 lists the zoom and numeric entry command functions.

Figure 4.6
Commands Focus keyboard shortcuts: Zoom and Numeric Entry.

Table 4.5   Zoom and Numeric Command Functions

Key(s)	Function	Notes
1,2,3,4,5	Recall Zoom Presets	Zoom values must be stored with the mouse and software.
- (hyphen key)	Track View Toggle*	Toggles the track view between two different states. • Audio tracks: Toggles between Waveform and Volume views. • MIDI/Instrument tracks: Toggles between Notes and Clips view. • VCA tracks: Toggles between Volume and Trim value. • Aux/Master tracks: N/A.
= (numeric keypad equals key)	Capture Timecode	Auto-enters the current incoming LTC when a timecode field is highlighted in a dialog box (such as Spot mode).
= (numeric keypad equals key)	Capture Timecode	Activates the Main Counter in the Edit window for numeric entry (similar to * on the numeric keypad). When timecode is being received, pressing the key a second time enters the currently received timecode into the Main Counter.
E	Zoom Toggle	Activates Zoom Toggle based on your preferences.
R, T	Zoom In/Out	Zooms audio and MIDI playlist displays horizontally in/out.
/ (numeric keypad)	Start/End/Length	Activates numeric entry for the Start/End/Length fields in the Edit window.
* (numeric keypad)	Enter Main Time	Activates the Main Counter in the Edit window for numeric entry.

* Track View Toggle: On MIDI or Instrument tracks, switches between Notes and Clips (non-Zoom Toggle mode), or Notes and Velocity (Zoom Toggle mode).

Edit Functions

The pink color-coded Commands focus keys shown in Figure 4.7 allow single-key access to various edit functions. Table 4.6 lists the editing shortcuts.

Figure 4.7
Commands Focus editing shortcuts.

Table 4.6   Edit Command Functions

Key(s)	Function	Notes
A and S	Clip Trim	Trims clip to current cursor location: • A = Trim Start to Insertion • S =Trim End to Insertion
D,F,G	Fade In/Out/Crossfade	Fades a clip in/out based on the current cursor location: • D = Fade to start • G = Fade to end When a selection occurs across adjacent clips, the F key crossfades the clips together, or creates batch fades when the selection crosses multiple clip boundaries. These commands use the fade preset curve and duration from Preferences.
X,C,V	Cut, Copy, Paste	Standard cut, copy, and paste using single keystrokes.
B	Separate Clip	Separates (breaks) clips at current cursor location.
N	Insertion Follows Playback	Places the Edit insertion cursor where playback is stopped.*
Comma and period numeric keypad plus or minus	Nudge Forward/Back	Nudges forward or back by nudge amount.

Continues...

Table 4.6 Edit Command Functions (*continued*)

Key(s)	Function	Notes
M and /	Nudge by Next Value	Nudges forward or back by the next larger nudge value in Nudge List.
Up/Down	Mark In/Out	Moves the mark in/out point during playback.
H,J,K	Snap Clip	Snaps the selected clip to timeline location**:
		• H = Snap head of clip to the cursor
		• J = Snap clip sync point to the cursor
		• K = Snap tail of clip to the cursor
Y,U,I	Snap Clip to Timecode	Snaps the selected clip to incoming timecode ***:
		• Y = Snap head of clip to current timecode location
		• U = Snap clip sync point to current timecode location
		• I = Snap tail of clip to current timecode location

* Insertion Follows Playback is also represented by an icon in the toolbar, as shown in Figure 4.8.

** Requires that the Timeline and Edit selections be unlinked.

*** Requires that incoming timecode be present.

Insertion Follows Playback toggle on/off

Figure 4.8
Insertion Follows Playback toggle on/off.

The Snap to Play keys (H, J, and K) move the currently selected clip(s) to the timeline cursor position. These keys allow you to snap a single clip or a whole group of clips to a new location, which you can't do with the standard Snap technique (that is, Control-click on Mac, Start-click on Windows). This advanced way of moving clips to timeline locations works only if the Edit and Timeline selections are unlinked.

To snap a collection of clips to a new location:

1. Unlink the Timeline and Edit selections by clicking the **Link Timeline and Edit Selection** button in the Edit window toolbar to disable it, as shown in Figure 4.9.

Link Timeline and Edit Selection button

Figure 4.9
Link Timeline and Edit Selection button.

2. Select all the clips you want to move. Use the Object Grabber to select discontinuous clips.

3. Place the cursor in a timebase ruler at the position where you want the group of clips to start. (Note: Do not click in a track playlist.)

4. Press the **H**, **J**, or **K** key (Snap Start, Sync Point, or End to Play). All the clips will be shifted so that the start, sync point, or tail begins at the new time.

Navigation and Transport Functions

The blue color-coded Commands focus keys shown in Figure 4.10 allow single key access for navigation and transport functions. Table 4.7 lists these command functions.

Figure 4.10
Navigation and Transport shortcuts.

Tip: Note that several of the pink and blue Commands focus keys provide independent functions for both Timeline and Edit selections when Link Timeline and Edit Selections is disabled.

Table 4.7   Navigation and Transport Command Functions

Key(s)	Function	Notes
Q and W	Center Timeline Selection	Centers the current Timeline selection start (Q) or end (W) in the center of the Edit window.
Left and Right Arrow	Center Edit Selection	Centers the current Edit selection start (Left Arrow) or end (Right Arrow) in the Edit window.
[	Play Edit Selection	Plays the current Edit selection.
]	Play Timeline Selection	Plays the current Timeline selection.
P and semicolon (;) L and single quote (')	Navigation keys	Moves the cursor up/down tracks (P/;), or to previous/next clip boundaries (L/')*.
6, 7, 8, 9	Audition keys	Plays a short duration of audio based on the pre/post-roll amount (see the "Audition Commands" section later in this lesson).
Space bar/0 on numeric keypad	Play/Stop	The numeric keypad 0 can be used as a separate stop play command, as set in preferences.
1, 2 on numeric keypad	Fast Forward/Rewind	Numeric keypad 1 activates Rewind; numeric keypad 2 activates Fast Forward; to hear audio during Fast Forward/Rewind, select the option in preferences.
4 on numeric keypad	Enable Loop Playback	Toggles Loop Playback On/Off.
5 on numeric keypad	Enable Loop Record	Toggles Loop Record On/Off.
6 on numeric keypad	Enable QuickPunch	Toggles QuickPunch On/Off.
Period (.) on numeric keypad	Recall Memory Location	Type period, Memory Location number, period on the numeric keypad to recall.
Enter on numeric keypad	Store Memory Location	Press Enter on the numeric keypad for next available Memory Location or press period, Memory Location number, Enter on numeric keypad to store a specific Memory Location.
3 on numeric keypad and F12	Immediate Record	Enables record on the transport and starts recording immediately.

* Moves to next transient if Tab to Transients is enabled.

Tip: The numeric keypad Transport shortcuts listed in Table 4.7 are independent of Commands Keyboard Focus mode and are instead enabled when the Operation Preference's Numeric Keypad mode is set to Transport (see the "Numeric Keypad" section later in this lesson).

MIDI Functions

The green color-coded Commands focus keys shown in Figure 4.11 allow single-key access to MIDI recording functions.

- **F11**: MIDI Wait Note. (This function can be enabled/disabled in MIDI Preferences, and is disabled by default.)

- **Numeric keypad 7**: MIDI Metronome

- **Numeric keypad 8**: Countoff

- **Numeric keypad 9**: MIDI Merge

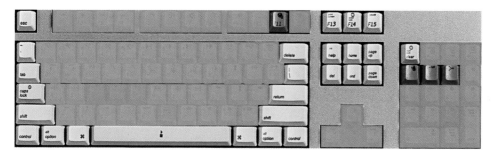

Figure 4.11
MIDI keyboard shortcuts.

Audition Commands

The alphanumeric keys 6–9 on the main keyboard (not on the numeric keypad) are used for auditioning (playing back) pre- and post-roll for the current edit selection in several ways, as shown in Table 4.8.

Table 4.8   Navigation and Transport Command Functions

Function	Focus Key	Mac	Windows
Play up to edit start by the pre-roll amount	6	Option+Left Arrow	Alt+Left Arrow
Play from edit start by the post-roll amount	7	Command+Left Arrow	Ctrl+Left Arrow
Play up to edit end by the pre-roll amount	8	Option+Right Arrow	Alt+Right Arrow
Play from edit end by the post-roll amount	9	Command+Right Arrow	Ctrl+Right Arrow
Play through edit start by the pre/post-roll amount	N/A	Option+Command+ Left Arrow	Ctrl+Alt+Left Arrow
Play through edit end by the pre/post-roll amount	N/A N/A	Option+Command+ Right Arrow	Ctrl+Alt+Right Arrow

Tip: Note that there is no way to access the "play through" functionality from the single stroke Commands focus keys.

Function Keys

Using the Function (F) keys on your computer keyboard, you can easily switch between the four Edit modes and six Edit tools. To access any of the Edit modes or tools, press the corresponding Function key: F1–F10. See Figure 4.12.

Figure 4.12
Edit mode and tool Function key shortcuts.

Shortcut: You can also enable/disable MIDI Wait Note (if enabled in MIDI preferences) by pressing F11, and Record by pressing F12.

Snap to Grid

You can use a keyboard shortcut to enable the Snap to Grid option, as listed in Table 4.9. To enable Snap to Grid while in an Edit mode other than Grid, do one of the following:

- Shift-click the **GRID MODE** button.

- Press **SHIFT+F4** to enable Snap to Grid while in another Edit mode.

Table 4.9   Snap to Grid Shortcuts

Snap to Grid Mode	Keyboard Shortcut
Shuffle	F1+F4
Slip	F2+F4
Spot	F3+F4

To access one of the six Edit tools:

1. Press the corresponding Function key (**F5**-**F10**).

Repeat presses of the Function key corresponding to the Zoomer, Trim, Grabber, or Pencil tool will toggle through the alternate modes for each tool, and repeat presses of Function key F4 will toggle between Absolute Grid and Relative Grid modes. You can also access the Smart Tool by pressing any two or more of the Function keys F6–F8 simultaneously.

Shortcut: You can lock the currently selected Edit tools (Zoom, Trim, Grab, and Pencil only) and Grid mode (Absolute or Relative) in place, preventing them from being inadvertently changed when using keyboard shortcuts, by choosing Options > Edit/Tool Mode Keyboard Lock or pressing Control+Shift+T (Mac) or Start+Shift+T (Windows).

Note: The Function key shortcuts (F1-F12) are always available and do not change when Commands Keyboard Focus mode is enabled or disabled.

 In the Mac OS, some of the Function keys may be in use for system tasks, such as Dashboard, Spotlight, and Exposé. For more information about configuring Mac OS shortcuts for Pro Tools compatibility, review the Mac OS System Optimization section of Lesson 1, "Pro Tools Hardware Configuration," or the Pro Tools Software Installation Guide.

Numeric Keypad

The numeric keypad can take on one of three modes–Classic, Transport, or Shuttle. The Numeric Keypad mode preference (found under the Operation tab in the Preference dialog box) determines how the numeric keypad will function. No matter which Numeric Keypad mode is selected, you can always use the keypad to select and enter values in the Event Edit Area, Location Indicators, and Transport fields.

To set the Numeric Keypad mode:

1. Choose SETUP > PREFERENCES and click the OPERATION tab.

2. Under the option for NUMERIC KEYPAD mode, select a keypad mode (Classic, Transport, or Shuttle). See Figure 4.13.

3. Click OK. The selected numeric keypad mode is always available and is not affected by the Keyboard Focus mode.

Figure 4.13
Numeric keypad preferences.

Classic Mode

This mode emulates the way Pro Tools worked in versions earlier than 5.0. With the Numeric Keypad mode set to Classic, you can:

■ Recall memory locations by typing the Memory Location number, followed by a period.

■ Play up to two tracks of audio in Shuttle Lock mode. (See the upcoming "Shuttle Lock Mode" section.)

Transport Mode (Default)

This mode allows you to set a number of record and play functions and also operate the Transport from the numeric keypad. See Table 4.10.

Table 4.10   Numeric Keypad Mapping for Transport Control

Function	Key
Click On/Off	7
Countoff On/Off	8
MIDI Merge/Replace Mode	9
Loop Playback On/Off	4
Loop Record On/Off	5
QuickPunch Mode On/Off	6
Rewind	1
Fast Forward	2
Record	3
Play/Stop	0

With the Numeric Keypad mode set to Transport, you can also:

■ Recall memory locations by typing period, the Memory Location number, and period again.

■ Play up to two tracks of audio in Shuttle Lock mode (see the next section).

■ Use Separate Play and Stop keys. When enabled, this option lets you start playback with the Enter key and stop playback with the 0 (zero) key on the numeric keypad. When this option is disabled, the numeric keypad zero key will toggle between playback/stop.

Shuttle Lock Mode

Shuttle Lock mode can be used when the Numeric Keypad Mode preference is set to either Classic or Transport. Shuttle Lock mode lets you use the numeric keypad to shuttle up to two tracks forward or backward at specific speeds: 5 is normal speed, numbers from 6 to 9 provide increasingly faster speeds, and numbers from 4 to 1 provide progressively slower speeds, with 0 equaling pause. If multiple tracks are selected, only the first two tracks are shuttled.

To play one or two tracks with the Shuttle Lock:

1. With Pro Tools HD (or Complete Production Toolkit), make sure the OPERATION preference for NUMERIC KEYPAD mode is not set to SHUTTLE.

2. With the SELECTOR tool, click in the track where you want playback to begin. To shuttle on two tracks, Shift-click in a second track.

3. Press the CONTROL (Mac) or START key (Windows) and a number on the numeric keypad: 0–9 (9 is fastest, 5 is normal playback speed, and 0 is pause).

   Once Shuttle Lock mode is initiated, Fast Forward and Rewind become highlighted in the Transport window.

4. Press additional keys to change the playback speed, or press the PLUS (+) or MINUS (–) key to switch the playback direction (plus for forward, minus for backward).

5. To pause playback, press numeric keypad ZERO (0) key.

To exit Shuttle Lock mode, do one of the following:

■ Press Stop in the Transport window or Avid supported worksurface.

■ Press the space bar.

Tip: In the Operation tab of preferences, you can customize the Custom Shuttle Lock Speed setting, allowing you to choose the highest fast-forward Shuttle Lock speed (key 9) to better match your editing and auditioning needs. The setting has a range of 50–800%.

Shuttle Mode

Shuttle mode on a Pro Tools HD and Complete Production Toolkit systems offers an alternative to Shuttle Lock mode. With the Numeric Keypad mode set to Shuttle, playback from the current Edit selection is triggered by pressing and holding the keys on the numeric keypad, with playback stopping once the keys are released. Various playback speeds are available in both forward and reverse, and holding the Shift key allows you to make selections while in Shuttle mode. In this mode, pre-roll and post-roll are ignored. Table 4.11 lists the keys for Shuttle mode.

Table 4.11   Numeric Keypad Mapping for Shuttle Mode

Function	Key
1× forward	6
1× rewind	4
4× forward	9
4× rewind	7
¼× forward	3
¼× rewind	1
½× forward	5+6
½× rewind	5+4
2× forward	8+9
2× rewind	8+7
¹⁄₁₆× forward	2+3
¹⁄₁₆× rewind	2+1
Loop selection (1× speed)	0*

* The Loop selection Shuttle Mode Numeric Keypad shortcut (0) works regardless of Loop Playback status.

With the Numeric Keypad mode set to Shuttle, you can also recall memory locations by typing period, the Memory Location number, and period again.

Note: Shuttle Lock mode is not available when the Numeric Keypad mode is set to Shuttle.

Review/Discussion Questions

1. What do the modifier keys Option/Alt and Option/Alt+Shift correspond to for most functions in Pro Tools?

2. In Pro Tools, when changing a sliding or rotary control, what happens when you press the Command key (Mac) or Ctrl key (Windows) while adjusting the control?

3. What is the keyboard shortcut to Solo Safe a track?

4. How many different Keyboard Focus options are available in the Mix and Edit windows?

5. What is the key command for activating Commands Keyboard Focus mode?

6. What do the different colors (yellow, pink, and blue) on a coded keyboard refer to?

7. With Commands Keyboard Focus enabled in the Edit window, which key would you press to switch a track containing the cursor from Waveform view to Volume view?

8. What are the Commands Keyboard Focus shortcuts for fade-in, fade-out, and crossfade?

9. What are the focus keys H, J, and K used for?

10. What is the focus key N used for?

11. What is the keyboard shortcut to enable Loop Record and QuickPunch?

12. What is the keyboard shortcut for enabling Loop Playback?

13. What focus key shortcuts are used to trim a clip's start and end to the cursor?

14. Explain the difference between Shuttle Lock and Shuttle modes using the numeric keypad.

Lesson 4 Keyboard Shortcuts

Shortcut	Description
Option-click (Mac)/Alt-click (Windows)	Apply changes to all/multiple tracks
Option+Shift-click (Mac)/Alt+Shift-click (Windows)	Apply changes to selected tracks
Shift+R	Record Enable tracks containing edit cursor
Shift+I	Enable TrackInput Monitoring mode on tracks containing edit cursor
Shift+M	Mute tracks containing edit cursor
Shift+S	Solo tracks containing edit cursor
Command-click Record button (Mac)/ Ctrl-click Record button (Windows)	Record safe track
Command-click Solo button (Mac)/ Ctrl-click Solo button (Windows)	Solo safe track
Command-click Plug-in/Send (Mac)/ Ctrl-click Plug-in/Send (Windows)	Plug-in Bypass/Send Mute
Command-click Send Selector (Mac)/ Ctrl-click Send Selector (Windows)	Toggle Send Single or Assignments view
Command-click Mix window data display (Mac)/ Ctrl-click Mix window data display (Windows)	Toggle Mix window volume/peak/sample delay display
Command-click control or parameter (Mac)/ Ctrl-click control or parameter (Windows)	Finer resolution control/parameter adjust
Option-click control or parameter (Mac)/ Ctrl-click control or parameter (Windows)	Set to default
Option+Command-click first track's assignment (Mac)/ Ctrl+Alt-click first track's assignment (Windows)	Cascade input, output, or send assignment
Option+Command+1 (Mac)/Ctrl+Alt+1 (Windows)	Activate Commands Keyboard Focus mode
Option+Command+2 (Mac)/Ctrl+Alt+2 (Windows)	Activate Clips List Keyboard Focus mode
Option+Command+3 (Mac)/Ctrl+Alt+3 (Windows)	Activate Groups List Keyboard Focus mode
Option+Command+4 (Mac)/Ctrl+Alt+4 (Windows)	Move Focus to Edit window from MIDI Editor
Option+Command+5 (Mac)/Ctrl+Alt+5 (Windows)	Move Focus to MIDI Editor from Edit window
1, 2, 3, 4, or 5 (on alphanumeric keyboard)	Zoom presets 1–5

Lesson 4 Keyboard Shortcuts

Shortcut	Description
6 (on alphanumeric keyboard) or Option+ Left Arrow (Mac)/6 (on alphanumeric keyboard) or Alt+Left Arrow (Windows)	Play up to edit start by pre-roll value
7 (on alphanumeric keyboard) or Command+ Left Arrow (Mac)/7 (on alphanumeric keyboard) or Ctrl+Left Arrow (Windows)	Play from edit start by pre-roll value
8 (on alphanumeric keyboard) or Option+ Right Arrow (Mac)/8 (on alphanumeric keyboard) or Alt+Right Arrow (Windows)	Play up to edit end by pre-roll value
9 (on alphanumeric keyboard) or Command+ Right Arrow (Mac)/9 (on alphanumeric keyboard) or Ctrl+Right Arrow (Windows)	Play from edit end by pre-roll value
Option+Command+Left Arrow (Mac)/ Ctrl+Alt+Left Arrow (Windows)	Play through edit start by pre/post-roll value
Option+Command+Right Arrow (Mac)/ Ctrl+Alt+Right Arrow (Windows)	Play through edit end by pre/post-roll value
O (on alphanumeric keyboard)	Copy Edit selection to Timeline selection
0	Copy Timeline selection to Edit selection
Hyphen key	Toggle Track View
Numeric keypad equals (=) key	Capture Timecode
Q or Left Arrow	Center Timeline selection start
W or Right Arrow	Center Timeline selection end
E	Zoom Toggle
R	Zoom Out horizontally
T	Zoom In horizontally
Y	Snap start of selected clip to timecode
U	Snap sync point of selected clip to timecode
I	Snap end of selected clip to timecode
H	Snap start of selected clip to playhead
J	Snap sync point of selected clip to playhead
K	Snap end of selected clip to playhead

Lesson 4 Keyboard Shortcuts

Shortcut	Description
P	Move Edit Selection/Cursor Up
Semicolon (;)	Move Edit Selection/Cursor Down
L	Tab Back
Apostrophe (')	Tab Forward
Right Bracket (])	Play timeline selection
Left Bracket ([)	Play edit selection
A	Trim Start to Insertion
S	Trim End to Insertion
D	Fade to Start
G	Fade to End
F	Crossfade Selection
Z	Undo
X	Cut
C	Copy
V	Paste
B	Separate Clip
N	Insertion Follows Playback (disable/enable)
Minus (–) or comma (,)	Nudge earlier by nudge value
Plus (+) or period (.)	Nudge later by nudge value
M	Nudge earlier by next larger nudge value
Forward slash (/) (on alphanumeric keyboard)	Nudge later by next larger nudge value
Enter on numeric keypad	Store memory location
F11	Enable MIDI Wait Note
F1	Enable Shuffle mode
F2	Enable Slip mode
F3	Enable Spot mode
F4	Enable/Toggle Grid mode
F5	Enable/Toggle Zoomer tools
F6	Enable/Toggle Trim tools

Lesson 4 Keyboard Shortcuts

Shortcut	Description
F7	Enable Selector tool
F8	Enable/Toggle Grabber tools
F9	Enable/Toggle Scrubber tool
F10	Enable/Toggle Pencil tools
Press two or more (F6–F8)	Enable Smart tool
F1+F4	Enable Snap to Grid-Shuffle
F2+F4	Enable Snap to Grid-Slip
F3+F4	Enable Snap to Grid-Shuffle
Control+Shift+T (Mac)/Start+Shift+T (Windows)	Lock Current Edit tools in place
Numeric keypad 7	Click On/Off
Numeric keypad 8	Countoff On/Off
Numeric keypad 9	MIDI Merge On/Off
Command+Shift+L or numeric keypad 4 (Mac)/ Ctrl+Shift+L or numeric keypad 4 (Windows)	Loop Playback On/Off
Option+L or numeric keypad 5 (Mac)/ Alt+L or numeric keypad 5 (Windows)	Loop Record On/Off
Command+Shift+P or numeric keypad 6 (Mac)/ Ctrl+Shift+P or numeric keypad 6 (Windows)	QuickPunch On/Off
Numeric keypad 3 or F12	Immediate Record
Numeric keypad 2	Fast Forward
Numeric keypad 1	Rewind
Period (.)+Memory Location number+period (.)	Recall Memory Location
Control+numeric keypad 1–9 (Mac)/ Start+numeric keypad 1–9 (Windows)	Shuttle Lock Mode Play
Numeric keypad plus(+)/minus(−)	Shuttle Lock Mode Forward/Reverse
Numeric keypad 0	Shuttle Lock Mode Pause
Numeric keypad 6	Shuttle Mode 1× forward
Numeric keypad 4	Shuttle Mode 1× rewind
Numeric keypad 9	Shuttle Mode 4× forward
Numeric keypad 7	Shuttle Mode 4× rewind

Lesson 4 Keyboard Shortcuts

Shortcut	Description
Numeric keypad 3	Shuttle Mode ¼× forward
Numeric keypad 1	Shuttle Mode ¼× rewind
Numeric keypad 5+6	Shuttle Mode ½× forward
Numeric keypad 5+4	Shuttle Mode ½× rewind
Numeric keypad 8+9	Shuttle Mode 2× forward
Numeric keypad 8+7	Shuttle Mode 2× rewind
Numeric keypad 2+3	Shuttle Mode ⅟₁₆× forward
Numeric keypad 2+1	Shuttle Mode ⅟₁₆× rewind
Numeric keypad 0	Shuttle Mode Loop selection (1× speed)
With Grabber tool, Control-click clip (Mac)/ with Grabber tool, Start-click clip (Windows)	Snap clip to edit cursor
With Grabber tool, Control+Shift-click clip (Mac)/ with Grabber tool, Start+Shift-click clip (Windows)	Snap clip's sync point to edit cursor
With Grabber tool, Control+Command-click clip (Mac)/ with Grabber tool, Control+Start-click clip (Windows)	Snap clip's end to edit cursor

Tactile Control of Pro Tools

In this exercise, you will get a chance to practice keyboard editing shortcuts while editing the *Agent MX Zero* movie trailer.

Media Used:

310P Exercise 04.ptxt (Pro Tools session)

Duration:

30 minutes

GOAL

■ Recall and use editing keyboard shortcuts to work faster

Getting Started

After completing Lesson 4, which covered many of the common keyboard shortcuts that are available in Pro Tools, you will now get a chance to practice using them on your own.

1. Open **310P EXERCISE 04.PTXT**, located on the book DVD in the **EXERCISE MEDIA / 310P CLASS AUDIO FILES v10 / 310P EXERCISE 04** (or other location specified by the course instructor) directory.

2. In the **SAVE NEW SESSION AS** dialog box, name the session as desired, saving into an appropriate location on a valid storage volume.

Keyboard Editing Shortcuts

This exercise contains four separate sets of editing tasks, with each set containing 10 individual editing commands. Using only the keyboard, perform each of the following tasks as quickly as possible, and then write down the commands you used to achieve the task using the space provided.

Note: Some of the single tasks require multiple keyboard shortcuts to complete.

As an example, the first step of task 1 has been completed for you. You should be able to complete a single group of 10 editing tasks in about 3–5 minutes (not counting the writing).

Tip: During this exercise, try to use keyboard shortcuts exclusively. Avoid using menus and the mouse as much as possible, except in situations that require modifier keys in combination with a mouse action. Feel free to refer back to the preceding lesson topics as necessary.

Caution: Some of the shortcuts required in this exercise were taught in previous books in the Avid Learning Series. If necessary, you can choose Help > Pro Tools Shortcuts from within Pro Tools or refer to the shortcuts answer key at the end of this exercise.

Task 1: Keyboard Editing Shortcuts

Step #	Task Description	Commands Used to Complete Task
1.	Recall Memory Location 1 (Task 1).	Press period+numeric keypad 1+period
2.	Change all track sizes from small to medium.	
3.	Enable Commands Keyboard Focus mode.	
4.	Select all clips in the 2-pop clip group.	
5.	Nudge the 2-pop clip group three frames earlier to align its start to timecode number 00:59:58:00.	
6.	Edit-lock the 2-pop clip group.	
7.	Move the edit selection to the FX_01 track.	
8.	Enable Tab to Transients.	
9.	Tab to the first waveform modulation in the FX_01 track.	
10.	Delete from the insertion cursor back to the start of the clip.	

Task 2: Keyboard Editing Shortcuts

Step #	Task Description	Commands Used to Complete Task
1.	Recall Memory Location 2 (Task 2).	
2.	Disable Tab to Transients.	
3.	On the MX_01 track, move the insertion cursor to the start of the AMXZ Cue_02C clip.	
4.	Select from the cursor to the end of the MX_01 track.	
5.	Extend the selection to include the MX_02 track.	
6.	Move all selected clips on the MX_01 and MX_02 tracks two seconds later.	
7.	Place the insertion cursor on the MX_01 track at timecode number 01:01:09:17.	
8.	Add a sync point at the current cursor location.	
9.	Place the insertion cursor three frames later to timecode number 01:01:09:20.	
10.	Using the mouse while holding a Modifier key, snap the AMXZ Cue_07F clip's sync point to the gunflash occurring at timecode number 01:01:09:20.	

Task 3: Keyboard Editing Shortcuts

Step #	Task Description	Commands Used to Complete Task
1.	Place short fade-ins and fade-outs (about one second each) on both music clips on the MX_01 track.	
2.	Recall Memory Location 3 (Task 3).	
3.	Disable all active groups.	
4.	Solo the FX_02 track.	
5.	On the FX_02 track, zoom in until the AMXO-Alarm_03B clip is visible, then select the clip (including the fades).	
6.	Copy the clip to the Clipboard.	
7.	On the FX_02 track, paste copies of the AMXO-Alarm_03B clip at timecode numbers 01:00:32:14 and 01:00:34:15.	
8.	Clear the solo on the FX_02 track.	
9.	On the FX_01 track, move the insertion cursor to timecode number 01:00:56:21.	
10.	Change the Nudge increment to 6 frames.	

Lesson 5

Post Production Recording Techniques

This lesson details the steps for controlling an Avid PRE or other compatible third-party microphone preamps using Pro Tools with an Avid worksurface.

Media Used: 310P Exercise 05.ptxt

Duration: 45 minutes

GOALS

- Set up and control a PRE-compatible mic preamp from the Pro Tools software
- Control a PRE-compatible mic preamp from an Avid worksurface
- Record Foley using a PRE-compatible mic preamp
- Record MIDI Foley using the Structure sampler plug-in

Introduction

When combined with Pro Tools and an Avid worksurface, the Avid PRE microphone preamp can be part of a very fast and powerful workflow.

Third-Party Support for Avid PRE Communications Protocol

The Avid PRE communications protocol is an open standard using MIDI. A number of third-party manufacturers offer multi-channel microphone preamps that support the Avid PRE communications protocol. After installing the appropriate Pro Tools software drivers, these devices are configured in Pro Tools in the same manner as an Avid PRE.

Note: Some features of the Avid PRE might not be available on all third-party microphone preamps. Please consult the appropriate manufacturer to determine operational differences.

Microphone preamps currently supporting the PRE communication protocol include:

- Aphex 1788A and 188
- Focusrite Liquid 4PRE
- Grace Design M802
- Millennia Music & Media Systems HV-3R
- Prodigy Engineering Anima
- Summit Audio MPE-200

On the Web   For a complete listing of third-party microphone preamps supporting the Avid PRE communications protocol, go to www.avid.com.

Controlling PRE from Pro Tools

Once you have configured a PRE in the Peripherals and I/O Setup windows, it can be controlled directly from tracks in either the Mix or Edit windows.

Connecting, configuring and enabling an Avid PRE using the Pro Tools software is discussed in the "PRE" section of Lesson 1, "Pro Tools HD Hardware Configuration."

To control a PRE channel from a track in the Mix window:

1. Choose TRACK > NEW, and create a new mono Audio or Aux Input track.

2. From the track INPUT SELECTOR, choose the input path that is mapped to the PRE channel you want to use.

3. As shown in Figure 5.1, the parameters for the PRE channel can now be controlled from the Mic Preamp controls at the top of the channel strip. If you can't see the PRE controls at the top of the channel strip in the Mix window, choose VIEW > MIX WINDOW VIEWS > MIC PREAMPS, or choose MIC PREAMPS from the MIX WINDOW VIEW SELECTOR pop-up menu at the bottom of the Mix window.

Tip: You can also display the Mic Preamps view in the Edit window by choosing View > Edit Window Views > Mic Preamps.

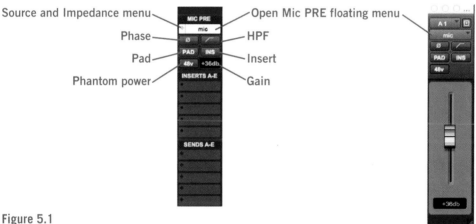

Figure 5.1
Mic PRE track controls (left) and a mic PRE floating window (right).

You can also access PRE controls from a floating window.

To open a Mic Preamp window:

1. Click on the Mic Pre Input display (which is the top box in the channel strip labeled MIC, LINE, or DI).

To open multiple Mic Preamp windows:

1. Shift-click each window button when opening a new window or untarget an open window.

Stereo and Multi-Channel Operation

Pro Tools can control multiple PRE channels from a single multi-channel track.

To control a stereo pair of PRE channels in Pro Tools:

1. Create a stereo path in the Inputs tab of the I/O Setup dialog box. The path should be mapped to the pair of analog interface inputs that are assigned to the two PRE channels your stereo source is connected to.

2. Choose TRACK > NEW, and create a new stereo Audio or Aux Input track.

3. Choose your stereo input path from the track INPUT SELECTOR.

The preamp controls at the top of the channel will now control both PRE channels simultaneously.

PRE Parameters

The following PRE parameters can be controlled from the Pro Tools software:

- **Input**: This control mirrors the main track Input Selector.

- **Phase**: Reverses the phase of the signal (at the pre-amp stage, that is, before it reaches your Pro Tools audio interface).

- **HPF**: Switches in the channel's High Pass Filter. The filter has a cut off frequency of 85Hz, with an 18dB/octave rolloff. Use the HPF to reduce microphone proximity effects, breath, wind, rumble, and hum.

- **Pad**: Enables/disables the –18dB gain pad (gain reduction).

- **Insert**: This switch routes the input via the PRE channel's Insert connection. PRE's back panel has eight pairs of Send and Return jacks for inserting external analog processors (such as compressors or EQs) into the audio path. Inserts are post the output trims. If you do not have your signal routed through an external processor, enabling the Insert will effectively mute your signal. When PRE's internal oscillator (test signal) is active, the Insert switch routes the oscillator signal to that channel's Send output, as well as the main DB-25 output. This enables you to test the signal path across the insert.

■ **Source**: Clicking the Source Selector brings up a pop-up menu with two separate sections. As shown in Figure 5.2, the top half of the menu lets you select an input source by type (Mic, Line, DI). The bottom half lets you select the input impedance for the PRE channel (1.5kOhms, 15kOhms, or 1.5MOhms). By default these are linked, so when you choose Mic, the impedance switches to 1.5k; choosing Line switches impedance to 15k, and choosing DI (Instrument) switches impedance to 1.5M. When your input source is set to Mic, you can go back into the menu and select any of the three impedance settings. If you select Line, you can choose either 1.5kOhms or 15kOhms. If you select DI, the only available input impedance is 1.5MOhms, which cannot be changed.

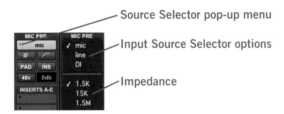

Figure 5.2
Avid PRE Source Selector menu.

Tip: The default Impedance settings of 1.5kOhms is appropriate for most good quality microphones. However, you can check the output impedance of your microphone to see if a higher input impedance setting is necessary. The input impedance should be at least 5-10 times the output impedance of the mic. Therefore, if your mic has an output impedance rating over 300Ohms, consider trying a higher input setting.

■ **48V**: Toggle 48V Phantom Power on/off. 48v automatically switches off when either Line or DI are chosen as the input source. Phantom Power should be switched off until you've connected your microphone and before disconnecting your microphone.

■ **Gain**: The main gain control has a range from 0dB to +69dB and is adjusted in fixed steps of approximately 3dB. For this reason, it is recommended that you not adjust the gain during recording.

On the Web

You can also control an Avid PRE using a supported Avid worksurface. Each worksurface has slightly different methods of entering Mic PRE mode, displaying PRE settings, and changing parameters. For more information about controlling an Avid PRE using an Avid worksurface, consult the worksurface's documentation or go to www.avid.com.

Recording Foley

When recording Foley into Pro Tools using an Avid worksurface and a PRE-compatible microphone preamp, you can work quickly and efficiently. Since a PRE-compatible microphone preamp can be easily accessed from most Avid work-surfaces, you can first dial in the proper preamp settings and mic levels, and then use the track arming, record mode, and transport controls to quickly and easily record your Foley takes. After recording, you can then audition, edit, and sync your Foley so that it aligns perfectly with the picture. All of the recording, auditioning, and editing functions can be easily accessed using your Avid worksurface, allowing you to progress from recording Foley to a final check of your completed Foley with minimal effort.

Recording Foley with a Avid PRE via Aux Input Tracks

Some Pro Tools operators like to bring inputs into Pro Tools via Aux Inputs and then bus them to record tracks. This allows you to record with plug-ins inserted, and make adjustments to the recording level from the Pro Tools mixer. Although in most cases this is a matter of preference, it may be advisable when using an Avid PRE. This is because it is recommended not to make gain adjustments on the PRE unit itself during recording. PRE's gain is not continuously variable; it changes in steps of about 3dB, and this would be audible if changed in the middle of a take. Recording via an Aux Input track allows you to use the Aux track's fader to make any on-the-fly level adjustments.

Caution: Recording an audio source using a PRE via an Aux Input track is post A/D converter, so lowering the Aux Input fader level will not help if clipping your audio interface inputs from the PRE.

Note: Keep in mind that this is a workaround for making last minute adjustments during recording, and is not a substitute for setting the optimum gain on your PRE before recording.

To set up and record Foley into Pro Tools:

1. Verify that all necessary control room monitoring and talkback/listenback have been configured properly.

2. Choose SETUP > PREFERENCES > OPERATION page, and then enable MUTE RECORD-ARMED TRACKS WHILE STOPPED, as shown in Figure 5.3.

   Although enabling this preference is optional, it will allow you to move and adjust microphone positions while the Pro Tools transport is stopped and the audio track is still record-armed. This will stop any audible bumps from reaching and possibly damaging your control room speakers.

Figure 5.3
The Mute Record-Armed Tracks
While Stopped preference.

3. Enable either **Loop Record** or **QuickPunch**, record enable the desired Foley track, and adjust your PRE **Input Gain** as necessary.

4. Create an edit selection with the appropriate amount of pre-roll and start playback, allowing the Foley artist to rehearse or practice before recording.

Tip: **Foley artists work almost exclusively with either visual streamers (called wipes) as a visual cueing system for their recordings, or use beep tones (similar to ADR recording). Although the Pro Tools hardware cannot generate wipes, you can create them using third-party software products such as Gallery Software's VirtualVTR Pro, Figure 53's Streamers, KIWA International's VoiceQ, or hardware solutions, such as Colin Broad's VS-1, CueLine's ProCue 1M1, or Horita's ADQ-50.**

5. When ready, record the Foley, making sure to name record files and create multiple Foley takes as needed.

Tip: **After the Foley recording session is completed, you can edit the Foley as necessary using any of the standard Pro Tools editing features.**

Recording Foley Using MIDI (Alternative)

If your post production project has the budget, you should probably use real Foley artists, since it will save an immense amount of time getting the Foley to sound correct and natural. Although recording Foley as MIDI is a less costly alternative to recording audio Foley, it usually requires a skilled operator to get the desired sound. Despite the inherent difficulties in getting MIDI recorded Foley to sound natural, for projects with a tight budget where real Foley is cost prohibitive, you can record Foley into Pro Tools as MIDI using a software-based sampler plug-in inserted on an Instrument track.

Although there are several plug-in based sampler options that are available for Pro Tools from third-party manufacturers, the most powerful and processor-efficient plug-in sampler for Pro Tools is Avid's Structure plug-in, shown in Figure 5.4.

Although Structure Free comes with all Pro Tools systems, the feature set of Structure Free may not be suitable for Foley workflows. For more information about Structure plug-in options and features, go to www.avid.com/US/products/Structure.

Figure 5.4
Avid Structure sampling plug-in for Pro Tools.

To record Foley as MIDI directly into the Pro Tools timeline using the Structure plug-in:

1. Verify that you have the Avid Structure plug-in installed.

2. Verify that you have digital video online for the scene where you will be recording Foley.

3. Create a new stereo Instrument track.

4. Using the stereo Instrument track's INSERT SELECTOR, choose MULTICHANNEL NATIVE PLUG-IN > INSTRUMENT > STRUCTURE (STEREO).

5. Do one of the following:

   - Load and map the desired Foley sample files into your sampler plug-in.

Tip: Importing and mapping sample files, as well as creating custom Structure patches, is beyond the scope of this book. For more information about creating custom Structure patches, consult the *Structure Plug-in Guide* for more details.

- From the **QUICK BROWSE** menu (for **FAVORITE** folders), choose the desired preset, as shown in Figure 5.5.

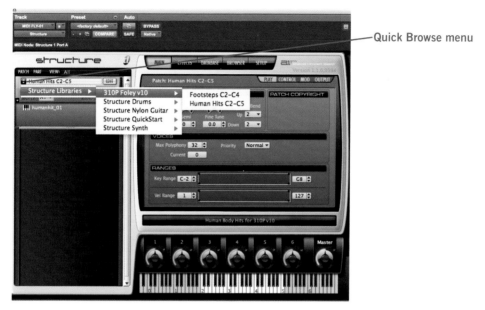

Figure 5.5
Selecting a Structure plug-in preset using the Quick Browse menu.

Tip: For simplicity, two different Foley presets for Structure have been provided
      for use in this book. These can be loaded from the Structure plug-in window
      by choosing Quick Browse (menu) > 310P Foley v10 > Footsteps C2-C4 or
      Human Hits C2-C5.

6. Record enable your Instrument track, and use your MIDI keyboard to trigger the Foley samples as precisely as possible.

7. After recording, you can then edit the MIDI Foley notes to match your picture exactly (using the Notes View track display).

Sample-Based MIDI in Post Production

When working with MIDI tracks in post production, you have the option of creating or modifying MIDI tracks to be tick-based or sample-based. Although there are many reasons to assign MIDI tracks to tick-based timing for musical applications, when working with MIDI tracks in post production that will be used to trigger sound effects or Foley, these MIDI tracks will always need to have sample-based timing references.

Since sample-based MIDI tracks use an absolute time reference, this type of MIDI track is ideally suited for Foley, sound effects, and other post production audio triggered via MIDI that requires absolute timing that will not alter sync location, even after tempo and meter changes occur. For example, if Foley footsteps are loaded into the Structure plug-in, and then triggered from an Instrument track in sync with the picture (starting at timecode number 01:15:10:12), this track's timing reference *must* be sample-based. This will ensure that absolute sync is maintained, even if tempo and meter changes occur after syncing the Instrument track to the picture, as illustrated in Figure 5.6

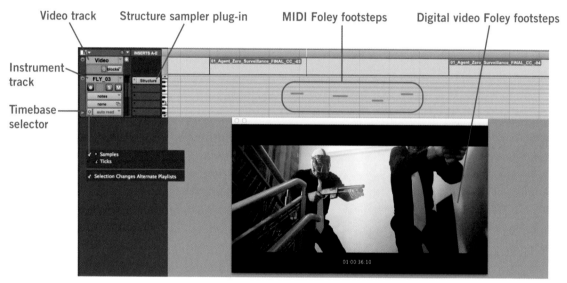

Figure 5.6
Recorded MIDI-based Foley using the Avid Structure sampler plug-in.

Review/Discussion Questions

1. What is the standard communications protocol used by an Avid PRE that allows it to receive settings changes from the Pro Tools software?

2. Which controls on an Avid PRE can be controlled from the Pro Tools software?

3. What is the high-pass filter's cutoff frequency on an Avid PRE?

4. How many decibels of gain reduction does the Pad provide on an Avid PRE?

5. What is the smallest gain change you can make on an Avid PRE?

6. What is the purpose of using an Aux Input track for an Avid PRE's signal input into Pro Tools instead of using an Audio track?

7. How is the Mute Record Armed Tracks While Stopped operation preference useful when recording Foley?

8. How do Foley artists know when to start performing a Foley audio cue?

9. Why is it often preferable to record audio Foley rather than MIDI Foley?

10. Why are sample-based Instrument tracks useful when recording Foley for post production projects?

Recording and Editing Foley

In this exercise, you will be recording Foley (both as audio and MIDI) directly into Pro Tools, and then editing the Foley. In the post-sound industry, most audio Foley is recorded professionally using at least one separate Pro Tools engineer running the recording system in the control room, and another Foley artist in the sound studio. For this exercise, it is recommended to use two people, so that you can alternate between the roles of Pro Tools engineer and Foley artist. It also might make it easier to record Foley sharing roles in this manner, since you won't have to worry about trying to be the Foley artist and the Pro Tools engineer simultaneously. As an alternative to this approach, you can also record and perform the Foley entirely on your own using one Pro Tools system (with adequate pre-roll). In a classroom environment with multiple Pro Tools systems, you may need to take turns (one at a time) recording the footsteps using your hands inside shoes "walking" on a table top.

Media Used:

310P Exercise 5.ptxt (Pro Tools session)

Duration:

45 minutes

GOALS

- Set up and configure a PRE-compatible microphone preamp for use with Pro Tools

- Set up and configure Pro Tools to record audio Foley

- Edit audio Foley to synchronize with picture

- Set up and configure Pro Tools to record MIDI Foley

- Edit MIDI Foley to synchronize with picture

Getting Started

Note: When taking this class at an Avid Learning Partner, your instructor will advise you as to the best way to record Foley at the training facility based upon the number of available Pro Tools systems, the classroom setup, and the monitoring capabilities of the systems. If you do not have the ability to record audio Foley using Pro Tools, skip ahead to the "Recording MIDI Foley into Pro Tools" section of this exercise.

1. Open **310P EXERCISE 05.PTXT**, located in the **EXERCISE MEDIA/310P CLASS AUDIO FILES v10/310P EXERCISE 05** folder on the DVD (or other location specified by the course instructor).

2. In the Save New Session As dialog box, name the session as desired, saving into an appropriate location on a valid storage volume.

When the session opens, the following 13 tracks shown in Figure 5.7 will be available in your session:

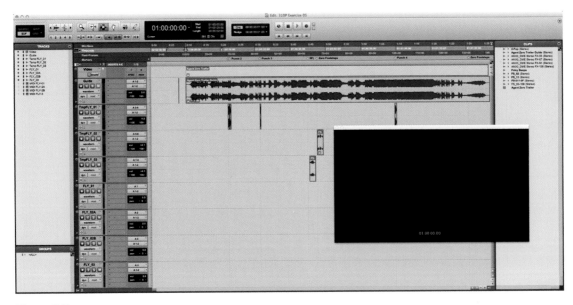

Figure 5.7
Edit window at the start of 310P Exercise 5.

- **Video**: QuickTime video reference for Foley recording.
- **Guide**: Stereo guide track mix of the trailer containing dialogue, sound effects, Foley, and music.

■ **Temp FLY_01**: Temporary Foley track example of punches for the scene.

■ **Temp FLY_02**: Temporary Foley track example of the two men's footsteps in the stairwell for the scene.

■ **Temp FLY_03**: Temporary Foley track example of Agent MX Zero's footsteps for the scene.

■ **FLY_01**: Source audio track for recording the Foley audio punches.

■ **FLY_02A**: Source audio track for recording the Foley audio footsteps of Man 1 in the stairwell.

■ **FLY_02B**: Source audio track for recording the Foley audio footsteps of Man 2 in the stairwell.

■ **FLY_03**: Source audio track for recording the Foley audio footsteps of Agent MX Zero.

■ **MIDI FLY_01**: Source MIDI track for recording the Foley MIDI punches.

■ **MIDI FLY_02A**: Source MIDI track for recording the Foley MIDI footsteps of Man 1 in the stairwell.

■ **MIDI FLY_02B**: Source MIDI track for recording the Foley MIDI footsteps of Man 2 in the stairwell.

■ **MIDI FLY_03**: Source MIDI track for recording the Foley MIDI footsteps of Agent MX Zero.

Recording and Editing Foley

This exercise gives you the opportunity to practice recording and editing Foley using PRE controlled from the Pro Tools software or using an (optional) Avid worksurface.

Note: If you do not have the ability to record audio Foley in Pro Tools, skip ahead to the "Recording MIDI Foley into Pro Tools" section of this exercise.

Enabling PRE for Remote Control from Pro Tools

Before you can start recording Foley into Pro Tools, you need to verify that the Avid PRE is set up and ready to be controlled by Pro Tools.

To set up PRE to be controlled by Pro Tools:

1. Make the proper audio and MIDI connections to PRE.

2. Configure MIDI in AMS (Mac) or MSS (Windows).

3. Declare and enable PRE in the Peripherals dialog box.

4. Map PRE outputs to an audio interface's inputs within the I/O Setup dialog box.

 For more detailed instructions regarding each of the above steps, refer back to Lesson 1 of this book.

Tip: You can also control an Avid PRE using a supported Avid worksurface (if available). For more information about controlling an Avid PRE from your Avid worksurface, consult your worksurface's User Guide.

Recording Audio Foley into Pro Tools

Assuming all microphone, PRE, and Pro Tools software settings are configured correctly, you are ready to record up to seven separate Foley cues into Pro Tools using the *Agent MX Zero* movie trailer. The Foley cues you need to record are detailed in Table 5.1.

Table 5.1 Audio Foley Recording Cues

Memory Location #	Approximate TC Start	Description	Recommended Props	Rec Track
1	01:00:12:07	Punch 1	Fruits/vegetables or stick hitting meat	FLY_01
2	01:00:12:16	Punch 2	Fruits/vegetables or stick hitting meat	FLY_01
3	01:00:21:11	Punch 3	Fruits/vegetables or stick hitting meat	FLY_01
4	01:00:35:00	Man 1-2 stairs footsteps	Shoes on cement surface or shoes on tabletop	FLY_02A-B
5	01:00:37:13	Agent MX Zero footsteps	Shoes on cement surface or shoes on tabletop	FLY_03
6	01:00:59:18	Punch 4	Fruits/vegetables or stick hitting meat	FLY_01
7	01:01:20:16	Agent MX Zero footsteps	Shoes on cement surface or shoes on tabletop	FLY_03

Tip: Listen to the temp audio Foley tracks to get an idea of how your recorded
      Foley should sound.

1. Before recording, you should watch the listed Foley cues several times so
    that you are familiar with them and can develop your own ideas on how
    to best create and record the perfect Foley performance for each cue.
    Memory locations are provided to help you quickly locate each Foley cue.
    (See Figure 5.8.)

Figure 5.8
Foley cues saved as memory locations for easy cueing.

2. Set proper inputs and record levels for the Foley record tracks.

Tip: You can use the audio clip, "Foley Beeps," in the Clips List for Foley cueing
      if desired.

3. Before recording the Foley cues, you will probably want to enable the
    following Pro Tools features:

    • QuickPunch

    • Operation page preference: Mute Record-Armed Tracks While Stopped

4. When all settings are correct, you can record the Foley cues onto each
    designated track. It is recommended to record multiple takes of each Foley
    cue using Loop Record, so that later you can choose the best take for final
    use in the project.

*In the Avid
Learning Series*   You can record multiple Foley takes in succession without stopping
    using Loop Record. For more information about loop recording, see
    "Loop Recording" in the Pro Tools 110 and 210P books.

Recording MIDI Foley into Pro Tools

In this section of the exercise, you will try recording the same previously listed
Foley cues into Pro Tools using the Structure software plug-in sampler, with punches
and footsteps pre-loaded and triggered using a MIDI or USB keyboard (or other
controller).

To record MIDI Foley into Pro Tools using digital picture:

1. If you recorded audio Foley in the previous section, mute all of your audio Foley tracks, and then hide all of them in the Track List.

2. From the Track List, show all four of the MIDI FLY instrument tracks.

3. Using Table 5.2, record all of the Foley cues as MIDI onto their specified instrument tracks.

Table 5.2   MIDI Foley Recording Cues

Memory Location #	Approximate TC Start	Description	Rec Track	MIDI Note Ranges
1	01:00:12:07	Punch 1	MIDI FLY_01	C2-C5
2	01:00:12:16	Punch 2	MIDI FLY_01	C2-C5
3	01:00:21:11	Punch 3	MIDI FLY_01	C2-C5
4	01:00:35:00	Man 1-2 stairs footsteps	MIDI FLY_02A-B	C2-C4
5	01:00:37:13	Agent MX Zero footsteps	MIDI FLY_03	C2-C4
6	01:00:59:18	Punch 4	MIDI FLY_01	C2-C5
7	01:01:20:16	Agent MX Zero footsteps	MIDI FLY_03	C2-C4

All four instrument tracks already contain the Structure plug-in with a corresponding patch pre-loaded for each Foley cue, as indicated in Table 5.2. For example, the first memory location will be recorded on the MIDI FLY_01 instrument track. The track already contains a pre-mapped Structure patch containing a variety of human punches mapped chromatically in octaves C2-C5 of your keyboard. You will use this instrument track to record the punches that Agent MX Zero delivers to his assailants. See Figure 5.9.

4. Using the table, record as many of the Foley cues as MIDI onto their respective tracks as time permits.

Tip: Be sure to use the Temp FLY audio tracks as your guide to get an idea of how the Foley should sound.

5. Before recording, audition and practice triggering the Foley footsteps from your MIDI keyboard or other MIDI controller.

Figure 5.9
Structure Sampler plug-in with "Human Hits C2-C5" patch pre-loaded.

6. When you are ready, record multiple passes of the MIDI Foley cues listed in Table 5.2 until you are satisfied with the performance.

Tip: Instead of using two separate Instrument tracks to record the two men running down the stairs in Foley Cue #4, you can use MIDI Merge with Loop Playback enabled to record and layer two sets of separate footsteps on a single instrument track.

Editing Foley

After all of the Foley cues are recorded to your satisfaction, you are now ready to choose your best Foley takes and edit the final Foley takes to match the picture.

1. Audition your various Foley record takes (both audio and MIDI) for each of the Foley cues and decide which one is your best take, compiling them onto one track, using playlist comping techniques.

**In the Avid
Learning Series**

Selecting alternate record takes is covered in both the Pro Tools 110 and 210P books, while voiceover and ADR comping using playlists is covered in the Pro Tools 210P.

2. Edit each final Foley take as necessary, using any of the editing techniques you've learned.

Tip: Feel free to use a reverb plug-in or any other plug-ins that will help to make your audio or MIDI Foley recordings sound more realistic.

3. When you're satisfied with all of your Foley edits, save the session.

4. For your MIDI Foley, record the final edited MIDI Foley tracks onto audio tracks using any available buses.

Editing Workflows

This lesson focuses on the various editing workflows and techniques used for film and television.

Media Used: 310P Exercise 06.ptxt

Duration: 45 minutes

GOALS

- Understand post production editing workflows for a television drama, film, and an advertisement
- Understand the audio search options available for Pro Tools
- Create sound effects beds using plug-ins
- Use Elastic Audio TCE and pitch shift for sound design
- Use Pro Tools advanced editing shortcuts

Introduction

When editing sound for film and television, it is important to understand and utilize workflows that make sense and allow you to work quickly and efficiently. The workflows and editing techniques discussed in this lesson will help you edit and finish projects on time, using industry proven shortcuts to get the job completed without wasting time.

Examples of Post Production Editing Workflows

The specific television, film, and advertising workflows listed in this section are real client workflows that were completed exactly as indicated. Because post production is full of many different workflows, it is important to understand that these workflows are just examples, and are not intended to serve as a rigid guide that all similar projects should follow. Many times, personal preferences, budgets, experience, time constraints, and the available hardware and software will influence the choice of workflow. Because of all of these factors, there are many other valid workflows that might look very different from the ones presented in this section.

Television Drama

This is an example of a workflow used for an episode of a 60-minute European TV drama based in a hospital. The production uses Avid Media Composer systems to edit the video footage and a Pro Tools|HDX system with Avid Mojo SDI to do the audio dubbing. All the systems are clients on an Avid ISIS 7000 network, which speeds up the production process, as this is a tightly scheduled production that goes from shooting to editing very quickly.

On set there are minimal microphones, so there is likely to be a maximum of four tracks of sync sound (location sound). Once shot, the picture footage and sync sound are transferred into the Avid Media Composer systems where the episode is cut together. Titles are then added to the beginning and end of the episode. If stereo sync sound is available, it is used. Otherwise, the Avid editor chooses which of the sync sound tracks to use.

Once the episode is cut together, an AAF export is created from Media Composer and the audio is exported with long handles and placed in the audio editor's workspace on the Avid ISIS 7000 server. The audio editor has a Pro Tools template already set up, which includes sound effects libraries, routing, and track layout. The exported AAF file is then imported into the template session, ready for the audio post production process to begin.

Next, the audio editor listens through the episode to check the audio. After creating a checkerboard of the dialogue audio clips across several tracks, clips are pulled in and taken out to find the best dialogue possible. Most of the production dialogue is usable from the sync sound, and for any that is not, the audio editor fills out an ADR request form to get the talent in to redo any necessary lines of dialogue.

While going through the episode, the audio editor adds any necessary sound effects, such as room atmospheres, off-mic talking, phones ringing, and so on, which are reused from previous episodes. Sometimes there is the need to manually edit the Foley footsteps, which the audio editor first records into Pro Tools and then fits to the necessary scenes.

While playing through the episode, the audio editor is constantly automating and balancing the levels using Latch automation mode. At this point, plug-ins will be added to the mix as needed, including EQ, Dynamics, and Reverb, to best match the actors to the scene. Once play-through is finished, the audio editor plays the session again and adjusts any levels where necessary.

The actor arrives to record ADR and, if necessary, the audio editor manually lip syncs the actor's ADR recordings to the scene using Elastic Audio.

On the Web

The Synchro Arts AudioSuite plug-in, VocALign Project or VocALign Pro (purchased separately), can be used to auto-sync ADR to the original production dialogue. For more information, go to synchroarts.com.

A picture re-cut often occurs during this process, so the audio editor receives a new AAF export from the Avid picture editor, which requires re-editing the session to match the new picture cut.

Once completed, the session is bounced to a stereo BWF/WAV file in Pro Tools, and then made available to the Avid picture editor's workspace on the Avid ISIS 7000 server. The picture editor then inserts the file into the final sequence, making the production ready to air.

Film

Making a film and assembling all of the parts comes with many issues and problems that need to be worked around, as generally one film is not the same as the next when it comes to the production. This example workflow discusses the Pro Tools session track layout of a film project, including the experience of one of the dialogue editors. The dialogue editor is using a Pro Tools|HDX system, Avid Artist Series controllers (Artist Control and an Artist Mix), and a BlackMagic Design DeckLink Extreme PCIe video card for QuickTime video playback to an external monitor.

Pre-production meetings are important as they generally define how the film is going to be shot. At these meetings it is determined what equipment will be used to edit the film, as well as the frame rates, bit depth, and sample rates for the project. Sometimes (although not always) the sound supervisor meets with the picture editor to discuss their workflow at these pre-production meetings. When this does not occur, problems can ensue.

The film project referenced for this sample workflow is shot on film media for delivery to the cinema, which in turn means that it was shot at 24FPS and delivered at 24FPS. A decision has been made to deliver watermarked QuickTime video cuts to the audio editors using a secure Internet-based file transfer technology from Aspera called DigiDelivery.

 For more information about DigiDelivery, go to www.asperasoft.com.

On the Web

The studio producing the film feels this is a secure way to deliver their picture, thereby not letting it get copied and released on the Internet due to stray parcels "going missing" from the couriers. This also means that the movie can be edited and mixed at 24FPS film speed throughout the whole process. The only issue to resolve is that the dailies will be telecined and sent to the Avid Editor on Sony HDCAM-SR 23.976FPS videotapes. When the telecine is complete, the Avid Editor digitizes the 23.976FPS HDCAM-SR videotapes into a 24p Media Composer project that changes the speed of the audio and video back to film speed (using a reverse telecine-like process), thereby allowing editing at 24FPS film speed. This also means that the Pro Tools sessions can be worked on at 24FPS running at true film speed (with no audio pulls necessary).

When the dailies are digitized into an Avid Media Composer picture editing system, the assistant editor logs and digitizes all the multi-track location sound as well as the stereo guide. This is very useful to the audio editors later in the process. The location sound is recorded on a *Sound Devices 788T* field recorder, and then copied via FireWire into the Avid picture editing system. The picture editor starts to create the film, choosing the scenes he wants from the best takes of the dailies that are currently available. Once a reel is compiled, a watermarked QuickTime video is created and sent to the sound supervisor to begin work on the track organization and layout. The sound supervisor is working with a team of editors specializing in various disciplines, such as a dialogue, ADR, Foley, and background and specific sound effects. Reels are distributed to the sound editors as they are received from the picture editor.

Since the sound editors are using Pro Tools with a BlackMagic DeckLink Extreme video display card, they import the QuickTime video directly into a Pro Tools session file template containing all the track names, track layout, and settings. After setting the proper QuickTime Video Sync Offset in Pro Tools, the sound editors watch the audio and video on an external video monitor with frame accuracy.

The dialogue editor's session template has a simple layout containing the following audio tracks:

- **Dialogue 1–8**: The dialogue is arranged in a checkerboard layout across these eight tracks. For simplicity and time purposes, the dialogue is not edited and split into separate tracks by character.

- **Dialogue FX 1–8**: These tracks contain any production sound effects such as background sound effects, effects recorded on location, and footsteps.

- **Filler Tracks**: As the title suggests, these are tracks used for filling in holes, such as when ADR is added and room tone is required, or a background is needed.

- **Strip Tracks**: These are tracks from the original production sound, and act as comparison tracks (for example, when ADR is added) to compare this to the original production sound.

- **ADR Tracks**: The production sound for this film is high quality, so they would like to use as much as possible, but there are instances in the film where ADR is necessary. An ADR request is filled out and the necessary talent is brought in.

On this production, all of the multi-track location sound is sent to the sound supervisor as an AAF from the assistant editor, who previously imported it from the field recorder into the Avid Media Composer system. This makes it possible for the editors to re-conform their sessions when any re-cuts occur.

With the tracks laid out, then the next step is to go through the first reel and check for anomalies in the audio, such as hums and lip smacks in the dialogue. It is also necessary to keep up to date with the re-cuts of the reels as they come in from the picture editor. Audio editors have many tasks to complete in order to match the existing audio to the new picture cuts, including ascertaining what changes have been made, finding the appropriate audio to match the changes, and then manually re-conforming the session to precisely match the changes.

As new picture cuts are delivered and the changes are made to the audio, the editor uses a combination of clip-based gain adjustments and snapshot automation to balance the volume levels, but no dynamic automation is used. Although volume automation is added, no panning automation added, since this is left to the mixing engineer. Any plug-ins that are used to eliminate hum or noise in the dialogue and production sound are printed to disk.

Auto-Conforming Software

Since the process of manually conforming audio to new picture changes is usually very time consuming, you may wish to consider a third-party software auto-conforming solution. Auto-conforming software can help a sound editor conform audio much more quickly and most times with even better accuracy. Conforming software takes a cut list, EDL, AAF, or change list from the picture editing software, compares the Pro Tools session with it, and then automatically syncs the session's audio to the changes. Although most of the conforming is done automatically by the software, the sound editor would still need to verify and adjust the audio edits to match the new picture change, even after using an auto-conforming solution. Depending on your workflow and the conforming solution you choose, results will vary.

Once the session is ready for the mix engineer, the editor uses the Save Copy In command to put the session and all related media files on a transfer hard drive and take it to the mixing theatre (dub stage).

While in the mixing theatre, the sound supervisor makes any changes that the picture editor and mix engineer request, and if any new cuts arrive, makes those necessary changes as well.

As the mix is going on, the studio executives want to check how the film is progressing, and order pre-dub versions of the film that they can watch and comment on. This means rough mixes of the audio must be quickly assembled. It is the responsibility of the sound supervisor to get a stereo bounced file of the current state of the audio over to the picture editor, who will then add the audio to the video and create a review version for the executives.

With the technology currently available, changes are made right up to the last moment, so it is crucial to keep up with all of the picture cuts that occur. It is left to the mix engineers to then deliver the final DM&E (dialogue, music, and effects) stem mixes on whichever format the studio requires.

DM&E Stems

Dialogue, music, and effects stems are individual audio sub-mixes of only dialogue, music, and sound effects that are used for international distribution of film and television projects. Separating the original project's audio tracks into individual dialogue, music, and sound effects sub-mixes makes it easier to replace the original recorded dialogue with the local indigenous language of the intended market, and then combine and re-mix the original music and sound effects elements with the newly recorded dialogue.

Advertising

Advertising post production is a fast paced and varied business, this workflow is a real-life example of how a job gets completed. The system used includes a Pro Tools|HDX system running an Avid Mojo SDI, an Avid PRE, a SYNC HD, and an ICON D-Control ES (32-Fader) worksurface.

Advertising executives come into the session with a (Sony) HDCAM-SR video-tape of the project that contains multiple versions of various lengths of the project, with some temp sound effects and music. The source tape gets digitized into Media Composer by the transfers department, who then export the picture (with any temp sound) to the audio engineer working on the project. The first version of the advertisement will be imported as an AAF file into a Pro Tools session, using the project's original source timecode. Any temp audio will be imported along with the AAF video export into the Pro Tools timeline. The work now begins.

First, a voiceover is recorded with multiple versions, different phrases, and tonal qualities until the executives have what they require. The audio engineer records the voiceovers using the track playlist function of Pro Tools for speed. The voiceovers are compiled and mixed with any music that has come from the original Avid export. If no music is present, suitable music is found that fits the advertising content. The selected music is then imported and spotted into the session. Once the advertising executives are happy with the way the music and voiceover sounds, the sound design is the next task.

The sound textures, layers, and overall sound design are created based on the needs of the advertisement. This is an especially creative and varied process, which can also combine Foley recording, such as footsteps (where required).

Once the first version of the advertisement is complete, the engineer moves down the Pro Tools timeline to the next version. The engineer will then add whatever is necessary to each different length advertisement version, usually by copying, pasting, and editing along the timeline from the first version.

Once all versions are completed and mixed, the audio is then laid back to a source videotape. When laying back multiple versions to linear tape, the audio engineer will use the Redefine Current Time Code Position dialog box in Pro Tools to place the ads at the correct timecode positions on the final master tapes.

 Outputting audio to linear videotape and the Redefine Current Time Code Position dialog box will be covered in Lesson 10, "Advanced Layback."

Sound Library Searching and Management

When doing creative sound design for professional post production projects, you will often need to search and retrieve audio from very large sound libraries. In this section of the lesson, you will learn about some of the options that are available for searching and importing audio into your Pro Tools sessions.

Pro Tools Workspace Browser Recap

As described in the Pro Tools 201 and Pro Tools 210 books, the Workspace Browser can be used to search, catalog, and import audio into your Pro Tools sessions, allowing complex searches (such as AND, OR, and wildcard searches) using multiple search criteria across multiple volumes. See Figure 6.1.

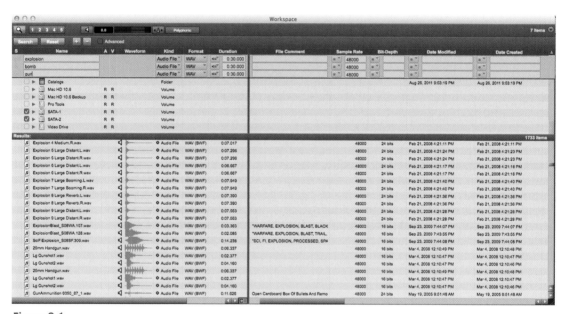

Figure 6.1
Pro Tools Workspace browser search.

Although the built-n DigiBase searching and importing features within Pro Tools are powerful and sufficient for most users, some additional features are offered by third-party sound library management software companies that are currently not available within the DigiBase browsers. In the following sections of this lesson, you will learn about two of these third-party software solutions: Soundminer Inc.'s Soundminer and Creative Network Design's Netmix Pro.

Soundminer

Soundminer Inc. offers a variety of products aimed at audio asset management for multiple large music and sound effect libraries—or simply for your own files. The original product, Soundminer, was commercially released in 2002 to replace "modified off-the-shelf database programs originally intended for traditional office work," or "mouse-click intensive stock network browsers that simply could not navigate through hundreds of thousands of search returns with any kind of speed."

Soundminer's original product in 2002 was the first product to incorporate a graphical waveform editor and player, a search engine, and metadata editing in one standalone application. In addition, Soundminer quickly became known for fast searches of vast databases. Figure 6.2 shows Soundminer V4Pro.

Figure 6.2
Soundminer V4Pro. (Image provided courtesy of Soundminer, Inc.)

Soundminer enjoys broad industry support by both music and effect library titles (Hollywood Edge, Sound Ideas, Opus 1 Music, and so on) and DAWs such as Pro Tools. A large collection of sound effects libraries and music libraries now ship pre-indexed and databased with Soundminer metatags, making searching even faster. Some of these libraries even include some version of the Soundminer software.

On the Web

For more information about Soundminer software, go to www.soundminer.com.

NetMix Pro

Like Soundminer, NetMix Pro is a sophisticated cross-platform software program for advanced music and sound effects library management. With NetMix Pro, users can organize, search, audition, and transfer music cues, sound effects, ADR takes, and field recordings directly into Pro Tools, Avid Media Composer, and other professional production tools.

NetMix Pro's features include:

- Google-style Boolean full-text searching

- Synonym search (search for "car" and NetMix Pro will find "automobile" as well)

- Clip editor with pitch control

- Sophisticated bin structure for organizing sounds by projects

- Multi-user database support

- QuickTime SyncAudition

- ReWire support

- Multi-track sequence clip editor (to preview soundbeds before spotting into Pro Tools)

NetMix Pro can be extended with MetaPlug (an AudioSuite plug-in) that allows users to archive sound effects, ADR, and Foley takes with embedded metadata directly from Pro Tools back to the NetMix Pro database with the click of a button. See Figure 6.3.

On the Web

For more information about NetMix Pro software, go to www.netmixpro.com.

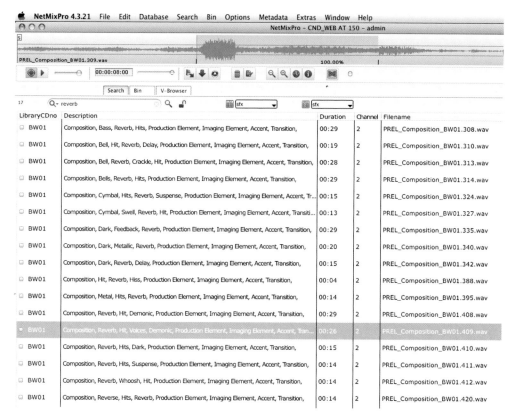

Figure 6.3
NetMix Pro Sound library management software. (Image provided courtesy of Creative Network Design, Inc.)

Sound Effects Creation and Design Using Plug-ins

Due to the popularity of Pro Tools, a large number of Pro Tools-compatible plug-ins are available from Avid as well as third-party developers. Although many of these can be used for creating sound effects for post production projects, there are a number of basic core plug-ins that can be used to create a wide diversity of sound effects for film and television. It is important to understand that creative sound design many times involves processing with more than one plug-in, such as pitch shift, reverb, EQ, and time compression–expansion, which allows very accurate control and details in the final sound. Although some attempt is made to provide usage examples in the following section, it is not possible to list all of the possible uses for a particular plug-in, since the possibilities are endless.

Caution: Editors who are involved in sound design should take great care to avoid printing or writing EQ, reverb, compression, limiting, panning, or any other similar plug-in effects into the audio files, because these decisions are better left to the re-recording (or dubbing) mixer on the final dub stage.

Reverse Plug-in

The Reverse plug-in is a very simple yet useful plug-in, allowing you to play audio backwards. Using the Reverse plug-in, shown in Figure 6.4, you can take a very simple, easily identifiable sound effect, and make it sound completely different, many times unrecognizable from the original. In addition, reversing could be used when events or actions with sound are shown in reverse, such as a bullet being shot or glass breaking, and then re-forming. There are many examples of creative sound design that start with the simple reversing of the original audio.

Figure 6.4
Reverse plug-in.

Tip: When using the AudioSuite plug-in versions of D-Verb and Mod Delay III, you have the option to reverse the selected audio, allowing you to create reverse reverb and delay effects.

Pitch Shift

Since both the X-Form and Time Shift plug-ins allow you to shift the pitch of your audio up or down 24 semitones (two octaves in musical terminology) with or without changing the speed, they are very useful for taking standard sound effects from sound effects libraries, and changing them to sound completely different. For example, dialogue could be pitch-shifted up or down to sound like alien, cartoon, supernatural, demonic, or psychotic-styled character voices. In another example, a basketball sound effect could be pitch-shifted down to sound like a bomb or other low-frequency sound effect. In a simpler example, sound effects like footsteps, finger taps, and gunshots could be pitched up/down in small increments to make them appear as different, rather than the same sound effect used multiple times in succession. Again there are many applications and interesting effects that can be created with both the X-Form and Time Shift plug-ins, shown in Figure 6.5.

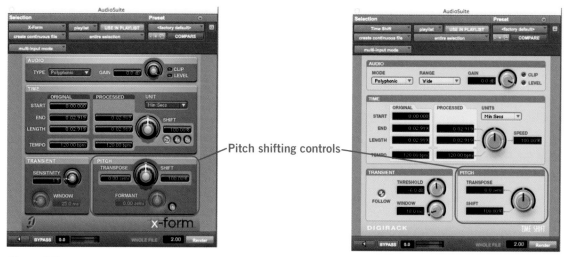

Figure 6.5
X-Form (left) and Time Shift (right) pitch shifting plug-ins.

Tip: Since the X-Form plug-in uses a high-quality algorithm for pitch shifting and
time compression-expansion that yields superior sound quality, under most
circumstances, you should use the X-Form plug-in over the Time Shift plug-in,
unless you wish to use the additional generated artifacts created by the Time
Shift plug-in as part of the creative effect. If the optional X-Form plug-in is not
available on your system, you can use the Time Shift plug-in instead.

Time Compression-Expansion

Time compression-expansion (TCE) processes audio in the time domain, using
either the X-Form or Time Shift plug-in. TCE can be used to change the speed of
the audio with or without changing the original pitch. As discussed in the previous
section, you can independently process audio in the frequency domain, shifting
the pitch of the audio up or down, with or without changing the speed. The X-Form
and Time Shift plug-ins have many post production and sound design uses, as they
can easily change the speed of dialogue, ADR, music, or sound effects without
changing the original pitch. For example, an ADR line could be slowed down to
match the picture, a clock ticking sound effect could be sped up or slowed down
to perhaps match a character's distorted, non-linear perception of time, the pitch
and speed of a motor could be adjusted, or the pace of footsteps could be slowed
or quickened to match the desired walking or running pace needed.

Tip: In Pro Tools, time compression-expansion and pitch shifting are normally completely independent audio processes, although when selecting the Varispeed processing option, time and pitch are linked using a proportional relationship, whereby increasing speed raises pitch, and decreasing speed lowers pitch. Using Varispeed, a doubling of the speed (or halving of the overall length of audio) causes a +1 octave pitch shift, and a halving of the speed (doubling the overall length of audio) causes a –1 octave pitch shift.

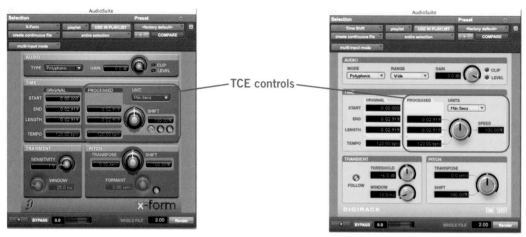

Figure 6.6
X-Form (left) and Time Shift (right) time expansion-compression plug-ins.

Delay

The Mod Delay III plug-in shown in Figure 6.7 repeats the input audio at a specified time interval. Delay effects also allow feedback, which feeds the output of the delay back into the input. You can also add a Low Frequency Oscillator (LFO) effect, which continuously oscillates the pitch of the audio at a rate of up to 20Hz, using the Depth and Rate controls. LFO effects are typically used on musical instruments (such as guitars and electric pianos), but they can also be used to create unique sounds for dialogue and sound effects, especially when using extreme settings. Digital delays are often used for flashback, dream, and hallucination sequences in film and television, but can also be used to add a thicker and fuller sound to background and specific effects, as well as to create repeating sound effects appropriate for the acoustical environment they are meant to represent.

Note: The Mod Delay III plug-in is available as a Native and AudioSuite plug-in on all Pro Tools systems, and additionally runs as a DSP plug-in on Pro Tools|HDX hardware.

Figure 6.7
Mod Delay III plug-in.

Eleven

Although the Eleven plug-in shown in Figure 6.8 was designed for the more obvious use of simulating various vintage and modern guitar amplifier/cabinet effects for music, it can also be used in post production to create fuzz or distorted effects for audio communications like two-way radios, FM or AM radio, low fidelity speakers, effects for lights flickering, air conditioning, or any other audio needing general distortion or buzz.

Figure 6.8
Avid Eleven plug-in.

D-Fi

D-Fi consists of four separate plug-ins for DSP, Native, and AudioSuite processing. The D-Fi plug-ins form a unique sound-design toolkit for processing and deconstructing audio in several retro and synthesis-oriented ways.

Tip: For more information concerning the parameters and uses of the D-Fi plug-in bundle (and any other Avid plug-ins), consult the *Audio Plug-Ins Guide*.

Lo-Fi

The Lo-Fi plug-in, shown in Figure 6.9, provides retro and down-processing effects, including:

- Bit-rate reduction

- Sample rate reduction

- Soft clipping distortion and saturation

- Anti-aliasing filter

- Variable amplitude noise generator

Figure 6.9
Lo-Fi plug-in.

Lo-Fi can be used for lowering the audio quality to simulate limitations of the sound-producing device depicted, such as the public address speaker at a train station, an old sound recording from a previous era, a problematic communications link, a rough-running engine sound, or any other situation that requires lower audio fidelity.

Sci-Fi

The Sci-Fi plug-in, shown in Figure 6.10, is ideal for blending and synthesizing additional harmonic content with your existing audio.

The Sci-Fi plug-in provides four types of analog synthesizer-type effects:

- **Ring modulation**: This effect modulates the signal amplitude with a carrier frequency, producing additional harmonic content that are the sum and difference of the two signals. Although the carrier frequency is supplied by the Sci-Fi plug-in itself, the modulation frequency is determined by the Effect Frequency control.

Figure 6.10
Sci-Fi plug-in.

■ **Freak Mod (frequency modulation)**: This effect is a frequency modulation processor that modulates the signal frequency with a carrier frequency, producing harmonic sidebands that are the sum and difference of the input signal frequency and whole number multiples of the carrier frequency. Frequency modulation produces many more sideband frequencies than ring modulation and an even wilder metallic characteristic. The Effect Frequency control determines the modulation frequency of the Freak Mod effect.

■ **Resonator+** and **Resonator–**: These two similar effects add a resonant frequency tone to the input audio signal. This frequency is determined by the Effect Frequency control. The difference between the Resonator+ and the Resonator– synthesis modules is that Resonator– reverses the phase (polarity) of the effect, producing more of a hollow sound than Resonator+.

The Sci-Fi plug-in can be used for adding brighter, harmonic content to the audio it processes, creating audio effects for science-fiction type projects, or other applications you discover.

Recti-Fi

The Recti-Fi plug-in, shown in Figure 6.11, provides additive harmonic processing effects through waveform rectification.

Figure 6.11
Recti-Fi plug-in.

The Recti-Fi plug-in includes the following:

- Sub-harmonic synthesizer

- Full wave rectifier

- Pre-filter for adjusting effect frequency

- Post-filter for smoothing generated waveforms

The Recti-Fi plug-in can be used for multiplying the harmonic content of the audio, and then adding sub-harmonic or super-harmonic content to the audio it processes. It works especially well for beefing up gunshots, body blows, and explosions without adding amplitude.

Vari-Fi

The Vari-Fi plug-in, shown in Figure 6.12, provides a pitch-change effect similar to a tape deck or record turntable speeding up from or slowing down to a complete stop.

Figure 6.12
Vari-Fi plug-in.

Features of Vari-Fi include the following:

- Speed up from a complete stop to normal speed

- Slow down to a complete stop from normal speed

Note: There is no real-time Native or DSP version of the Vari-Fi plug-in. Instead, the Vari-Fi plug-in is only available as an AudioSuite plug-in.

Besides using Vari-Fi for the obvious (simulating the speeding up or slowing down of a turntable or other audio device), you can also use it for speeding up or slowing down engine sounds (airplanes, cars, trucks, spaceships), factory machinery, or electronic equipment; simulating weather effects, explosions, space and alien weapons; and creating any other effects or other applications you can think of.

Sound Effects Creation and Design Using Elastic Audio

As discussed in the Pro Tools 110 and 210P books, in addition to creating rendered time-compression expansion effects using plug-ins, Pro Tools systems support a track-based real-time time compression and expansion (TCE) and pitch-shifting feature known as Elastic Audio. Pro Tools Elastic Audio uses high-quality transient detection algorithms, beat and tempo analysis (for music applications), and real-time TCE/Pitch Shift processing algorithms, borrowed from the X-Form plug-in technology (previously discussed). Elastic Audio provides a high degree of control over transient detection and TCE processing on an event-by-event basis, which has many uses for music and sound design for picture.

With Elastic Audio, Pro Tools analyzes entire audio files for transient "events." For example, an event can be a whole or partial music cue, a word, phrase, or sentence of dialogue, a Foley recording (such as footsteps), or any length specific or background sound effect. These detected events can then serve as control points for "warping" the audio. Pro Tools can warp (TCE) audio events automatically, such as automatically conforming musical cues to the session tempo, or you can warp audio manually using the standard editing tools in the track's Warp view.

In the Avid Learning Series

For a description of warping audio using a track's Warp view, consult the Pro Tools 110 course book or the *Pro Tools Reference Guide*.

Elastic Audio is useful in many different post production workflows, including editing music to picture, conforming audio, editing ADR, sound design, and creating special effects.

Enabling Elastic Audio Tracks

Any audio track in your Pro Tools session can be Elastic Audio–enabled. Elastic Audio tracks can be sample- or tick-based. Sample-based Elastic Audio–enabled tracks let you apply real-time or rendered Elastic Audio processing by editing in Warp view, applying Quantize, and using the TCE Trim tool. However, only tick-based Elastic Audio tracks (useful for music) will automatically apply Elastic Audio processing based on tempo changes.

When using previous generations Pro Tools|HD hardware, Elastic Audio is disallowed on *explicitly voiced tracks*. It is therefore necessary to use dynamic voice allocation (dyn) for tracks on which you want to use Elastic Audio.

To enable Elastic Audio on a track:

1. Create a new audio track or choose an existing audio track.

2. Click the track's Elastic Audio Plug-In Selector (shown in Figure 6.13), and select the Elastic Audio plug-in appropriate to your track material and the results you want from the pop-up menu:

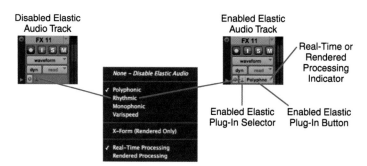

Figure 6.13
Elastic Audio track with plug-in pop-up menu.

- **Polyphonic**: The Polyphonic plug-in is a general, all-purpose algorithm that is effective with a wide range of material. For audio containing complex harmonic and frequency content and multi-instrument mixes, use the Polyphonic plug-in.

- **Rhythmic**: The Rhythmic plug-in is best suited to material with clear attack transients, such as an alarm or clock ticking sound effect or music with a strong rhythm or beat.

- **Monophonic**: The Monophonic plug-in is best suited to monophonic material where you want to keep the formant relationships intact, such as with dialogue or ADR lines. The Monophonic plug-in is also well suited to monophonic instrumental lines, such as a solo piano, flute, or violin passages.

- **Varispeed**: Use the Varispeed plug-in to link time and pitch changes for tape-like Varispeed change effects.

- **X-Form (Rendered Only)**: The X-Form plug-in provides the highest quality time compression and expansion algorithms for music, dialogue, sound design, and sound effect loop applications. However, the X-Form Elastic Audio plug-in is for Rendered Elastic Audio processing only and cannot process in real-time.

Any audio clips on the track will temporarily go offline while they are analyzed and come back online when the analysis is finished. The waveforms for audio clips that are offline for Elastic Audio analysis appear grayed out.

When recording to a real-time Elastic Audio–enabled track, once recording is stopped, the newly recorded audio will temporarily go offline while it is analyzed and will come back online as soon as the analysis is finished.

3. From the track's Elastic Audio Plug-In Selector menu, select either Real-Time Processing or Rendered Processing.

Tip: Real-Time Elastic Audio processing is immediate, but it is more demanding of system resources. Rendered Elastic Audio processing is non-real-time, and is less demanding of system resources. If you are working on a system with limited resources, use Rendered Elastic Audio processing.

Elastic Audio Clip-Based Pitch Transposition (Polyphonic, Rhythmic, and X-Form Only)

In addition to using Pro Tools Elastic Audio time compression-expansion capabilities for creative sound design, you can also change the pitch of whole audio clips in semitones and cents in the range of plus/minus two octaves.

Pitch transposition can be applied to Elastic Audio clips using the Elastic Properties window or the Transpose window.

Note: Elastic Audio pitch transposition is not supported when using the Monophonic or Varispeed algorithms.

To transpose the pitch of an audio clip in the Elastic Properties window:

1. Make sure the clip, or clips, you want to transpose are on Elastic Audio–enabled tracks (using the Polyphonic, Rhythmic, or X-Form algorithm).

2. With the Grabber or Selector tool, select the audio clip you want to transpose. Only clips that are completely selected will be affected.

3. To open the Elastic Properties window, do one of the following:

   - Choose CLIP > ELASTIC PROPERTIES.

   - Right-click the selected clip and choose ELASTIC PROPERTIES.

   - Press OPTION+NUMERIC KEYPAD 5 (Mac) or ALT+NUMERIC KEYPAD 5 (Windows) to open the Elastic Properties window.

4. Adjust the Pitch Shift settings by the desired amount in semitones and cents. See Figure 6.14.

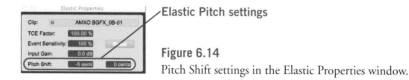

Elastic Pitch settings

Figure 6.14
Pitch Shift settings in the Elastic Properties window.

Tip: You can also transpose the pitch of an audio clip on an Elastic Audio–enabled track within the Transpose window by choosing Event > Event Operations > Transpose, or pressing Option+T (Mac) or Alt+T (Windows).

Removing Clip Pitch Shifting

If you have applied any pitch shifting to a clip, you can remove pitch shifting and revert the clip to its original pitch. This can be useful when you are not satisfied with the results and want to revert to the pre-pitch shifted clip.

To remove clip pitch shifting:

1. Select the clip for which you want to remove the pitch shifting.

2. Do one of the following:

   - Choose CLIP > REMOVE PITCH SHIFT.

   - With any editing tool, right-click the clip and then select REMOVE PITCH SHIFT.

   - With any editing tool, right-click the clip, choose ELASTIC PROPERTIES, then set the Pitch Shift semitones and cents settings to O (zero).

   - Choose EVENT > EVENT OPERATIONS > TRANSPOSE, OPTION+T (Mac) or ALT+T (Windows), then set the Pitch Shift semitones and cents settings to O (zero).

Tip: Remove Pitch Shift can only be applied to clips and cannot be applied to Clip Groups. To remove pitch shifting from Clip Groups, you must first Ungroup the clips, then apply Remove Pitch Shift, and then finally Regroup those clips.

Disabling Elastic Audio Tracks

There may be times when you want to disable Elastic Audio processing to free up system resources, revert to the original unprocessed audio, or commit the Elastic Audio processing to new (rendered) files.

To disable Elastic Audio on a track:

1. From the track's Elastic Audio Plug-In Selector, select None–Disable Elastic Audio.

2. If the track had any Elastic Audio–based processing, you will be prompted to Cancel, Revert, or Commit, as shown in Figure 6.15.

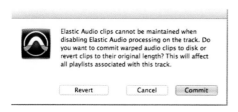

Figure 6.15
Commit Elastic Audio dialog box.

- **Cancel**: Leaves Elastic Audio enabled on the track.

- **Revert**: Removes any Elastic Audio processing, reverts clips on the track to their original duration, and disables Elastic Audio on the track.

- **Commit**: Renders and commits any Elastic Audio processing on the track, writes new files into the Audio Files folder (depending on Disk Allocation), and disables Elastic Audio on the track.

Clips that are committed, either by disabling Elastic Audio on a track or by moving a clip to a track without Elastic Audio enabled, are written to disk as new audio files, using the track's Disk Allocation setting. These new audio files include the audio in the clip, plus any fades, and also an additional five seconds of audio before and after the clip, if available.

Alternate Playlists

Disabling Elastic Audio on a track affects all playlists on the track. All playlists on the track are either committed or reverted, depending on which option you choose.

Tip: When new tracks are created, Elastic Audio can be automatically enabled on the new tracks if the Enable Elastic Audio On New Tracks option is enabled in the Processing tab of Preferences.

Pro Tools Advanced Editing Shortcuts

When editing in Pro Tools, your goal is to always work as quickly and efficiently as possible. To do this, you will use the mouse sparingly and always use the shortest number of keystrokes possible. Continually moving your hand between the keyboard and mouse slows your working speed, so using keyboard shortcuts whenever possible will allow you to keep your hand on the keyboard for longer periods of time, thereby increasing your speed and overall work output. Although keyboard shortcuts were discussed in depth in Lesson 4, "Tactile Control of Pro Tools," the editing options discussed in this section are some of the preferred keystrokes of Pro Tools editors, since they are both fast and efficient.

For fine-tuning an audio clip's placement on a track, several nudging shortcut options are available.

Changing Nudge Increments

Other Pro Tools books in the Avid Learning Series describe how to nudge a single selected clip, multiple selected clips, or a selection using the numeric keypad Plus (+) or Minus (–) keys. You can also change nudge increments using a simple keyboard shortcut.

Caution: Unless stated otherwise, the nudge shortcuts listed in this section require you to use the numeric keypad Plus (+) or Minus (–) keys, and do not support the equivalent alphanumeric Keyboard Focus shortcuts.

To change or toggle through the available nudge increments shown in Figure 6.16, simply press Option+Command (Mac) or Ctrl+Alt (Windows) followed by numeric keypad Plus (+) or Minus (–) keys.

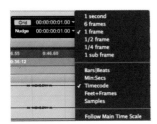

Figure 6.16
Nudge menu options increased/decreased with a keyboard shortcut.

Nudging by Next Nudge Value

In addition to nudging clips by the current Nudge value, you can also nudge clips by the next-larger value in the Nudge pop-up. For example, if the Nudge value is set to 1 frame and you want to nudge by a larger value, you can nudge by the next-larger Nudge value of 5 frames.

To nudge later or earlier by the next-larger Nudge value:

1. Enable COMMANDS KEYBOARD FOCUS.

2. With the Selector or Grabber tool, select the clips that you want to nudge.

3. Press SLASH (/) on the alphanumeric keyboard to nudge the selected material later by the next Nudge value. Press **M** to nudge the selection earlier.

Shortcut: You can also nudge by the next Nudge value without enabling Commands Keyboard Focus. While holding the Control key (Mac) or the Start key (Windows), press the alphanumeric Slash (/) or M key.

Nudging a Clip's Contents

Often a clip's start point will reside at the correct timecode or film frame location, but the material within the clip will start too late or early. You can nudge a clip's audio waveform within the clip's start and end boundaries without changing the clip's start and end points.

This "sliding" of clip contents is possible only if there is additional media (handles) residing outside the clip's start and end points—from the clip having been trimmed or edited from a larger clip.

To nudge the contents of a clip without changing the clip's start and end points:

1. Configure the NUDGE value as desired.

2. With the Grabber tool, select the clip whose contents you want to nudge.

3. While holding the CONTROL key (Mac) or START key (Windows), press PLUS (+) or MINUS (–) on the numeric keypad to move the material by the current Nudge value. Figure 6.17 shows the before and after.

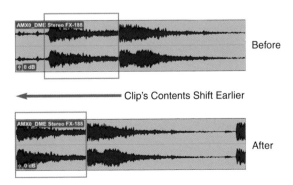

Figure 6.17
Nudging an audio clip's contents.

Trimming with Nudge

You can also trim the start and end points of a clip by nudging them.

To trim a clip's start or end point by the current Nudge value:

1. Configure the NUDGE value as desired.

2. Select the clip you want to trim.

3. Choose one of the following:

   - **To trim the clip's start point by the current Nudge value**: While holding OPTION (Mac) or ALT (Windows), press PLUS **(+)** or MINUS **(−)** on the numeric keypad.

   - **To trim the clip's end point by the current Nudge value**: While holding COMMAND (Mac) or CTRL (Windows), press PLUS **(+)** or MINUS **(−)** on the numeric keypad.

Nudging and Audio Selection

You can also nudge the start and end points of an edit selection.

To nudge the start or end point of an edit selection by the current Nudge value:

1. Configure the NUDGE value as desired.

2. Make an edit selection.

3. Choose one of the following:

   - **To nudge the selection start by the current Nudge value**: While holding OPTION+SHIFT (Mac) or ALT+SHIFT (Windows), press PLUS **(+)** or MINUS **(−)** on the numeric keypad.

   - **To nudge the selection end by the current Nudge value**: While holding COMMAND+SHIFT (Mac) or CTRL+SHIFT (Windows), press PLUS **(+)** or MINUS **(−)** on the numeric keypad.

Grouped Playlist Synchronization

In addition to the shortcuts mentioned in the previous sections, it is also useful to apply track grouping when creating and cueing playlists of layered audio spanning multiple tracks.

Multitrack Editing Using Playlists

As discussed in the Pro Tools 210P book, Pro Tools playlist functionality provides an ideal way to store and manage multiple record takes or edit versions within a single track. Playlists on tracks that are grouped are synchronized, so creating and cueing playlists on any single track will perform the same function across all tracks in the group. This is particularly useful when creating and editing alternate versions of specific or background sound effects, music, or group ADR that are layered across multiple grouped tracks.

To create multitrack edits using synchronized playlists:

1. Create a group of all the tracks you wish to synchronize for multi playlist editing.

2. In any track in the group, choose one of the following:

   - To create a new playlist, choose **NEW** from the **PLAYLIST SELECTOR**.

   - To create a duplicate playlist, choose **DUPLICATE** from the **PLAYLIST SELECTOR**.

   The first time you create a new or duplicate playlist on a grouped track, new playlists will be created across all tracks in the group, and each new playlist will have the track's name with the suffix ".01" for take 1.

3. Place and edit the clips on the new track playlists as desired.

4. For additional playlists, choose **NEW** or **DUPLICATE** from the **PLAYLIST SELECTOR**. New playlists will be created across all tracks in the group.

5. Place and edit the clips on the new .02 playlists as desired.

6. To go back and audition any playlist, switch any track to the desired playlist number, and all other track playlists in the group will follow.

Shortcut: You can also create a new playlist on the first selected track by pressing Control+Backslash (\) (Mac) or Start+Backslash (\) (Windows). You can also create a duplicate playlist on the first selected track by pressing Control+Command+Backslash (\) (Mac) or Ctrl+Start+Backslash (\) (Windows).

Adding Tracks During an Editing Session

Pro Tools is capable of handling a situation in which you decide to add additional tracks to your group, even after you've already begun editing and creating synchronized playlists on the existing tracks. All you need to do is add a track to your group and create the next playlist take. Pro Tools will create empty dummy takes on the new tracks so that the playlists stay synchronized across all the tracks in the group.

To add new tracks to the group:

1. Create the new tracks.

2. Choose one of the following:

   ● In the **GROUP LIST** pop-up menu, choose **MODIFY GROUP**.

   ● Right-click on the group in the **GROUP LIST**, and choose **MODIFY GROUP**.

   ● Press **CONTROL+COMMAND+G** (Mac) or **CTRL+START+G** (Windows).

The Modify Groups dialog box will appear:

Figure 6.18
Modify Groups dialog box.

3. In the Modify Groups dialog box, select the group that you wish to modify from the ID menu.

4. In the left-hand list, select the new tracks you wish to add to the group, click the **ADD** button, and then click **OK**.

After modifying and adding the tracks to the group, when you create a new or duplicate playlist on any track group member, the new tracks will get a new playlist with a suffix number matching the rest of the group. Also, empty playlists will be created in the new tracks for all previously created playlists.

Review/Discussion Questions

1. What is audio conforming?

2. Why would someone want to use a third-party sound librarian software program such as Soundminer or NetMix Pro over the Pro Tools DigiBase browsers?

3. List some plug-ins mentioned in the lesson that could be used for post production sound design.

4. What is the Vari-Fi plug-in used for?

5. What is Elastic Audio and Elastic Pitch? Provide some examples of how Elastic Audio and Elastic Pitch can be used for post production.

6. Which Elastic Audio algorithms cannot be used with Elastic Pitch?

7. What is the key command to change nudge increments (Mac or Windows)?

8. What are the Keyboard Focus commands to nudge an audio clip later and earlier by the next higher nudge value?

9. What is the key command to nudge an audio clip's contents (Mac or Windows)?

10. What is the key command to trim a selected audio clip's start and end using the current Nudge value (Mac or Windows)?

11. List the key command to create a new playlist and a duplicate playlist on the first selected track (Mac or Windows).

Lesson 6 Keyboard Shortcuts

Shortcut	Description
Option+numeric keypad 5 (Mac)/ Alt+numeric keypad 5 (Windows)	Open Elastic Properties window
Option+T (Mac)/Alt+T (Windows)	Open Transpose window
Command+Option+numeric keypad Plus (+) or Minus (–) (Mac)/ Ctrl+Alt+numeric keypad Plus (+) or Minus (–) (Windows)	Increase/decrease nudge increments
Control+Slash (/) (Mac)/Start+Slash (/) (Windows)	Nudge later by the next-larger Nudge value
Control+M (Mac)/Start+M (Windows)	Nudge earlier by the next-larger Nudge value
Control+numeric keypad Plus (+) or Minus (–) (Mac)/ Start+numeric keypad Plus (+) or Minus (–) (Windows)	Nudge the contents of a clip
Option+numeric keypad Plus (+) or Minus (–) (Mac)/ Alt+numeric keypad Plus (+) or Minus (–) (Windows)	Trim a clip's start point by the current Nudge value
Command+numeric keypad Plus (+) or Minus (–) (Mac)/ Ctrl+numeric keypad Plus (+) or Minus (–) (Windows)	Nudge the selection start by the current Nudge value
Option+Shift+numeric keypad Plus (+) or Minus (–) (Mac)/ Alt+Shift+numeric keypad Plus (+) or Minus (–)	Trim a clip's end point by the current Nudge value
Command+Shift+numeric keypad Plus (+) or Minus (–) (Mac)/ Ctrl+Shift+numeric keypad Plus (+) or Minus (–) (Windows)	Nudge the selection end by the current Nudge value
Control+Backslash(\) (Mac)/Start+ Backslash(\) (Windows)	Create a new playlist on the first selected track
Control+Command+Backslash(\) (Mac)/ Ctrl+Start+ Backslash(\) (Windows)	Create a duplicate playlist on the first selected track
Control+Command+G (Mac)/Ctrl+Start+G (Windows)	Modify groups

Sound Effects Design Using Plug-ins

In the previous lesson, you learned how some of the Pro Tools plug-ins can be used for creative sound design. In this exercise, you will create your own custom sound effects for a television commercial for Schweppes Tonic Water.

Media Used:

310P Exercise 6.ptxt (Pro Tools session)

Duration:

60 minutes

GOALS

- Import audio and video into a Pro Tools session
- Apply creative sound design and editing techniques to a commercial

Getting Started

In this exercise, you will be creating and designing sound effects for Part 2 of a two-part television commercial for Schweppes Tonic Water. Part 1 is already completely edited and mixed, so you will be concentrating your efforts on Part 2 of the commercial.

1. Open 310P Exercise **06**.PTXT, located in the Exercise Media/310P Class Audio Files v10/310P Exercise 06 folder on the book's DVD (or other location specified by the course instructor).

2. In the Save New Session As dialog box, name the session as desired, saving into an appropriate location on a valid storage volume.

After the session opens, the Edit window will include one video track containing Part 1 of the Schweppes Tonic Water commercial and 10 mono audio tracks (see Figure 6.19).

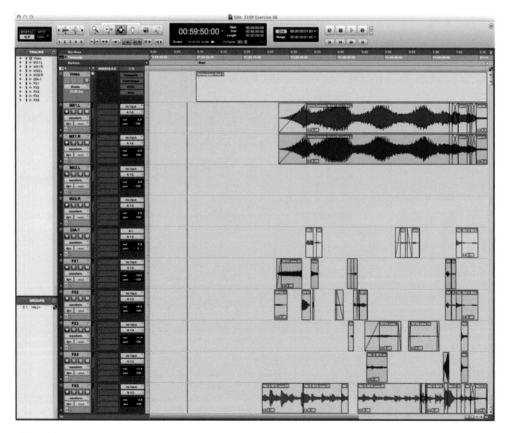

Figure 6.19
Exercise 6 starting Edit window view.

Because the picture editor needed more time to complete the edits for the second half of this commercial, the current session contains only the video and audio for Part 1 (or the first half of the commercial). This means that you will need to import the video and audio for Part 2, while maintaining perfect sync.

Importing Video and Audio

In this section of the exercise, you will import audio and video for the Schweppes commercial.

To import video and audio:

1. Place the edit cursor on the **VIDEO** track, then (using the **TAB** key), tab to the end of the **SCHWEPPES PART 1** video clip, so that the Edit cursor is blinking at timecode number 01:01:01:19.

2. Import into the Clip List the QuickTime video clip, **SCHWEPPES PART 2**, located in the **EXERCISE MEDIA/310P CLASS VIDEO FILES v10/310P EXERCISE 6 VIDEO/SCHWEPPES VIDEO PART 2** folder on the book's DVD (or other location specified by the course instructor).

Shortcut: You can import video using the keyboard shortcut Option+Command+ Shift+I (Mac) or Ctrl+Alt+Shift+I (Windows).

3. When the Video Import Options dialog box appears, configure the settings as shown in Figure 6.20.

Figure 6.20
Video Import Options dialog box.

The **SCHWEPPES PART 2** video from the Schweppes commercial should now be on the Main video track immediately following the **SCHWEPPES PART 1** video clip, as shown in Figure 6.21.

Figure 6.21
Schweppes Video Part 1 and 2 on the Main video track.

Next you will import the audio for Part 2, overlaying the audio onto your existing audio tracks from Part 1.

4. Using the Import Session Data command, open the SCHWEPPES PART 2 SEQ.AAF audio file, located in the EXERCISE MEDIA/310P CLASS AUDIO FILES V10/310P EXERCISE 06/AAF AUDIO IMPORT directory on the book's DVD (or other location specified by the course instructor).

Shortcut: You can Import Session Data using the keyboard shortcut Option+Shift+I (Mac) or Alt+Shift+I (Windows).

5. The source track's playlists must be overlaid onto the destination track's playlists using the Import Session Data command's Main Playlist option, Import–Overlay new on existing playlists. See Figure 6.22.

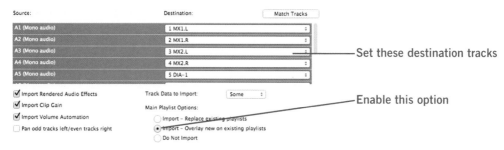

Figure 6.22
Import Session Data track import settings.

6. The source track's playlists should be overlaid on the destination track's playlists, as shown in Table 6.1.

Shortcut: You can cascade tracks in the Import Session Data dialog box by pressing Command+Option (Mac) or Ctrl+Alt (Windows).

After import is complete, you should now have all of the audio and video for Parts 1 and 2 of the Schweppes Tonic Water commercial as shown in Figure 6.23.

Table 6.1   Track Import Mapping Assignments

Source Tracks	Destination Tracks
A 1	MX1.L
A 2	MX1.R
A 3	MX2.L
A 4	MX2.R
A 5	DIA-1
A 6	FX1
A 7	FX2
A 8	FX3
A 9	FX4
A 10	FX5

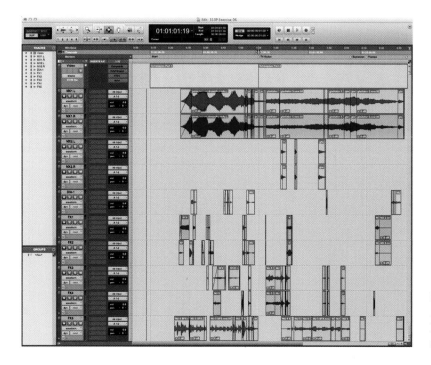

Figure 6.23
Schweppes Commercial
Import of Part 2 Audio
and Video Complete.

7. Take some time to play the commercial and become familiar with the
    audio and video before continuing to the next section of this exercise.

Creative Sound Design

Now that you have imported all of the audio and video that you will need for the scene, you will import and edit sound effects for the scene and use plug-ins for creative sound design. Although most of the sound effects and music are already edited and placed in sync with picture, there are several sound effect layers that you will be adding to Part 2 of the commercial.

You will be designing sound for the following three sound effects:

- TV/Radio flicker

- Explosion

- Flames crackle

To create the sound effects:

1. To locate the exact place where the sound effects should be placed, you can recall the corresponding memory locations that have been provided for you in the session; then watch the scene to decide how you will create the sound effects for the scene.

2. Some sound effect files have been provided that you might want to import. The files are located in the Exercise Media/310P Class Audio Files v10/310P Exercise 6/Sound Effects directory on the book's DVD (or other location specified by the course instructor).

   Although there are no specific requirements regarding which sound effects and plug-ins you use to create the sound effects for Part 2 of the Schweppes commercial, you must adhere to these requirements:

   - Create separate synchronized grouped audio track playlists for each of the three required sound effects, so that you are creating complex sound textures across multiple audio tracks.

   - Use keyboard shortcuts and your Avid worksurface (if available) to access plug-ins and create automated effects.

   - Use some of the plug-ins discussed in the previous lesson.

   - Think "outside the box" and be as creative as possible.

   Although you are free to use any creative sound design you want, consider the following plug-in usage suggestions:

   - **TV/Radio flicker**: Use the Signal Generator plug-in with White or Pink Noise or the Eleven plug-in.

- **Explosion**: Use the Recti-Fi and Reverb plug-ins.
- **Flames crackle**: Use plug-in processing to give the flames a different, more modern sound, so that it is less obvious that you're using a flames crackling sound effect. You could experiment with any of the D-FX and Digital Delay plug-ins, or use Elastic Audio.

Note: Although you can use any types of automation for your creative sound design, do not spend time mixing this project, since this is an editing/sound design exercise (not a mixing exercise).

Tip: If time permits, feel free to add any other creative sound design elements to the session.

3. Save your session when you are finished.

Pro Tools HD/HDX Mixing Concepts

This lesson explores the technology behind the different Pro Tools mixers available for Pro Tools. You will learn how to optimize your use of each system, see how to preserve the highest possible audio quality, and gain an understanding of the differences between systems and the ramifications of moving projects back and forth between systems.

Media Used: 310P Exercise 07.ptxt

Duration: 75 minutes

GOALS

- Understand the relationship between bit depth, dynamic range, and dither

- Understand the differences between the different Pro Tools mixers (Pro Tools HD|Native versus Pro Tools|HD versus Pro Tools|HDX)

- Understand the differences between Pro Tools|HD TDM architecture and Pro Tools|HDX architecture

- Understand the differences between 48-bit fixed-point mixing and 64-bit floating-point mixing

- Understand the factors that affect DSP usage

- Recognize the differences between DSP plug-ins and Native plug-ins

- Recognize appropriate use of Native plug-ins with Pro Tools|HD and Pro Tools|HDX

- Understand jitter

Introduction

Having a solid understanding of digital audio and the theories behind the Pro Tools mixer will give you the foundation upon which to build best practices to optimize your recordings and mixes. This lesson begins by re-acquainting you with some vital digital audio concepts that will help you appreciate the differences between the various Pro Tools platforms. You will also learn about the DSP-accelerated hardware architecture of both Pro Tools|HD and Pro Tools|HDX, as well as how DSP resources are managed. The heart of this discussion will delve into the differences between double-precision 24-bit environments (48-bit fixed-point processing) and dual-precision 32-bit environments (64-bit floating-point processing). This lesson also discusses how to optimize voice usage with Native plug-ins on DSP-accelerated systems. The lesson concludes with a short discussion of jitter and how it affects the sample rate clock.

Bit Depth, Dynamic Range, and Dither

Before comparing the different Pro Tools systems, it will help to review the principles of digital audio. By doing so you will come to understand the practical reasons behind using high resolution audio processing and maximizing headroom, footroom, and dynamic range.

Quantization and Quantization Errors

When an analog audio signal is digitized into Pro Tools, the analog-to-digital convertor (ADC) chip in the audio interface takes a rapid series of measurements of the amplitude (level) and interval (frequency) of the signal. When enough measurements are taken over a small window of time (i.e., when using a sufficient sample rate), a precise reproduction of the original signal can be stored within the human hearing range as a digital file.

Each measurement (sample) is recorded as a quantized or digitized number. The larger the range of numbers available to record measurements, the more accurately the original signal will be represented (for example, 24-bit/192kHz sampling will always record a more precise signal than 16-bit/44.1kHz). But the measurements always reference a finite scale—with common audio interface converters (delta sigma)—these are called *quantization units*. Each sample's amplitude must be rounded to the nearest step along this finite, or quant, scale, so there will always be a minute difference between the original signal and the signal described by the measurement scale. This difference is known as "quantization error."

In Figure 7.1, the actual audio signal is superimposed on a quantization grid. Notice that the grid does not have the resolution required to capture the sound at the precise amplitude at the precise time.

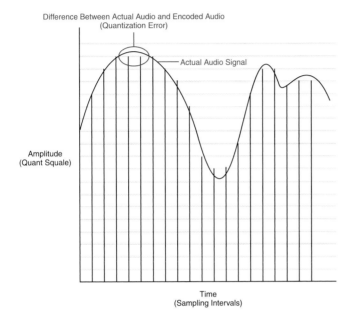

Figure 7.1
Quantization errors between actual audio signal and sampling resolution.

However, the finer the resolution of the measuring system (higher sample rates, larger bit depths), the smaller the quantization error will be.

Bit Depth and Dynamic Range

Computers use a binary number system to represent values as a series of 0s and 1s, with each 0 or 1 represented by a single binary digit, or bit. When recording digital audio, the number of bits that will be used to store each sample is determined when you create a session in Pro Tools (or later if you change the bit depth in the Session Setup window). You have your choice of 16-bit, 24-bit, or 32-bit float. More bits means more steps on the measurement scale, and therefore finer resolution. However, larger bit depths and higher sampling frequencies require significantly more storage space and processing power.

To clearly illustrate how bit depth affects resolution, consider a 3-bit system, which has 8 steps of measurement. Figure 7.2 shows a sine wave at progressively quieter levels and how it is measured by a 3-bit system. The first waveform is the loudest the system can represent. The second is quieter and is only crossing over one step either side of the center point. The final waveform is too quiet to be represented at all by the system.

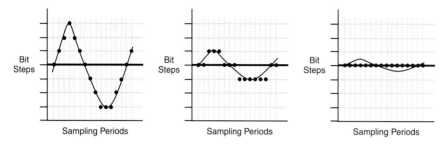

Figure 7.2
A very loud, very quiet, and undetectable signal in a 3-bit (8-step) digital audio system.

This figure shows how dynamic range (the difference between the quietest signal and the loudest signal a system can reproduce) is related to the bit depth. In this 3-bit example, you could only pull down the fader for a signal recorded at maximum level by -18dB before the signal would become too quiet for the system to reproduce. In fact it works out that for every bit you add, the dynamic range of the system is increased by approximately 6dB (6.02dB to be exact). See Table 7.1.

Table 7.1   Theoretical versus Usable Dynamic Range with Common Bit Depths

Bit Depth	Theoretical Dynamic Range	Practical Dynamic Range Limit
1	6.02dB	N/A
16	96dB	84dB
24	144dB	132dB
32	192dB	180dB

As you can see from Table 7.1, using higher bit depths will increase dynamic range. But modern converter technology is limited to roughly 128dB of dynamic range. This is because the two least-significant bits of the sampling word (or bit depth) are reserved for noise floor. A signal cannot go from program material to nothing —it must pass through a noise floor. For example, even though 16-bit audio files have a theoretical dynamic range of 96dB, their usable dynamic range is 84dB. This explains why most CD players quote a dynamic range of 84dB when the theoretical dynamic range is 96dB for a 16-bit audio file.

With 24-bit files, the usable dynamic range matches closely to human hearing. But with floating-point, your audio files and the mixer have more dynamic range than human perceptibility, resulting in a digital file that can retain more of its original signal, even with extreme gain changes during mixing and processing.

Comparing Different Pro Tools Mix Engines (PT Native, PT|HD, and PT|HDX)

With a fundamental understanding of bit depth and quantization, we can move on to the mixing differences between Pro Tools host-based (or *Native*) systems, Pro Tools|HD systems, and Pro Tools|HDX systems.

Pro Tools Native Mixers

Developed and released originally with Pro Tools LE in 1998, the Pro Tools Native mixer employed floating-point processing for mixing and plug-in processing. Floating-point mixing, rather than fixed-point mixing (discussed next), was deployed because it lends itself to modern computer platforms such as Intel-based processors (x86 architecture) and previous Apple/IBM G4/G5 processing architecture. In fact, nearly all host-based digital audio mixing platforms use 32-bit floating-point calculations (and some even 64-bit architecture) at their core. How well the mixer is implemented on the host is the subject of fierce debate. However one thing is certain: Programming 32-bit floating-point mixing well on a host processor (especially when considering summing errors, dithering, and precision) takes a fair bit of processing power and digital audio knowledge. To do 64-bit mixing requires even more of both.

Pro Tools|HD Mixer

Released in 1994 and developed entirely on the Motorola 56k DSP platform, the Pro Tools TDM mixer evolved over the subsequent 17 years using purpose-built DSP chips linked together with a patented real-time audio system known as TDM (time division multiplexing). While the Motorola DSPs provided the raw processing power required for recording, processing, and mixing, Digidesign's custom-designed TDM chips allowed the audio to move between DSPs and audio interfaces in real time—similar to how audio passes through a digital console. The primary advantages of a TDM-based system versus a host-based system are as follows:

- Mixing and processing tasks are offloaded to dedicated DSP processing cards rather than using the host computer CPU.

- Additional DSP cards can be installed into the same computer to increase computing power rather than buying a new computer to get more power.

■ Input-to-output throughput latency is reduced to undetectable levels rather than having to wait through a buffer cycle on a host-based system to hear your live input.

During the past 19 years, the TDM mixer evolved from 16-bit to 24-bit to 48-bit mixing. Moving to a double-precision 24-bit environment (48-bit fixed-point processing) improved headroom, footroom, processing accuracy, and audio detail, resulting in a much improved mixer. With the addition of automatic delay compensation in the Pro Tools|HD platform, Pro Tools quickly became a de facto mixing platform for the entire audio industry. Yet this powerful, scalable, expandable system uses standard consumer-grade computers as a host rather than costly fixed-architecture mixing consoles or purpose-built audio processing platforms that quickly become obsolete. In fact, mixes created on Pro Tools III TDM systems (version 3.3 or higher) can still be opened 16 years later on today's Pro Tools|HD or HDX systems (plug-in availability may vary).

Pro Tools|HDX Mixer

The Pro Tools|HDX platform combines the best of both worlds—dedicated DSP processing, expandability, and the predictability of the Pro Tools|HD platform paired with an expanded 64-bit floating-point mixer, increased delay compensation times, contemporary 32-bit floating-point DSPs, and an improved interchange capability with host-based Pro Tools systems. Built upon 32-bit floating-point DSPs from Texas Instruments and large FPGAs to handle inter-DSP communication at full 32-bit word lengths, the HDX card increases power and performance to roughly four times that of the previous Pro Tools|HD Accel cards. To summarize, HDX increases the capability of a Pro Tools HD system by doing the following:

■ Using a 64-bit floating-point mixer that offers increased headroom, dynamic range, resolution, and accuracy.

■ Retaining 64-bit mixing values when mixers span DSP chips.

■ Employing the same mixer as host-based Pro Tools systems, ensuring common-sounding mixes when moving projects to different Pro Tools 9/10 systems.*

■ Using a full 32-bit data path from audio file to final mix bus, removing many truncation and dithering points in the Pro Tools|HD mixer.

■ Expanding automatic delay compensation buffers up to 16,383 samples.

■ Providing twice as many DSPs as Pro Tools|HD (HDX = 18 versus Pro Tools|HD = 9) per card, running at faster clock speeds (HDX = 350+ MHz versus Pro Tools|HD Accel PCIe = 220 MHz).

* When using AAX plug-ins.

Having reviewed the general differences between the Pro Tools mix engines, let's look further into floating-point processing versus fixed-point processing.

Fixed-Point Versus Floating-Point Processing Overview

As mentioned previously, Pro Tools|HD hardware uses 48-bit fixed-point processing, while host-based Pro Tools systems and HDX hardware use a different mathematical system—dual-precision 32-bit floating-point, also known as 64-bit floating-point processing. While at first glance 64-bit floating-point processing offers more bits than 48-bit fixed-point processing, how the bits are used, how numbers are represented, and what types of calculations are used affect rounding errors, resolution, and accuracy. This section briefly explains the two approaches as well as their benefits and challenges. Later in this lesson, we will revisit these topics, after gaining a more thorough understanding of how the entire mixer works.

Fixed-Point Processing

In fixed-point coding, numbers are represented linearly in binary and constrained by the number of available bits—24 in the case of a digitized signal from an HD I/O interface, through the TDM connection to the DSPs on the Pro Tools|HD cards. In contrast to floating-point systems, fixed-point systems have a consistent noise floor that is roughly –144dB below 0dBFS (for 24-bit sessions), resulting in good low-level detail, predictable summing characteristics, and predicable dithering results due to a fixed bit for noise floor (least significant bit, or LSB). Pro Tools|HD uses a 48-bit mixer to combine signals together. The increased bit depth offers increased detail and resolution. In addition, the Pro Tools|HD mixer uses a 56-bit accumulator for extra computational headroom when inputting values into a mixer before calculating results and rounding down to a final 48-bit result.

To demonstrate how increased resolution works, imagine applying an audio process to a signal (such as gain or EQ). Take two numbers: the amplitude of a signal and some amount of gain change being applied to the signal (using the more familiar decimal system here):

0.96 (original signal amplitude) × 0.612 (negative gain) = 0.58752 (resulting signal amplitude after gain change)

You can see that multiplying the numbers produces a new number with more digits than the original number. If you were limited to our initial resolution (two decimal places), the result would be rounded to 0.59.

With a 24-bit signal, this rounding error may be small, but it could become significant over successive processes. Pro Tools|HD uses a 48-bit fixed-point scheme, which doubles the digital word length to 48 bits by using two 24-bit words to represent 48 bits. This reduces the amount of rounding required and adds a tremendous amount of resolution after the decimal point. When binary numbers are used, the 48-bit scheme provides 281,474,976,710,656 discrete values.

You might think about bit depth like this: Each added bit represents 6.02dB of added dynamic range, so a 24-bit system has a theoretical dynamic range of 144dB, while a 48-bit system has a theoretical dynamic range of 288dB. While increasing bit depth increases dynamic range, it also provides more decimal points to store the digital audio. That means increasing audio bit depth not only provides increased dynamic range, but it also provides the added benefit of higher resolution or accuracy when storing the amplitude values of the audio samples.

Floating-Point Processing

In floating-point coding, numbers are represented using the scientific notation of mantissa/significand (base number) and exponent (multiplier). For example, the number 256,000,000 is illustrated in Figure 7.3.

Number   256,000,000

Exponent
(Multiplier)

Floating-Point Equivalent   256E6

Mantissa
(Base Number)

Figure 7.3
Floating-point equivalent
of a decimal number.

With floating-point notation, the value 256,000,000 requires only four numbers to represent (2, 5, 6, and 6). This allows the floating-point system to store very wide ranging values by changing the exponent as compared to fixed-point processing, where the scale is fixed and cannot be adjusted (except by widening the bit depth). With audio, wide range translates to very large dynamic ranges and higher audio quality.

With 32-bit floating-point systems, 1 bit is reserved for the sign, 23 bits are reserved for the mantissa, and 8 bits are reserved for the exponent. With 64-bit floating-point systems, 1 bit is reserved for the sign, 52 bits are used for the mantissa, with 11 bits used for the exponent. In the simplified decimal example in Figure 7.3, which has three digits for the mantissa and one for the exponent, you can store all the numbers from 0 to 999 with the exponent set to 0. To go above 999, you would need to increment the exponent by 1 (which multiplies the mantissa by 10). The number series would then span from 10 to 9990 in steps of 10.

With a system that can represent very wide ranges, yet has a word depth larger than 24-bit, 64-bit floating-point mixers have the ability to retain and process more mathematical resolution because of their expanded word length and reliance on the exponent to provide increased dynamic range. This is commonly referred to as moving the window around the bit tree. The practical translation is that 64-bit floating-point provides much more headroom and dynamic range without losing any low-level detail when mixing or processing audio.

Comparing Pro Tools|HD Versus HDX Versus Native Mixers

Moving projects between Pro Tools|HD using dual 24-bit (48-bit) DSP architecture and host-based Pro Tools systems using 64-bit floating-point processing appears identical. But underneath, they have slight variances (such as pan depths, headroom, and clipping characteristics) that may lead to slightly different-sounding mixes. Much of that difference depends upon what version of Pro Tools you are using.

Pro Tools|HDX with Pro Tools 10.x software fundamentally changes this paradigm. While retaining the on-demand power, scalability, and stability of Pro Tools|HD, Pro Tools|HDX uses 32-bit floating-point DSPs to re-create the same 64-bit floating-point mixer used on host-based Pro Tools systems 10.x or later. This allows a mix created on a Native Pro Tools system to run on the dedicated DSPs of Pro Tools HDX and sound identical, while completely off-loading the host-based processor for other tasks (such as processor-intensive virtual instruments). When using AAX-based plug-ins, sessions automatically switch between Native and DSP versions of the plug-ins.

However, if you find yourself faced with moving projects between Native and DSP-accelerated systems, it's good to understand the differences.

Common Mixing Errors When Moving from Pro Tools Host-Based to Pro Tools|HD

As noted, Pro Tools host-based systems (or Pro Tools LE) have always used floating-point mixing. This was done to take advantage of modern computing processors to mix and process signals efficiently. However, the product was aimed at consumers who were not necessarily professional audio engineers. It would be quite easy to clip a sum point in the LE mixer or the internal plug-in process. Therefore, the following measures were put into place to alleviate common mixing problems:

- Signals summed at a bus point, if clipped, would be rounded to just below clip on Pro Tools LE. The same bus point, if shown on Pro Tools|HD, would show clip. This would typically result in a mix that looked and sounded fine on a Pro Tools LE system but might clip on a Pro Tools|HD system.

- If a plug-in was inserted on the bus point, as is often the case with Aux Submasters, the Pro Tools LE mixer would not allow a clipped signal to pass to the first instance of a plug-in on that summed track. To alleviate the problem, the signal was rounded down using floating-point mixing to reduce the level below clip before passing it to the first plug-in on the Aux Submaster. Again, if the mix was moved to a Pro Tools|HD mixer, you could see clipping at the input of the plug-in, requiring you to rebalance the mix to alleviate the problem.

- Pro Tools LE had 36dB of headroom in the mixer, while Pro Tools|HD has 56dB of headroom in the mixer. But people could not understand how Pro Tools|HD could clip while Pro Tools LE would not. In actuality, Pro Tools was modifying gain stages in the Pro Tools LE mixer without it being very obvious.

- Pro Tools LE used 32-bit floating-point calculations for processing with RTAS (Real-Time AudioSuite) plug-ins, whereas Pro Tools|HD uses 24/48-bit DSP (or TDM) plug-ins. While the sound and algorithms were meticulously programmed by the manufacturers to yield similar sound, some DSP plug-ins are not available in Native versions, and vice versa. However, when moving mixes from LE to TDM, a TDM system can still run plug-ins as Native versions.

- Pro Tools|HD has had automatic delay compensation running for years. But automatic delay compensation was not introduced to host-based Pro Tools systems until Pro Tools 9, although host-based plug-ins could always auto-compensate on audio/disk tracks, assuming there was no look-ahead functionality built into the plug-in.

- Pro Tools LE used −3dB pan laws, whereas Pro Tools|HD used −2.5. This meant that additional time would be required to rebalance a mix when moving from Pro Tools LE to Pro Tools|HD for tracks that were panned to the center position or dynamically panned across center. Prior to Pro Tools 9, TDM systems could be forced to use a 3dB pan law by removing the stereo mixer plug-in, and using the surround mixer plug-in for both stereo and surround-sound mixes. With Pro Tools 9 and later software, pan laws are adjustable on a session by session basis from within the Session Setup window.

All of these issues are resolved when moving host-based Pro Tools 9 or later sessions to HDX because of the common 64-bit mixer and the introduction of AAX plug-ins, which can run either on the host or on the HDX 32-bit DSPs.

DSP-Based Mixers and DSP Usage

Now that you have a better understanding of fixed-point versus floating-point processing and how the mixer architecture applies to dynamic range and resolution, it's time to review the hardware components of Pro Tools|HD and Pro Tools|HDX. Understanding these differences can help you to create better sounding mixes and point you in the right direction when troubleshooting issues.

Pro Tools|HD and TDM

As mentioned earlier, the Pro Tools|HD platform is composed of DSP chips mounted on a PCIe card that interconnect using a data highway called time division multiplexing (TDM). Figure 7.4 shows a Pro Tools|HD Accel card.

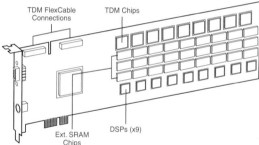

Figure 7.4
Pro Tools|HD Accel card.

TDM is a widely used technology in which multiple digital channels or streams of data are sent via a single bus. Instead of using individual physical connections for each stream (connecting one DSP to another DSP), a very high data transmission speed is used, with each stream allocated a "timeslot" to go from DSP to DSP (or interface). This means that connections between points connected to a TDM bus can be made and changed simply by changing which timeslot a point is listening to.

Pro Tools|HD-series cards feature Avid's TDM II architecture. Channels from sources such as disk tracks, sends, or buses can be combined together or *multiplexed* onto a data highway (TDM bus) so that all signals can propagate throughout the system simultaneously and be accessed within a single sample period.

TDM II runs fast enough to accommodate many audio signals at the same time. Each separate audio signal, or *stream*, takes up a single timeslot on this multiplexed bus. One of most powerful features of the TDM II architecture is that a single timeslot can be used to broadcast data to many destinations simultaneously. Data can also be sent bi-directionally and privately between DSP chips, which effectively provides a very large number of available timeslots. This provides a huge number of potential connections for routing, processing, and mixing audio signals within Pro Tools.

On Pro Tools|HD cards, the DSP chips are arranged serially, with 512 connections, or timeslots, between each chip. Many more than 512 connections are technically possible, as signals only need to use slots on the bus between the chips at their source and destination. (See Figure 7.5.)

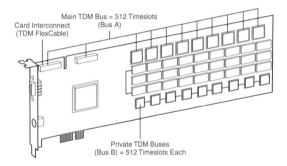

Figure 7.5
Main TDM bus and private buses between chips.

HDX Architecture

The Pro Tools|HDX platform is similar to Pro Tools|HD in that it has dedicated DSP chips mounted on a PCIe card. However, that is where the similarity ends.

The first thing to note is the HDX card has twice as many DSPs as the previous generation (as shown in Figure 7.6), providing roughly 1.5 times the processing power of Pro Tools|HD.

Another substantial difference between Pro Tools|HDX and Pro Tools|HD is that Pro Tools|HDX does not have TDM chips—rather, all DSPs are connected to a central FPGA (field programmable gate array). This star configuration of DSPs connected to a single FPGA allows the FPGA to control what signals go to which DSPs in a timely and efficient manner, yielding the following benefits:

- By having one FPGA chip connected to each DSP, expert programming is employed to keep latency between chips to a minimum.

- By using an FPGA instead of fixed ASIC chips for data communication, new programming changes and firmware updates can be easily applied. This provides the potential for new features and improvements without having to update hardware with costly hardware exchanges.

The DSP chips used on the HDX card are quite different from those used on previous generation Pro Tools|HD hardware. Rather than using fixed-point processing DSP (Motorola 56k family), the HDX card employs Texas Instruments 32-bit floating-point DSPs. This allows Pro Tools to have a common mixing and processing environment that spans both DSP-accelerated systems and host-based Pro Tools systems. Also, these 32-bit floating-point DSPs are much more powerful than their predecessors, allowing you to mix more signals, employ more signal processing, and have higher track counts than previous Pro Tools|HD systems per chip. In fact, at 48kHz, HDX cards are typically four times more powerful than previous generation Pro Tools|HD Accel cards.

HDX cards also utilize uniform DSP cores. This means that any plug-in can run on any DSP core. This was not the case with previous generation Pro Tools Accel cards, which had an assortment of different external RAM components for DSP chips. In rare circumstances, you could seemingly have enough free DSPs for a particular plug-in that used external RAM (such as a reverb), but because the available DSPs did not have external RAM, a DSP shuffle would occur.

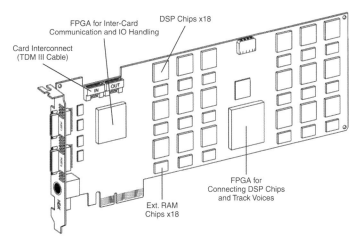

Figure 7.6
Diagram of HDX card architecture.

Pro Tools|HD DSP Shuffle

When a new session is opened, Pro Tools|HD attempts to reload all the plug-ins and mixers onto any DSPs that have already been allocated. But when running low on DSP resources, the software will automatically perform a DSP shuffle to optimize DSP mixing—typically when a new plug-in is inserted that may not necessarily have a free DSP to load on.

HDX (and previous generation Pro Tools|HD) also offers the ability to convert any plug-in that runs on the DSP to a Native version (assuming an equivalent plug-in is available on the system). This means that if you need more processing power, you can always use the power of the host computer to complement your dedicated DSP processes.

Note: When converting between DSP and Native versions of plug-ins, there could be audible sonic differences.

At the time of print, Pro Tools|HDX systems support up to three HDX cards maximum. However, the hardware system is designed to eventually support up to seven total HDX cards installed in a single system.

Mixer Creation

Now that you have a better understanding of the core technology powering the Pro Tools DSP-accelerated hardware, it's time to look at the technology that powers the Pro Tools HD mixer. Each time you open a session, a mixer is created on your DSP chips. You learned in earlier courses that plug-ins use DSP chips. So do mixers, except that mixers can span more than one chip and communicate with each other at full 64-bit word lengths with HDX and 48-bit word lengths with Pro Tools|HD. When you go beyond a certain number of mixer channels (including audio tracks, Aux Input tracks, Instrument tracks, and sends), Pro Tools will use another DSP to expand mixer capacity.

As in the analog world, every auxiliary send (internal mix bus) or output bus that you use demands that a summing mixer exist for that group output. On an analog console, the number of these summing mixers is dictated by the physical layout of the console (for instance, a 24-bus console has 24 buses). In the Pro Tools mix environment, this number is variable (up to 256 internal mix buses and up to 192 mono or 96 stereo output buses) depending on the number of output mixes or sends that you choose to create. Pro Tools allocates DSP power as it is needed, in order to build the mixers for each session as additional buses are used.

Monitoring Mixer Usage with the System Usage Window

Pro Tools HD software provides an easy way to track how much processing powering is being used for mixing on the DSP chips from within the System Usage window, shown in Figure 7.7.

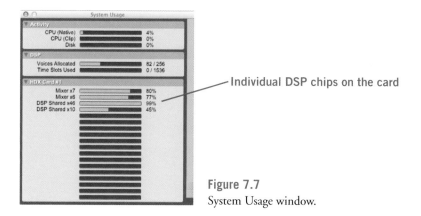

— Individual DSP chips on the card

Figure 7.7
System Usage window.

Each mixer will use a DSP chip. The number of mixers that share the DSP chip for mixing can vary, depending upon their configuration.

Stereo

Each TDM stereo mixer has the dimensions $N \times 2$, meaning that it mixes a variable number of inputs to an output pair. For example, a session with 48 tracks would require a 48×2 mixer. If one of the tracks is assigned to Output 3–4, however, two mixers are required—one 47×2 mixer routed to Output 1–2, and one 1×2 mixer routed to Output 3–4. Depending upon the number of tracks and the width of the mixer (stereo versus mono), two separate $N \times 2$ mixers typically fit on a single DSP chip. However, as more tracks are added or more discrete buses are used, Pro Tools will be forced to use another DSP for mixing without having used the first DSP 100%.

In Figure 7.8, a single mixer is created for 48 channels to a pair of outputs on a Pro Tools|HDX system. The DSP is only at 49% for all 48 tracks.

In Figure 7.9, a send is used across all channels to a second set of outputs. Notice that the DSP usage gauge has increased to 69% but has successfully created two distinct 48×2 mixers on the same DSP chip. This is the equivalent of a 96×4 mixer. Also notice that the DSP gauge for the DSP chip now says Mixer x2.

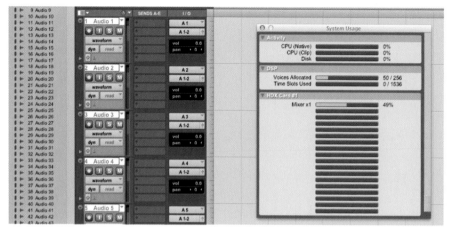

Figure 7.8
System Usage window showing DSP mixing resources.

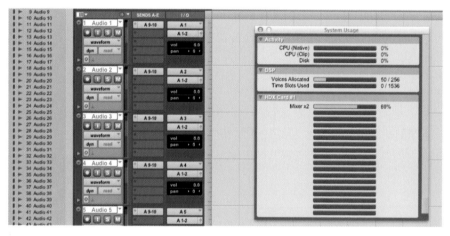

Figure 7.9
System Usage window showing two 48 × 2 mixers on a single chip.

In Figure 7.10, a second send has been used across all tracks to go to a third set of outputs. At this point the mixer cannot run three distinct 48 × 2 mixers on a single DSP chip, so it assigns the third 48 × 2 mixer to a second DSP chip. Notice that the DSP gauge says Mixer x1.

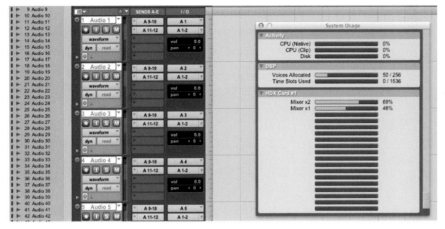

Figure 7.10
System Usage window showing three 48 × 2 mixers on two DSP chips.

Multichannel

When using surround paths, each surround mixer can have a variable number of outputs as well as a variable number of inputs. For example, the 5.1 format requires six outputs. However routing to this output is usually done through various multichannel buses (LCR, 5.0, 5.1). In Figure 7.11, 32 tracks are assigned to four different auxiliary submasters; two are 5.0 mix buses, and two are 5.1 mix buses. These submasters are subsequently bussed to a single 5.1 output bus going to the interface. Notice that two different DSPs are employed for this mix; the first DSP is used for the submixing, and the second DSP is used for the final output bus to the interface.

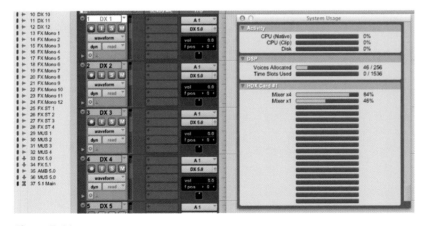

Figure 7.11
System Usage window showing four 32 × 5.0/5.1 mixers on a single DSP.

Adding more internal buses for effects (such as reverb) will also contribute to the number of DSPs required. In Figure 7.12, two mono buses have been added for two different reverb sends across all source tracks. Notice that 75% of a single DSP chip has now been utilized for these sends.

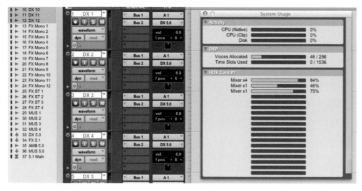

Figure 7.12
System Usage window showing additional DSP mixers for internal effects.

As the track count grows in high-sample rate production (such as 96kHz), more and more of the DSPs will be required for mixing.

Identifying Which Mixers Are Used on What DSPs

With Pro Tools 10.x and HDX, the System Usage window provides detailed information on the number of mixers and their configuration on a single DSP.

To get a listing of what mixers are running on individual DSPs:

1. Open the System Usage window (**WINDOW > SYSTEM USAGE**).

2. Hover the mouse over a DSP gas gauge that has a mixer process running, as shown in Figure 7.13. A pop-up display will appear showing the processes running on that DSP chip.

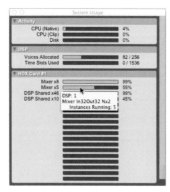

Figure 7.13
System Usage window showing detailed mixer information.

Dither

When you reduce the bit depth of a signal, you run the risk of eliminating, or truncating, program material in the least significant bits. For example, when moving from 24 bits to 16 bits, any low-level audio in the bottom 8 bits gets truncated, which can cause audible quantization errors. In an effort to mask the quantization errors, you have the option of adding dither, which creates an artificial "noise floor" at the least significant bit (LSB), ultimately helping to mask the quantization errors caused by the original truncation of the file. The LSB represents the quietest amplitude level that can be recorded by a digital system. Hence, dither creates a noise floor at the quietest level that can be represented at a given bit depth. Dither is applied in several instances:

- When a signal in the Pro Tools|HD mixer is sent from the mixer to a physical output (when using the dithered mixer).

- On Pro Tools|HD, when a signal is processed in a higher bit depth plug-in process (48-bit for Pro Tools|HD) and is sent back to the mixer chips.

- When choosing **Export Clips as Files** from the Clips List to a lower bit depth file. In this case dither is automatically applied.

Why Dither Works

Perceptually, the effect of dither is to de-correlate the quantization distortion from the original signal by exaggerating signal activity around the LSB. In other words, instead of hearing a slightly distorted version of the original signal, you hear the original signal plus some very quiet uncorrelated noise, which is preferable.

Figure 7.14 is a recording of dither noise that POW-r dither uses (discussed in the next section). The dither signal has been amplified by stacking four Trim plug-ins at +12dB on top of each other (thus boosting the signal 48dB).

Figure 7.14
Waveform of POW-r dither Type 3.

This seemingly random waveform again would be introduced near the bottom of a 24- or 32-bit signal, in order to mask the quantization error.

Not all dither is the same. In fact, POW-r dither gives you three different algorithms to choose from, as discussed in the next section.

When to Apply Dither Plug-ins

Because dither masks low-level quantization errors that occur during file truncation, it should be used after all gain-based processing has occurred, as the final step when converting a high bit depth audio file to a lower bit depth file. Often this is done when creating the final mix of a 24-bit music project going to 16-bit for CD replication. Adding dither allows the low-level signals of a high bit depth audio file to still be perceived to some extent in the reduced-bit version.

Note: When converting 32-bit floating point files to 24-bit fixed-point files, truncation is applied with no dither, although dither is applied if further reducing the bit depth of the fixed-point file.

Dither is added at the least significant bit, which will typically be the noise floor. Once the conversion is completed, the new audio file will have an increased noise floor, but the quietest parts and finest details of the recording will be heard through the dither.

When trying to decide if dither is necessary, consider the following:

- Audio signals with quiet passages will have less distortion if dither is applied.

- Dither should always be applied when converting from a fixed-point file to a lower bit depth, assuming no further processing or summing will be applied.

- Dither is not needed when converting to a higher bit depth.

Caution: Dither should never be applied during a sample rate conversion. The noise added at the least significant bit interacts with the sampling conversion algorithm and may lead to a slightly degraded sound while converting. If you must reduce the bit depth of a file and sample-rate convert it (such as creating a 16-bit/44.1kHz version of a file from a 24-bit/48kHz master file), break the process into two steps—convert the file's sample rate first to the target sample rate but retain the bit depth (in this case 44.1kHz but still a 24-bit file). Open the new file at the new sample rate in a new 44.1kHz session and then reduce the bit depth with dither.

Dithering Down to 16-Bit for CD

Music that has been recorded and mixed at 24-bit must at some point be reduced to 16-bit for CD reproduction. If you are providing a final CD-ready master, this may become your responsibility. Dither should normally be used in this situation to preserve some of the benefit of the 24-bit mix.

In the Avid Learning Series   Dither plug-ins are introduced in the Pro Tools 110 course.

Caution: If you are supplying a finished mix that will be worked on further by a mastering engineer, you should not reduce the bit depth or apply dither.

Flavors of Dither

A number of plug-ins provide dither, including the Dither and POW-r Dither plug-ins that are included with all Pro Tools systems. Some dither plug-ins, including POW-r Dither, provide different types of dither that suit various types of program material. Other "mastering" plug-ins, such as Maxim, provide dither at their output stage. One thing they all have in common is that they must be the very last process in the signal chain before going to the outputs or being recorded via Bounce to Disk. Dither must therefore be the last insert on a Master Fader (which is the only track type that supports post-fader inserts). Figure 7.15 shows both the POW-r Dither and Maxim plug-ins.

Figure 7.15
The POW-r Dither plug-in (left) and Maxim plug-in (right) both provide dither.

DigiRack Dither

The DigiRack Dither plug-in shown in Figure 7.16 uses basic dither with a single noise-shaping option. The DigiRack Dither plug-in does not provide any selectable noise-shaping options. Instead, it uses a standard dithering setting to retain a linear frequency response when reducing resolution. This does not always translate into the best stereo mix. Instead, consider using the POW-r Dither plug-in when reducing the resolution of a final stereo mix, since it provides selectable noise-shaping options.

Figure 7.16
DigiRack Dither plug-in.

POW-r Dither

POW-r Dither (*Psycho-Acoustically Optimized Word Length Reduction*) is an algorithm created by the POW-r Dither Consortium, composed of John La Grou (Millenea Media), David McGrath (Lake Audio, now part of Dolby Labs), Daniel Weiss (Weiss Electronics), and Dr. Glenn Zelniker (Z Systems). Their algorithm provides a method to reduce word length (or bit depth) while retaining a high degree of perceived dynamic efficiency and very low noise. This plug-in has three different settings, optimized for different program material. You should listen carefully in a studio-quality monitoring environment to judge which option provides the best results on your mix.

- **Type 1:** Has the flattest frequency spectrum in the audible range of frequencies, modulating and accumulating the dither noise just below the Nyquist frequency. Recommended for less stereophonically complex material such as solo instrument recordings and spoken word.

- **Type 2:** Has a psycho-acoustically optimized low order noise-shaping curve. Recommended for material containing some stereophonic complexity. Also recommended if the final mix is slightly bright or edgy.

- **Type 3:** Has a psycho-acoustically optimized high order noise-shaping curve. Recommended for full-spectrum, wide stereo field material. Also recommended if the final mix is right where you want it and you don't want any imaging or clarity to be lost when reducing the word lengths.

Caution: Applying any further processing, especially gain-based processes after applying Type 2 or 3 dither, can make the dither audible in certain frequency bands.

The Pro Tools HD Mixer

At this point you have a solid understanding of the theories behind the Pro Tools mix environment. In this section you will explore the Pro Tools mixer in more detail to uncover more similarities and differences between the two DSP-accelerated platforms. Understanding exactly what is (and isn't) happening when you mix signals in Pro Tools can be a great asset. It will allow you to proceed with confidence, knowing that your mixing methods are not detrimental to sound quality.

First we'll introduce the main topics; then we'll go back and explore them more deeply while looking at how an audio signal is handled on its way through Pro Tools.

Double-Precision Processing

Pro Tools's audio interfaces can digitize analog signals or receive digital signals at a maximum bit depth of 24 bits (32-bit float files can also be used, but the actual PCM audio resolution of the converter is still 24 bits). We saw earlier that 24 bits equals a theoretical dynamic range of 144dB, which is a much more dynamic range than the human ear can perceive. This is the maximum resolution of audio signals when they come into the system, leave the system digitally, or arrive at the DACs for conversion back to analog signals. However, the Pro Tools mixer uses 48-bit values (Pro Tools|HD) or 64-bit values (Pro Tools Native or HDX) when mixing and processing signals to retain clarity and detail and avoid unnecessary rounding errors. The other advantages to using large bit depth mixers are headroom, footroom, and processing capacity.

Headroom

The 48-bit mixer and the 64-bit mixer both offer a huge amount of headroom for mixing together signals without clipping. In fact, mix buses in Pro Tools|HD have 54dB of headroom above the maximum for any individual channel. This means that you can mix 128 tracks of maximum-level, in-phase audio, with every fader at +12, and still not clip the bus internally. With 64-bit floating-point processing, the mixer headroom provides more than 1,500dB of dynamic range.

Tip: In real-world terms, this means that you will never clip a bus input when mixing signals. Master Faders on buses and outputs can be used to scale the final result to a level that doesn't clip when the signal returns to 24 bits or 32-bit float in the Native/HDX mixer.

Footroom

With the 48-bit mixer, you can pull signals down drastically without losing any of the original resolution. If the mixer worked at 24-bit, pulling a fader down would immediately start reducing the resolution of the signal. In fact, with the 48-bit mixer, faders can be pulled down to nearly –90dB before any of the original resolution is lost. With the 64-bit mixer, the full 32-bit floating point word traveling through the system is also retained, even when pulling a fader down to inaudible levels.

Tip: In practical terms, this means that you don't need to worry too much about where your faders are positioned. Your original recordings will be represented with all their resolution intact in the mix. Also, it makes no difference whether you set your faders low and have the master high or vice versa, but employing proper gain stages throughout your mix will always yield better results.

Eventually, your mix must leave the mixer and be sent across the HD Mixer to the outputs or to analog outputs via the DACs (digital to analog converters). This requires going back to a standard 24-bit signal. With the 48-bit mixer, this is either achieved simply by discarding the bottom 24 bits (truncation) and then applying dither. Remember, the difference between these two methods is only slight; although you are discarding half your bits, they represent only extremely fine details of the signal that are below –144dB. Using dither will reduce quantization noise below this level, at the expense of the noise floor at –144dB.

The 64-bit mixer uses two 32-bit words to represent the audio, with the first 23 bits of data in each 32-bit word representing the actual bits of audio. However, throughout the entire mix and summing process, those 32 bits have never been lost. So again, when the signal is converted from 64-bit, to 32-bit, to 24-bit, the entire 24-bit signal is maintained.

Master Faders allow you to choose which 24 bits (or 32 bits on HDx and Native mixers) make up the signal that reaches a bus or output. This will be explained in more detail in the next section.

Looking in More Detail: An Audio Signal's Tale

This section reviews the entire path of the audio signal, how quantization is minimized, how summing characteristics are different between fixed-point and floating-point processing, and where truncation points occur in each system.

Analog to Digital Conversion

A signal that enters the input of an Avid HD I/O is digitized at 24-bit resolution. The 24-bit signal has a theoretical dynamic range of 144dB. The ADCs on the HD I/O have an incredible dynamic range of 122dB on the ADC side, so there is plenty of resolution in the 24-bit signal.

On a Pro Tools|HD system, once the signal is digitized, it is transferred over the TDM bus at 24-bit resolution to the DSP chips for plug-in processing. With Pro Tools|HDX, the signal is converted on the HDX card to 32-bit floating point and transferred to the DSPs.

Tip: To take full advantage of the 64-bit mixer resolution, it is recommended to create your session using the 32-Bit Float Bit Depth setting. This will allow you to use Elastic Audio at full resolution and offer a way to print your final mix to disk at a 32-bit float file.

Plug-in Processing

Audio signals in the Pro Tools mixer are often processed with plug-ins. However, the data pathway used to get to the plug-ins is different, depending upon which mixer you use.

Pro Tools|HD

DSP plug-in processing is carried out at 24-bit or 48-bit resolution, depending on how the plug-in is coded. Plug-ins that process at 48-bit resolution take advantage of the ability of 24-bit DSP chips to perform double-precision processing (using two 24-bit words). The 48-bit result of such calculations is converted back down to 24-bit resolution in order to be passed on to the next plug-in or back to the mixer. Figure 7.17 shows an overview of the signal path in the Pro Tools mixer.

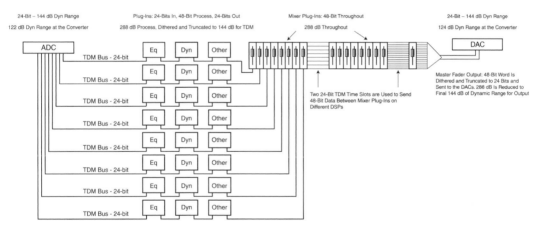

Figure 7.17
Pro Tools|HD system diagram.

48-Bit Mixing

Once the signal has left the inserts, it is added to the Pro Tools mixer. At this stage the 24-bit word is multiplied by another 24-bit word that represents the fader and pan positions, producing a 48-bit word that stays at 48-bit resolution throughout the mixer. Although connections in the TDM bus are 24-bit, two 24-bit timeslots are used to pass the two 24-bit words of mixer data between DSPs, maintaining an internal dynamic range of 288dB. As already stated, the additional 24 bits provide the mixer with a larger amount of headroom and footroom above and below the original 24-bit word, making the mixer very difficult to clip as you add more inputs to the mix bus. Specifically, nine bits are reserved for levels above 0dBFS, providing 54dB of headroom. Fifteen bits are added to the other end of the 24-bit word. The practical implications of this are that you can do the following:

- Sum 128 tracks of correlated, full-code audio with all the faders at +12dB without clipping the input of the bus.

- Pull down any channel fader to around –90dB without losing any of the original 24 bits.

The DSP chips on a Pro Tools|HD card use a 56-bit register, meaning that 56 bits are available on the chip to store the results of any calculations. Let's consider in more detail why reserving extra bits maintains resolution when processing digital audio. The diagram shown in Figure 7.18 represents four points in time in a 24-bit mixer.

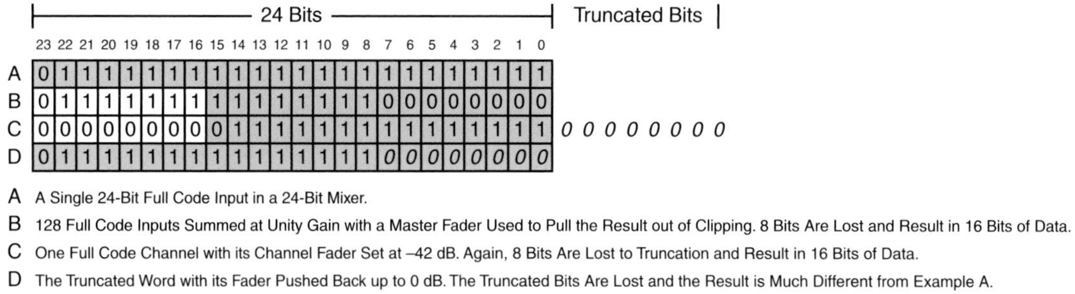

	24 Bits	Truncated Bits

A   A Single 24-Bit Full Code Input in a 24-Bit Mixer.

B   128 Full Code Inputs Summed at Unity Gain with a Master Fader Used to Pull the Result out of Clipping. 8 Bits Are Lost and Result in 16 Bits of Data.

C   One Full Code Channel with its Channel Fader Set at –42 dB. Again, 8 Bits Are Lost to Truncation and Result in 16 Bits of Data.

D   The Truncated Word with its Fader Pushed Back up to 0 dB. The Truncated Bits Are Lost and the Result is Much Different from Example A.

Figure 7.18
24-bit mixer truncation points.

- **Row A:** Shows the original, full-code input channel as it appears at the mixer. There is no initial multiplication performed, so it is at full level at both the DAC and the mixer.

- **Row B**: Shows 128 summed channels of full code 24-bit audio. A master fader would have to be used to pull the output level down by –42.1dB to pull it out of clipping, but the penalty in this system is a loss of eight bits.

- **Row C**: Shows an individual channel reduced by 42dB. Since there are no footroom bits available, the lowest bits are simply cut off, and the result is a 16-bit word.

- **Row D**: Shows the truncated word with its fader pushed back up to 0dB. The truncated bits are lost and cannot be recovered.

In the Pro Tools 48-bit mixer, however, this is not the case. The DSPs use a 56-bit register for performing 48-bit calculations, with eight additional bits provided for overflow to avoid rounding errors. There is enough headroom to sum 128 full-code tracks at +12 without internally clipping, as well as enough low level resolution to pull channel faders down to –90dB without losing any of their original bits, as shown in Figure 7.19.

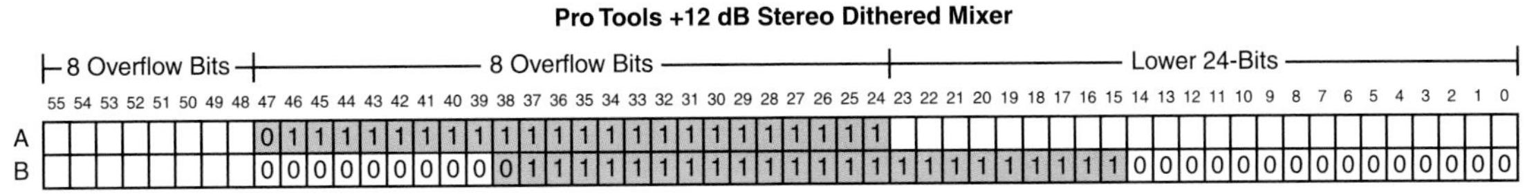

Pro Tools +12 dB Stereo Dithered Mixer

├─ 8 Overflow Bits ─┤├──────── 8 Overflow Bits ────────┤├──────── Lower 24-Bits ────────┤

55 54 53 52 51 50 49 48 47 46 45 44 43 42 41 40 39 38 37 36 35 34 33 32 31 30 29 28 27 26 25 24 23 22 21 20 19 18 17 16 15 14 13 12 11 10 9 8 7 6 5 4 3 2 1 0

A □ □ □ □ □ □ □ □ 0 1 1 1 1 1 1 1 1 1 1 1 1 1 1 1 1 1 1 1 1 1 1 1 1

B □ □ □ □ □ □ □ □ □ □ □ 0 0 0 0 0 0 0 0 0 0 0 1 1 1 1 1 1 1 1 1 1 1 1 1 1 1 1 1 1 1 1 1 1 1 1 0 0 0 0 0 0 0 0 0 0 0 0 0 0 0 0 0

Figure 7.19
24-bit full code signal as placed in the 56-bit register in the Pro Tools mixer.

Dithered Versus Non-Dithered Mixers (ProTools|HD Hardware Only)

Whether or not dither is applied at the final output stage of the Pro Tools HD mixer is determined by which mixer plug-in is currently active.

The following four mixer plug-ins are supplied with Pro Tools HD software:

- Stereo mixer
- Surround mixer
- Stereo dithered mixer
- Surround dithered mixer

Caution: Pro Tools HD PCIe hardware systems only support having one of each set of mixer plug-ins installed at any one time. If both plug-in types from the same set are installed, an error message will occur when launching Pro Tools.

The mixer you wish to use must be placed manually in the Plug–ins folder before launching Pro Tools. The dithered mixer plug-ins use slightly more DSP resources than the non-dithered versions.

To switch mixer plug-ins:

1. Quit Pro Tools.
2. Do one of the following:
   - On Windows systems, open the PLUG-INS (UNUSED) folder (PROGRAM FILES\ COMMONFILES\DIGIDESIGN\DAE).
   - On Macintosh systems, open the PLUG-INS (UNUSED) folder on your Startup drive (LIBRARY/APPLICATION SUPPORT/DIGIDESIGN).

3. Locate the mixer plug-in that you want to use, and drag it to the Plug-ins folder.

4. Open the **PLUG-INS** folder, locate the mixer plug-in version that you no longer want to use, and drag it to the **PLUG-INS (UNUSED)** folder.

5. Launch Pro Tools.

It is important to note that the dithered mixer dithers signals at outputs only, and not internal bus destinations. This means that when submixing tracks using buses, Pro Tools mixers are able to pass full 48-bit words to each other. The dithered mixer also has no effect when audio is routed to/from the HD hardware's DSP chips for DSP plug-in processing. Finally, when using a dithered mixer, you must still insert a dithering plug-in on the Master Fader if down converting from 24 bits to a 16-bit master recording (the dithered mixer in this example only dithers down from 48 bits to 24 bits).

Pro Tools|HDX

HDX architecture allows a plug-in process to operate at 32-bit, 64-bit, or 80-bit floating-point utilizing dual precision. (See Figure 7.20.) Unlike Pro Tools|HD, there is no truncation when passing a signal from the mixer to the plug-in process and back again. The 32-bit floating-point value is shifted to allow the signal to pass into the plug-in without truncation. If a plug-in processes at 64-bit floating-point, the plug-in manufacturer will employ a conversion process on the file before it passes out of the DSP chip and back to the mixer DSP chip.

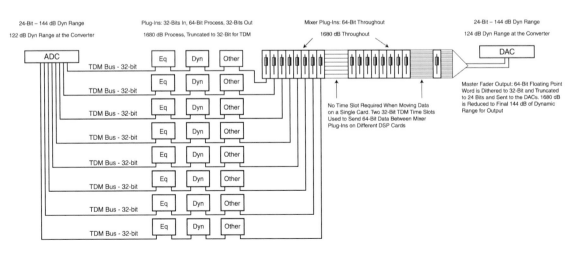

Figure 7.20
Pro Tools|HDX system diagram.

64-Bit Floating-Point Mixing

After analog audio entering an HD-series audio interface is converted to a digital signal, it then enters the mixer at a bit depth matching the session settings (16-, 24-, or 32-bit float). If the bit depth is anything less than 32-bit float, the signal is padded with zeros to fill out the full 32-bit data path of Pro Tools|HDX.

At this stage, the 32-bit streams are summed into a 64-bit mixer. However, HDX differs from Pro Tools|HD in that the data path through the various DSP chips remains at 32-bit (rather than truncating to 24-bit). This allows a file recorded as 32-bit float to pass through the entire mixing and processing path without any truncation or dithering, much like a 24-bit signal on a Pro Tools|HD system. Also different is how the DSPs pass audio between themselves. Unlike Pro Tools|HD, Pro Tools|HDX does not require any timeslots to move data from one DSP to another on the same HDX card—the FPGA chip connects DSPs together. This results in very low latency when stacking multiple plug-in processes on top of each other in the mixer. TDM is still used in multiple HDX card systems to pass signals between cards. Pro Tools|HDX offers 1536 timeslots (at 44.1/48kHz). As already stated, HDX uses floating-point mixing, so headroom is never a factor. With 64-bit summing, resolution is preserved even when applying extreme gain changes and panning with hundreds of tracks in a session. To summarize:

- HDX uses 32-bit data paths to preserve fidelity and accuracy throughout the mixer.

- Using floating-point processing allows you to build very large, complex mixers using less DSP.

- Using an FPGA chip to manage voices allows a single card to have more available voices and frees DSP for other processes.

- The combination of an FPGA chip managing voices, floating-point mixing, and more powerful DSP results in a four-fold increase in processing power versus previous generation Pro Tools|HD Accel cards.

- 32-bit floating-point processing prevents internal clipping in plug-ins.

- 64-bit summing allows for an extraordinarily high number of tracks to sum and not clip the inputs of the HD mixer. For example, 512 audio tracks at full code would still not clip the input of a master bus. However, the master bus fader would need to be lowered to –90dB to avoid clipping the outputs.

Tip: If you plan to do extreme Elastic Audio operations and want maximum fidelity, or plan to print your mixes internally, you should record audio at 32-bit float.

Note: Due to the nature of 64-bit floating-point mixing, a separate dithered mixer is not required.

Master Faders

Master Faders play an important role in gaining the full benefit of the 48-bit mixer or 64-bit mixer, allowing you to adjust the level of any bus or output. Now that you've had an insight into the HD mixer, you will be able to appreciate a different view of exactly what Master Faders are doing. A Master Fader shifts the audio signal up and down within the 48-bit workspace of the mixer with Pro Tools|HD hardware. With floating-point mixers, it is essentially changing the exponent of the 32-bit word to either boost or cut the output. This becomes particularly significant when the signal returns to 24 bits, such as when being bussed or routed to an audio interface output.

With fixed-point processing, you can think of a Master Fader as creating a 24-bit window into the 48-bit mixer. In the case where several signals are being mixed together, creating a signal that spills over into the headroom bits, a Master Fader is used to manually scale the signal back down into the main 24-bit range. With the floating-point mixer, the Master Fader is adjusting the 32-bit floating-point value in the 64-bit mixer by adjusting the exponent and keeping the mantissa in place. This allows the Master Fader to create a window below the clip that you can then pass on to the interface outputs. You can experience this firsthand, and hear a master fader recover an output from clipping, by working through the exercise at the end of this lesson.

Appropriate Use of Native Plug-ins

On DSP-accelerated systems, you primarily use DSP-based plug-ins to keep the host CPU(s) free for other tasks. However, host-based (or Native) plug-in processing, whether AAX or RTAS, can still play an important role and provides a "best of both worlds" solution.

Native plug-ins are generally used in the following situations:

- When no DSP version of a plug-in is available. Some plug-ins, most notably the AIR instruments, are available only for the Native format. However, the new AAX plug-in format offers a way for formerly Native only plug-ins to run on DSP chips if the plug-in manufacturer recodes the plug-in for the AAX DSP format.

- When the DSP chips are maxed out. If a large mix uses up all of the available DSP resources (primarily for mixing), you can add additional plug-ins by using Native versions. With Pro Tools|HDX, these plug-ins are seamless.

■ When moving a session to a system with fewer DSP cards. In this situation, the second Pro Tools system may have insufficient DSP resources to load all the plug-ins in the mixer configuration. However, plug-ins that have Native equivalents can be converted.

To convert DSP plug-ins to Native:

1. Open the plug-in window. Whether the plug-in is active or inactive due to insufficient DSP resources, the process is the same.

2. At the top right of the plug-in window, click the word **DSP**. A pop-up menu will appear. Choose **CONVERT TO NATIVE** as shown in Figure 7.21.

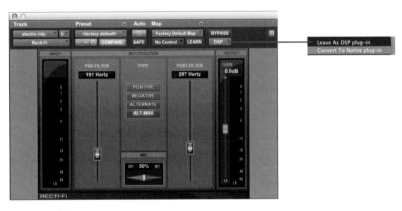

Figure 7.21
Converting a plug-in from DSP to Native.

Native Plug-ins on Aux Input and Master Fader Tracks

When using Native plug-ins on Aux Inputs or Master Faders in DSP-accelerated systems, be aware that voices are required to take the signal from the DSPs to the host processor and back again into the DSP-based mixer. The following sections describe issues around this.

Voice Usage and Total Latency for Native Plug-ins

With Pro Tools|HD or Pro Tools|HDX, inserting a Native plug-in on an audio track does not require additional voices, as long as it is inserted before a DSP plug-in. The Native DSP process is performed on the host before the audio is sent into the DSP-based mixer. However, a Native plug-in inserted on an Aux Input or Master Fader has no way to route the signal from the DSPs to the host CPU without using a voice. The voice allows the signal to leave the DSP mixer and travel along the PCI bus to the host CPU. Another voice is used to return to the mixer.

This means that the initial insert of a Native plug-in will take up two additional voices per channel (one voice for input and one voice for output) and incur latency equal to the buffer amount chosen in the Playback Engine dialog box. The latency from the buffer must be applied for each journey to and from the CPU, so effectively twice the buffer size, plus whatever the delay of the plug-in is. When a Native plug-in is inserted on a track, additional voices are used when the following conditions occur:

- The Aux Input channel has both inputs and outputs assigned.

- The track is a Master Fader track.

- The plug-in is inserted on an Instrument track that does not contain an instrument plug-in. (The track is being used with an external hardware instrument with an input assigned.)

- The plug-in is inserted after a DSP plug-in on any kind of track.

For example, the initial insert of a Native plug-in on a mono Aux Input track uses two voices (one channel with two voices), while the initial insert of that plug-in on a stereo Aux Input track uses four voices (two channels with two voices each), as shown in Figure 7.22. Again, the latency from the buffer must be applied for each journey to and from the CPU, so effectively twice the buffer size, plus whatever the delay of the plug-in is.

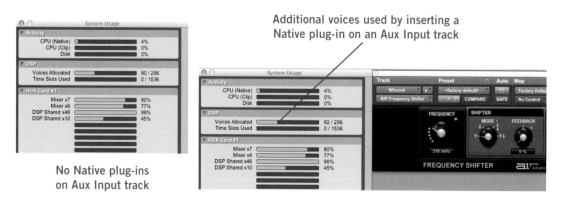

Figure 7.22
Adding a Native plug-in to an Aux Input increases voice count.

Tip: When a track has no input assigned or the input is made inactive, as in the case of an Instrument track or Aux Input that is used for a Native instrument plug-in, only one extra voice is used per channel for the plug-in.

Subsequent Native plug-ins on the same track do not take up additional voices because there is actually no passing back and forth from the host CPU. At this stage, as the audio is being processed by the CPU, it simply continues to process each Native plug-in (much like the Native mixer) and then the voice is used to return the audio to the DSP mixer. However, if passing back and forth between DSP and Native plug-ins, additional voices are used for each trip to and from the CPU. In Figure 7.23, a DSP-based plug-in is inserted between two Native plug-ins, requiring twice the number of voices.

Figure 7.23
Inserting a DSP plug-in between two Native plug-ins doubles the voice requirement.

Caution: As a general rule, avoid inserting DSP plug-ins between Native plug-ins on any kind of track—this causes unnecessary voice usage and may cause additional latency.

Furthermore, one additional voice is used for each occurrence of any of the following conditions when using voices for Native plug-ins on a track:

■ When you use an external side-chain for a Native plug-in on that track

■ When you select multiple outputs for that track (one voice used for each output)

■ When you select an AFL/PFL Path output in the Output tab of the I/O Setup dialog box (one voice used for each channel)

Mixing Native and DSP Plug-ins on an Audio Track

On a DSP-accelerated system, when Native and DSP plug-ins are combined on an audio track, the order in which they are inserted has different results:

- **Native plug-ins grouped before DSP plug-ins:** No additional voices will be used, and no processing latency will occur. This is because Native processing happens before the signal is brought into the DSP mixer. Native plug-ins will be bypassed when either Record or TrackInput monitoring is enabled for that track.

- **DSP plug-ins grouped before Native plug-ins:** Each initial insert of a Native plug-in after a DSP plug-in will cause processing latency and will use extra voices. Native plug-ins will stay active while either Record or TrackInput monitoring is enabled for that track. If Native plug-ins are stacked after each other, no additional voices will be used.

When combining Native and DSP plug-ins on an audio track, choose one of the following two strategies based on your recording needs:

- To ensure that Native plug-ins stay active when you record-enable a track or use TrackInput monitoring, group all DSP plug-ins before Native plug-ins.

- To conserve voices and minimize processing latency, group all Native plug-ins before DSP plug-ins.

- For best results, convert all Native plug-ins to DSP (if DSP equivalents exists) while recording to reduce latency and allow for record enables.

Jitter

An entirely different subject from digital mixing is jitter. Every digital audio system requires a clock that determines when samples occur during digitization (recording) and digital-to-analog conversion (playback). For example, when working at 44.1kHz, the system's frequency clock must make sure all the samples occur exactly one 44,100th of a second apart. Any variation in the time spacing between samples is called jitter.

Recall the sampling diagram in Figure 7.1. The x-axis represents time, and you can see samples equally spaced along this axis. Now, imagine if during recording or playback the sample clock were unstable, causing some samples to occur too late or too early. This inaccuracy would deform the shape of the waveform, distorting the signal at either the recording or playback stage.

The Pro Tools HD frequency clock is derived from the crystal oscillator in either the Loop Sync Master audio interface or the Avid SYNC Peripheral, if present.

Loop Sync connections distribute the clock from the master device. Although the connections are daisy-chained (which removes the need for many clock outputs on the first device), the clock is essentially being delivered directly to each interface from the master. In some studios, you may see an alternate (third-party) clock source being distributed to the interfaces.

Review/Discussion Questions

1. Define the term "quantization error."

2. What is dynamic range? What is the theoretical dynamic range for a 24-bit signal?

3. Which Pro Tools 10 mixers use fixed-point processing? Which Pro Tools 10 mixers use floating-point processing?

4. How is the Pro Tools|HDX mixer different from Native Pro Tools mixers?

5. What is the bit depth used for data pathways on Pro Tools|HD? What is the bit depth on HDX?

6. What are some advantages of the Pro Tools|HDX mixing architecture versus Pro Tools|HD?

7. What happens to voice count when you place Native plug-ins on Aux Inputs, Instrument tracks, or Master Faders on a DSP-accelerated hardware system?

8. How many additional voices would a stereo instance of a Native EQ3 1-band plug-in require if placed on an Aux Input track with the input set to no input? How many voices would be required if the same Native EQ3 plug-in was placed as the only plug-in on a stereo audio track?

Lesson 7 Keyboard Shortcuts

Shortcut	Description
Select the track nameplate and press Option+Shift+D (Mac)/ Select the track nameplate and press Alt+Shift+D (Windows)	Duplicate tracks
Command+Option+M (Mac)/Ctrl+Alt+M (Windows)	Narrow Mix window
Command+move control (Mac)/Ctrl+move control (Windows)	Fine control adjust
Control+Command+Down Arrow (Mac)/ Ctrl+Start+Down Arrow (Windows)	Zoom Edit window tracks to full-screen size

Mixer Experiments

This exercise allows you to experiment with 32-bit float files, the 64-bit Pro Tools mixer, and the different dithering options for Pro Tools.

Media Used:

31OP Exercise 7.ptxt (Pro Tools session file)

Duration:

30–45 minutes

GOALS

- Understand gain staging in the HD mixer
- Identify how pan depth settings affect mix levels
- Explore the advantages of 32-bit float files over fixed-bit depth files
- Explore DSP usage in the HD mixer
- Understand dither
- Identify how Native and DSP plug-ins affect voice usage

Getting Started

This exercise contains mixing scenarios to demonstrate headroom availability in the Pro Tools mixer, DSP use with mixers, dithering options, and how the use of Native plug-ins affects voice count. We'll start by exploring how pan laws and gain staging affect clipping in Pro Tools and what steps you can take to prevent the clips. We'll then move on to explore how different mixer configurations affect DSP usage. We'll also review dithering options for Pro Tools and how dither affects sound. We'll end the exercise by examining how Native plug-ins affect voice count when used on Aux Input tracks, Instrument tracks, or Master Faders, as well as ramifications when mixing Native and DSP plug-ins on the same track.

Caution: Before starting this exercise, if you are using previous-generation Pro Tools|HD DSP-accelerated hardware, you must switch the playback engine from HD TDM to an alternate Native playback engine option that you are able to monitor sound through.

To open the 310P Exercise 7 session:

1. Open the **310P EXERCISE 07.PTXT** session file, located on the book's DVD (or other location specified by the course instructor).

2. In the **SAVE NEW SESSION AS** dialog box, name the session as desired, saving into an appropriate location on a valid storage drive.

The session includes several tracks and a signal generator to demonstrate clipping and mixing headroom in Pro Tools.

Gain Staging and Mixing

To demonstrate the tremendous amount of headroom in the Pro Tools mixer, we will be using the Signal Generator plug-in on a single Aux Input track that in turn will feed other Aux Input tracks to simulate a full mix. In Figure 7.24, you'll notice the Signal Generator plug-in is located on a source Aux Input track (called Sine), which in turn is feeding another mono Aux Input track (Aux 1) through an internal mix bus (Bus 1). The second Aux Input track is feeding a stereo Aux Input Submaster via a stereo internal mix bus (Sub Mix).

Pan Depths

We'll start by reviewing the effect of different Pan Depth settings in the Session Setup window. Understanding the Pan Depth setting is critical when re-creating an exact mix in a different studio or when opening older Pro Tools sessions created on different Pro Tools hardware.

Figure 7.24
Signal Generator used as signal source for mixing example.

Caution: Before opening the session, mute your main monitors. During this exercise, use caution when unmuting your monitoring system to hear examples or detect minute clip points. This exercise uses full code audio (extremely loud) for demonstration purposes.

To see the effect of different pan laws:

1. Make sure that PRE-FADER METERING is disabled in the OPTIONS menu.

2. Check that your monitoring system is muted before beginning. Unmute your Signal Generator plug-in. Notice that the first two Aux Input Submasters are identical in signal level, but the Aux Submaster is lower by –3.0dB as shown in Figure 7.25. This is due to the default Pan Depth setting. Move the pan on the Aux 1 track fully left and right and see how the signal is affected. Return the pan pot to 0 or center when done. You can quickly reset the parameter by OPTION-CLICKING (Mac) or ALT-CLICKING (Windows) on the PAN knob.

Figure 7.25
Pan Depth effect on sources panned center.

3. To change the pan depth, open the Session Setup window by choosing
   Setup > Session or by pressing **Command+ 2** (Mac) or **Ctrl+2**
   (Windows) on the numeric keypad. Change the **Pan Depth** setting to
   -2.5. Notice that the level on the Submaster track rises correspondingly
   (when the Aux Input track feeding it is panned center). See Figure 7.26.

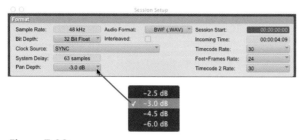

Figure 7.26
Changing the Pan Depth setting in Session Setup.

Peak Level Indication

During this exercise, it will be useful to switch the track indicator at the bottom of the track into peak level mode (pk level). This is done by Command-clicking (Mac) or Ctrl-clicking (Windows) until the indicator says "pk x.xx." If you wish to change all tracks to peak level indication, use Option+Command-click (Mac) or Ctrl+Alt-click (Windows).

In this mode, the numeric indicator is on infinite hold. If you wish to reset an individual indicator, simply click it with the mouse. To reset all tracks in pk level mode, use Option-click (Mac) or Alt-click (Windows).

---

4. Return the **PAN DEPTH** to **–3.0** and close the Session Setup window and the Signal Generator plug-in window.

Gain Staging

When mixing many signals together, it's important to monitor your gain staging. However, the Pro Tools mixer affords tremendous amounts of headroom. With large amounts of headroom, it becomes difficult to clip the input of a mixer, but it remains easy to clip the output. You can resolve the audio clipping in one of three ways:

■ Reduce the gain on the source tracks.

■ Reduce the output gain of the Submaster track.

■ Place a Master Fader inline and assign it to the bus feeding the Submaster track.

Caution: When using the Pro Tools 64-bit mixer, although unlikely, it is theoretically possible to clip the output of a bus and not be able to correct the problem by turning down an Auxiliary Submaster controlling the bus. It is therefore recommended to use a Master Fader inline to scale down the input to the bus in order to correct or recover the clipped signal.

The first solution is simple and a good rule of thumb, but in complex mixes it may become time consuming to change the gain on the source track and rebalance the mix. To complicate matters, the signal reaching the Submaster may be hitting a plug-in source first before going to the output. Changing the source track may affect the sound. In these cases, it may be more appropriate to reduce the input signal feeding the Submaster by placing a Master Fader track inline to reduce the volume.

To see how much headroom the mixer has:

1. Start by selecting the **AUX 1** track and duplicating it once by doing one of the following:

   - Selecting the track nameplate and choosing **TRACK > DUPLICATE**

   - Right-clicking the track name and choosing **DUPLICATE** (see Figure 7.27)

   - Selecting the track nameplate and pressing **OPTION+SHIFT+D** (Mac) or **ALT+SHIFT+D** (Windows)

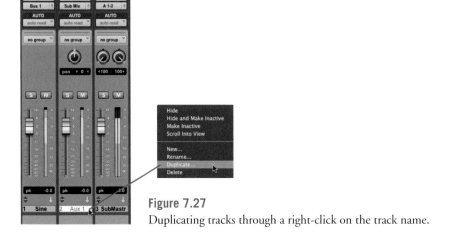

Figure 7.27
Duplicating tracks through a right-click on the track name.

2. Click **OK** in the Duplicate Tracks dialog box to make a single duplicate track. Notice that the Submaster track is now clipping. (See Figure 7.28.)

Figure 7.28
Adding another full code track to the mix bus has clipped the Submaster.

3. To remove the clip, lower the Submaster track fader by –3.1dB. This will eliminate the clip, and the audio will sound fine again.

4. With the duplicated Aux Input track still selected (Aux1.dp1), choose the **DUPLICATE** command again and specify **62** duplicates this time. At this point, it may be wise to switch to narrow track view so you can see more tracks at once by pressing **COMMAND+OPTION+M** (Mac) or **CTRL+ALT+M** (Windows).

5. Zoom your window so you can see as many tracks as possible and scroll to the right until you see the Submaster Aux Input track again. Notice how the tracks are clipping the Submaster. Lower the Submaster fader until the clip is removed (about –33.1), as shown in Figure 7.29. Carefully lower the volume on your monitoring system and unmute it to hear when the Submaster fader goes from clip to no clip (usually 0.1dB will make the difference). You may need to use Fine control when moving the fader by holding down **COMMAND** (Mac) or **CTRL** (Windows) when moving the fader.

Figure 7.29
Lowering the Submaster Aux Input track to remove clipped audio.

At this point you should have 64 tracks (excluding the Sine tone source track) at full code feeding the Submaster track, and you should have had to reduce the fader by only –33.1dB.

6. With the 62 duplicate tracks you created still selected, choose the **DUPLICATE** command again and choose 8 duplicates. Pro Tools will attempt to create 496 additional Aux Input tracks. However, Pro Tools only allows 512 Aux Input tracks total in a session. A dialog box will appear, indicating that you have reached the maximum allowed by Pro Tools, and 510 Aux Input tracks will now be in the session feeding the Submaster track. (See Figure 7.30.)

One or more tracks were not duplicated because it would exceed the number of allowed tracks in the current Pro Tools configuration.

OK

Figure 7.30
Maximum number of allowed track type reached.

7. Scroll to the far right of the Mix window until you see your Submaster Aux Input track. Notice that it is clipping again. Again lower the fader until the clip disappears on the Aux Submaster's track meter. This should be about –51.2. You now have 510 tracks at full code feeding a single stereo bus, and you are still not clipping the input of the bus.

Using a Master Fader to Trim the Bus

Another method for reducing the signal enough to eliminate clipping the Sub Mix bus is to insert a Master Fader to control, or trim, the bus before reaching the Submaster Aux Input track, allowing you to leave the Submaster track at unity gain.

To control a bus with a Master Fader:

1. Start by selecting only the last Aux Input track before the Submaster track. Create a new stereo Master Fader track.

2 The Master Fader track will be inserted before the Submaster track in the Mix window and will default to controlling the Main A 1–2 Outputs. In Figure 7.31, the Mix window has been restored to normal track width for easy viewing.

Figure 7.31
Using a Master Fader to trim a bus level before reaching the Submaster Aux Input.

3. Click on the **OUTPUT PATH SELECTOR** for the Master Fader track and choose **BUS > SUB MIX** for the output. Notice that it is still clipped. Now lower the Master Fader until the clip is removed on the meter (about –51.2). Return the Submaster track to unity (0.0dB) and notice that the signal is no longer clipped as well.

32-Bit Float Files

Now that we have a simulated session, there may be a time when you bounce a file or receive a file that is recorded so close to clip it is actually clipped. If using 32-bit float files, you can eliminate the clip by using the AudioSuite Gain plug-in to reduce the level to below clip. This is possible only with 32-bit floating-point files; 24-bit fixed-point files do not offer this ability.

Caution: The Bit Depth setting in the Session Setup window should already be set to 32 Bit Float. If it is not set to 32 Bit Float, change the setting now before continuing with this exercise.

We'll start by creating a new stereo track in our session and routing to it from our Submaster track. We'll increase the gain on our Master Fader to simulate a +12dB clip and then remove it with the AudioSuite Gain plug-in.

To remove a clip in a 32-bit float file:

1. Select the Submaster track and create a new stereo audio track. Route the output of the Submaster track to Bus 5–6. Route the input of the new stereo track to Bus 5–6. Arm the track for recording. Your setup should look like Figure 7.32.

Figure 7.32

Routing a track for recording.

2. Raise the Master Fader track to **–39.2dB**. This will now be clipping your record-enabled audio track.

3. Record a five-second pass.

4. In the Session Setup window, switch the **Bit Depth** to **24 Bit** and then record another five-second record pass on the same track starting after the first (32-bit float) clip.

5. Switch to the Edit window and scroll to the bottom. Your clipped recordings should be there. Place the cursor on the track and quickly zoom to full screen size by pressing **Control+Command+Down Arrow** (Mac) or **Ctrl+Start+Down Arrow** (Windows). (See Figure 7.33.)

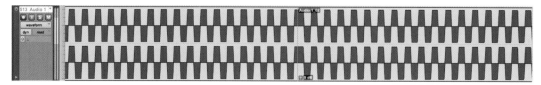

Figure 7.33
Recorded 32-bit float and 24-bit clipped files.

6. Zoom in to see the waveforms on the track. Notice how both clips are clipped, as shown in Figure 7.34.

Figure 7.34
Choose the AudioSuite Gain plug-in.

7. To attempt to remove the clipped signal on both audio clips, select both audio clips and choose **AudioSuite > Other > Gain**.

8. In the Gain plug-in window, use the slider or the **Gain Amount** field to set the gain to **–12.0dB**. Click **Render** in the AudioSuite Gain plug-in. Notice that the sine wave is returned to an unclipped state on only the first (32-bit float) clip in Figure 7.35, but the second (24-bit) clip has not had its clip removed in Figure 7.36. The ability to remove audio clips from 32-bit float files is a unique feature that is not shared by fixed-bit audio files.

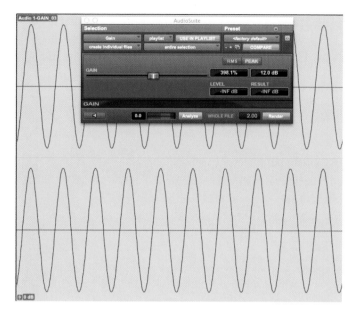

Figure 7.35
32-bit float clipping removed by
using the AudioSuite Gain plug-in.

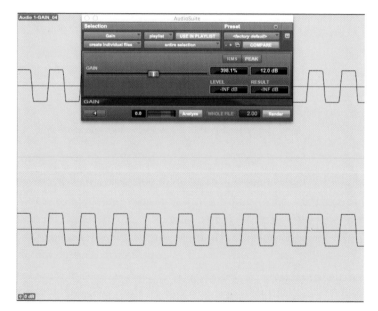

Figure 7.36
24-bit clipping can not be removed by
using the AudioSuite Gain plug-in.

Caution: Before continuing with the next section of this exercise, if you are using
previous-generation Pro Tools|HD DSP-accelerated hardware, you must
switch the playback engine of the session to **HD TDM (96 voices, 3 DSPs)**.

Understanding Mixer Creation and Use

As you build larger and larger mixes in Pro Tools, it becomes necessary to understand when new mixers are created and how to monitor resources dedicated for mixing. By understanding the process, you can craft mixers that efficiently use the available DSP in Pro Tools HD systems or understand error messages that state you have run out of DSP processing power.

As you learned previously in the lesson, stereo mixers are created when tracks are summed together into $N \times 2$ mixers. When doing a simple mix, where all tracks are routed to a single pair of outputs, monitoring use is usually not required. But when adding internal mix buses for effects, building discrete output mixes, or mixing in surround, it becomes important to create your mix wisely to utilize DSP chips efficiently.

To monitor how much DSP power is taken by a mixer:

1. If **Delay Compensation** is enabled, disable it now in the **Options** menu.

2. Delete all of the tracks from the previous portion of the exercise. Next, create 48 mono audio tracks.

3. The tracks will automatically be routed to outputs 1–2. To see how much DSP is used for 48 channels to a stereo output bus (48×2), open the System Usage window under **Window > System Usage**. Figure 7.37 shows the System Usage window using Pro Tools|HDX hardware.

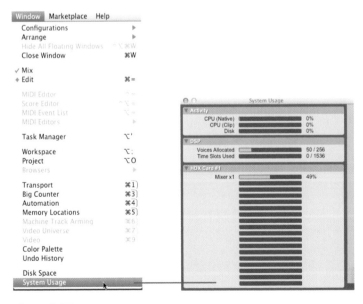

Figure 7.37
Opening the System Usage window using Pro Tools|HDX hardware.

4. Create a stereo Aux Input track and route all 48 tracks into the stereo Aux Input using the Sub Mix internal bus you created earlier in the exercise. Notice that the mixer usage may increase slightly because you have created a 48×2×2 mixer. This is a common configuration when "mixing in the box."

5. If we now split the 48 tracks into four mix output groups and route each of the groups individually to an external summing system, we will use more DSP resources. To see the difference, start by routing tracks 1–12 to Outputs 1–2. Next, route tracks 13–24 to Outputs 3–4, tracks 25–36 to Outputs 5–6, and tracks 37–48 to Outputs 7–8. We have effectively built a 48×4×4 mixer. On Pro Tools|HDX systems, you can see what mixes a DSP is servicing by hovering the mouse over the DSP gauge as shown in Figure 7.38.

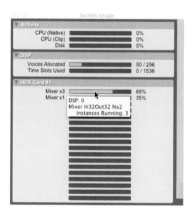

Figure 7.38
Hovering the mouse over the DSP usage gauge shows how many Nx mixers are used.

The first three sets of mixers are using the first DSP chip on the card, and the last 12 channels are using the second DSP chip of the card.

6. Create a send across each track to Outputs 9–10. Notice that the DSP Manager allocates and utilizes DSP to be as efficient as possible.

If you then switch the send to an internal mix bus, the send will utilize a different amount of DSP.

Tip: If using Pro Tools|HD hardware, it may be necessary to choose Purge Cache from within the System Usage window in order for the DSP usage meters to update after a change.

Dither

As you learned earlier, dither is used when doing bit-depth reductions. How the dither interacts with the audio is an extremely subjective matter that requires auditory experimentation. In this section of the exercise, we examine what dither looks like when amplified to audible levels and the sonic characteristics of each type of dither.

To hear dither:

1. Delete all tracks previously created in this exercise. Create a single mono Aux Input track. Be sure to show all 10 insert positions (A–J).

2. Place the POW-r Dither plug-in on insert A, a Native Maxim plug-in on insert B, and an DigiRack Dither plug-in on insert C. Bypass the Maxim and Avid Dither plug-ins as shown in Figure 7.39.

Figure 7.39
Inserting POW-r Dither, Maxim, and Dither plug-ins on a track.

3. On insert D, insert a Native **TRIM** plug-in. Set the Trim plug-in for **+12DB** mode at the top of the plug-in display and raise the gain **+12DB**. (See Figure 7.40.)

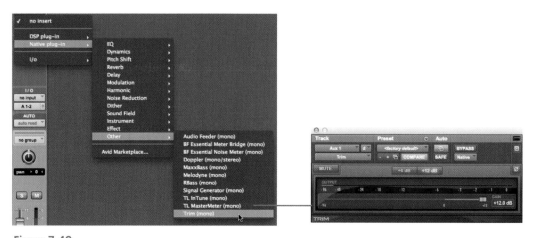

Figure 7.40
Adding a Trim plug-in on a track to boost the signal.

4. Copy the plug-in to the next four insert positions (e–h) by **OPTION-DRAGGING** (Mac) or **ALT-DRAGGING** (Windows) on the plug-in nameplate. This will amplify the dither noise, making it sound like pink noise. (See Figure 7.41.)

5. Open the POW-r Dither plug-in window and click on the **TYPE** menu. Switch between the dithering algorithms to hear the differences. Which algorithm you choose depends upon the source material being bounced. For full program mixes, Type 2 or Type 3 is recommended. (See Figure 7.42.)

Figure 7.41
Stacking Trim plug-ins on top of each other to create +60dB of gain.

Figure 7.42
Changing POW-r Dither algorithms.

6. Next, bypass the POW-r Dither plug-in and click on the **MAXIM** plug-in to open the window. Un-bypass the Maxim plug-in and enable its built-in **DITHER** option. The Maxim plug-in supports peak limiting and dithering in the same plug-in. (See Figure 7.43.)

Figure 7.43
Enabling dithering options in Maxim.

Tip: When the **Dither On** button is unlit, all dithering and noise-shaping options are deactivated. This allows you to use Maxim for peak limiting without dithering or noise shaping. It also allows you to use other dithering algorithms while peak limiting (such as POW-r Dither).

7. Next, bypass the Maxim plug-in and un-bypass the Dither plug-in. Note the difference in sonic characteristics.

This is just a simple experiment to demonstrate how different dithering options have different noise characteristics. Learning how dither interacts with program material takes time and effort beyond the scope of this course. However, if you have time, take a 24- or 32-bit mix you are very familiar with and run through all the dither algorithms as you bounce the files to a 16-bit stereo pair. Burn the results to a CD-R and listen to them in a critical listening environment to see how the different dither algorithms impart a sonic signature on your mix.

Voice Usage with Native Plug-ins and Mixed DSP/Native Plug-in Combinations

Another topic covered in the lesson was the need for voices when adding Native plug-ins to Aux Input, Instrument, and Master Fader tracks on DSP-based Pro Tools|HD and HDX systems. In this section of the exercise you will place Native plug-ins on audio tracks and Aux Input tracks while monitoring voice usage through the System Usage window. You will also combine Native and DSP-based plug-ins on the same track to see how it affects voice usage.

Native Plug-ins on Aux Input Tracks and Voice Count

To see how voices are taken when using Native plug-ins on a track:

1. Delete all tracks previously created in this exercise. Create a mono audio track, a stereo audio track, a mono Aux Input track, and a stereo Aux Input track.

2. Set the mono Aux 1 track to mono input bus 1, and the stereo Aux 2 track to stereo inputs bus 7–8, as shown in Figure 7.44.

Figure 7.44
Creating mono/stereo Audio and Aux Input tracks.

3. Open the System Usage window by choosing **WINDOW > SYSTEM USAGE**. (See Figure 7.45.)

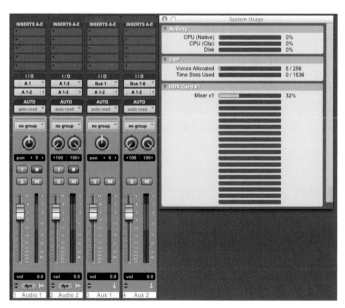

Figure 7.45
System Usage window showing the number of active voices.

Ghost Voices

Even though you only have three voices used on the audio tracks (one for the mono track and two for stereo) you may see five or more voices allocated. An extra stereo pair is used for auditioning sounds in the DigiBase browsers as well as import and fade dialog boxes when an audition path has been defined in the I/O Setup dialog box. Also, when using AFL/PFL, two additional voices will be used for the solo bus.

4. Remember that Native plug-ins on audio tracks require no additional voices. To test this, place a Native version of the EQ3 7-Band plug-in on the mono audio track. (See Figure 7.46.)

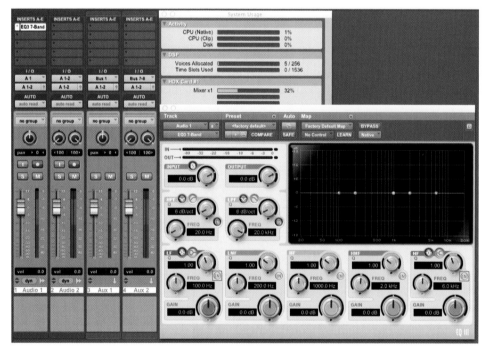

Figure 7.46
Only Native plug-ins on audio tracks require no extra voices.

5. Next, move the EQ3 7-Band plug-in to the mono Aux Input track. Notice that the voice usage increases by two voices. (See Figure 7.47.)

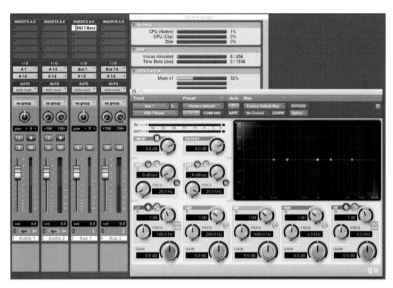

Figure 7.47
Placing a Native plug-in on a mono Aux Input requires an extra voice.

6. Next, place a Native multichannel version of the Channel Strip plug-in on the stereo Aux Input track. Notice that the voice usage increases by two voices. Adding Native plug-ins to an Aux Input track will always increase the voice count by the channel width of the track (i.e., mono = one voice, stereo = two voices, 5.1 = six voices). (See Figure 7.48.)

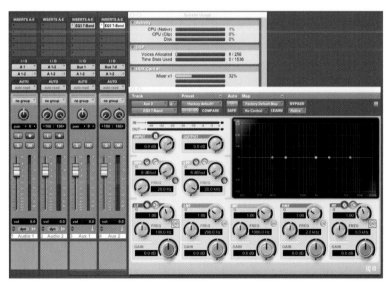

Figure 7.48
Adding a multichannel plug-in increases voice count by the channel width.

Mixing Native and DSP Plug-ins on Audio Tracks

As stated above, placing Native plug-ins on audio tracks typically does not require voices. When the audio is played back in Pro Tools, the audio is processed at the CPU before being passed to the Pro Tools mixer. In essence, the audio arrives pre-processed into the Pro Tools mixer. However, when you insert a Native plug-in after a DSP plug-in on any type of track, the signal must route back to the host, be processed, and return to the DSP mixer channel. This requires double the number of voices.

To see how voices are taken when using Native plug-ins on audio tracks:

1. Remove all plug-ins on the tracks before continuing. Now place a DSP-based version of **EQ3 1-Band** at insert A on the mono audio track. Next, place a Native Air Frequency Shifter plug-in (under Harmonic). Notice that the voice usage increases by two voices. (See Figure 7.49.)

Figure 7.49
Placing a Native plug-in after a DSP plug-in increases voice count.

2. Place a DSP-based EQ3 1-band at insert position C. Notice that the voice usage has not increased.

3. Next, add a Native Air Enhancer plug-in (under Harmonic). Notice that the voice count only increases by one. It has not increased by two because it already has a voice to return to the DSP mixer. (See Figure 7.50.)

4. Feel free to experiment with the stereo audio track to see how voices are affected there. Essentially, each time a stereo audio signal travels to the host CPU and returns to the DSP mixer, Pro Tools requires two pairs of voices (four voices total).

Figure 7.50
Inserting DSP plug-ins between Native plug-ins leads to more voice usage.

To see how voices are taken when using Native plug-ins on Aux Input tracks:

1. Remove all plug-ins from the audio tracks. Add a Native Channel Strip plug-in to the mono Aux Input track. Notice that the voice count increases by two.

2. Next add a DSP-based EQ III 1-band on insert B, followed by a Native Air Enhancer on insert C; notice that the voice count has increased.

3. Repeat the process on the stereo Aux Input track and note how many voices are required for this very simple process.

While it may not be readily apparent why voice management is necessary in 44.1/48kHz sessions, it becomes much more apparent when mixing for surround and higher sample rates. With surround mixing, multichannel Aux Input tracks require as many voices as channels for the track. For example, inserting a Native version of a 5.1 compressor on a 5.1 Aux Input Submaster will require 12 voices. If a DSP plug-in is then placed after the 5.1 compressor and followed by a Native plug-in, the Aux Input will require 24 voices to process the audio on the single track.

Lesson 8

Advanced Mixing Techniques

This lesson discusses advanced mixing and routing techniques for post production, including Pro Tools advanced automation functionality.

Media Used: 310P Exercise 08.ptxt

Duration: 75 minutes

GOALS

- Configure common Pro Tools mixing preferences and utilize delay compensation
- Use advanced mixing and submixing techniques
- Use advanced automation features

Introduction

A number of advanced signal routing and automation features focus on the way Pro Tools automation is used in real-world workflows. Many of these less well-known functions become essential as you become fluent with the process of automating your post production projects.

Common Mixing Preferences

Pro Tools provides a number of preference settings that allow you to customize the setup for your mixing environment. Some of the common preference settings that you might want to change include the Solo mode settings, the default Send level setting, and various automation preference settings.

Solo Modes

Pro Tools provides various solo modes that affect how the Solo button works. The Pro Tools 100- and 200-level books introduced Solo in Place (SIP), as well as AFL/PFL solo. When using Solo in Place (SIP), it is considered a "destructive" solo mode. In other words, when a track is soloed, the mix is changed and listeners can only monitor the track or tracks that are soloed. With Pro Tools HD hardware systems, you have two additional "non-destructive" solo modes, which pass the soloed track out a different output pair configured in the Output tab of the I/O Setup window.

The currently active solo mode is specified using the submenu under Options > Solo Mode, as shown in Figure 8.1.

Figure 8.1

Solo mode options in the Options menu.

The additional solo modes available with Pro Tools HD hardware systems are as follows:

- **After Fader Listen** (**AFL**): In this mode, the Solo button routes the track's post-fader/post-pan signal to the AFL/PFL path output. This signal will also include any insert processing on the track.

  With AFL, the level you hear is dependent on the fader level for that track. Additionally, there is a separate master level setting for AFL that affects the output of any or all tracks you solo in AFL mode. This level setting is independent of the PFL level setting.

■ **Pre-Fader Listen** (**PFL**): In this mode, the Solo button routes the track's pre-fader/pre-pan signal to the AFL/PFL path output. This signal will also include any insert processing on the track.

With PFL, the fader level and pan are ignored, and the level you hear is dependent on the audio file's recorded level. Additionally, there is a separate master level setting for PFL that affects the output of any or all tracks you solo in PFL mode. This level setting is independent of the AFL level setting.

Note: AFL and PFL Solo modes require the Surround Mixer plug-in and significantly more DSP resources.

Note: When using previous-generation Pro Tools|HD PCIe hardware only, if Mute Frees Assigned Voice is enabled, muted tracks will not be audible in AFL/PFL mode when assigned to explicit voices.

These Solo modes are considered "non-destructive" modes. When soloing a track, the mix is left as is, and the soloed signal is sent along a separate solo bus to a different output of the audio interface. The primary application for non-destructive solo is for tracking sessions. However, AFL/PFL is also useful during mixing, with the exception of surround, as the solo bus is stereo only and signals cannot be soloed in their mix pan position in AFL/PFL. Using a stereo mixing example, suppose you have orchestral music tracks submixed to a stereo Aux Input track and you are using a small amount of reverb on the violin, viola, and cello tracks. To hear the submixed orchestral music tracks, you can simply solo the Aux Input through the AFL/PFL bus. If you want to hear just the reverb, you can solo the reverb return track. Without AFL/PFL, you would need to solo safe your Aux Inputs and solo the source tracks. For the reverb, you would have to put the send into pre-fader send first, and then solo the reverb return.

Tip: When using an ICON-based mixing system, the XMON monitoring system will automatically switch over to monitor the AFL/PFL bus and mute the main outputs so you can hear your solo signal across your main monitors. If you are not using an ICON-based system, you will need to configure the outputs to mute when solo is engaged (known as AFL/PFL mutes).

Configuring AFL/PFL Operation

In order to use either of the non-destructive modes, you must configure an AFL/PFL bus to monitor the output. You configure this through the I/O Setup dialog box. AFL/PFL is useful when you want to solo tracks in the control room without affecting the cue mix going to the live room or, in broadcast situations, when you want to leave the main mix in place, but solo different sources on a different set of speakers or headphones.

To configure an AFL/PFL bus:

1. Open the I/O Setup dialog box and click on the **OUTPUT** tab.

2. Create a new stereo output path or use an existing stereo path. Name the path using a descriptive name, such as **AFL/PFL OUT,** so that the path's function is clearly identified.

3. Route the path to the physical output of the audio interface that you want to use for AFL/PFL operation. Figure 8.2 shows the stereo output path AFL/PFL Out routed to interface output 3–4 in the Output tab of the I/O Setup dialog box.

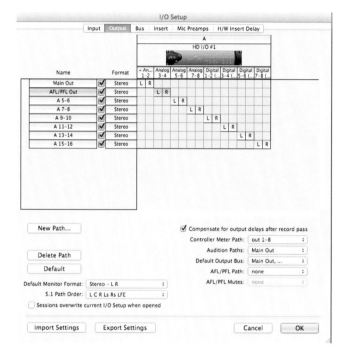

Figure 8.2
AFL/PFL path routed to interface outputs A 3–4.

4. Physically connect the chosen outputs to your monitoring system. If you're using an XMON monitoring system, this is the TB/LB/UTIL connector on the rear of the XMON.

5. Next, click on the **AFL/PFL PATH** drop-down menu at the bottom of the I/O Setup dialog box and choose the new output path you just created, as shown in Figure 8.3. This will activate the AFL/PFL bus.

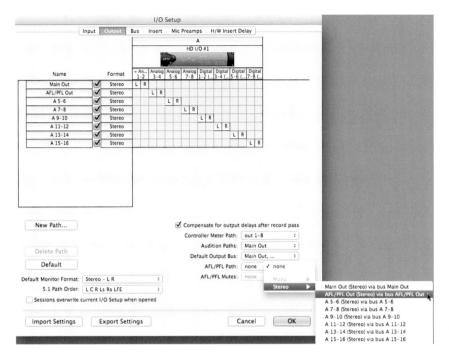

Figure 8.3
AFL/PFL Path
drop-down menu.

AFL/PFL Mutes

If you are using an XMON monitoring system with an ICON system, you do not need to configure the AFL/PFL mutes. However, if you are not using an ICON system, you may need to configure the AFL/PFL mutes to silence the main output path.

When you solo a track in AFL/PFL mode, the main mix continues to pass audio out the main outputs, while the soloed tracks are sent to the AFL/PFL output path assigned in the I/O Setup dialog box. If you do not mute the main output path, you will continue to hear the main mix, thus obscuring the AFL/PFL solos. You can manually mute the main output through your monitoring system or console, or you can have Pro Tools automatically mute the main output.

The following example demonstrates the use of AFL/PFL mutes without an ICON system. A multi-track stereo Pro Tools mix is being monitored through speakers connected to the inputs of an external mixing board using HD I/O outputs A 1–2. The AFL/PFL output path A 3–4 is also connected to the inputs of the mixing board, while the stereo mix is simultaneously being recorded to a VTR (video tape recorder) using Pro Tools multed (or duplicated) outputs A 5–6. Since the main mix output path has have been multed to an alternate set of outputs, it will be possible to solo any individual audio tracks and monitor the AFL/PFL soloed tracks on the control room speakers, while continuing to record the full mix undisturbed to the VTR.

To configure an AFL/PFL solo path using AFL/PFL mutes (without an ICON system):

1. Connect output paths of the audio interface to the external mixing board and additional devices as required. In this example, outputs A 1–4 of the HD I/O interface are connected to the external mixing board inputs, and multed outputs A 5–6 are connected to the VTR inputs as shown in Figure 8.4.

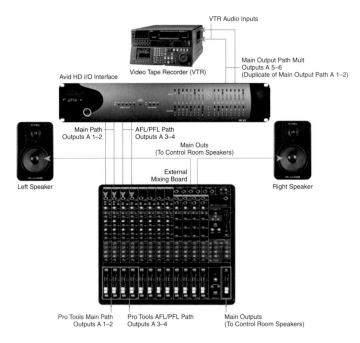

Figure 8.4
Avid HD I/O connected to an external mixing board and a VTR for using AFL/PFL mutes.

2. Choose **Setup > I/O** and in the **Output** tab of the I/O Setup dialog box, choose an AFL/PFL monitoring path, and also set the AFL/PFL mutes to the same path as your main output monitoring path. In the example in Figure 8.5, the main output monitoring path is set to outputs A 1–2, the AFL/PFL Path is set to outputs A 3–4, with the AFL/PFL Mutes set to outputs A 1–2.

Controller Meter Path: out 1–8	
Audition Paths: A 1–2	**Figure 8.5**
Default Output Bus: A 1–2, …	AFL/PFL path and AFL/PFL mutes
AFL/PFL Path: A 3–4	chosen in the I/O Setup dialog box.
AFL/PFL Mutes: A 1–2	

3. To mult the outputs of all of your Pro Tools tracks, select the tracks you wish to mult, and then hold CONTROL+OPTION+SHIFT (Mac) or START+ALT+SHIFT (Windows) while choosing the desired multed output path that you wish to remain undisturbed by the AFL/PFL solos. This example is using output path A 5–6, which is connected to the inputs of the VTR.

4. After you have configured the aforementioned options including the AFL/PFL Path and AFL/PFL Mute, choose OPTIONS > SOLO MODE > AFL or PFL. You should now be able to solo tracks using the AFL/PFL Output path during playback, without disturbing the full multed output mix (in this example, interface outputs A 5–6).

How to Change AFL/PFL Solo Bus Level

With AFL, the level you hear is dependent on the fader level for a track. However, with PFL you will be listening to the recorded level as well as any insert processing. Fortunately, there is a way to set your solo bus level for both AFL and PFL. Once you set a level in AFL mode, you can set a different level in PFL mode and vice versa (levels can be set independently for the two modes).

To change the AFL or PFL solo level in the software:

1. Select the desired solo mode (**AFL** or **PFL**).

2. Command-click (Mac) or Ctrl-click (Windows) and hold on any SOLO button on any track. A small fader will appear.

3. Adjust the level as needed using the fader control.

   To set the solo level for the other non-destructive mode, switch to that mode and repeat this process.

Note: After enabling Solo Safe in SIP solo mode (which is advisable when mixing), the solo status is retained when switching between SIP and AFL/PFL solo modes.

Advanced Delay Compensation

As you learned in the *Pro Tools 201* book, the Pro Tools software provides ADC (Automatic Delay Compensation) for managing DSP and host-based delays from plug-in inserts, and mixer routing (busing and sends). With Delay Compensation enabled, Pro Tools maintains phase coherent time alignment between tracks that have plug-ins with differing delays, tracks with different mixing paths, tracks that are split off and recombined within the mixer, and tracks with hardware inserts.

This section will cover advanced delay compensation techniques that will allow you to correct for delays that occur when integrating Pro Tools with external hardware devices.

Delay Compensation and Hardware Inserts

Hardware inserts are compensated for in two ways:

- Latency caused by going out and returning via your Avid audio interfaces is compensated for automatically.

- As shown in Figure 8.6, the user can enter the latency value incurred by other devices in the audio signal path (typically digital effects devices) into the I/O Setup dialog box.

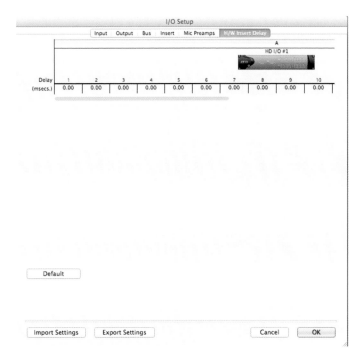

Figure 8.6
I/O Setup: H/W (Hardware) Insert Delay page.

Measuring Hardware Insert Latency

To determine the latency of outboard devices, you can consult the device's documentation. However, if this information is not available, you can measure the latency yourself.

In order to do this, you need to play an audio signal out through an HD audio interface and then record the returning audio signal back into the system. You can then measure the delay in the Edit window.

To measure hardware insert latency:

1. Set the DELAY COMPENSATION ENGINE to SHORT, LONG, or MAXIMUM in the Playback Engine dialog box.

2. Verify that Automatic Delay Compensation is enabled by choosing OPTIONS > DELAY COMPENSATION.

3. Change your session's MAIN TIME SCALE to SAMPLES.

4. Create two audio tracks (for this example the two audio tracks will be referred to as Audio 1 and Audio 2).

5. On the Audio 1 track, place an I/O (hardware) insert using an available audio interface path.

6. Route the tracks as follows:

   • Route the I/O insert on Audio 1 through the corresponding audio interface output connected to the device's inputs.

   • Connect the device's output to the corresponding audio interface input and route it to the input of Audio 2.

7. Choose SETUP > I/O, and the enable COMPENSATE FOR INPUT DELAYS AFTER RECORD PASS (in the INPUT tab) and also enable COMPENSATE FOR OUTPUT DELAYS AFTER RECORD PASS (in the OUTPUT tab).

8. Use the Signal Generator AudioSuite plug-in to place a short tone on Audio 1.

9. Record-enable Audio 2 and then record the I/O insert signal returning onto Audio 2.

Note: Calculating hardware insert delay in this manner is only useful when using gain-based processing (such as EQ or compression). If using a multi-effects processor, be sure to disable any pre-delay or other time-based processing.

10. Zoom in very close so you can see the start of the two sections of tone. In order to determine the exact delay amount, use the Selector tool to select the gap between a zero crossing on the original waveform, and the corresponding zero crossing on the recorded waveform, and then read the Edit Selection Length field.

Tip: To ensure that your offset length measurement is accurate, you might want to measure the gap between zero crossing points in more than one location.

After you have determined the exact hardware insert delay offset in samples, you will need to do one simple mathematical calculation to determine the correct H/W Insert Delay compensation setting in milliseconds.

11. Divide the sample offset number by your session's sample rate (in kHz), and then enter the result into the corresponding field of the H/W Insert Delay tab of the I/O Setup dialog box.

The example in Figure 8.7 has a 12 sample offset number and a session sample rate of 48kHz:

12 samples / 48kHz = 0.25 milliseconds (ms)

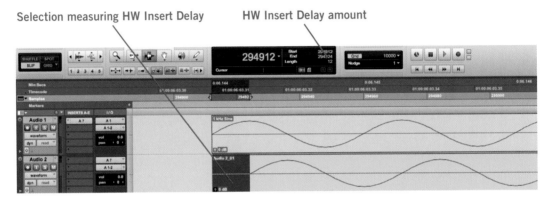

Figure 8.7
Measuring Hardware Insert Latency in the Edit window.

12. In the I/O Setup dialog box, enter the sample delay in milliseconds into the appropriate **H/W Insert Delay** field.

Compensation for Input/Output Delays After Record Pass (Pro Tools HD Hardware Systems Only)

All audio that passes in or out of any audio interface has a small amount of sample delay, which varies depending upon the type of connection being used (such as analog or AES/EBU) and the actual interface. When these varying sample delays occur, it will cause a phase offset that can be audible. To correct these offsets, Pro Tools HD systems have a delay compensation setting that can be separately enabled/disabled on both input and output in I/O Setup dialog box.

Compensation for Input Delays After Record Pass

This feature (which can be enabled/disabled in the Input tab of the I/O Setup dialog box, shown in Figure 8.8) provides automatic compensation for any analog or digital input delay. This option should be enabled in order to maintain phase coherence and correct for sample delays that occur while audio is passing through the analog and digital input connectors of your HD-series audio interface.

Although this option can be enabled for post overdub recording situations (such as ADR or Foley recording), it is probably not necessary, since the ADR talent or Foley artist will automatically adjust their performance to compensate for monitoring delays on both input and output.

☑ Compensate for input delays after record pass

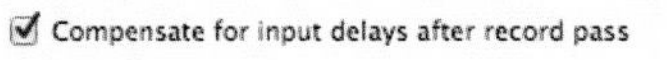

Figure 8.8
I/O Setup dialog box showing the Compensate for Input Delays After Record Pass option.

Note: When recording from a digital source, both the Compensate for Input Delays After Record Pass and the Compensate for Output Delays After Record Pass options should be enabled, since making multiple digital generational copies would continue to offset the audio by the delay of the HD-series audio interface digital I/O, further increasing the amount of samples offset with each successive digital copy.

Compensation for Output Delays After Record Pass

This feature (which can be enabled/disabled in the Output tab of the I/O Setup dialog box shown in Figure 8.9) provides automatic compensation for any analog or digital output delay. Although this option can be enabled for post-overdub recording situations (such as ADR or Foley recording), it is probably not necessary, since the ADR talent or Foley artist will automatically adjust their performance to compensate for monitoring delays on both input and output.

☑ Compensate for output delays after record pass

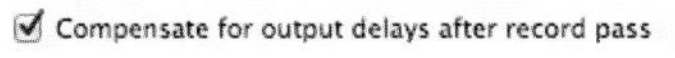

Figure 8.9
I/O Setup dialog box showing the Compensate for Output Delays After Record Pass option.

Delay Compensation and Recording

When a track is record-enabled, delay compensation is suspended for that track in order to allow a latency-free monitoring path. However, other tracks are still compensated, so with large delays, there could be timing issues between what is being recorded and the existing material. For example, when using the maximum amount of delay compensation with Pro Tools|HDX hardware (16,383 samples), you can have delays up to 371ms at 44.1kHz (or 341ms at 48kHz). Therefore, it may be best to disable delay compensation when recording.

Tip: MIDI tracks do not have latency issues, as they are automatically shifted earlier in time after recording to correct any delay.

Mix Bus Techniques

When working with large post production sessions that contain high track counts, working with groups, sub-groups, and VCA masters can greatly simplify the process of mixing so many tracks. In this section of the lesson, you will learn some useful techniques for routing and combining audio signals in the Pro Tools mixer.

Audio Sub-groups Versus Mix/Edit Groups

Most traditional large-format mixing consoles use the word "group" in a different sense than that used in Pro Tools. Mix groups in Pro Tools are more akin to what some consoles would call a "gang," with several faders' relative positions being tied together. Traditionally groups on a large-format mixing console are entirely separate mix buses. On consoles with groups, each input channel on the desk can be routed either to a group or to the main mix bus. The groups buses can then be output directly from the desk, or added into the main mix bus.

The Pro Tools 200-level courses cover the idea of using Aux Input tracks and VCA Masters to control submixes. This is exactly the same concept as an audio sub-group.

Stem Mixing Recap

As discussed in the *PT 210P Post Production Techniques* book, stem mixing is a working method where elements from your mix are grouped together into a smaller number of submixes, or stems. Each of these stems is like a mini mix of its own, with the main mix being a mix of the stems. There are a number of advantages to working like this:

- Large mixes are simplified and broken down into more manageable chunks.

- Decisions about balances between dialogue, sound effects, ADR, Foley, and music can be left until the end of the project, since it is easy to change these.

- Effects can be applied to sections of the mix as groups. For example, you can apply compression to all of the dialogue tracks, instead of individual tracks. This can really help a mix "gel" together.

- All the stems can be recorded separately. This makes it easy to re-balance the mix at a later time, even on different equipment.

- With stems, it is easy to record different variations of the mix. Typically delivery requirements include separate stem mixes of dialogue, music, and sound effects (called DM&E mixes), making it easy to export post production projects to international markets for re-dubbing of dialogue in the country's native language. With stems, you can easily set up these mixes.

Master Faders Versus VCA Masters

In the previous lesson, you learned that Pro Tools software (excluding legacy Pro Tools|HD systems) uses 64-bit floating point summing to provide extensive headroom when mixing signals, and to allow for large gain changes to any channel without a loss of resolution. You also learned that Master Faders scale the levels of buses and outputs. So, how are these concepts used in a real mix?

When to Use Master Faders

In Pro Tools, although internal buses are 64-bit floating point at the summing point and 32-bit floating after and between inserts, any audio path to an interface output represents a return to 24-bit fixed point. When you are using stem mixing, you need to be aware that any of your submixes could be clipped when sent to a bus, resulting in a clipped signal at the input of the Aux Input channel. Pulling down the fader on the Aux Input will only result in a quieter (but still clipped) signal. With the new design of the Pro Tools mixer (used by all Pro Tools systems with the exception of HD TDM), the potential to clip the input to a bus is greatly reduced, making this much less of an issue for Pro Tools|HDX, Pro Tools|HD Native, and host-based systems when compared to legacy Pro Tools|HD systems.

How to Determine When a Submix Is Clipping

You will be able to see if any of your submix stems are clipping if you use a Master Fader. The Master Fader's track meters will give you a true reading of the input level of the Aux submix channel. Also, be aware that plug-in clip indicator lights are for plug-in outputs only. This means that if there are any plug-ins on an Aux Input track, the top plug-in will be the point at which the signal arrives, but it will not light red to indicate clipping on the input bus. Instead, a plug-in's clip indicator measures clipping on output only. In addition, an Aux track's metering will only show post insert metering, so often a clipped bus routing to the Aux track will not be apparent in the Aux Input's track meter. Therefore, the only way to determine if the input bus of an Aux Input track is clipping is by the use of a Master Fader.

Tip: As an alternative to viewing a Master Fader track in order to check for clipping, you can instead click the Maximize button in an audio track's Output window to view an additional output display that shows the overall sum level of all tracks in the session that are routed to the corresponding output path. This is the same metering as on the Master Fader and is very useful if you do not need to scale the audio levels.

Master Faders as Bus Trims

If you determine that a submix is clipping, a Master Fader can be assigned to the bus, and used to attenuate its input. You can think of a Master Fader as an input trim control for the Aux submix channel that it's assigned to control, ensuring that an optimal signal enters the bus and is passed on to the Aux Input track. Figure 8.10 is using two separate stereo Master Faders called FX Bus and Main Out as input trim controls for their respective path assignments.

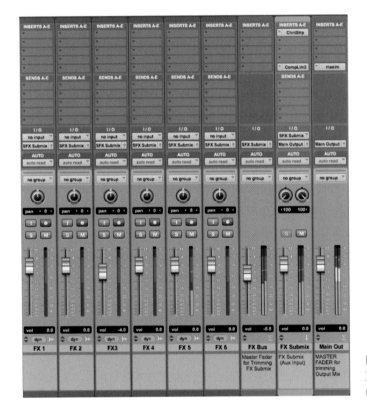

Figure 8.10
FX Bus Master Fader reducing signal level to avoid clipping on the SFX Submix bus.

Should You Use Master Faders for Every Bus?

Should a Master Fader or VCA Master be used on every submix? In real-world scenarios, a balance is generally found between practicality and the optimal mixing path. Using Master Faders on all summing points (including reverb sends), or grouping and managing every last section of your mix with VCA Masters would be excessive and unnecessarily complex. A better practice is to record with plenty of headroom and use modest submix levels. You can then make up the desired gain amount at the final mix bus, and use a Master Fader to optimize at this stage. If you notice that a bus is clipping earlier in the signal path, use a VCA Master or Master Fader as necessary.

Using VCA Masters to Adjust Source Tracks

Reducing the levels of tracks that are being summed to a bus has exactly the same result as trimming the bus with a Master Fader (unless the source faders fall below –90dBFS). You can therefore also deal with clipping submixes by attenuating all of the faders on the tracks feeding the bus. If the source tracks are grouped, a VCA Master Fader makes this job much easier, especially when the tracks are automated. You will explore the relationship between VCA Masters and automation in the next section.

VCA Master Automation

The *PT 201: Pro Tools Production II* book describes how VCA Master Faders can be used to control all members of a mix group. You saw a situation where this can be useful in the previous section. In this section, you will learn about the relationship between VCA Masters and automation.

VCA Composite Volume Graphs

Figure 8.11 shows a group of five sound effects tracks (FX1–FX5), with a VCA Master assigned to the group. This group has been automated before the VCA Master was created. In this situation, the VCA Master provides an easy way to freely adjust the overall level of the group, without interfering with the automation of the tracks or committing to a Trim pass.

In Volume view, a second graph is drawn in blue that indicates the actual fader position. This is the composite result of the original volume automation and the VCA Master's volume automation, summed together.

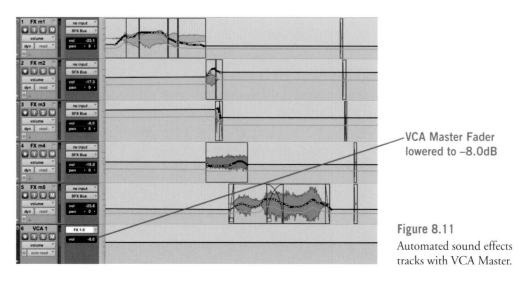

VCA Master Fader
lowered to –8.0dB

Figure 8.11
Automated sound effects tracks with VCA Master.

VCA Automation

VCA Masters can also be automated, providing an alternative (or addition) to recording Trim automation on group members. In Figure 8.12, the VCA Master has been automated to fade down the whole group during one section of the sound effects.

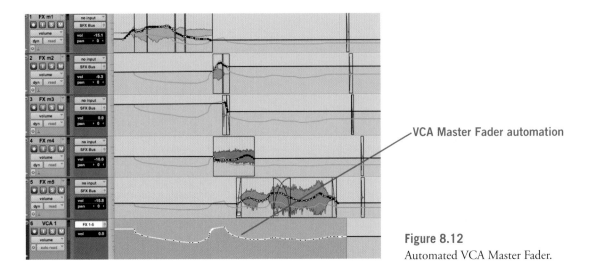

VCA Master Fader automation

Figure 8.12
Automated VCA Master Fader.

The blue composite playlist automation graphs that show the actual fader paths are no longer simply scaled (trimmed) versions of the original track automation. Instead, they are now composites of the track automation and the VCA Master automation.

Coalescing VCA Automation

After writing VCA automation, you lose the ability to make simple level adjustments with the VCA Master, because the fader is now tied to its own automation graph. Subsequent passes must be recorded to this graph, or you can use Trim mode on the VCA Master to adjust the existing automation. At this point, the final fader positions of the group members are the composite of up to four layers of automation: the original track volume, the original track's un-coalesced trim automation, the VCA Master Fader automation, and the VCA Master's Trim graph. Often it's more manageable to commit the VCA automation to the tracks. This process is called *coalescing*, in the same way as committing Trim automation is referred to as coalescing.

Note: When applying VCA Master automation to an audio track, it is not possible to obtain more than +12dB of total fader gain.

To coalesce VCA Master automation to group members, do one of the following:

■ Choose Track > Coalesce VCA Master Automation.

■ Right-click on the VCA Master's track name and choose Coalesce VCA Master Automation, as shown in Figure 8.13. Figure 8.14 shows the result.

Figure 8.13
The Coalesce VCA Master Automation command.

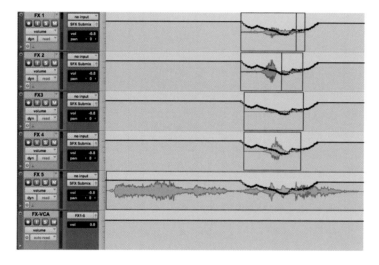

Figure 8.14
Coalesced VCA Master automation.

Coalescing writes the composite (blue) graphs to the main volume playlists on the group member tracks, and clears volume automation from the VCA Master.

Overriding VCA Master Automation on a Group Member Track

This is an advanced technique that allows you to "protect" certain tracks in a group from the effect of a VCA Master automation pass. In the previous example, the VCA Master was used to pull down the sound effects track levels (FX1–FX5) during a scene in a film project. Now, imagine that you wanted to pull down all of the sound effects tracks except FX4. Pro Tools has a special way of handling this situation. When you write automation directly to a group member, it overrides any VCA Master automation affecting the track. In other words, any automation moves that you record on a group member's fader are absolute, and will play back exactly as you recorded them. This means they are not relative to any existing VCA Master automation.

In Figure 8.15, track FX4's volume fader has been held still in Touch mode during the dip in the VCA Master's automation. The assumption is that you want the FX4 track's volume fader to remain stationary (ignoring the VCA Master's volume dip). Pro Tools achieves this by adjusting the track's main volume playlist to cancel out the effect of the VCA Master automation at this section.

This technique can be used at the same time that you write VCA Master automation, or during a subsequent pass.

Caution: While writing automation using Latch mode (especially with Latch Prime enabled) on a group member track that is under the control of a VCA Master, if a track parameter is accidentally touched or bumped, you may end up inadvertently writing or altering existing automation on the group member track, causing it to no longer follow the VCA Master's automation.

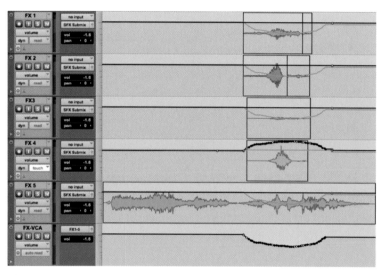

Figure 8.15
Writing automation directly to group members overrides VCA Master automation.

Latch Prime

In post production mixing, it is common to configure some parameters of the mix while playback is stopped, and then have those parameters start writing from the positions you've set. Typical examples include setting static pans for sound effects, or setting plug-in parameters that will be used for the duration of a scene. Before the Latch Prime feature was added to the software, this was only possible by switching the tracks containing those parameters into Write mode. This would mean that all enabled parameters on those tracks would start writing. Latch Prime addresses this issue by allowing you to force selected mixer parameters to begin writing from the start of playback, without switching the channel into Write mode.

Priming While Stopped

When Latch Prime is enabled, any parameters that you touch or click in Latch (or Touch/Latch for parameters other than volume) while playback is stopped are "primed" for automation recording. Any track that has primed controls inverts its automation mode indicator from red text on a white background, to white text on a red background (just as any automation mode indicator does when writing automation). When you begin playback, the parameters that you have touched or clicked will begin writing.

To enable latch priming:

1. Choose **SETUP > PREFERENCES** and then select the **MIXING** tab.

2. In the **AUTOMATION** section, enable **ALLOW LATCH PRIME IN STOP**, as shown in Figure 8.16.

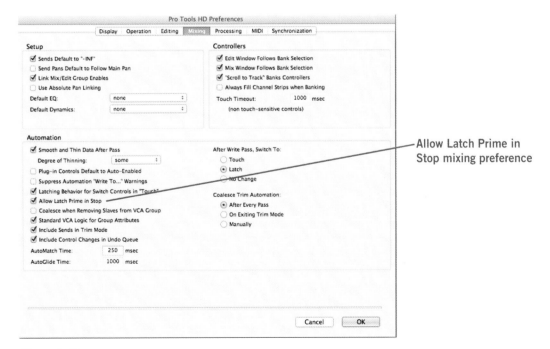

Allow Latch Prime in Stop mixing preference

Figure 8.16
Locating the Allow Latch Prime in Stop mixing preference.

Un-Priming Controls

Like AutoMatch (discussed in the *PT Pro Tools Production II* book), if you have primed controls, but want to reset them and prevent them from dropping into record when you start playback, you can take all controls, or individual tracks, out of Latch Prime.

To reset individual tracks, Command-click (Mac) or Ctrl-click (Windows) on the Automation Mode Selector on the track in either the Mix or Edit window or on an Avid worksurface.

You can reset all track controls by clicking the AutoMatch button in the Automation window, as shown in Figure 8.17.

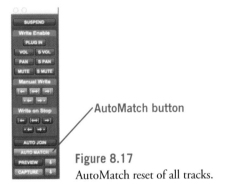

AutoMatch button

Figure 8.17
AutoMatch reset of all tracks.

Writing Static Automation Mixer Settings

In addition to writing dynamically changing automation values, there are times when you may need to write static (non-changing) automation values.

Writing Static Automation Versus Real-Time Automation

The 100- and 200-level Pro Tools books in the Avid Learning Series describe various ways to record mixer automation in Pro Tools. In many cases you will write dynamic automation, that is, recording real-time adjustments to parameters on the mixer and plug-ins. The Pro Tools 201 book covers techniques for writing static automation, using the Write to All/End/Start/Next/Punch commands in the Automation window.

These commands all write flat parameter settings over a range of time, freezing parts of the mixer in a particular configuration throughout a section of the session. This type of static automation is also sometimes referred to as *snapshot* automation, because the settings are unchanging over a specified period of time (like a camera snapshot).

Note: When referring to Pro Tools static automation as "snapshot automation" in this way, it should not be confused with the completely different and somewhat unrelated snapshot capture buffers that are supported on Avid ICON series worksurfaces.

A section of static automation can be as simple as a single plug-in bypass, or as complicated as a mixer-wide recall of levels, pans, mutes, sends, and plug-in settings.

There are many post production projects where it is appropriate to write static automation in this way, including:

■ Writing static automation data for alternating or repeating scenes.

■ Smoothing out and leveling volume changes in dialogue or narration that was recorded outdoors or in other non-controlled recording environments.

■ Matching audio levels or plug-in effects for camera angle perspective changes.

■ Copying and pasting multiple static automation graphs to tracks simultaneously, for any desired length of time (regardless of source automation length).

The Two Families of Write Commands

Before you look at some workflows, it's important to understand the distinction between the Write to Start/All/End/Punch/Next commands in the Automation window, and the Write to Current and Write to All Enabled commands in the Edit menu. Although they have similar names and purposes, they are not the same commands, and have a number of differences. See Figure 8.18.

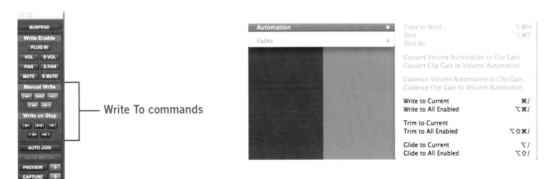

Figure 8.18
The Write commands in the Automation window (left) and the Edit > Automation commands (right).

Write to All/End/Start/Next/Punch Commands

The Write to All/End/Start/Next/Punch commands (in the Automation window) can be used during playback and stop (if using Write, Latch Prime, or Preview and Capture), writing automation to all parameters that are currently writing, or (as you'll learn shortly) parameters that are isolated in Preview mode.

To review the material from the Pro Tools 201 book:

■ **Write to All**: Writes the current settings of all currently writing mixer/plug-in parameters to the Timeline selection (or the whole session if there's no Timeline selection).

■ **Write to End**: Writes the current settings of all currently writing mixer/plug-in parameters from the current time to the end of the Timeline selection (or to the end of the session if there's no Timeline selection).

■ **Write to Start**: Writes the current settings of all currently writing mixer/plug-in parameters from the current time to the start of the Timeline selection (or to the beginning of the session if there's no Timeline selection).

■ **Write to Next**: Writes the current settings of all currently writing mixer/plug-in parameters from the current time to the next automation breakpoint on each automation playlist.

■ **Write to Punch**: Writes the current settings of all currently writing mixer/plug-in parameters from the current time back to the point where they began writing.

Write to Current and Write to All Enabled

Write to Current and Write to All Enabled (and their variants) only write to parameters on tracks containing an Edit selection, and within the current Edit selection's time range. The Write to Current and Write to All Enabled commands are considered automation playlist Edit commands, and are unaffected by track automation modes. (See the keyboard shortcuts listed in Table 8.1.)

■ **Write to Current**: Writes the setting(s) of the currently displayed automation playlist(s), within the Edit selection. This means that only one parameter can be written per track. For this reason, it is much more common to use Write to All Enabled.

■ **Write to All Enabled**: Writes the current settings of all automation parameters within the current Edit selection, except for parameter types that are not enabled in the Automation window.

Table 8.2 lists a summary of the differences between the Write commands.

Table 8.1   "Write To" Keyboard Shortcuts

Function	Keyboard Shortcut
Write to Current	Command+Forward Slash (/) (Mac) or Ctrl+Forward Slash (/) (Windows)
Write to All Enabled	Command+Option+Forward Slash (/) (Mac) or Ctrl+Alt+Forward Slash (/) (Windows)

Table 8.2   Summary of Differences Between the Write Commands

Write to All/End/Start/Next/Punch	Write to Current/All Enabled
Located in the Automation window	Located in the Edit > Automation menu
Writes to currently writing/isolated parameters	Writes to any/all automation enabled parameters
Writes within the Timeline selection on all tracks writing automation	Writes within the Edit selection, and only to tracks that contain the Edit selection
Not active if automation is suspended	Can still write when automation is suspended
Will only write to tracks in Write, Touch, Latch, and Touch-Latch mode (with or without Trim enabled)	Will write to track selections even if the track is in Off or Read mode

Workflow 1:
Using Write to All Enabled with Suspend

When working on post production mixes, using the Write to All Enabled command in combination with the Automation window Suspend command is a very powerful mixing feature, allowing you to temporarily disable all of the currently written automation graphs and then experiment with different automation parameter settings. After suspending the automation and altering the existing automation settings, you then have the option to overwrite the previous automation or cancel your changes and revert back to the original automation.

To use the Write to All command with automation Suspend:

1. Make an edit selection on the tracks containing automation that you wish to alter and disable INSERTION FOLLOWS PLAYBACK (if enabled).

2. If you are not familiar with the existing automation on the tracks, play back the existing automation and note which automation parameters will require changes.

3. In the Automation window, click the **Suspend** button to suspend all automation playback and writing (see Figure 8.19).

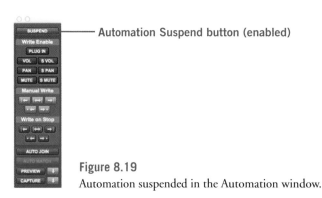 ———— Automation Suspend button (enabled)

Figure 8.19
Automation suspended in the Automation window.

4. Start playback and alter the existing automation parameters on the tracks containing the edit selection as required.

5. When you are satisfied with your new changes to the automation parameters, verify that the parameters you wish to overwrite are enabled in the Automation window.

Tip: If you wish to revert back to the existing automation without applying the new automation parameter changes to the edit selection, disable Suspend in the Automation window.

6. To apply your new changes to the Edit selection, choose **Edit > Automation > Write to All Enabled** or press **Option+Command+ Forward Slash (/)** (Mac) or **Ctrl+Alt+Forward Slash (/)** (Windows). The new automation parameter settings overwrite the previously existing automation, although this action can be undone.

Now that you understand how the Write to All Enabled command can be used with automation Suspend, the following section of this lesson describes how Preview mode can be used to apply static automation mixer settings to sections of your post production projects, and discuss which methods are appropriate in different situations.

Preview Mode

When Preview mode is activated in the Automaton window, mixer or plug-in automation plays back normally. However, in an automation write mode such as Latch, as soon as you touch any control that is write-enabled, that parameter becomes "isolated" from its automation. The parameter will not play back or write automation, and will continue to ignore its corresponding automation graph until you exit Preview mode, or invoke one of the Write or AutoMatch commands. Unlike using Suspend, which globally disables all automation in the session, Preview mode allows you to choose which automation graphs will play back, and which ones will not.

Preview mode is useful because it allows you to experiment with mixer and plug-in settings while Pro Tools plays back, without writing automation and without fighting with any automation that already exists for those parameters. Preview mode also inhibits changes to automation graphs containing no automation on write-enabled tracks. This is not the case if you simply Suspend automation, or switch the tracks to Auto Off mode. This means your previous mix can be completely recovered just by exiting Preview.

Basic Outline

The basic workflow for using Preview mode is similar in all situations:

1. Put the tracks you wish to change into Latch, Touch, or Touch/Latch mode.

2. Enable Preview mode in the Automation window (or using an Avid worksurface). See Figure 8.20.

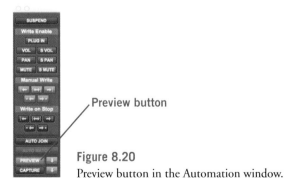

Preview button

Figure 8.20
Preview button in the Automation window.

3. During playback, configure mixer and plug-in settings without disturbing the existing mix or automation.

4. Using Punch Preview, write the new settings.

Writing Isolated Parameters

Any changes you make in Preview mode can be discarded by exiting Preview, or you can choose to write your current settings as automation in a number of different ways.

Workflow 2: Using Preview with Write to All

In this workflow, you will see an example of how to use Preview mode to disable existing automation and experiment with new mixer and plug-in settings while playing a Timeline selection. After adjusting the mixer and plug-ins controls to the proper settings during playback, the modified automation settings can then be written to the Timeline selection using the Manual Write to All command in the Automation window.

To write new static mixer settings using Preview mode and Write to All:

1. Make a Timeline selection corresponding to the area you wish to automate.

2. Put the tracks you wish to automate into **LATCH**, **TOUCH**, or **TOUCH/LATCH** mode.

3. Enable **PREVIEW** mode in the Automation window.

4. Enable **LOOP PLAYBACK**.

5. Start playback.

6. While Pro Tools plays back, adjust the necessary mixer and plug-in settings on the write-enabled tracks to get the sound you need.

   When you are satisfied with the new mixer and plug-in settings, you are ready to commit it to automation. (You can also cancel the changes you've made by disabling Preview mode.)

7. Click the **PUNCH PREVIEW** button (shown in Figure 8.21).

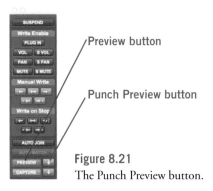
Preview button

Punch Preview button

Figure 8.21
The Punch Preview button.

8. Click the **MANUAL WRITE TO ALL** button in the Automation window.

   Every parameter that you've touched or moved since entering Preview mode will be written at its current level to the Timeline selection. If you've changed parameters on more than one track, automation will be written to the Timeline selection on all of the modified tracks.

   You can test that the procedure was successful by playing through the automated sections, and watching the mixer/plug-in parameters snap to new positions.

Figure 8.22 shows an example of using this workflow, where Channel Strip plug-in mixer settings were first auditioned in real-time using Preview, and then written to the Timeline selection using Punch Preview, followed by Manual Write to All. This allowed track volume and plug-in parameter changes to automate to match interior/exterior camera perspectives.

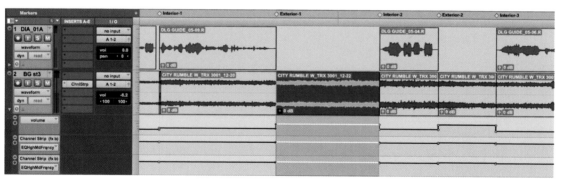

Figure 8.22
Automation graphs indicating the new mixer and plug-in settings changing for each interior/exterior perspective.

Workflow 3: Preview Using Cue Up and Punch

In Workflow 2, you found the mixer and plug-in settings you wanted during playback, and then wrote the settings to the Timeline selection using Punch Preview followed by Manual Write to All.

Instead of punching in on-the-fly and using Manual Write to All, you can use Punch Preview while the transport is stopped. Isolated parameters will begin writing when you start playback. This option is often preferable as it allows you to cue up the start point of the automation precisely. So why would you do this instead of just selecting the whole range and using one of the Write commands? This method disables Preview mode as part of the function of Latch Priming the parameters, allowing you to begin writing a basic static mix, while still allowing you to make dynamic adjustments at the same time. This works well with linear mixing tasks, such as working through a post production project riding the levels on music and sound effects tracks, while also writing static automation on several dialogue tracks at the same time.

Usage Example

A scene from a film contains several sound effects tracks with many different clips at varying levels. The clips need a lot of volume automation to fit them into the mix with the dialogue and music tracks. This requires a combination of static volume changes and dynamic volume fader rides. After playing through the session, a balance is set that works for the first part of the scene. The next section is selected, and Preview mode is activated in order to set new levels. After new levels are set, Pro Tools is cued to the start of the selection, Punch Preview is invoked, and then playback is started. The basic static mix is written during playback, and dynamic adjustments are made for the rest of the scene as needed. At each new section, the process is repeated.

To preview and then Punch Preview from a standing start:

1. Start playback.

2. Do one of the following:

   - Enable PREVIEW mode and adjust automation parameters during playback.

   - To preview-isolate all currently write-enabled controls, Option-click (Mac) or Alt-click (Windows) the PREVIEW button in the Automation window during playback.

   - To preview-isolate all currently write-enabled controls on only the selected tracks, Option+Shift-click (Mac) or Alt+Shift-click (Windows) the PREVIEW button in the Automation window during playback.

3. Stop playback.

4. Position the playback position at the point where you want to start writing the Preview settings and do one of the following:

   - To punch in on all currently isolated controls, click the PUNCH PREVIEW button in the Automation window.

   - To punch in on all currently isolated controls on only the selected tracks, Option+Shift-click (Mac) or Alt+Shift-click (Windows) the PREVIEW button in the Automation window.

   All isolated parameters on tracks in Touch, Latch, Touch/Latch, or Write mode will become primed for writing automation. Tracks in Touch will be switched to Latch, to facilitate the punch.

5. Start playback. The isolated parameters will begin writing from the playback position.

Tip: Punching Previewed mix settings in Stop is similar to using the Latch Prime in Stop feature described earlier in this lesson. Latch Prime in Stop does not need to be enabled in order for Punch Preview to work while in Stop.

Suspending Preview Mode

While in Preview mode, you can temporarily suspend Preview mode, allowing you to toggle and compare between preview values and existing automation.

To suspend Preview mode:

1. Command-click (Mac) or Control-click (Windows) the **Preview** button in the Automation window or Avid worksurface.

Preview and Trim Mode

The Preview and Punch Preview commands work with Trim automation in the same way as regular automation. Using real-time Trim mode with Preview allows you to re-balance your track levels, by first letting you to preview your new track volume offset (delta change), and then writing the new change using Punch Preview.

To use Preview with Trim mode to re-balance audio track levels:

1. In the Automation window, verify that volume is write-enabled.

2. Select the desired audio tracks and enable **Trim with Latch** mode on the selected tracks.

Tip: Although this workflow step most often uses Trim with Latch mode, Touch, Touch/Latch, and Write modes with Trim are also supported.

3. Start playback.

4. Do one of the following:

   - Enable **Preview** mode and adjust the volume automation parameters during playback.

   - To preview isolate all currently write-enabled controls, Option-click (Mac) or Alt-click (Windows) the **Preview** button in the Automation window during playback.

   - To preview isolate all currently write-enabled controls on only the selected tracks, Option+Shift-click (Mac) or Alt+Shift-click (Windows) the **Preview** button in the Automation window during playback.

5. Stop playback.

6. Position the playback position at the point where you want to start writing the Preview settings and do one of the following:

   - To punch in on all currently isolated controls, click the **PUNCH PREVIEW** button in the Automation window.

   - To punch in on all currently isolated controls on only the selected tracks, Option+Shift-click (Mac) or Alt+Shift-click (Windows) the **PUNCH PREVIEW** button in the Automation window.

   All isolated parameters on tracks in Touch, Latch, or Write mode will become primed for writing automation. Tracks in Touch will be switched to Latch, to facilitate the punch.

7. Start playback. The isolated parameters will begin writing from the new trim values you configured from the playback position. Pro Tools saves Trim status when capturing, so if you attempt to Punch Capture Trim values while displaying a non-Trim automation playlist, Pro Tools will automatically apply the values to the corresponding Trim playlist.

Capture Mode and Punch Capture

The Capture button, located in the Automation window (shown in Figure 8.23), by default operation captures the settings of any parameters that are currently writing automation, but can also be forced to capture selected or all parameters regardless of their write state. Once captured, these settings can then be written to other locations in the session using Punch Capture. When working with long format post production projects (such as film), you can save time by capturing automation from an earlier point in the project, and then applying it to similar audio at a later point in the project.

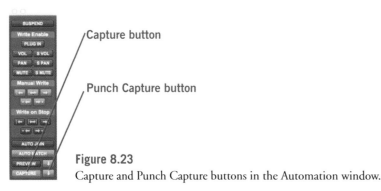

Capture button

Punch Capture button

Figure 8.23
Capture and Punch Capture buttons in the Automation window.

Tip: Capture grabs parameter settings at a single point in your session instead of continuously changing automation data over time. In other words, Capture takes a "snapshot" of the currently writing settings, Capture Selected takes a "snapshot" of only the mixer settings for the selected tracks, and Capture All takes a "snapshot" of the entire mixer, if auto-enabled.

Basic Operation

To capture settings that are currently writing, click the Capture button in the Automation window.

To capture all parameters on all tracks, regardless of whether they are writing, Option-click (Mac) or Alt-click (Windows) on the Capture button.

To capture all parameters on selected tracks, regardless of whether they are writing, Option+Shift-click (Mac) or Alt+Shift-click (Windows) on the Capture button.

To punch the captured parameters, click the Punch Capture button in the Automation window.

The following options apply to Punch Capture:

- Activating Punch Capture while the transport is stopped will activate Latch Prime in Stop mode.

- Option-click (Mac) or Alt-click (Windows) the Punch Capture button to switch any affected tracks into Latch mode (if they weren't already). If Capture All was used, this will effectively Punch All, although the Automation Enable buttons can be used to write-protect or isolate specific automation parameters.

- Option+Shift-click (Mac) or Alt+Shift-click (Windows) the Punch Capture button to punch controls on the selected tracks.

Capture/Punch Capture Workflow Examples

When using Capture/Punch Capture in a post production workflow, several Capture methods are available:

- **Capturing the actively writing parameters**: Although the basic outline for using Capture is to capture parameters that you are actively writing, this method has rather limited applications.

- **Capture all**: Taking a snapshot of the whole mixer is often useful, especially when you've finished mixing a particular scene in a film, and you want to transfer the (static) mix to a similar section of the film. This is not as heavy-handed an approach as it might seem, as there are several ways to limit how much of the snapshot is actually punched.

■ **Capturing selected tracks**: Taking a snapshot of the mixer settings for only selected tracks is often useful, especially when you've finished mixing a combination of tracks, and you want to transfer the (static) mix on those tracks to a similar section of the film. If there are specific automation parameter settings that you wish to ignore, there are several ways to limit how much of the snapshot is actually punched.

Workflow Example 1: Capturing the Actively Writing Parameters

In this workflow example, you are writing EQ parameter settings to balance a number of dialogue tracks in a scene from a film. You have decided to grab the EQ settings you've set and use them for a repeat of a similar scene later in the project.

To capture the actively writing parameters:

1. Place the dialogue tracks in Latch mode.

2. Start playback, and then adjust the EQ parameter settings during the first passage of dialogue.

3. When you find the proper settings, click the **CAPTURE** button to capture the EQ parameter settings that you want to use later (during the second passage of dialogue). The Punch Capture button lights to indicate that a captured value is ready to punch.

4. Punch the captured settings by parking Pro Tools at the beginning of the second passage of dialogue, and then clicking the **PUNCH CAPTURE** button.

   The EQ settings that you previously captured will jump to their settings from the Capture point. This will be your starting point for adjusting the EQ parameters during the second passage of dialogue. The tracks with the punched parameters will indicate that they are primed by changing their automation mode indicators to red.

5. Resume writing at the captured settings by starting playback. The EQ settings will begin to write automation at their previous levels from the first passage of dialogue. You can now adjust the EQ settings from this starting point as desired.

6. Stop playback (or if you have a Timeline selection, invoke one of the Write To commands and stop playback).

Workflow Example 2: Capture All and Write

Consider a scene for a film where a number of tracks need different plug-in settings and volume levels for simulating alternating scene locations of a very live and reverberant stairwell and a more acoustically neutral room. Levels are different,

EQ settings are different, and there is a very different reverb setting needed for the stairwell and the room. You start by setting up the mix for the room, and this becomes the default mixer setup for the whole session. Next you work on the stairwell settings, writing the different settings as automation, using the Preview and Write workflow described in this lesson.

Now you want to capture all the settings for the first stairwell scene and apply them to a later scene occurring in the same stairwell.

To capture the settings and apply them to the later scene:

1. Park Pro Tools in the first stairwell scene. The mixer will update to reflect the automation settings at this location in the session.

2. Take a snapshot of the entire mixer by Option-clicking (Mac) or Alt-clicking (Windows) on the **Capture** button.

Caution: **You can only capture the automation parameters across the entire mixer for automation parameters that are write-enabled in the Automation window.**

3. Make a Timeline selection that entirely encompasses the second stairwell scene.

4. Punch the captured mixer snapshot by clicking the **Punch Capture** button. All automation parameters in the mixer (including plug-ins) on all tracks that are in either Latch or Touch mode will jump to the captured settings and be primed.

Shortcut: **Instead of punching to all write-enabled tracks, you can punch to only the selected tracks by pressing Option+Shift+Punch (Mac) or Alt+Shift+Punch (Windows) or all tracks regardless of write-enable status by pressing Option+Punch (Mac) or Alt+Punch (Windows).**

5. Write the snapshot to the second stairwell scene by clicking the **Manual Write to All** button in the Automation window. The punched settings will be written throughout the Timeline selection.

Punch Capture and Write To Commands

As mentioned in the "Workflow Example 1 and 2" sections, after issuing a Punch Capture command, the affected controls are writing automation (in Latch mode), so any of the automation Write To commands can be used to extend the punched value in the same manner as other automation.

Capture and Trim Mode

The Capture and Punch Capture commands work with Trim automation in the same way as regular automation. Pro Tools saves Trim status when capturing, so if you attempt to punch capture Trim values while displaying a non-Trim automation playlist, Pro Tools will automatically apply the values to the corresponding Trim playlist.

Using real-time Trim mode with Capture allows you to re-balance your track levels, by first letting you to capture currently writing trim volume offset (delta change), and then writing the new trim value at a different track location using Punch Capture.

To capture Trim automation and punch in the volume trim values at a different location on audio track:

1. In the Automation window, verify that the volume is write-enabled.

2. Select the desired audio tracks and enable Trim with Latch mode on the selected tracks.

Tip: Although this workflow step most often uses Trim with Latch mode, Touch, Touch/Latch, and Write modes with Trim are also supported.

3. Start playback and begin writing new trim automation.

4. Do one of the following:

   - To capture all currently writing trim controls, click the **CAPTURE** button in the Automation window during playback.

   - To capture all currently writing trim controls on only the selected tracks, Option+Shift-click (Mac) or Alt+Shift-click (Windows) the **CAPTURE** button in the Automation window during playback.

5. Stop playback.

6. Position the playback position at the point on the track where you want to start writing the Punch Capture trim settings and do one of the following:

   - To punch in on the currently isolated trim controls, click the **PUNCH CAPTURE** button in the Automation window.

   - To punch in on the currently isolated trim controls on only the selected tracks, Option+Shift-click (Mac) or Alt+Shift-click (Windows) the **PUNCH CAPTURE** button in the Automation window.

   All isolated trim controls on tracks in Touch, Latch, or Write mode will become primed for writing automation. Tracks in Touch will be switched to Latch, to facilitate the punch.

7. Start playback.

The isolated parameters will begin writing from the new trim values you configured from the playback position. Pro Tools saves Trim status when capturing, so if you attempt to Punch Capture Trim values while displaying a non-Trim automation playlist, Pro Tools will automatically apply the values to the corresponding Trim playlist.

Capture and Preview Mode

You can preview and modify captured automation values in Preview mode before punching the values to the automation playlist.

Loading Captured Values into Preview

To capture multiple automation values and use them to preview:

1. Make sure the track where you want to preview the value is enabled for automation (Touch, Latch, or Touch/Latch).

2. Make sure the automation type you want to preview is enabled in the Automation window (Volume, Pan, Mute, Send level, Send pan, Send mute, or Plug-In).

3. Capture the automation values that you want to preview in another location on the track.

4. Go to a location where you want to preview the captured automation states, and click the Preview button in the Automation window.

5. Click the Punch Capture button. The affected controls will be isolated and updated to the captured values and the Punch Preview button in the Automation window will light to indicate the preview value is available to punch.

6. Start playback and adjust the isolated control to audition the changes.

7. When you are ready to punch the preview value to the automation playlist, click the lit Punch Preview button.

Capturing Values While in Preview Mode

When you are in Preview mode, you can capture the values of isolated controls and apply them elsewhere on a track. By capturing Preview values this way, the Preview values can be stored and then recalled at a later point regardless of whether the Preview values were subsequently changed after this capture, effectively allowing three states of automation to be active at one time, the underlying automation, the previewing automation, and the automation previously captured from Preview.

To capture a preview value:

1. Activate PREVIEW mode and isolate a control.

2. Start playback and adjust the isolated control to audition the changes.

3. When you are ready to capture the previewed value, click the CAPTURE button in the Automation window. The Punch Capture button in the Automation window will light to indicate a captured value is available to punch.

AutoJoin Mode

Latch mode is arguably one of the most commonly used automation modes in post production, and it makes it possible to have several faders writing at once, without needing to keep them held in position. One problem, however, is that if playback is stopped in the middle of a pass, you will be left with sudden jumps in the automation graphs. The Join and AutoJoin functions address this situation.

Tip: Instead of using AutoJoin, you can also use Write Automation to Next Breakpoint on Stop in the Automation window.

Join

The solution to the situation described above is to drop all the parameters that were previously writing back into writing during the next automation pass, before the point where playback was stopped. This could be achieved manually by touching the appropriate faders during the next pass to start them writing again. However, this can be a complex situation to manage manually. The Join command immediately drops all the parameters that were writing automation in the previous pass back into automation writing.

Note: The Join command can only be accessed when using an Avid-compatible worksurface. For more information about using the Join command using an Avid worksurface, consult the corresponding worksurface guide.

AutoJoin

AutoJoin automates the process of resuming automation writing from one pass to the next. With AutoJoin enabled, Pro Tools will remember where playback was stopped and which faders were writing in Latch mode. With that information, if the engineer stops to go back and check or redo part of an automation pass, Pro Tools will resume writing automation for all previously writing controls at the precise position that the previous pass was stopped.

When playback is stopped, a red line will appear to show where the AutoJoin will take place, as shown in Figure 8.24.

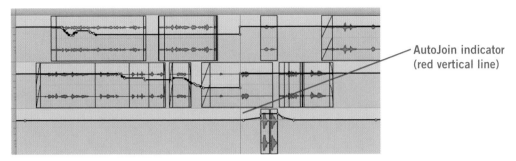

AutoJoin indicator
(red vertical line)

Figure 8.24
A red line indicates where writing in Latch mode was last stopped.

Activating AutoJoin Mode

In the absence of an Avid worksurface, AutoJoin mode can also be enabled in the Automation window, by clicking the AutoJoin button, as shown in Figure 8.25.

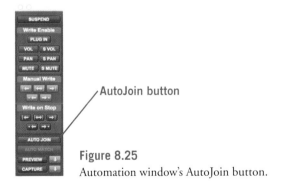

AutoJoin button

Figure 8.25
Automation window's AutoJoin button.

Using AutoJoin

Example of AutoJoin workflow:

1. Enable **AUTOJOIN** from the Automation window or supported Avid work-surface.

2. Start an automation pass with several faders writing in Latch mode.

3. Stop playback and locate the playback cursor to an earlier point. A red line will appear to show where playback was stopped.

4. Start playback.

5. Touch one of the faders to rewrite automation data. The other faders will drop into Latch record when you reach the point where playback was previously stopped.

Caution: When writing automation using AutoJoin, if you decide to abort an automation pass, do not stop playback until passing the red line. Otherwise, subsequent automation passes will not resume writing of the desired parameters. Instead, automation will resume writing using the last written parameters from the aborted pass.

Miscellaneous Automation Techniques

In addition to the advanced automation techniques you have learned in this lesson, some additional automation mute and glide techniques are available.

Resuming Recording of Mute Automation

When working with mute automation, you may have the need to extend previously created mute automation to match a new picture cut. In the following example, the BG-FX1 track contains two separate sections of mute automation, as shown in Figure 8.26.

Figure 8.26
BG-FX1 mute automation graph.

After receiving a new picture cut, you may find that you need to extend the time where the first mute is active on the BG-FX1 track, as shown in Figure 8.27.

Figure 8.27
BG-FX1 extended mute automation graph.

Without editing the mute graph, this would be difficult to overwrite using real-time automation, because each time that you click the Mute button, it toggles to the opposite state.

However, by holding a modifier key, you can extend the mute automation in its present state, instead of toggling it. This will work in Touch, Latch, and Touch/Latch modes.

To extend (or overwrite) mute automation:

1. Make sure that MUTE automation is write-enabled in the Automation window.

2. Switch to TOUCH, LATCH, or TOUCH/LATCH mode on the tracks you want to update.

3. Begin playback before the point containing the mute automation you want to extend.

4. Command-click (Mac) or Ctrl-click (Windows) on a MUTE button. The Mute button will not change its state, but instead will begin to write its current state to the automation graph.

Note: In Write, Latch, and Touch/Latch modes, the mute automation will continue to be written until you stop playback. In Touch mode, you will need to keep the button or mouse held down to keep overwriting and replacing changes in mute state.

Extending Automation

Sometimes you need to extend an existing area of static automation later in time. Consider the following example: You have faded a track's volume all the way down during an automation pass, and then stopped playback before you reached the end of the audio. See Figure 8.28.

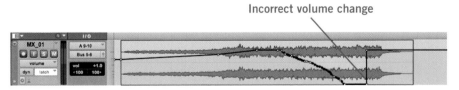

Figure 8.28
Audio clip with incorrect volume automation.

There are a number of ways to resolve this issue, but two quick and precise ways are to use either the Edit > Automation > Write to All Enabled Parameters or the Edit > Automation > Write to Current commands (covered earlier in this lesson).

To extend all automation later in time:

1. Use the **SELECTOR** tool to select from a point near the end of your pass up to the point you want to extend the automation parameter to, as shown in Figure 8.29.

Selection for extended automation

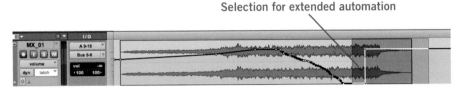

Figure 8.29
Audio clip area selected for extending volume automation.

2. Choose **EDIT > AUTOMATION > WRITE TO ALL ENABLED,** or press **OPTION+ COMMAND+FORWARD SLASH (/)** (Mac) or **ALT+CTRL+FORWARD SLASH (/)** (Windows). Figure 8.30 shows the corrected volume automation.

Caution: Using Edit > Automation > Write to All Enabled will write the current automation values to all enabled automation graphs in the selection, which could overwrite and replace existing automation that you wish to keep.

Corrected automation

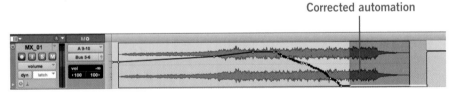

Figure 8.30
Audio clip with corrected volume automation.

This works because automation parks at the beginning of the selection, so these settings are written throughout the selection when you choose the Write To command.

Choosing Which Parameters Are Written

As an alternative to the preceding workflow, provided the Allow Latch Prime in Stop mixing preference is enabled and you are using an Avid worksurface, you can also use the Write to All command to choose exactly which parameters are extended. In the above example, only the volume automation needed to be extended.

To extend select automation parameters later in time:

1. Use the SELECTOR tool to select from a point near the end of your pass up to the point you want to extend the automation parameter to.

2. Touch the parameters that you want to write (in the example, this would just be the volume fader).

3. Choose WRITE TO ALL in the Automation window or on an Avid work-surface.

Glide Automation

The Glide automation commands let you manually create an automation transition (or glide) from an existing automation value to a new one, over a selected area. This is useful in post production projects, since it allows controls to smoothly glide (or morph) from one setting to the next, providing smoother and more precise transitions between automated controls (such as plug-ins or volume faders).

To apply Glide automation to the current automation parameter type:

1. In the Automation window, make sure the automation type is write-enabled.

2. Using the TRACK VIEW SELECTOR, choose the graph you want to automate.

3. With the SELECTOR tool, select the source tracks and area you want to write the Glide automation to.

4. If there is no automation on the track, verify that the track automation is at the correct starting point, and then choose EDIT > AUTOMATION > WRITE TO ALL ENABLED. If there is already automation on the track, this step can be skipped.

5. Change the automation parameter to the desired value at the end of the selection. For example, to glide the volume from Unity Gain (0.0 dB) to –Infinity, move the VOLUME fader to –INFINITY.

6. Do one of the following:

   - Choose EDIT > AUTOMATION > GLIDE TO CURRENT.

   - Press OPTION+FORWARD SLASH (/) (Mac) or ALT+FORWARD SLASH (/) (Windows).

To apply Glide automation to all current enabled automation parameters:

1. In the Automation window, make sure the automation type is write-enabled.

2. In each track that you want to automate, click the TRACK VIEW SELECTOR and choose the automation type you want to automate.

3. With the **Selector** tool, select the source tracks and area you want to write the Glide automation to.

4. If there is no automation on the track, verify that the track automation is at the correct starting point, and then choose **Edit > Automation > Write to All Enabled**. If there is already automation on the track, this step can be skipped.

5. In each track that you want to automate, change the automation parameter to the desired value at the end of the selection.

6. Do one of the following:

   - Choose **Edit > Automation > Glide to All Enabled**.

   - Press **Option+Shift+Forward Slash (/)** (Mac) or **Alt+Shift+Forward Slash (/)** (Windows).

Figure 8.31 shows an example of an EQ plug-in with the starting EQ parameters before the glide command, and the ending parameters after the glide command.

New glide automation

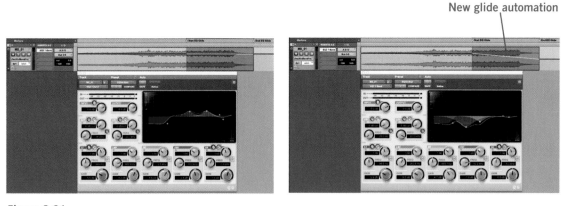

Figure 8.31
Track selection with 7-band EQ3 starting glide value (left) and ending glide value (right).

Glide Automation Considerations

When Glide automation is applied to automation data, it behaves as follows:

■ When a selection is made, the automation value at the start of the selection is the start point of the Glide automation and the end of the selection is the end point of the Glide automation. The Glide automation that is created between the two is based on the length of the selection and the end value that is selected.

- If a selection is made and automation data exists before the start of the selection, automation breakpoints are written at the start and end points of the Glide automation.

- If automation breakpoints follow the selection, they are not changed, but the value selected for the end of the selection is written from the end point up until the next breakpoint.

- If no automation breakpoints follow the selection, the value selected for the end of the selection is written to the end of the track.

- If no selection is made, a breakpoint is written to the current location, and the value selected for the Glide automation is written to the next breakpoint.

Tip: As an alternative to using the Edit > Automation > Glide commands, you can create static "snapshots" of your preferred starting and ending settings, then use the Edit > Cut Special automation commands to smooth the transitions.

Trim Automation

Pro Tools lets you use trim automation values as snapshots and apply the relative changes (delta values) to the selected automation by using the Trim Automation command. This works in much the same way as the Write Automation command, except that it writes delta values instead of absolute values to automation data.

You can use trim values in writing "snapshot" automation to any automatable parameter, such as trimming a pan setting in order to move pan automation more toward the left or right speaker, scaling a reverb decay graph higher or lower to change room size, or even scaling an EQ gain graph higher or lower to make an EQ brighter or duller sounding near the center frequency. You can also apply the Trim to automation to more standard automation graphs such as volume and send level, to re-balance track or send levels without the need to completely replace the existing automation.

To create a snapshot of relative changes in automation data:

1. If using Trim to All Enabled, in the Automation window, make sure that the automation parameters you want to edit are write-enabled. Deselect any automation parameters you want to preserve.

2. Select the area of the track you want to edit. All automated controls update to reflect the automation at the beginning of the selection.

3. Move the controls for the parameter by the amount you want to change the data.

4. Choose EDIT > AUTOMATION and do one of the following:

- To write the current delta value to only the currently selected automation graphs, choose TRIM TO CURRENT, COMMAND+SHIFT+FORWARD SLASH (/) (Mac) or CTRL+SHIFT+FORWARD SLASH (/) (Windows).

- To write the current delta value for all automation parameters enabled in the Automation window, choose TRIM TO ALL ENABLED, OPTION+ COMMAND+SHIFT+FORWARD SLASH (/) (Mac) or CTRL+ALT+SHIFT+ FORWARD SLASH (/) (Windows).

Automation Workflows

Now that you understand most of the major automation mixing features that are available in the Pro Tools HD software and Pro Tools with Complete Production Toolkit, it is important to review some of the common post production automation workflows. All automation data that is created in Pro Tools can be organized into one of the following general categories:

- Real-time first (or initial) passes of automation data written dynamically using the mouse or an Avid worksurface.

- Real-time update (or corrective) passes of automation data written dynamically using the mouse or an Avid worksurface.

- Non-real-time graphically created or edited automation data in the Edit window, including the Edit > Automation commands.

There are many different and valid ways of creating a finished post production mix. There is no single right way or correct way to mix. Many of the factors that will determine how you go about creating your final mix are dependent upon many different things, including your own personal preferences for automating your mix, the available Avid worksurface, genre, the specific requirements of the post production project you are working on, and the time constraints and budget of the project.

Keeping all of these factors in mind, and accepting the fact that approaches to mixing vary wildly between individuals with many variations in automation workflows, the following basic workflow example shows how a post production project could successfully progress from an unmixed fully edited project to a completed, highly polished, fully automated final mix. Everyone mixes differently, and this is only an example of some of the things that might need to be done.

1. Tracks are re-named and re-ordered (as needed) so that similar tracks are located adjacent to each other in the Mix window.

2. Tracks are color-coded, and Show-Hide memory locations are created to facilitate quick and easy navigation to essential tracks during the mix.

3. Auxiliary subgroups and Master Faders are created for related tracks such as dialogue, music, and effects.

4. Window Configurations are created and saved to facilitate the use of numeric keypad shortcuts to instantly recall commonly used Mix window views (such as viewing Send A only, EQ or Compressor plug-ins windows for Submaster tracks and Master Fader tracks, and so on).

5. Non-automated (static) EQ, compressor-limiter, reverb, delay, and any other non-automated inserts/sends are created with initial plug-in parameter settings adjusted as needed. Where needed, snapshot (static) plug-in automation is created and copied using the Write to Current and Write to All Enabled commands.

6. Plug-ins that will require dynamic (changing automation) are inserted with initial plug-in parameter settings, and the necessary parameters for automation are enabled.

7. Non-automated (static) volume, pan, and send assignments are set for individual tracks, submasters, and Master Faders, trying to establish a good starting balance between all tracks.

8. A rough first-pass of the automated volume/pan mix is created using an Avid worksurface with Write, Touch, and Latch.

9. A rough first-pass of the automated plug-in/send mix is created using an Avid worksurface with Write, Touch, Touch/Latch, and Latch.

10. After a rough mix is created, additional plug-ins are added (as needed).

11. The following is completed:
    - Preview mode is used to experiment with automation changes and existing automation is updated using Punch Preview.
    - Capture mode is used to capture automation values and the captured values are written to similar sections of the project using Punch Capture.

12. All automated parameters are fine-tuned and updated using automation modes and an Avid worksurface using basic automation modes with Trim mode, Write to Start/End/All, Automatch, AutoJoin, and Glide automation.

13. Submaster and Master Fader tracks are adjusted and fine-tuned as necessary, making sure no clipping or excessive levels are occurring on all tracks in the mix. Limiters and compressors may be used to help tame the levels of the mix.

14. Similar track elements are soloed to ensure that the balance, panning, and inserts/sends are correct.

15. Edit window automation graphs are used to fine-tune, correct, and create automation data that is difficult to create using an Avid worksurface.

16. The mix is listened to critically and then automation is added or deleted, as required.

17. After taking a break from listening, the automated mix is listened to again with fresh ears (after one day has passed, if possible).

18. Any final adjustments are made. Client provides feedback (if client was not present during mix).

19. Final feedback is incorporated from client and final changes are made to the mix. The final automated mix of the project is saved.

Review/Discussion Questions

1. In Pro Tools, where do you enter a hardware insert delay value?

2. How could you tell if five mono sound-effects tracks, all routed to stereo bus 5–6, were clipping on the input to their respective Auxiliary Submaster track?

3. How do you coalesce VCA Master automation to group members?

4. What is the Allow Latch Prime in Stop mixing preference used for?

5. What are the two families of Write To commands?

6. How is using Preview mode on an audio track different from just placing the track in automation off?

7. While in Preview mode, what is the keyboard shortcut that allows you to temporarily suspend Preview mode, allowing you to toggle and compare between preview values and existing automation?

8. Explain the basic function of Capture mode.

9. What is AutoJoin and how is it useful for mixing?

10. Explain what the menu option Edit > Automation > Glide to Current does.

Lesson 8 Keyboard Shortcuts

Shortcut	Description
Control+Option+Shift and select additional output path (Mac)/ Start+Alt+Shift and select additional output path (Windows)	Mult track outputs
Command-click Solo button (Mac)/Alt-click Solo button	Change AFL/PFL solo level
Command-click Automation mode selector (Mac)/ Ctrl-click Automation mode selector (Windows)	Un-prime control on track
Command+Forward Slash (/) (Mac)/ Ctrl+Forward Slash (/) (Windows)	Write to Current
Command+Option+Forward Slash (/) (Mac)/ Ctrl+Alt+Forward Slash (/) (Windows)	Write to All Enabled
Option-click the Preview button (Mac)/ Alt-click the Preview button (Windows)	Preview isolate all currently write-enabled controls
Option+Shift-click the Preview button (Mac)/ Alt+Shift-click the Preview button (Windows)	Preview isolate all currently write-enabled controls on only the selected tracks
Option+Shift-click the Punch Preview button (Mac)/ Alt+Shift-click the Punch Preview button (Windows)	Punch Preview all currently isolated controls on only the selected tracks
Command-click the Preview button (Mac)/ Ctrl-click the Preview button (Windows)	Suspend Preview mode
Option-click Capture button (Mac)/ Alt-click Capture button (Windows)	Capture entire mixer settings
Option+Shift-click the Capture button (Mac)/ Alt+Shift-click the Capture button (Windows)	Capture all currently writing controls on selected tracks
Option-click the Punch Capture button (Mac)/ Alt-click the Punch Capture button (Windows)	Punch Capture All
Option+Shift-click the Punch Capture button (Mac)/ Alt+Shift-click the Punch Capture button (Windows)	Punch Capture selected tracks
Command-click the Mute button (Mac)/ Ctrl-click the Mute button (Windows)	Extend automation mute while writing
Option+Forward Slash (/) (Mac)/ Alt+Forward Slash (/) (Windows)	Glide to Current
Option+Shift+Forward Slash (/) (Mac)/ Alt+Shift+Forward Slash (/) (Windows)	Glide to All Enabled

Lesson 8 Keyboard Shortcuts

Shortcut	Description
Command+Shift+Forward Slash (/) (Mac)/ Ctrl+Shift+Forward Slash (/) (Windows)	**Trim to Current**
Option+Command+Shift+Forward Slash (/) (Mac)/ Ctrl+Alt+Shift+Forward Slash (/) (Windows)	**Trim to All Enabled**

Advanced Mixing and Routing

In this exercise, you will be mixing the opening five minutes of the short film, *Agent MX Zero*, applying many of the advanced mixing techniques you learned in the previous lesson and throughout this course.

Media Used:

310P Exercise 08.ptxt (Pro Tools session)

Duration:

90 minutes

GOALS

■ Create auxiliary track stems

■ Enable Delay Compensation

■ Create a mix to picture

Getting Started

In this exercise, you will be mixing the opening five minutes of the short film, *Agent MX Zero,* using many of the shortcuts, advanced mixing techniques, and routing techniques you've learned throughout this book so far. The session used for this exercise contains a QuickTime video track and approximately 60 audio tracks that need to be mixed.

1. Open **310P EXERCISE 08.PTXT**, located on the book DVD in the **EXERCISE MEDIA/310P CLASS AUDIO FILES v10/310P EXERCISE 08** folder (or other location specified by the course instructor).

2. In the Save New Session As dialog box, name the session as desired, saving it into an appropriate location on a valid storage volume. Figure 8.32 shows the starting Edit window.

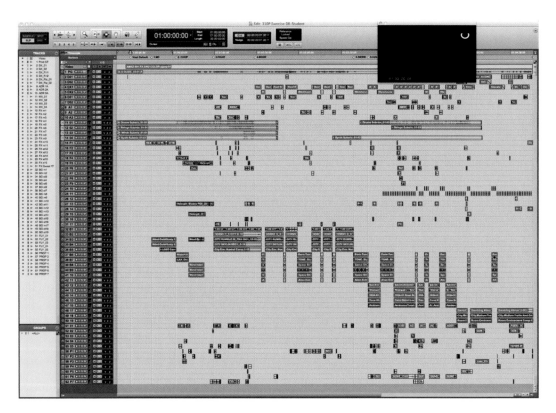

Figure 8.32
310P Starting Edit window view.

The opening scene from *Agent MX Zero* that you have been provided contains completely edited tracks that are synchronized to the picture. You are now going to create a final automated stereo mix of the project, in preparation for final layback and output.

Tip: Assuming you know how to use an Avid worksurface (and one is available) and you have a good understanding of keyboard shortcuts, try to use the Avid worksurface and keyboard shortcuts as much as possible during this mixing exercise. Using keyboard shortcuts in combination with an Avid worksurface will allow you to work as quickly as possible.

Creating Auxiliary Track Stems

Before beginning a mix to picture, it is usually helpful to create Auxiliary sub-groups of your common tracks, Master Faders, and VCA Masters, making them easily accessible and arranged in a logical manner. As you've learned in the *PT 210P: Post Production Techniques* book, sub-groups allow you to apply plug-in effects globally to similar tracks. They also provide centralized volume, pan, mute and send controls from one single channel strip.

Although there are no specific directions in this exercise for creating Auxiliary sub-groups, Master Faders, and VCA Masters, feel free to create these tracks for dialogue, music, and sound effects, and route signals within the Pro Tools mixer as necessary.

Enabling Delay Compensation

Before starting to create a final mix to picture, you need to enable Delay Compensation so that your audio tracks remain in phase with each other as you use inserts, sends, and buses.

To enable Delay Compensation, choose Options > Delay Compensation.

Tip: After enabling Delay Compensation, if you are prompted to choose a Delay Compensation Engine setting in the Playback Engine dialog box, choose the shortest available delay compensation option. You can always increase the setting later (if necessary).

Guidelines for Creating a Mix for the Opening Scene of *Agent MX Zero*

Before starting to mix, playback the session and get familiar with all of the audio that has been provided. Depending upon your level of mixing experience, you may already have many ideas for creating a finished mix. In case you need help getting started, below are some general guidelines you can follow:

- Automate a reverb plug-in (such as ReVibe) so that it is only applied to the dialogue and sound effects that take place in the stairwell, to simulate the natural reverb characteristics of the stairs. Used different reverb settings for outside and inside perspectives as well.

- Use an automated pan for the helicopter's approach (near the start of the scene).

- Try adding a 7-band EQ 3 to each of the dialogue and ADR tracks separately, and then solo each track, trying to make them sound cleaner, removing any hiss, hum, or rumble that might be present. Also match the production and ADR dialogue frequencies to make them match as closely as possible.

- EQ Agent MX Zero's voice differently when it is heard through Agent Sierra's headset versus a direct on-camera shot.

- Make sure that the dialogue is always audible in the mix and is not over-powered by sound effects or music.

- Use clip-based gain (see Figure 8.33) to raise the level of some of the nearly inaudible dialogue and sound effects.

— Clip-based gain fader

Figure 8.33
Adjusting clip-based gain.

- Process the DX_Ftz_01 track with EQ and the Lo-Fi plug-in to make the audio sound more like a live wireless communications feed. (You can un-mute the Prod GT track to listen to processed versions of the dialogue in order to get some ideas.)

- Match the warning alarm volume levels to be consistent with the different camera perspectives (for example, in the stairwell, in the lobby, from Agent Sierra's perspective).

Tip: Mute the music tracks while you work on automating levels between the DIA, ADR, and SFX tracks.

■ Add a small amount of reverb to the music tracks.

■ Insert the Focusrite d3 compressor/limiter plug-in (or other favorite compressor/limiter plug-in) on all Submaster and the Master Fader tracks, using an appropriate amount of compression/limiting. Figure 8.34 shows the Focusrite d3 Compressor/Limiter plug-in.

Figure 8.34
Focusrite d3 Compressor/Limiter plug-in.

Creating a Mix to Picture

Other than the general guidelines listed above, there are no other specific directions for creating a mix of the *Agent MX Zero* opening scene, although you should try to create a finished mix with good balance and intelligibility between all of the tracks, with no clipping. Although the tracks are already color-coded and arranged in a logical order, feel free to make any changes you desire.

Tip: If you'd like to listen to a reference mix of the opening scene for some ideas, there is a finished split-stereo reference mix of the scene available in your session, listed as the last track (hidden and inactive). Your mix does not have to sound exactly like the reference mix to be correct.

If possible, try using all of the following in your mix:

■ Real-time recorded automation using Write, Touch, Latch, and Trim automation modes

■ Real-time recorded automation using AutoJoin, Automatch, Latch Prime, and Glide

■ Punch Preview and Capture

■ Write to: All, Start, and End

- Write to: Current and All Enabled

- Real-time automation

- Automation snapshots

- DSP and Native plug-in inserts

- Sends and Returns (Auxiliary Inputs)

- Submaster Auxiliary Inputs

- Master Faders

- Edited graphical automation data

- Pan and Mute automation

- Automated plug-in parameters

- Audio processed using AudioSuite plug-ins and Elastic Audio

- Individually muted automation parameters

When you are satisfied with your stereo mix of the scene, save your session.

Mixing Using Satellite Link

This lesson discusses linking multiple Pro Tools systems using Satellite Link for large-scale mixing projects.

Media Used: 310P Exercise 9 DX-MX.ptxt, 310P Exercise 9 FX.ptxt, 310P Exercise 9 Video LE.ptxt, and Agent MXZRO.mov

Duration: 45 minutes

GOALS

- Apply large-scale mixing techniques using Satellite Link
- Configure Satellite Link preferences for mixing

Introduction

As discussed in the *Pro Tools 210P Post Production Techniques* book, the Satellite Link option is a powerful feature that allows multiple Pro Tools HD–series hardware systems and a Video Satellite system to synchronize transport functions. In this lesson, you will learn how the Satellite Link option can be used for managing large-scale mixing projects.

Large-Scale Mixing Techniques Using Satellite Link

Although some smaller post production mixes can be done with one Pro Tools system, larger post production projects can have high track counts or plug-in processing requirements beyond the capabilities of a single Pro Tools HD system. For these larger projects, the Satellite Link option can be used to link up to 12 Pro Tools HD–series hardware systems together, so that the required processing power is divided among the linked systems.

Why Synchronize Multiple Pro Tools Systems?

There are several reasons you might want to synchronize multiple Pro Tools systems together when using Pro Tools for post production applications:

■ Recording or mixing using Pro Tools for playback on projects that have very high track counts that exceed the maximum track count of any single Pro Tools HD–series hardware system.

■ Organizing common audio track elements on different Pro Tools systems such as dialogue, ADR, and music on Pro Tools System 1, and sound effects and Foley on Pro Tools System 2.

■ Composing with virtual instrument plug-ins that exceed the available processing power on one computer, for increased processing capability.

■ Synchronizing multiple Pro Tools systems for playback or recording that physically exist in different locations within a large post production facility.

■ Redundancy for critical recording or playback functions that have no tolerance for downtime due to computer system malfunctions.

Pro Tools HD Satellite Link Mixing Scenario

In this scenario, two Pro Tools HD–series hardware systems and one Pro Tools Video Satellite LE system will be synchronized for mixing a 23.976FPS HD film project using Satellite Link. All dialogue, ADR, and music will be mixed on Pro Tools HD System 1, all background and specific sound effects will be mixed on Pro Tools HD System 2, and a high-definition QuickTime video will play back on a Video LE Satellite system. The system details are as follows and are shown in Figure 9.1:

- **Pro Tools HD System 1**: (Administrator system) dialogue, ADR, and music (189 audio tracks total) with D-Command ES (32-faders)

- **Pro Tools HD System 2**: Background and specific sound effects (250 audio tracks total) with D-Control ES (32-faders)

- **Pro Tools Video Satellite LE System**: 23.976FPS HD QuickTime (H.264) playing back via a BlackMagic design DeckLink HD Extreme PCIe card

After the Pro Tools HD–series hardware systems and the Video Satellite LE system are configured and declared as Satellites, they can be placed in a linked state from the Administrator machine or from another Satellite.

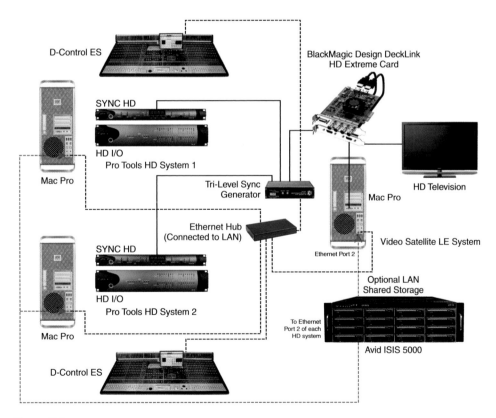

Figure 9.1
Two HD-Series Pro Tools systems and a Video Satellite LE system connected using Satellite Link with optional Avid ISIS 5000 network storage.

When systems are linked, the following features and commands can be controlled across all linked systems:

- Linking and unlinking of the system

- Transport controls (Stop, Play, Fast Forward, and Rewind)

- Play selections

- Scrub/Shuttle location

- Channel solo (including Solo Clear)

- Clearing system errors (for example, DAE errors)

Using Shared Storage

Computers that are connected to storage devices that are not accessible to other computers over a LAN are using what is commonly referred to as local storage. Although local storage is adequate in smaller home and project studios, for larger post production facilities, using exclusively local storage would be a serious workflow limitation. For these larger facilities, the ability to move and share files quickly is the key to completing projects on time, which is why shared storage is an attractive alternative to local storage. When working in post production facilities that contain multiple audio- and picture-editing workstations, the term *shared storage* refers to utilizing centralized storage devices for audio and video playback and recording that can be accessed (or shared) by all systems over some type of local area network (LAN), using either Ethernet or fiber-channel networking technology. These networked shared-storage technologies can allow sharing of media in two ways:

- **Real-time:** Real-time recording and playback of shared audio and video over a dedicated high-speed network is supported, although since Pro Tools now supports audio playback using a RAM-based disk cache, networked audio playback and sharing over standard LANs is now possible as well. Audio can now be streamed and pre-loaded from the storage device over the network to a RAM-based cache on a remote system, allowing all of the audio in a session to be stored in RAM for immediate playback. Despite this new Pro Tools disk cache feature, audio recording, video recording, and playback over a network would still require a fast dedicated network such as Avid ISIS, since the Pro Tools disk cache feature only supports Pro Tools audio playback, and not recording.

- **Push-pull:** Without a dedicated high-speed network (such as Avid ISIS), video recording and playback would require local storage. After storing the video locally, it could then be copied (pushed-pulled) to another system's local storage connected to the same LAN. With the exception of disk cached audio playback, without a connection to a high-speed network, you would be forced to transfer video media files over a LAN to each system's local storage device.

Because multiple systems can share the same project files over a LAN, shared storage offers a huge time savings advantage over local storage; it eliminates the extra time needed to export, transfer, and import projects and media between multiple systems using only local storage.

Other shared storage advantages include:

■ Immediate facility-wide access to online and offline media

■ Simultaneous file sharing for real-time project collaboration

■ Centralized access to sound and video media libraries (such as music and sound effects libraries)

■ Integrated media management tools

■ Redundant components and background media recovery tools for high reliability and protection from file loss in the event of a hard drive failure

Pro Tools 10 supports the use of shared storage solutions from Avid and other third-party companies, which can be used with Pro Tools HD–series hardware systems in conjunction with the Satellite Link option. This means that a Pro Tools HD system can be linked to up to 11 other Pro Tools HD systems using any combination of local or networked storage.

When using networked or shared storage, performance is not guaranteed and is dependent on a variety of factors, including:

■ Type of storage (such as SATA, FireWire, or SAS)

■ If using a RAID array, the number of disks in a RAID volume and the level of RAID volume used

■ Network topology (such as Gigabit Ethernet, 10 Gigabit Ethernet, or Fiber Channel)

■ Number of simultaneous users, network traffic, and data load on the network

Tip: When running Pro Tools HD or Pro Tools with Complete Production Toolkit, you can assign more RAM than the size of your session being opened using the Playback Engine dialog box's Disk Cache setting. This will eliminate hard disk playback errors since all audio is streaming directly from RAM.

Configuring the Satellite Link Network

Although configuring a Pro Tools Satellite Link network using a Video Satellite is covered in the *PT 210P Post Production Techniques* book, the topic is repeated here for this specific scenario example.

Caution: Satellite Link is not supported on a wireless network.

Configuring Clock and Positional Reference Settings

As discussed in Lesson 3, "Synchronizing Pro Tools with Linear Video," and in the *210P Post Production Techniques* class, in order for a Pro Tools system to maintain proper speed and sync with video and other systems, you must have both a common clock reference and positional reference between all systems.

When using and synchronizing systems using the Satellite Link option, you should verify that all of the following settings are identical between systems:

- Session Start
- Timecode Rate
- Clock Reference
- Positional Reference
- Video Ref Format

Caution: Failure to match all of the above settings between all systems in a Satellite Link network will cause sync issues.

To set up two Pro Tools HD–series hardware systems and a Video Satellite LE system for Satellite Link operation, one Pro Tools HD system on the network must be designated an Administrator system.

Other systems on the network are set up as Satellite systems, and then added to the network from the Administrator system.

Configuring an Administrator System

To configure a Pro Tools HD–series hardware system as a Satellite Link Administrator:

1. Choose SETUP > PERIPHERALS and click the SATELLITES tab.

2. In the SYSTEM NAME text box, enter a name for the system.

3. Under MODE, choose ADMINISTRATOR.

Caution: Only one Pro Tools HD–series hardware system in a Satellite Link network can be enabled as the Administrator.

4. Under ADMINISTRATOR, choose the current system from the SYSTEM 1 pop-up menu, as shown in Figure 9.2.

5. Make sure your IP address and Ethernet port are displayed correctly under ADVANCED NETWORK SETTINGS, as shown in Figure 9.3.

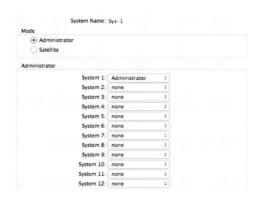

Figure 9.2
Configuring the Administrator system from the Satellites page of the Peripherals dialog box.

Ethernet Port menu

Figure 9.3
Choosing an Ethernet port in Satellites tab's Advanced Network Settings.

Tip: Dynamic IP addresses should not be used with Satellite Link networks because the Satellite Link network will need resetting each time a machine is restarted. Instead, each machine should have a unique fixed IP address for the interface port being used for Satellite Link. The IP address Pro Tools uses is set when Pro Tools launches, so you should not change the computer's IP address while Pro Tools is open.

6. Verify that the TCP/UPD port number is correct and then click **OK**.

Tip: All systems on the same Satellite Link network must use the same TCP/UDP port number, although you can designate different Satellite Link networks on the same LAN by using unique TCP/UDP port numbers for each separate Satellite Link network. For most Satellite Link networks, the default TCP/UDP port number of 28282 will work. On some larger corporate and institutional networks, the default TCP/UDP port number of 28282 may be unavailable. In such cases, the alternative TCP/UDP port number 10,000 usually works.

Note: No iLok authorization is required for the Administrator machine, but a separate Satellite Link iLok authorization is required for each Pro Tools HD Satellite, Video Satellite, or Video Satellite LE system in the Satellite Link network.

Configuring Satellite Systems

Repeat the following steps for each Pro Tools system you want to configure as a Satellite Link Satellite:

1. Choose SETUP > PERIPHERALS and click the SATELLITES tab.

2. In the SYSTEM NAME text box, enter a name for the system.

3. Under MODE, choose SATELLITE, as shown in Figure 9.4.

> System Name: Sys-2
>
> Mode
> ○ Administrator
> ⦿ Satellite

Figure 9.4
Configuring a Satellite in the Satellites tab of the Peripherals dialog box.

4. Make sure your IP address and Ethernet port are displayed correctly under ADVANCED NETWORK SETTINGS (as discussed in the previous section).

5. Verify that the TCP/UPD port number is correct and then click OK. The Pro Tools HD Satellite is now ready to be linked to the Pro Tools Administrator system.

To set up a Video Satellite LE system as a satellite:

In the Avid Learning Series

To configure a Media Composer Video Satellite or Pro Tools Video Satellite LE system, refer to Lesson 3 of the *PT 210P Post Production Techniques* book.

1. On the Video Satellite LE system, choose SETUP > PERIPHERALS and click the SATELLITES tab.

2. In the SYSTEM NAME text box, enter a name for the system.

3. Under MODE, choose ENABLE SATELLITE MODE. See Figure 9.5.

> System Name: Vid Sat
>
> Mode
> ☑ Enable Satellite Mode

Figure 9.5
Configuring a Video Satellite LE system from the Satellites page of the Peripherals dialog box.

4. Make sure your IP address and Ethernet port are displayed correctly under ADVANCED NETWORK SETTINGS (as discussed previously).

5. Verify that the TCP/UPD port number is correct and then click **OK**. The Video Satellite LE system is now ready to be linked to the Pro Tools Administrator system.

Adding Satellites to the Network

When systems have been configured as Satellites, they become available on the Administrator system. The Satellite systems are then declared from the Administrator system to build the Satellite Link network.

Note: Avid Satellite Link option with Pro Tools 10.x allows you to link up to 12 Pro Tools HD–series hardware systems (or 11 HD-series systems and a single Video Satellite or Video Satellite LE system). In order to use more than five Satellite systems, all linked systems must be running Pro Tools 10 (or higher).

To declare Satellite systems:

1. On the Administrator system, choose **Setup > Peripherals** and click the **Satellites** tab.

2. Under **Administrator**, declare the systems you want to use as Satellites from the **System 2-12** pop-up menus. See Figure 9.6.

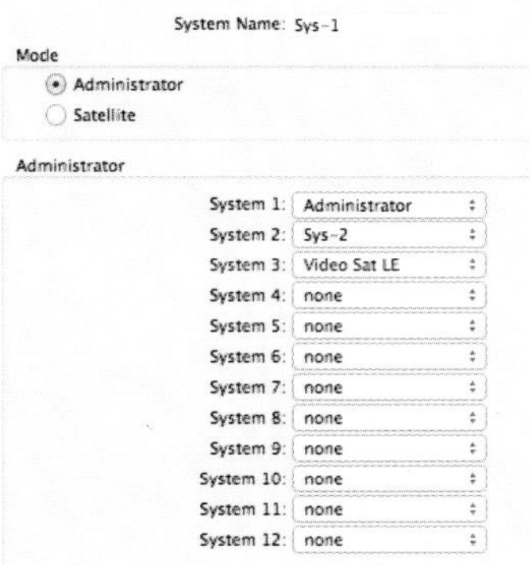

Figure 9.6
Two Pro Tools HD–series hardware systems and one Video Satellite LE System declared in the Peripherals dialog box.

Linked Satellite systems (up to a maximum of 12) appear in the Synchronization section of the Transport window. Figure 9.7 shows a total of 3 linked Pro Tools systems.

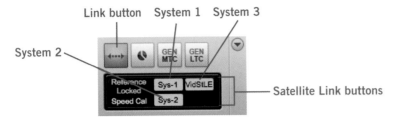

Figure 9.7
Two Pro Tools HD–series hardware systems and one Video Satellite LE system in the Synchronization section of the Transport window.

Satellite Link Controls Recap

As described in Lesson 3 of the *PT 210P Post Production Techniques* book, when a Pro Tools system has been declared as a Satellite, the following Satellite Link controls appear in the Transport window:

- **Link button**: Controls the link status of the local system.

- **Satellite Link buttons**: Control the link status of the other Satellite systems. On every system, one of these buttons corresponds to that system's main Link button.

Link buttons highlight to indicate linked status. To display Satellite Link controls in the Transport window, choose View > Transport > Synchronization and View > Transport > Expanded. See Figure 9.8.

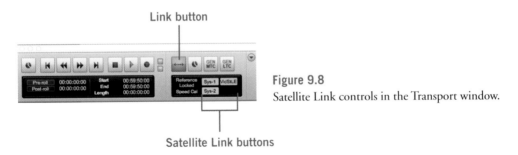

Figure 9.8
Satellite Link controls in the Transport window.

- To link or unlink the local Pro Tools system, click the **LINK** button in the Transport window.

- To link or unlink other Satellite systems, click the corresponding **SATELLITE LINK** button in the Transport window.

- To link or unlink all declared Satellite systems, Option-click (Mac) or Alt-click (Windows) on the **LINK** button or on any **SATELLITE LINK** button in the Transport window.

Linking Systems During Playback

You can link or unlink a system while it or any other linked system is playing back ("join in play"), and the transports will play in sync. In cases where both systems are playing back, the newly linked system will cue to the location of the linked system on which playback was initiated.

Tip: You can also control, link, and unlink Satellites using an approved Avid worksurface. For more information about controlling Satellites using an Avid worksurface, consult the Avid worksurface guide.

Satellite Linking Preferences

Once your Satellite Link network is enabled, there are a number of Pro Tools preferences that can be configured for finer control of your system, based on your specific scenario.

Linking Play Selections

You can set linked Pro Tools systems to transmit and receive play selections with other Satellite systems in the Synchronization page of Preferences, shown in Figure 9.9. This lets you configure your setup to selectively mirror Edit window selections between designated systems.

- If you are working in a multi-user dub stage environment where dialogue, FX, and music reside on different systems, it can be useful to set those systems to only transmit play selections, and set the recorder/video Pro Tools system to only receive play selections.

- If you are working in a single-user mix environment and are moving between systems, it can be useful to set all systems to transmit and receive play selections, so that you can work with the same selection on any system.

Figure 9.9
Satellites Synchronization Preference options.

To set Satellite Pro Tools systems to mirror play selections on other Satellite systems:

1. On the systems where you will be making play selections, do the following:

   ● Choose SETUP > PREFERENCES and click the SYNCHRONIZATION tab.

   ● In the SATELLITES section of the SYNCHRONIZATION tab, enable TRANSMIT PLAY SELECTIONS.

2. On the systems that you want to mirror the play selections, do the following:

   ● Choose SETUP > PREFERENCES and click the SYNCHRONIZATION tab.

   ● In the SATELLITES section of the SYNCHRONIZATION tab, enable RECEIVE PLAY SELECTIONS.

3. Make sure the systems are linked.

Solo Linking

You can set linked Pro Tools systems to transmit the solo status of their tracks and receive solo status information from other Satellite systems.

■ If you are working in a multi-user dub stage environment where dialogue, FX, and music reside on different systems, it can be useful to set those systems to send and receive solos, and set the recorder/video Pro Tools system so that it does not transmit or receive solos.

■ If you are working in a single-user mix environment and are moving between systems, it might be useful to set all systems to transmit and receive solos (excluding the recorder system), so that solos propagate across all systems. You would still probably want the recorder system in this scenario to not receive selections, although it would be useful to have it set up to transmit solos as long as nothing is soloed while printing.

When using solo linking, the following options affect soloing on linked systems as follows:

■ **Solo Safe**: When Solo Linking is enabled, tracks on all systems retain their Solo Safe status.

■ **Solo Clear**: When Solo Linking is enabled, a Solo Clear operation—Option-clicking (Mac) or Alt-clicking (Windows) on a Solo button or clicking the Solo Status indicator—clears all solos on systems set to receive solos.

To configure Satellite Pro Tools systems to transmit or receive solo status:

1. On the systems where you will be transmitting solos, do the following:

   - Choose SETUP > PREFERENCES and click the SYNCHRONIZATION tab.

   - In the SATELLITES section of the SYNCHRONIZATION tab, enable TRANSMIT SOLOS.

2. On the systems that you will be receiving solos, do the following:

   - Choose SETUP > PREFERENCES and click the SYNCHRONIZATION tab.

   - In the SATELLITES section of the SYNCHRONIZATION tab, enable RECEIVE SOLOS.

3. Make sure the systems are linked.

Using Solo Link Without Linking Transport Controls

You can set a Satellite on Pro Tools Satellite Link network to always send its solo status, whether linked or unlinked, so that you can solo tracks across systems without linking their transport controls. This can also be useful if you are synchronizing multiple Pro Tools systems to an external synchronizer, since it will still allow you to take advantage of the Solo Link feature.

To set a Satellite Pro Tools system to always solo, even when it is not linked:

1. Choose SETUP > PREFERENCES > SYNCHRONIZATION.

2. In the SATELLITES section of the Synchronization tab, enable the SOLO INDEPENDENT OF LINKED STATE option.

3. Click OK to close the Preferences window.

Solo Link Behavior in the Solo Modes

This section will discuss how the various solo options work in conjunction with a Satellite Link network.

- **Solo in Place**: With Solo Link, when using Solo in Place, the mode of solo operation is determined by the system transmitting the solo. If a linked system is in Solo Latch mode, soloing a track on that system adds to the number of tracks in solo, regardless of the solo mode of other systems set to receive solos. If a linked system is in Solo X-OR mode, soloing a track on that system cancels all other system's solos, regardless of the solo mode of other systems set to receive solos.

■ **AFL and PFL Modes:** With Solo Link, AFL and PFL solos on a linked system have no effect on other systems. An AFL-soloed track on a linked system can be muted by a Solo In Place (SIP) on another system. To avoid this, use PFL instead of AFL.

Satellite Link Operation

By default, linked systems will continue to operate if one of the systems experiences an error and stops playback. Any error message on a linked system appears in the tooltip for the corresponding Satellite Link button in the Transport window. You can also set each system to stop playback of all linked systems when it experiences an error.

To clear an error dialog box on a linked system, in the Transport window on another linked system, Shift-click the Satellite Link button for the affected system.

To set a linked system to stop its transport when an error occurs on the system:

1. Choose SETUP > PREFERENCES; choose the SYNCHRONIZATION tab and enable DAE ERRORS STOP ALL LINKED SYSTEMS.

Once this preference is enabled on a single linked systems, if an error occurs on the system, a stop command will be sent to all other linked systems, regardless of their individual preference setting.

Satellite Link Playback and Modal Dialog Boxes

Linked systems will stop playback (or prevent playback from starting) if a modal dialog box (such as the I/O Setup, Hardware Setup, or Playback Engine dialog box) is opened on any linked system. To avoid interrupting playback on another system when opening a modal dialog box, unlink the system before opening the dialog box.

Review/Discussion Questions

1. When mixing large-scale post projects, why would you need to link multiple Pro Tools HD–series hardware systems?

2. Using the Avid Satellite Link option, what is the maximum number of Pro Tools HD–series hardware systems that can be linked?

3. What is the exact menu path that allows you to connect and link Pro Tools Satellites to the Administrator system?

4. How can the Pro Tools Disk Cache setting in the Playback Engine dialog box allow Pro Tools systems to play back and stream audio over a standard LAN?

5. How many Administrator systems can be enabled simultaneously in a single Satellite Link network?

6. What is the keyboard shortcut that allows you to clear all solos of linked systems that are set to receive solos?

7. Why is it recommended that you use a PFL soloed track instead of an AFL soloed track on a linked system?

8. In a Satellite Link network with the default settings, what happens to the other systems when a single system has a playback error and stops playback?

Lesson 9 Keyboard Shortcuts

Shortcut	Description
Option-click Link button (Mac)/ Alt-click Link button (Windows)	Link/unlink Satellite systems
Option-click Solo button (Mac)/ Alt-click Solo button (Windows)	Solo clear on all Satellite systems set to receive solos

Mixing Using Satellite Link

In this exercise, you will be mixing audio for the opening scene of the short film, *Agent MX Zero* (as you did in Exercise 8). The one big difference in this exercise is that you will be mixing using audio playing back from two separate Pro Tools HD–series hardware systems using the Satellite Link option. If time and equipment allow, you can also link a third system, using Video Satellite or Video Satellite LE.

Media Used:

310P Exercise 9 DX-MX.ptxt, 310P Exercise 9 FX.ptxt, 310P Exercise 9 Video LE.ptxt, and Agent MXZRO.mov

Duration:

45-60 minutes

GOALS

- Configure and sync multiple Pro Tools systems using the Satellite Link option
- Mix on Pro Tools systems linked using the Satellite Link option

Overview

Note: Since this exercise requires multiple Pro Tools HD systems to complete, this exercise is primarily designed to be completed at an Avid Learning Partner facility or other facility where multiple Pro Tools HD systems are available. This is an optional exercise that can be skipped or completed in several different ways depending on your hardware setup and the total number of available Pro Tools systems.

Self-study learners can complete this exercise if you have access to two Pro Tools HD–series hardware systems with at least one Satellite Link iLok asset. Students using this book at an Avid Learning Partner can complete this exercise using any of the following:

- Working together as a class with their instructor guiding them, using the main teaching system and a second linked Pro Tools HD–series Satellite system.

- Pairing off, each working on a separate Pro Tools HD–series hardware system that can be linked to a second Pro Tools HD–series Satellite system (requires an even number of Pro Tools HD–series hardware systems).

- Sharing time (or rotating) on pairs of Satellite-linked Pro Tools HD–series systems at Avid Learning Partners that have an uneven number of Pro Tools HD–series hardware systems.

- Using any other setup configuration that your instructor deems a valid method for practicing and understanding how Satellite Link can be used for linking multiple Pro Tools HD–series systems for mixing.

Audio Monitoring

This exercise assumes that you will be first configuring a Pro Tools HD–series hardware system as an Administrator system (referred to in this exercise as *Pro Tools System 1*) and then linking to a second Pro Tools HD–series system (referred to in this exercise as *Pro Tools System 2*). It is also assumed that you have some method of routing and merging together the individual main outputs from Pro Tools System 1 and Pro Tools System 2, so that they can be monitored together on one set of shared speakers or headphone monitoring system. Ideally, both Pro Tools systems should be located in the same room. At the end of the exercise, you have the option to add and enable either a Video Satellite or Video Satellite LE system (if you have the required additional hardware.)

Matching Clock and Positional Reference Settings

As discussed in Lesson 3 and in the 210P Post Production Techniques class, for a Pro Tools system to maintain proper speed and sync with video and other systems, you must have both a common clock reference and positional reference between all systems.

When using and synchronizing systems using the Satellite Link option, you should verify that all of the following settings are identical between systems:

- Session Start: 00:59:50:00

- Timecode Rate: 23.976FPS

- Clock Reference: Video Reference (HD) or Video Reference (SD)

- Positional Reference: LTC

- Video Ref Format: 720p–23.976 (HD) or NTSC/PAL (SD)

Caution: Failure to match all of these settings between all systems in a Satellite Link network will cause sync issues.

Configuring Pro Tools System 2 (Satellite System)

To configure the Satellite system:

1. Open **310P Exercise 09-FX.ptxt**, located in the **Exercise Media/310P Class Audio Files v10/310P Exercise 09** folder on the book's DVD (or other location specified by the course instructor).

2. In the Save New Session As dialog box, name the session as desired, saving it into an appropriate location on a valid storage volume.

You are now ready to enable the Satellite system.

Enabling the Satellite System

To enable the Satellite system:

1. Choose **Setup > Peripherals** and then click the **Satellites** tab.

2. Make sure your IP address, Ethernet port, and TCP/UDP port number are configured correctly (as previously discussed).

3. In the **System Name** text box, enter a name, such as **Sys 2 FX**.

4. Under **Mode**, choose **Satellite** and then click **OK**. See Figure 9.10.

Figure 9.10
Configuring the Satellite system in the Satellites tab of the Peripherals dialog box.

The system is now ready to be linked to the Administrator system.

Configuring Pro Tools System 1 (Administrator System)

If you will be working on Pro Tools System 2, skip this section.

1. Open **310P Exercise 09-DX-MX**.ptxt, located in the **Exercise Media/310P Class Audio Files v10/310P Exercise 09** folder on the book's DVD (or other location specified by the course instructor).

2. In the Save New Session As dialog box, name the session as desired, saving it into an appropriate location on a valid storage volume.

After the session opens, you are ready to enable the Administrator system.

Enabling the Administrator System

1. Choose **Setup > Peripherals** and then click the **Satellites** tab.

2. Make sure your IP address and Ethernet port are displayed correctly under Advanced Network Settings. See Figure 9.11.

Figure 9.11
Choosing an Ethernet port in the Satellites tab's Advanced Network Settings.

3. Verify that the TCP/UDP port number is correct.

4. In the **System Name** text box, enter a system name, such as **Sys 1 DX-MX**.

5. Under **Mode**, choose **Administrator**.

6. Under **ADMINISTRATOR**, choose the current system from the **SYSTEM 1** pop-up menu. See Figure 9.12.

7. Click **OK**.

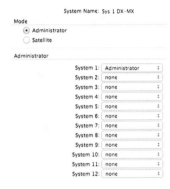

Figure 9.12

Configuring the Administrator system in the Satellites tab of the Peripherals dialog box.

Adding Satellites to the Network

After Pro Tools System 2 has been configured as a Satellite (covered in the first section of this exercise), it becomes available on the Administrator system (Pro Tools System 1).

Caution: You will not be able to enable Pro Tools System 2 as a Satellite on the Administrator system until Pro Tools System 2 has itself been enabled as a Satellite (as described in the next section of this exercise).

To declare Pro Tools System 2 as a Satellite system:

1. On the Administrator system, choose **SETUP > PERIPHERALS** and then click the **SATELLITES** tab.

2. Under Administrator, declare Pro Tools System 2 as a Satellite from the **SYSTEM 2** pop-up menu and then click **OK**. See Figure 9.13.

Figure 9.13

One Administrator and one Satellite system declared in the Peripherals dialog box.

The linked Satellite systems appear in vertical columns from left to right in the Synchronization section of the Transport window. See Figure 9.14.

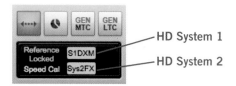

HD System 1

HD System 2

Figure 9.14
Two linked Pro Tools systems in the Transport window.

Mixing Using the Satellite Link Option (Pro Tools Systems 1 and 2)

1. Before staring to mix, choose **SETUP > PREFERENCES**, then click the **SYNCHRONIZATION** tab, and enable the Satellite preferences shown in Figure 9.15.

Figure 9.15
Satellite preferences.

With the preferences enabled as shown, both systems will be able to transmit and receive both solos and play selections. Feel free to change these preferences to your own liking or for your specific equipment setup.

2. If not already linked, link both systems in the Transport window, and then test playback to verify that the Satellite Link and audio playback monitoring is functioning correctly.

3. If you are working with another person, while linked during playback, practice writing and updating automation on Pro Tools System 1, while the other person simultaneously writes automation on Pro Tools System 2 (as applicable).

4. When you are finished, save the session on both systems.

Enabling a Video Satellite (Optional)

If you have additional time and the available hardware, software, and video routing capability, from the Administrator system, try enabling a (Media Composer) Video Satellite or Video Satellite LE system in addition to the two Pro Tools HD Satellites.

1. If you are using a Pro Tools 10 Video Satellite LE system, open the session called **310P EXERCISE 9 VIDEO SATLE.PTXT,** located in the **EXERCISE MEDIA/310P CLASS AUDIO FILES v10/310P EXERCISE 09** folder on the book's DVD (or other location specified by the course instructor).

2. In the Save New Session As dialog box, name the session as desired, saving it into an appropriate location on a valid storage volume.

   • If you are using a Media Composer Video Satellite, create a 23.976FPS Media Composer project, and then import the *Agent MX Zero* QuickTime file located in the **EXERCISE MEDIA/310P CLASS VIDEO FILES v10/ 23.976 HD CLASS VIDEO/AGENT MX ZERO MOVIE SC1.MOV** folder on the book's DVD.

In the Avid Learning Series

To review the steps for configuring and enabling a Video Satellite system, consult the *210P Post Production Techniques* book.

Advanced Layback

After you finish editing and mixing your post production projects, it will be necessary to layback or output your project to prepare it for distribution. Although there are a number of non-linear workflows used for post production audio deliverables (covered in the *PT 210P: Post Production Techniques* book), this lesson will cover the linear layback and output options that are also required for post production projects.

Media Used: 310P Exercise 10.ptxt, 310P Exercise 10-Master.ptxt, 310P Exercise 10-Slave.ptxt, and a linear video tape with LTC running from timecode numbers 00:59:00:00–01:05:00:00 (or later)

Duration: 60 minutes

GOALS

- Redefine timecode and feet+frames positions
- Create session offsets
- Perform a linear layback to video tape
- Configure speed corrections for film and video
- Record printmaster stems to a Pro Tools system using 9-pin deck emulation
- Create and save Machine Track Arming Profiles
- Understand how Satellite Link and 9-pin Machine Control can be used simultaneously

Introduction

In the post production industry, there are many different delivery formats and specifications that clients require for final delivery of edited and mixed audio projects. These delivery formats range from linear analog and digital tape formats, to non-linear digital file formats, and even Internet delivery of final files. Pro Tools can handle most linear and non-linear audio delivery requirements.

The common Pro Tools non-linear digital output formats are covered in *PT 210P: Pro Tools Post Production Techniques.* This lesson focuses instead on the common linear output delivery workflows for post production projects, including detailed steps and explanations.

Note: The first half of this lesson requires a professional SD or HD video tape recorder supporting RS-422 (9-pin) deck control and audio layback using Insert mode. Prior to starting this lesson, you will also need to record (or stripe) LTC onto a linear video tape, with the timecode starting at timecode number 00:59:00:00 and ending at timecode number 01:05:00:00, using either 29.97FPS (NTSC), 25FPS (PAL), or 23.976FPS (if using an HD video tape recorder). Refer to Appendix D, "Video Tape Duplication Instructions," for more details.

The second half of this lesson requires two Pro Tools HD–series hardware systems with the Machine Control option installed on both systems. Before continuing, you will need to verify that both Pro Tools systems are interconnected and set up to operate as 9-pin master and slave (as described in this lesson).

If you do not have access to the equipment required in this lesson, you can choose to skip this lesson.

Project Offset Options

In the post production world, it is very common for final edited or mixed Pro Tools projects to be delivered or transferred using timecode or feet+frames offsets that are different from the original values used. These changes are often necessary due to using different timecoded master tapes, changing between 23.976, 24, 25, and 29.97 frame rates, or other unforeseen changes. Pro Tools has several options for handling these changes.

Redefine Current Timecode Position

The Redefine Current Timecode Position command allows you to redefine the session start time. By placing the insertion point (or making a selection) and then entering a new timecode value for that location, the session start time will be recalculated based on the new, relative timecode location. Typically, this feature is useful for conforming, reel balancing, or re-syncing your session's audio using common known sync reference points such as the start of color bars and tones, pre-roll, head and tail 2-pop, or other easily identified visual references.

Using a more specific example, advertising commercial production typically creates different length commercials (60 seconds, 30 seconds, and 10 seconds) for the same product. All three versions of the commercial are usually loaded into the same Pro Tools session on the timeline, spaced 1–2 minutes apart. When each version of the commercial is completely edited and mixed, they are individually output to the same video tape, with the 30-second version starting at timecode number 01:00:00:00, the 10-second version starting at 01:01:00:00, and the 60-second version starting at 01:02:00:00. Using the Redefine Current Timecode Position dialog box allows you to easily output each separate commercial in the timeline to the correct starting timecode number on the corresponding video tape.

To redefine the current timecode of a session:

1. Set the **MAIN TIMESCALE** to **TIMECODE**.

2. In **GRID** mode, with the Grid increment set to **1 FRAME**, make a selection or place the insertion point at the desired location from which you want to recalculate the session time.

3. Choose **SETUP > CURRENT TIMECODE POSITION**.

   In the **REDEFINE CURRENT TIMECODE POSITION** dialog box, the current location of the insertion cursor (or insertion point) is shown. See Figure 10.1.

Figure 10.1
Redefine Current Timecode Position dialog box.

4. Enter the **DESIRED TIMECODE POSITION** and click **OK**.

   The session start timecode is adjusted earlier (or later) relative to the insertion point, based on the timecode number you entered. Exactly how much earlier or later depends on the current location of the insertion point. If you enter a timecode number that is greater than the current timecode position, causing media that exists on the timeline to move beyond the start of the session, the warning dialog box shown in Figure 10.2 will appear.

Unable to maintain original timecode
locations with the entered start time because
a clip and/or an alternate playlist would exist
outside the session boundaries. Click OK to
maintain relative position.

Cancel   OK

Figure 10.2
Unable to maintain timecode warning.

Redefine Current Feet+Frames Position

Similar to the Redefine Current Timecode Position command, the Redefine Current Feet+Frames Position command allows you to easily offset or realign your session's timecode position with any desired feet+frames value, based on the current Edit cursor location.

This feature is commonly used to match the feet+frames display with Academy leader, color bars and tones, Feet+Frames window burns, or other easily identified visual references.

To redefine the current feet+frames of a session:

1. Set the **Main Timescale** to **Feet+Frames**.

2. Set the **Edit** mode to **Grid**.

3. Set the **Grid** value to **Feet+Frames**, with a grid setting of **1 frame**.

4. Make a selection or place the insertion cursor at the desired location from which you want to recalculate the session's feet+frames location.

5. Choose **Setup > Current Feet+Frames Position**. In the Redefine Current Feet+Frames Position dialog box, the current location of the insertion cursor (or insertion point) is shown. See Figure 10.3.

Redefine Current Feet+Frames Position

Current Timecode Position: 01:00:00:00
Desired Feet+Frames Position: 12+00

Cancel   OK

Figure 10.3
Redefine Current Feet+Frames Position dialog box.

6. Enter the **Desired Feet+Frames Position** and then click **OK**.

The session's feet+frames start time is adjusted earlier or later relative to the insertion point, based on the feet+frames value you entered. Exactly how much earlier or later depends on the current location of the insertion point.

Using Session Offsets

Pro Tools lets you compensate for devices that are consistently offset by a fixed number of frames (such as some color-corrected video masters), or for source material that starts at a different time than the session.

Pro Tools provides four types of External Timecode Offset settings:

- **MMC (MIDI Machine control)**: MMC offsets can be entered for any devices connected via MMC.

- **9-Pin:** 9-Pin offsets for serial Machine Control can be entered if you are using Avid's Machine Control option.

- **Sync**: Sync offsets can be entered for Synchronization peripherals (such as the SYNC HD, the SYNC I/O, or a MIDI interface that provides MTC).

- **Satellite**: Satellite offsets can be entered for linked Satellite systems.

To configure session offsets:

1. Choose SETUP > SESSION or press COMMAND+NUMERIC KEYPAD 2 (Mac) or CTRL+NUMERIC KEYPAD 2 (Windows).

2. Expand the Session Setup window view to show the SYNC SETUP & TIMECODE OFFSETS view.

3. Enter offset values in the EXTERNAL TIMECODE OFFSETS section of the window, shown in Figure 10.4.

   Positive and negative offset values can be entered to offset Pro Tools's time-code display later or earlier. Unique values can be defined for each of these three types of offsets, or you can link all three to adjust them all in unison.

Figure 10.4
External Timecode Offsets in the Session Setup window.

Redefine External Timecode Offset

The Redefine External Timecode Offset command makes it easy to recalculate timecode offsets based on the current selection. This is particularly useful when synchronizing to a new picture cut that may have a different timecode from the original session.

To redefine the external timecode offsets:

1. Set the EDIT mode to GRID.

2. Set the GRID value to TIMECODE, with a unit setting of **1 FRAME**, as shown in Figure 10.5.

Figure 10.5
Grid value set to 1 frame.

3. Click the SELECTOR tool at a frame boundary where you can easily identify a picture sync point (for example, at the start of the picture or an edit).

4. Choose SETUP > EXTERNAL TIMECODE OFFSET.

5. Enter the desired TIMECODE position for the picture sync point you chose, and then click **OK**. See Figure 10.6.

Figure 10.6
Redefine External Timecode Offset dialog box.

After you redefine the timecode offset, the offset automatically updates in the Sync field under the External Timecode Offsets section of the Session Setup window, as shown in Figure 10.7.

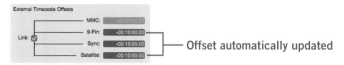

Figure 10.7
External timecode offsets (linked) in the Session Setup window.

Linear Layback Workflow

After completion of all recording, editing, mixing, and the required offsets, it is still fairly common to layback your audio mix to a linear tape machine such as a VTR, a timecode DAT machine, a Tascam DA-88/98, or another client-requested linear format. Although non-linear deliverables are increasingly becoming more common, non-linear output and layback are still used in many post production environments.

Configuring Machine Control for Audio Layback

When you are ready to lay back your finished audio mix to an external video deck, using Pro Tools HD PCIe hardware with the Machine Control option allows you to easily output your audio to video tape.

Hardware Connections

Before proceeding, verify that the following hardware connections have been made:

■ The 9-pin port on the video deck is connected to 9-pin port 1 or 2 on SYNC Peripheral (or other supported port).

■ The video deck is set to Remote mode (also make sure the tape is not write-protected).

■ The LTC Out of the video deck is connected to the LTC IN of the SYNC Peripheral (optional if using Serial Timecode for Positional Reference).

■ NTSC or PAL Video Reference is connected to both your video deck and SYNC Peripheral's Video Ref In (necessary if using Serial Timecode so that Pro Tools can lock to the frame edge).

Note: If you are using an HD linear video deck (such as Sony HD-CAM-SR format), you should connect and use Tri-Level sync instead of Bi-Level sync (Video Reference) for both the video deck and the SYNC HD.

■ Main stereo mix outputs (usually Outputs A 1–2) from the Pro Tools audio interface are routed to audio Inputs 1–2 of your video deck.

 For a review of the hardware connections listed here, consult Lesson 1, "Pro Tools HD Hardware Configuration, and Lesson 3, "Synchronizing Pro Tools with Linear Video."

Session Setup Settings

To prepare your Pro Tools session for audio synchronization and layback to an external NTSC or PAL video deck, configure the Session Setup window as shown in Figure 10.8.

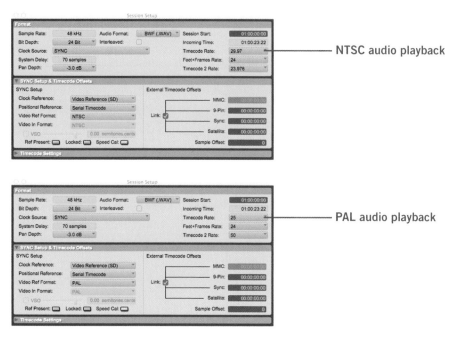

Figure 10.8
Session Setup window configured for NTSC audio layback (top) and PAL audio layback (bottom).

Enabling Machine Control

Assuming that your hardware and software settings have been configured correctly and your external machine is powered on and in remote mode, you are ready to enable Machine Control for audio layback.

 For detailed instructions on enabling Machine Control, please refer to Lesson 3.

Configuring Machine Track Arming

Pro Tools provides automatic, direct support for track-arming configurations of many common video decks. If your deck is supported, Machine Control will be able to identify and display your machine's particular track layout.

Even if your machine is not directly supported, the Machine Track Arming window allows you to designate the number of record tracks, arm the tracks, set the Record Protocol, and configure the record mode for the machine.

Caution: **Not all machines support independent arming of their audio tracks locally or remotely. In addition, some machines require a separate utility menu selection. Pro Tools remote track arming cannot operate in these situations.**

Identifying Your Machine

If Pro Tools does not recognize your machine, you can use the Generic 1 or Generic 2 machine profile. However, you should try a few test laybacks, using non-essential tapes or other non-vital material, to determine the best settings for your system.

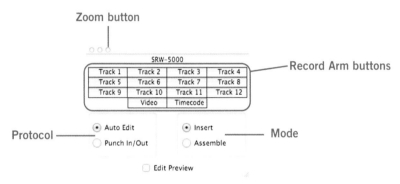

Figure 10.9
Machine Track Arm window using a Sony SRW-5000 VTR.

To display the Machine Track Arming window (shown in Figure 10.9), choose Window > Machine Track Arming, or press Command+numeric keypad 6 (Mac) or Ctrl+ numeric keypad 6 (Windows).

Zoom Button

A Zoom button is located in the upper-left corner of the Machine Track Arming window. In small view, only the Track Enable buttons appear. In large view, all the other controls of the window are visible. Once you configure these other controls for your setup, you may find it convenient to leave the Machine Track Arming window in small view, giving you access to just the Record Enable buttons.

Caution: Viewing the Machine Track Arming window in small view can be potentially dangerous, since the status of Insert or Assemble is not displayed
in small view.

Configuring the Number of Tracks

If your machine profile has been identified correctly in the Machine Type section
of the Machine Control tab of the Peripherals dialog box, the correct number of
record tracks will automatically appear.

If you are using a "generic" device profile, the number of available record tracks
defaults to eight, although if you attempt to record-enable more tracks than your
machine possesses, the extra tracks will be ignored. Be sure to double-check track
arming, as machines differ in how they map arming commands. Figure 10.10
shows the Machine Track Arming window using a Sony SRW-5000 and a Generic
profile.

Figure 10.10
Machine Track Arm window using a Sony SRW-5000 VTR (left) and a Generic Profile 2 (right).

After a machine profile is chosen, the Record Enable buttons are active. The
Record Enable buttons will be named with the appropriate machine-specific track
name. The button displays in red when armed.

Choosing a Record Mode

The Machine Track Arming window provides two choices for record mode:

- **Insert**: This mode is used to perform insert editing (punching in individual
  tracks) where one or more audio track is replaced by new material and the
  video material is retained.

- **Assemble**: Assemble mode should be used when you want to do either of
  the following: begin recording a program onto a completely blank tape
  (unformatted) or append program material to the remainder of a tape that
  already has a program on the tape you want to keep.

Note: Assemble mode is not appropriate for audio laybacks to video masters, because it replaces all the elements on the target tape.

Caution: Assemble mode should be used carefully because it arms all tracks on the target deck for recording, including the video track, timecode track, and control track. When performing an Assemble edit, all material on all tracks after the Edit In point will be replaced. Because a break in the control track will result at the Edit Out point, any remaining program material after an Assemble edit may be rendered unusable.

Tip: To avoid accidentally recording over program material, experiment with Assemble and Insert modes on a non-essential tape to familiarize yourself with the edit capabilities of your video deck.

Choosing a Record Protocol

The following two choices are available for configuring the recording protocol to be utilized by the target deck:

■ **Auto Edit:** This mode is a highly accurate way to ensure that the target deck will record only within the boundaries of an on-screen selection. If your deck does not support Auto Edit, use Punch In/Punch Out, as explained below.

In Auto Edit mode, the record start/end times are downloaded to the target deck (along with any pre-roll set in Setup > Peripherals > Machine Control), and the deck is responsible for performing the punch in/out at the specified times.

Because this protocol removes the vagaries of CPU timing from the remote recording process, Auto Edit is frame edge-accurate. It is also the best way to ensure that your machine will punch out correctly and avoid accidental erasure of audio, even in the event of a CPU error.

■ **Punch In/Out:** This mode uses Pro Tools to control the process of Punch In/Out. Instead of downloading the punch points (as in Auto Edit), Pro Tools actually performs them during the record pass. Because serial communication has inherent delays, timing with Punch In/Punch Out mode cannot guarantee frame-accuracy (though it will normally be within two to three frames).

Tip: When using the Punch In/Out record protocol, you can manually punch in/out on your external videotape recorder on the fly by pressing Record in the Transport window or on your worksurface.

Rules for On-screen Selections

The Record Protocol buttons allow you to choose between the two record protocol choices described above (Auto Edit and Punch In/Punch Out). Regardless of which choice is used, however, Pro Tools follows these rules for record selection:

■ If there is an on-screen selection, recording will take place over the period of the selection and punch out at the end of the selection.

■ If pre-or post-roll is enabled, recording takes place only in the selection area, not during pre- or post-roll.

■ If there is no selection (only a start location), recording will continue until it is manually stopped.

■ If you make a selection in Pro Tools that crosses the "midnight" boundary (00:00:00:00), make sure your deck can handle this situation. Experiment with a dispensable tape to familiarize yourself with the midnight crossover capabilities of your deck.

Using Edit Preview Mode for Machine Control Track Arming

In Pro Tools, before laying back audio to an external device, you can rehearse the layback using Edit Preview (Rehearse) mode. In Edit Preview mode, instead of performing an insert edit (recording) on the external device's armed tracks, the device switches to input monitoring without recording.

While in Edit Preview mode, the Transport Record button flashes yellow when armed and lights solid yellow when rehearsing. Armed tracks are indicated by yellow track buttons in the Track Arming window.

To rehearse a layback:

1. In Pro Tools, select the audio you want to rehearse for layback, or place the playback cursor at a start point.

2. Choose WINDOW > MACHINE TRACK ARMING.

3. In the MACHINE TRACK ARMING window, select EDIT PREVIEW.

4. In the MACHINE TRACK ARMING window, arm the tracks you want to rehearse by clicking the corresponding track buttons. The buttons light yellow to indicate EDIT PREVIEW is enabled and red to indicate EDIT PREVIEW is disabled (see Figure 10.11).

5. In the Pro Tools TRANSPORT window, select TRANSPORT > MACHINE.

6. Put Pro Tools Online.

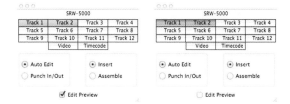

Figure 10.11
Machine Track Arming window in Edit Preview mode (left) and Record Armed (right).

7. In the Pro Tools **Transport** window, click **Record**. The **Record** button will flash yellow to indicate **Edit Preview** (Rehearse) mode is enabled. See Figure 10.12.

Figure 10.12
Armed Transport Record in Edit Preview mode.

8. In the Pro Tools **Transport**, click **Play**.

The machine will cue to the selection start or insert point and begin to play back. Pro Tools will then sync to the deck, and the deck will switch to Edit Preview mode, allowing input monitoring without recording.

Using Machine Track Arming for Layback

You learned about Machine Control shortcuts in Lesson 3. Now you will learn how to use remote track arming with Machine Control. The first step in using remote track arming is to configure the parameters of the Machine Track Arming window.

To configure machine track arming:

1. Make sure your machine is properly connected and Machine Control is enabled.

2. Open the **Transport** window (if not visible).

3. Enable **Transport = Machine** by pressing **Command+Backslash (\)** (Mac) or **Ctrl+Backslash (\)** (Windows) to toggle between the available Machine Control transports. See Figure 10.13.

Figure 10.13
Transport = Machine Enabled.

4. Open the MACHINE TRACK ARMING window by pressing COMMAND+6 (Mac) or CTRL+6 (Windows) on the numeric keypad. If the entire window is not visible, click the ZOOM box.

5. Verify that the number of record tracks is correct. The number of record tracks is based on the machine profile you chose when you first enabled Machine Control.

6. Select a Record Protocol (AUTO EDIT or PUNCH IN/OUT) in the MACHINE TRACK ARMING window.

7. Select a record mode (INSERT or ASSEMBLE) in the MACHINE TRACK ARMING window.

Caution: Assemble mode replaces all the tracks on the target tape deck—audio, video, control, and timecode. Use this mode with caution.

To perform a layback:

1. In Pro Tools, select the audio to layback, or place the playback cursor at a start point.

2. In the MACHINE TRACK ARMING window, arm the appropriate tracks.

3. Verify TRANSPORT = MACHINE has been enabled. Use COMMAND+ BACKSLASH (\) (Mac) or CTRL+BACKSLASH (\) (Windows) to toggle between the available Machine Control transports.

4. Press ONLINE+RECORD in the TRANSPORT window to arm recording.

5. Start playback.

Your machine will cue to the selection start minus all relevant pre-roll, and then begin to play back. Pro Tools will then sync to the deck, and the target deck will record as determined by your settings for Record Protocol and record mode. If you did not create an on-screen selection, deck recording will continue until you manually stop playback.

Speed Corrections

For video and film audio, there are many different standards being used worldwide, such as NTSC standard definition video, PAL standard definition video, high definition video, and film and cinema audio. Because each of these standards uses different clock references and frame rates, it is necessary to change the speed of the audio when converting between these standards. This section of the lesson will discuss the audio speed changes that are necessary to convert from video to film.

Film Speed Versus Video Speed

As you learned earlier in Lesson 2, "Troubleshooting a Pro Tools System," film referenced audio does not run at the same speed as video referenced audio, so consequently, speed changes known as *audio pulls* are necessary whenever you are converting between film, NTSC video, and PAL video referenced projects. Figure 10.14 illustrates the relationships between different film and video speeds.

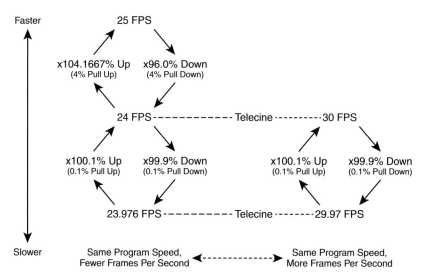

Figure 10.14
Speed correction for film, NTSC video, and PAL video using Pro Tools.

Unpulling Audio for Sprocketed Media

When editing and mixing audio with digital picture using either a NTSC or PAL digital video picture reference, your audio is running at video speed. If your final mix needs to end up on sprocketed media (such as film or mag dubbers), it may be necessary to change your speed prior to output from Pro Tools.

Note: Most film projects create print master audio stems in Pro Tools still referenced to video speed. The printmaster encoding process occurs during the film dub in a Dolby-approved facility (for Dolby delivery), with the audio corrected to film speed during the Dolby/DTS/SDDS/DCP encoding process. This makes unpulling audio in Pro Tools unnecessary for most film projects. For video referenced projects that are remaining on video (for example, television broadcasts), pulling/unpulling is also not necessary, although sample rate conversion might be required for delivery purposes.

NTSC to Film

If you are currently using the NTSC video format with a frame rate of 29.97FPS and an audio pull rate enabled, and you want to convert to film speed, it will be necessary to unpull (or speed up the audio 0.1%) in the Session Setup window.

To unpull NTSC video referenced audio for conversion to film speed:

1. In the **TIMECODE RATE** menu of the **SESSION SETUP** window, verify that **AUTO MATCH PULL FACTORS** is enabled, as shown in Figure 10.15.

Figure 10.15
Timecode Rate menu in the Session Setup window.

2. In the **TIMECODE RATE** menu of the **SESSION SETUP** window, change the frame rate from **29.97FPS** to **24FPS**.

The Auto Match Pull Factor option will automatically cancel the original Film-NTSC Pull Factor (originally 0.1% down), now showing an Audio Rate Pull Up/Down of None (or 0.1% up from the original pull rate). See Figure 10.16.

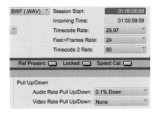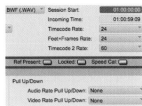

Figure 10.16
Original film referenced audio pulled down for NTSC video (left) and unpulled for film speed (right).

PAL to Film

If you are currently using the PAL video format with a frame rate of 25FPS and an audio pull rate enabled, and you want to convert to film speed, it will be necessary to unpull (or slow down the audio 4%) in the Session Setup window.

To unpull PAL video referenced audio for conversion to film speed:

1. In the **TIMECODE RATE** menu of the **SESSION SETUP** window, verify that **AUTO MATCH PULL FACTORS** is enabled, as shown in Figure 10.17.

Figure 10.17
Timecode Rate menu in the Session Setup window.

2. In the **TIMECODE RATE** menu of the **SESSION SETUP** window, change the frame rate from **25FPS** to **24FPS** (the standard frame rate for film).

The Auto Match Pull Factor option will automatically cancel the original Film-PAL pull factor (originally 4% up), now showing an Audio Rate Pull Up/Down of None (or 4% down from the original pull rate). See Figure 10.18.

Figure 10.18
Original film referenced audio pulled up for PAL video (left) and unpulled for film speed (right).

Creating Printmaster Stems Using Pro Tools 9-Pin Remote Deck Emulation

After the post production project is mixed and all audio offsets and pulls have been configured, one of the final steps is printing the mix into final printmaster stems (dialogue, sound effects, music, and Foley), and then exporting the stems for final delivery. Using Pro Tools 9-Pin Remote Deck Emulation mode, you can record-enable and print stems to a separate Pro Tools HD system (usually located in a machine room). This mode enables a form of *deck emulation* in Pro Tools.

When the 9-Pin Remote Deck Emulation Mode cable is used on a supported system, Pro Tools can respond to record-arming, transport, and other standard Sony P2 9-pin commands from another Pro Tools system or an external machine, essentially making Pro Tools operate as a virtual tape deck. In post production, it is common to control Pro Tools remotely using an external synchronizer or another Pro Tools system. By default, Pro Tools emulates a Sony BVW-75 model video deck, but it can also be configured to emulate other machines.

Connecting Machines for 9-Pin Remote Deck Emulation Mode

Before using 9-Pin Remote Deck Emulation mode in Pro Tools, you must connect Pro Tools using the 9-pin cables that are included in the Machine Control option box.

Note: The Machine Control option for Pro Tools includes separate boxed product with different cabling and adapters for Mac and Windows platforms. When purchasing the Machine Control option, you must choose the boxed product for your computer platform.

Machine Control Components

The Machine Control boxed product includes the following, based on your computer operating system:

Macintosh systems

- Machine Control Installer disc

- Serial Deck Control cable: male 8-pin mini-DIN to male 9-pin cable

- 9-pin Remote Deck Emulation cable: male 8-pin mini-DIN to female 9-pin cable

- Machine Control iLok activation card

Windows systems

- Machine Control Installer disc

- Serial Deck Control cable: RS-232 to RS-422

- 9-pin Turnaround adapter (for 9-Pin Remote Deck Emulation mode)

- Machine Control iLok activation card

Connecting a Machine for 9-Pin Remote Deck Emulation (Windows Systems)

To connect a machine for 9-Pin Remote Deck Emulation mode (Windows systems):

1. Connect the (supplied) turnaround adapter to an **RS-422** cable, preferably connected to a Rosetta Stone RS-232-422 adapter.

Note: For the best reliability on Windows systems with very long cable runs or Tamura synchronizers, Avid requires the Rosetta Stone RS-232 to RS-422 converter (models 2/8 or 2/9).

2. Connect one end of the cable to an available **COM** port on your computer and the other end to the 9-pin output of the machine.

Windows Computer COM Ports

The built-in COM ports on most Windows computers supports the RS-232 protocol, so an RS-232 to RS-422 converter box is recommended (but not required) for short cable runs and compatibility with Pro Tools's RS-422 machine control. Some newer Windows computers allow you to toggle the built-in COM ports between RS-232 and RS-422 compatibility. Check your Windows computer's documentation for more information about RS-232 and RS-422 compatibility.

In addition to connecting a Pro Tools 9-pin Master to a Pro Tools 9-pin Remote system, remote deck emulation mode on Windows is also qualified for use with the following controllers:

■ Soundmaster ION/ATOM

■ Colin Broad SR4

■ Tamura IZM-806

■ JSK MS-2901

The following controllers are not officially qualified and tested, but may still work:

■ Timeline MicroLynx, KCU, Lynx, and Lynx2

Connecting a Rosetta Stone RS-232 to RS-422 Converter (Windows Only)

To connect a Rosetta Stone RS-232 to RS-422 converter (Windows only) for remote mode use, connect the Avid Remote Mode adapter in the RS-422 path, and not the RS-232 path. You can extend the 9-pin cable on the RS-422 end if a longer run is needed. See Figure 10.19.

Note: Although using the 9-pin Out ports on a SYNC Peripheral for 9-Pin Remote Deck Emulation mode will not work in Pro Tools, you can use the 9-pin Out ports on a SYNC Peripheral when using Pro Tools as a 9-pin master.

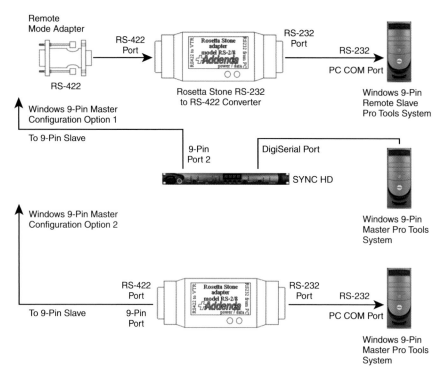

Figure 10.19
Windows: Connecting a Pro Tools 9-pin remote slave to a Pro Tools/SYNC HD master (option 1) or to a Pro Tools/Rosetta Stone master (option 2).

Connecting a Machine for 9-Pin Remote Deck Emulation (Macintosh Systems)

To connect a machine for 9-Pin Remote Deck Emulation mode (Macintosh systems):

1. Connect a KEYSPAN **USA-28XG USB** SERIAL ADAPTER (not provided) to a USB port on the computer.

2. Connect the supplied (black) Deck Emulation cable to the end of the serial adapter on the 9-pin remote system.

3. Connect the other end of the cable to the **9-PIN MASTER** Pro Tools system or other supported machine using a standard 9-pin cable or turnaround adapter (pictured in Figure 10.20).

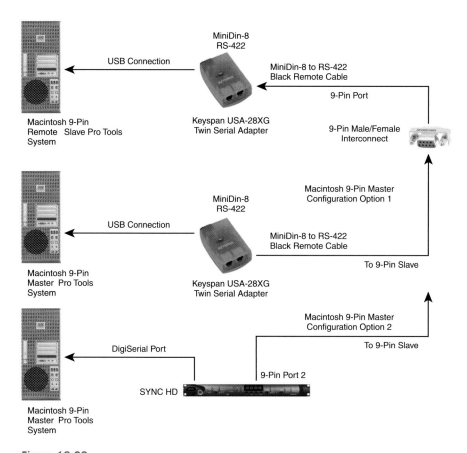

Figure 10.20
Mac System: Connecting a Pro Tools 9-pin remote slave to a Pro Tools/Keyspan USA-28X serial adapter master (option 1) or to a Pro Tools/SYNC HD master (option 2).

Configuring 9-Pin Remote Deck Emulation Mode

After all 9-pin deck emulation cables have been connected (described in the previous section), you can enable 9-Pin Remote (Deck Emulation) mode in Pro Tools.

To configure Pro Tools for 9-Pin Remote Deck Emulation mode:

1. Choose SETUP > PERIPHERALS and click the MACHINE CONTROL tab.

2. In the MACHINE CONTROL tab, enable 9-PIN REMOTE (DECK EMULATION) by checking the checkbox, as shown in Figure 10.21.

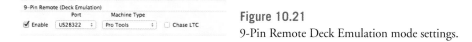

Figure 10.21
9-Pin Remote Deck Emulation mode settings.

3. Choose the appropriate port from the **PORT** menu.

4. Choose the appropriate machine profile (such as Pro Tools) from the **MACHINE TYPE** pop-up menu.

5. For Pro Tools to respond to all transport commands (including crawling and frame bumping), leave **CHASE LTC** disabled (default), which puts Pro Tools in **FULL REMOTE MODE**.

   - **Chase LTC disabled**: Pro Tools is in Full Remote mode, responding to all transport commands coming through the serial connection, including bump and crawl commands necessary for a tape machine to locate and cue.

   - **Chase LTC enabled**: When Chase LTC is enabled, Pro Tools can still respond to track arming and record commands. However, Pro Tools will chase incoming LTC instead of serial timecode, behaving as a master or slave device with the machine controller. By slaving Pro Tools to the LTC source instead of slaving the machine to Pro Tools timecode, you can avoid the waiting (and tape wear) that occurs while a machine transport locates and bumps tape to the cue point. Unlike Full Remote mode, Pro Tools waits until it receives only specific transport play, record, and track record commands from the machine (ignoring most other transport commands).

6. After all 9-pin remote settings have been configured, click **OK**.

7. When using Pro Tools as a remote timecode slave, set the **DELAY AFTER PLAY COMMAND** setting (located in **SETUP > PREFERENCES > SYNCHRONIZATION**) to 30 frames (as shown in Figure 10.22).

Figure 10.22

Synchronization preference page showing the Delay after Play Command setting.

Since Serial Timecode is bi-directional, any machine can become the positional timecode master if it is the first to go into play. The Delay After Play Command is therefore necessary for Pro Tools to reliably slave to timecode.

- When the Delay After Play Command preference is set to 30 frames, another machine is the timecode master. When online, Pro Tools behaves as a timecode slave device by delaying playback until its timecode can properly synchronize with the master device.

- When the Delay After Play Command preference is set to 0, Pro Tools is set up to function as the timecode master, and responds more quickly to transport commands. When online, Pro Tools locates and then plays when it gets a play command. One disadvantage of using Pro Tools as a timecode master device is that other linear slave machines may experience excessive frame bumping and tape wear in order to locate, cue, and synchronize with Pro Tools.

Tip: Generally, delay should be added only when Pro Tools is having problems starting and locking to a machine during playback or record. For example, if Pro Tools tries to lock, and the Transport window lights go from play to shuttle or fast-forward to rewind many times before locking, you should increase the Delay After Play Command setting by a few frames.

8. The IGNORE TRACK ARMING preference (located in SETUP > PREFERENCES > SYNCHRONIZATION), which is disabled by default, allows Pro Tools to follow remote track arming commands.

9. In the TRANSPORT window, click the **REM** (Remote) button to put Pro Tools into REMOTE mode. See Figure 10.23.

Remote button

Figure 10.23
Remote button in the Transport window (Chase LTC disabled).

Note: When you click the Remote button, if you did not enable Chase LTC, the Gen LTC (Generate LTC) button will automatically enable itself, which sets the Session Setup window's Positional Reference to Generate. This is required for Pro Tools to lock to the video reference with frame edge accuracy.

Note: When working with PAL video, after clicking the Remote button, check the Video Ref Format in the Session Setup window to make sure it is set to PAL.

10. In the SESSION SETUP window, shown in Figure 10.24, ensure that the following settings are configured:

- CLOCK SOURCE should be set to the AVID SYNC PERIPHERAL.

- CLOCK REFERENCE should be set to VIDEO REFERENCE.

- If CHASE LTC is disabled, POSITIONAL REFERENCE should be set to GENERATE.

- If CHASE LTC is enabled, POSITIONAL REFERENCE should be set to LTC.

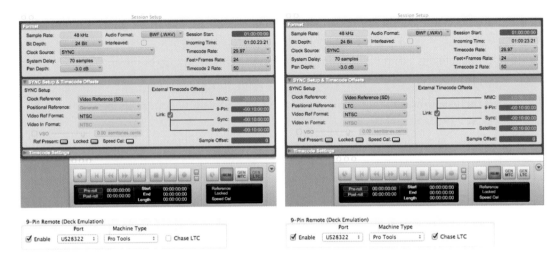

Figure 10.24
9-Pin Remote Deck Emulation settings: Chase LTC not enabled (left) and Chase LTC enabled (right).

Recording Stems Using 9-Pin Remote Deck Emulation Mode

As you learned earlier in this lesson, Pro Tools with Machine Control supports Auto Edit (selection-based) and Punch-In/Punch-Out (QuickPunch or TrackPunch) commands. Pro Tools must have QuickPunch, TrackPunch, or DestructivePunch enabled with tracks record-enabled when recording in 9-Pin Remote Deck Emulation mode with an edit controller.

Note: Preview, Edit, and Rehearse modes are not supported by Pro Tools 9-Pin Remote Deck Emulation.

Auto Edit Recording

When a machine sends Auto Edit commands to Pro Tools in 9-Pin Remote Deck Emulation mode, the edit in and out points are converted to a Pro Tools timeline selection. This selection, will then be used to record on all armed tracks when Pro Tools receives the Perform Auto Edit Record command.

Punch In/Out Recording

Punch-In/Punch-Out recording supports punch-on-the-fly, with Pro Tools in QuickPunch, TrackPunch, or DestructivePunch modes. In any of these record modes, tracks are armed before the record pass, and recording begins and ends when Punch-In and Punch-Out commands are received from the master machine.

Recording Printmaster Stems Using a 9-Pin Remote System

After all 9-pin settings for the 9-Pin Master and 9-Pin Remote Pro Tools systems have been properly configured, you are ready to record the printmaster stems.

To record the printmaster stems from the master Pro Tools HD system to the remote (slave) Pro Tools HD system:

1. Verify that the audio interface outputs from the master Pro Tools HD system are properly wired and routed to the inputs of the remote (slave) Pro Tools HD system, and that all other common system settings are correctly matched.

Tip: When recording audio from one Pro Tools system to another 9-pin remote slave system, it is recommended that you disable Chase LTC, so that the slave Pro Tools system can respond to all transport commands in Full Remote mode.

2. After the remote (slave) Pro Tools HD system has been configured to respond to 9-pin remote commands from the master Pro Tools HD system, enable 9-pin Machine Control from the master Pro Tools HD system.

3. Select a record mode by right-clicking the **Record** button in the **Transport** window on the **9-Pin Remote** Pro Tools systems, as shown in Figure 10.25.

Right-click on the Record button

Figure 10.25
Choosing a record option in the Transport window.

Tip: When re-recording updates or changes to existing printmaster stem files, choosing DestructivePunch will allow you to append whole or partial new recordings into previous printmaster audio files (without creating additional new files). This simplifies the process of creating the final printmaster delivery.

Note: When using DestructivePunch, Pro Tools will always fade in/out using a 100ms crossfade. Therefore, you should always check your punch points after using DestructivePunch to determine whether the audio needs to be re-punched (or the entire reel needs to be re-printed). You should also avoid punching into a reverb tail, other time-based effect, or track where a change in overall delay compensation has occurred since the previous recording.

4. In the MACHINE TRACK ARMING window of the 9-pin master Pro Tools HD system, arm the desired record tracks on the remote Pro Tools HD system and enable INSERT and PUNCH IN/OUT. See Figure 10.26.

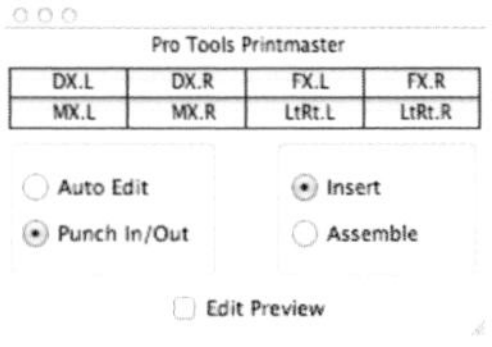

Figure 10.26
Machine Track Arming window of the master 9-pin Pro Tools HD system.

Tip: Although most professional theatrical releases would print surround stems, stereo stems are used in this book for simplicity.

5. Cue and begin machine playback and punch-record where desired.

Tip: If desired, you can continue to fine-tune and adjust any automatable parameters in Pro Tools as you are recording your final printmaster stems.

6. After the printmaster stem audio files have been recorded as shown in Figure 10.27, they can be transmitted for electronic delivery, or mastered and encoded to an optical format for theatrical release, with the most common digital formats being Dolby SR-D, SDDS, DTS, and DCP (Digital Cinema Package). For television projects, stems can be delivered for Dolby E (or other) encoding for DTV broadcast.

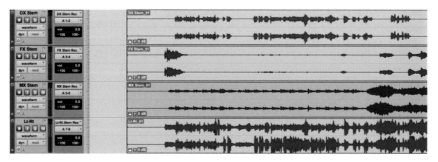

Figure 10.27
Dialogue, sound effects, music, and Lt-Rt stems printed on a Pro Tools HD 9-pin remote system.

Summary of Supported 9-Pin Commands

In 9-Pin Remote Deck Emulation mode (with Chase LTC disabled), Pro Tools with Machine Control can respond to the following 9-pin commands from compatible workstations, synchronizers, and other devices:

- Play
- Stop
- Pause
- Rewind
- Forward
- Cue To
- Poll Timecode
- Record Arm Track
- Set In/Out Point (for Auto Edit)
- Set Pre-/Post-Roll (for Auto Edit)
- Perform Auto Edit Record
- Perform Punch-In/Punch-Out Record (requires QuickPunch mode and voices)
- Return Status-Online, State, Tracks Armed
- Servo Lock
- Clear In Point

Creating a Machine Track Arming Profile

The Create Machine Track Arming Profile dialog box provides extensive control over Pro Tools track arming. You can customize arming, track naming, and mapping, and save configurations for different machines as Track Arming Profile files. These profiles can be imported and reused so that you can quickly reconfigure Track Arming as needed for future projects. You can also test track mapping, and remap tracks if needed.

Use the Create Machine Track Arming Profile feature to create profiles for machines that may not be included with Pro Tools, and to manage multiple profiles.

To create a Machine Track Arming profile, choose Setup > Machine Track Arming Profiles to open the dialog box shown in Figure 10.28.

Tip: When you create a new Machine Track Arming Profile, a Stop command is sent to any connected machine to protect elements on tape.

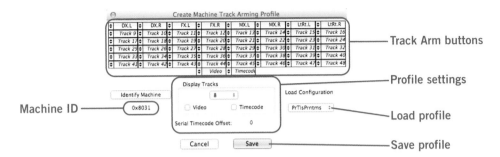

Figure 10.28
The Create Machine Track Arming Profile dialog box.

Choosing a Machine ID

To recognize your machine, click Identify Machine in the Create Machine Track Arming Profile dialog box. Machine Control will query the connected machine for its machine ID and then display the ID below the Identify Machine button.

Note: Although you can edit or replace the ID manually (if needed), the procedure for doing so is not covered in this book. For more information, please consult the Machine Control User's Guide.

Configuring and Saving a Profile

The Create Machine Track Arming Profile dialog box allows you to specify track names and track mapping.

Customizing Names for Track Arming Buttons

You can rename the Track Arm buttons displayed in each Machine Track Arming Profile to better describe the recording taking place. For example, an eight-track profile might be easier to use with tracks named DX.L, DX.R, FX.L, FX.R, MX.L, MX.R, Foley.L, and Foley.R, for eight tracks composed of stereo dialogue, stereo sound effects, stereo music, and a stereo Foley.

To edit the name of a track arming button:

1. In the CREATE MACHINE TRACK ARMING PROFILE dialog box, double-click the TRACK ARM button you want to rename.

2. Enter a new track name in the dialog box, and click **OK**. See Figure 10.29.

Figure 10.29
Entering a custom track name.

Remapping Tracks

You can remap track buttons to target different tracks on the machine.

To remap tracks:

1. In the **CREATE MACHINE TRACK ARMING PROFILE** dialog box, click the **TRACK** button you want to remap to display its **REMAP** pop-up menu, as shown in Figure 10.30.

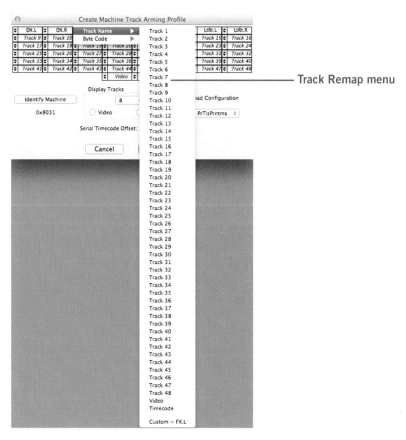

Figure 10.30
Remap pop-up menu in the Create Machine Track Arming Profile dialog box.

2. Choose a new target track in the REMAP pop-up menu.

Note: Remapping the byte codes to create a custom profile is beyond the scope of this class. Refer to the Machine Control Guide for more information.

Saving and Loading a Machine Track Arming Profile

Once you have configured and named the track arming buttons as desired, you can save the track arming profile for later use in other projects. To save a machine track arming profile, click the Save button at the bottom of the Create Machine Track Arming Profile dialog box.

By default, Machine Track Arming profiles are saved in the following directories:

- **Windows:** System Drive/Program Files/Avid/Pro Tools/DAE/Track Arming Profiles

- **Mac:** System Drive/Applications/Avid/Pro Tools/Track Arming Profiles

To load a previously saved Machine Track Arming profile:

1. Choose a machine profile from the LOAD CONFIGURATION selector.

Using Satellite Link with Machine Control

There may be times when you want to use Satellite Link and 9-pin serial deck control (Machine Control) simultaneously. This would allow you to sync multiple Pro Tools systems via Satellite Link, while driving other hardware devices connected to a 9-pin synchronizer. Machine Control can be used to operate a 9-pin synchronization device (such as a Soundmaster ATOM or a CB Electronics 9-pin synchronizer), allowing Pro Tools to act as a "timecode-only master" for other systems controlled by the synchronizer.

Satellite Link lets you use Machine Control on only one linked Pro Tools system at a time, using the following rules:

- When one linked Pro Tools system is already online, and you go online with another linked Pro Tools system, Satellite Link will automatically take the first system offline.

- Any linked Pro Tools systems set to Transport=Pro Tools will follow Satellite Link transport commands.

- You cannot use Transport=Machine when using Satellite Link.

Using Satellite Link Without Machine Control

Most post production printmaster workflows today involve interfacing Pro Tools systems with other 9-pin linear and non-linear hardware devices and synchronizers. As an alternative to using 9-pin Remote mode to print stems, in an all Pro Tools hardware scenario (without other external 9-pin devices), you could use Pro Tools Satellite Link to link multiple Pro Tools systems, with one system dedicated to recording the stems, while the other systems are playback devices feeding audio to the printmaster system. In this scenario, since remote track arming is not supported via Satellite Link, you would need to manually record-enable tracks locally on the printmaster record system, or use a remote computer monitor/keyboard and mouse control box, such as a KVM Switch or a software-only solution (such as Synergy) in order to record-enable the tracks on the printmaster record system from your desired location.

Review/Discussion Questions

1. Give some example scenarios that demonstrate the need to offset sessions.

2. List the four types of External Timecode Offset settings that are available in Pro Tools.

3. What is the Mac or Windows keyboard shortcut for opening the Machine Track Arming window?

4. What is the difference between choosing Insert versus Assemble mode when outputting audio to a linear tape?

5. Why are sample rate pulls necessary?

6. Why is it sometimes useful to have Pro Tools act as a 9-pin remote device?

7. Under what circumstances would you need to use a Rosetta Stone serial adapter?

8. When enabling Pro Tools as a 9-pin remote device, contrast the differences in how Pro Tools responds to machine control commands when the option Chase LTC is disabled versus enabled.

9. How is DestructivePunch recording useful when creating printmaster stems on a Pro Tools system?

10. What is a machine track arming profile?

11. Why is it sometimes useful to use 9-pin remote mode and Satellite Link option at the same time?

Lesson 10 Keyboard Shortcuts

Shortcut	Description
Command+numeric keypad 2 (Mac)/ Ctrl+numeric keypad 2 (Windows)	**Open Session Setup window**
Command+numeric keypad 6 (Mac)/ Ctrl+numeric keypad 6 (Windows)	**Open Machine Track Arming window**
Command+Backslash (\) (Mac)/ Ctrl+Backslash (\) (Windows)	**Toggle Machine Transport**

Advanced Layback Options

When working on any post production project, there are a variety of linear tape final delivery formats (such as HDCAM SR, D5, Digital Betacam, DVC-Pro, and DVCAM), as well as other non-linear delivery file formats such as QuickTime, AAF, OMFI, WAV, MXF, and MP3 (to name just a few). Since many of the common non-linear output options are covered in the *PT 210P: Post Production Techniques* book, this exercise focuses on the linear output options. This final exercise is divided into two separate parts. In Part 1 of this exercise, you will output a stereo mix to a linear video tape, while in Part 2, you will output DM&E mix stems from one Pro Tools system to another using 9-pin remote mode.

Media Used:

310P Exercise 10.ptxt, 310P Exercise 10-Master.ptxt, 310P Exercise 10-Slave.ptxt, and a linear video tape with LTC running from time numbers 00:59:00:00–01:05:00:00 (or later)

Duration:

60 minutes

GOALS

- Configure Pro Tools Machine Control for layback of a stereo mix to a VTR

- Use Pro Tools 9-Pin Remote mode to print stems from one Pro Tools master system to another slave system

Getting Started (Part 1)

Note: Part 1 of this exercise requires a professional SD or HD video tape recorder supporting RS-422 (9-pin) deck control and audio layback using Insert mode. Prior to starting this exercise, you will also need to record (or stripe) LTC onto a linear video tape, with the timecode starting at timecode number 00:59:00:00 and ending at timecode number 01:05:00:00, using either 29.97FPS (NTSC), 25FPS (PAL), or 23.976FPS (if using an HD video tape recorder). Refer to Appendix D for more details.

If you do not have access to a professional video tape recorder, skip ahead to the "Overview (Part 2)" section of this exercise.

1. Open **310P Exercise 10.ptxt** on the book DVD in the **Exercise Media/310P Class Audio Files v10/310P Exercise 10/Part 1** folder (or other location specified by the course instructor).

2. In the **Save New Session As** dialog box, name the session as desired, saving into an appropriate location on a valid storage volume.

   When the session opens, you should see the stems tracks shown in Figure 10.31.

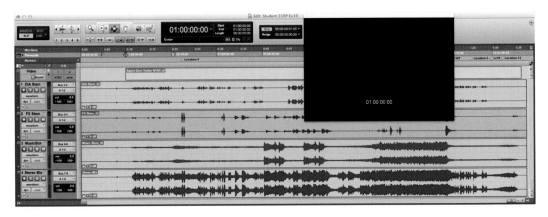

Figure 10.31
Stereo record stems from *Agent MX Zero* movie trailer.

Layback to Linear Videotape Using 9-Pin (RS-422)

You are now going to layback a stereo mix to a linear video deck, creating a final stereo video tape master of the project. Before you can begin the audio layback to linear video tape, you must do the following:

■ Verify the hardware connections

■ Configure the Session Setup window settings

■ Enable Machine Control

■ Arm tracks in the Track Arming window

Verifying the Hardware Connections

Before continuing, verify that the following hardware connections have been made:

■ 9-pin port on video deck is connected to 9-pin port 1 or 2 on SYNC Peripheral (or other supported port).

■ Video deck is set to Remote mode.

■ LTC OUT of video deck is connected to the LTC IN of the SYNC Peripheral (if not using Serial Timecode as the Positional Reference).

■ NTSC, PAL, or HD video sync is connected to both your video deck and SYNC Peripheral Video Ref ports.

■ Main stereo mix outputs (usually Outputs A 1–2) from your primary Pro Tools audio interface are routed to audio Inputs 1–2 of your video deck.

Configuring Session Setup Settings

To prepare your Pro Tools session for audio synchronization and layback to a standard definition or high definition external video deck, configure the Session Setup window settings as shown in Figure 10.32.

Note: Due to the method used to convert the 23.976FPS HD video master to the PAL video master, no audio sample rate pulls are necessary during layback to a PAL-formatted video tape master.

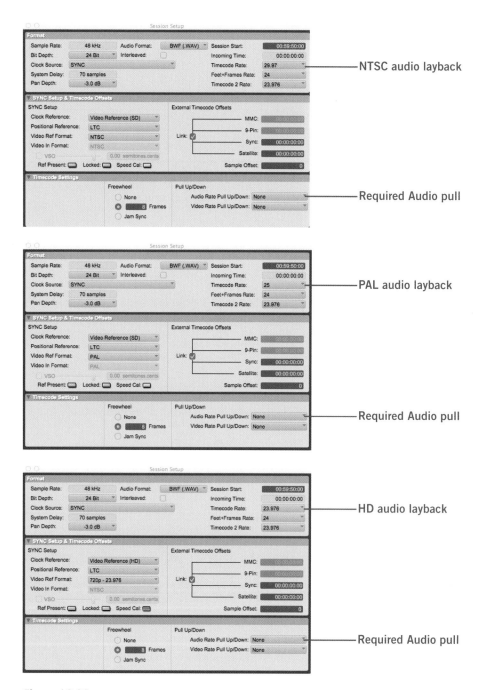

Figure 10.32
Session Setup window configured for NTSC audio layback (top), PAL audio layback (middle), and HD audio layback (bottom).

Enabling Machine Control

Assuming that your hardware and software settings have been configured properly and your external machine is powered on and in Remote mode, enable 9-pin (RS-422) Machine Control for audio layback.

 If you need a review of the steps for enabling 9-pin Machine Control, refer to Lesson 3.

Once serial Machine Control has been enabled, you are ready to configure and remotely record-enable tracks on your video deck using the Machine Track Arming window.

Using Machine Track Arming for Layback

Now that you are familiar with some of the Machine Control features and concepts taught in this lesson and Lesson 3, you will use remote track arming. The first step in using remote track arming is to configure the parameters of the Machine Track Arming window.

To configure track arming:

1. Make sure your machine is properly connected and Machine Control is enabled.

2. Open the TRANSPORT window (if not visible) by pressing COMMAND+1 (Mac) or CTRL+1 (Windows) on the numeric keypad. See Figure 10.33.

Figure 10.33
Transport = Pro Tools enabled.

3. Make sure TRANSPORT = MACHINE is enabled, as shown in Figure 10.34.

Figure 10.34
Transport = Machine enabled.

Shortcut: **You can toggle between machine transports by pressing Command+Backslash (Mac) or Ctrl+Backslash (Windows).**

4. Open the MACHINE TRACK ARMING window, shown in Figure 10.35, by pressing COMMAND+6 (Mac) or CTRL+6 (Windows) on the numeric keypad. If the entire window is not visible, click the ZOOM box.

Figure 10.35
Machine Track Arming window.

5. Verify that the number of record tracks is correct. The number of record tracks is based on the machine profile you chose when you enabled Machine Control.

6. Select the INSERT record mode in the MACHINE TRACK ARMING window.

7. Select the record protocol AUTO EDIT in the MACHINE TRACK ARMING window.

Caution: Do not choose Assemble mode, since this mode replaces all the elements on the target tape deck—audio, video, and timecode. Use this mode with caution.

To perform an audio layback to linear tape:

1. In the Edit window, solo the Stereo Mix track and then select the Stereo Mix clip for layback.

2. In the MACHINE TRACK ARMING window, arm the first two record tracks on your machine.

3. Verify that TRANSPORT = MACHINE has been enabled.

4. Press ONLINE+RECORD in the TRANSPORT window to arm recording.

5. Press PLAY in the TRANSPORT window.

   Your machine will cue to the selection start minus all relevant pre-roll, and then begin to play back. Pro Tools will then sync to the deck, and the target deck will record as determined by your settings for Record Protocol and record mode.

6. Once the audio layback is complete, disarm the machine-armed tracks and save the session.

Overview (Part 2)

In this part of the exercise, you will be using Pro Tools Remote 9-pin mode to record (or print) *Agent MX Zero* trailer stems from one Pro Tools system to another.

Note: In order to complete this section of the exercise, you will need two Pro Tools HD–series hardware systems with the Machine Control option installed on both systems. Before continuing, you will need to verify that both Pro Tools systems are interconnected and set up to operate as 9-pin master and slave (as described earlier in this lesson). If you are completing this exercise at an Avid Learning Partner, your instructor can assist you with verifying the system setup.

Because two separate Pro Tools HD–series hardware systems are required for this exercise, it is recommended that you complete this exercise with two people, one of you running the master Pro Tools HD system, and the other running the slave system. The master system operator will open and use a Pro Tools session containing digital picture and eight mono audio stem mix tracks from the *Agent MX Zero* movie trailer. The slave system operator will open an empty Pro Tools session and set up the system as a 9-pin remote slave. Then, using track arming and Machine Control commands originating from the master system, the slave system will record the audio stems from the master system.

Verifying the System Setup

Before proceeding, you need to verify the following:

1. Determine which Pro Tools HD systems are set up for 9-pin master/slave setup and operation.

2. The 9-pin master Pro Tools system is connected to the 9-pin remote slave Pro Tools system using the correct 9-pin remote cable.

Tip: For more information about setting up and configuring remote 9-pin Machine Control, refer back to the lesson or consult the *Avid Pro Tools Machine Control Guide.*

3. The master Pro Tools HD system's optical out (ADAT), TDIF, MADI, or (8-channel) AES/EBU connector is connected to the optical in (ADAT), TDIF, MADI, or (8-channel) AES/EBU connector of the slave Pro Tools system.

Note: When using a 96 I/O, you will need to use the Optical (ADAT) connectors, because TDIF and 8-channel AES/EBU connectors are not available on a 96 I/O interface. When using a HD Omni interface, you will also need to use the Optical (ADAT) connectors, because TDIF connectors are not available, and 8-channel AES/EBU connectors are only provided on output. If you are not wired for 8-channel audio from the master to slave system, you can use a single stereo AES/EBU audio routing assignment instead. If you are completing this exercise at an Avid Learning Partner, your instructor can assist you with verifying the system's audio connections.

Getting Started

1. Open **310P EXERCISE 10-MASTER.PTXT** (on the master system) and **310P EXERCISE-10-SLAVE.PTXT** (on the slave system) located on the book DVD in the **EXERCISE MEDIA/310P CLASS AUDIO FILES v10/310P EXERCISE 10/PART 2** folder (or other location specified by the course instructor).

2. In the **SAVE NEW SESSION AS** dialog box, name the session as desired, saving into an appropriate location on a valid storage volume.

   When the Master session opens, you should see the stems tracks shown in Figure 10.36.

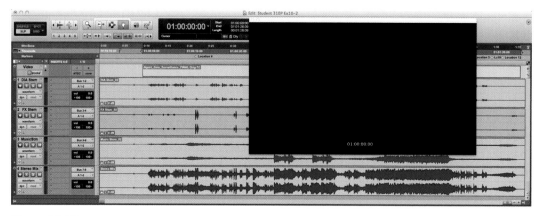

Figure 10.36
Master system stereo printmaster stems from *Agent MX Zero* movie trailer.

Tip: The master session already contains stereo dialogue, music, sound effects stems, and a stereo mix on tracks in the session.

Correcting a Session Offset

The slave Pro Tools session was mistakenly saved with the picture start at timecode number 01:02:00:00. This is a problem, because the master Pro Tools system that you will be using to control the slave system has the picture starting exactly at timecode number 01:00:00:00. To correct this problem, you can create the proper offset on the slave system using the Redefine Current Timecode Position feature in Pro Tools.

To offset the slave session to the correct timecode number:

1. Position the cursor at the start of the video (timecode number 01:02:00:00).

2. Choose SETUP > CURRENT TIMECODE POSITION to view the dialog box shown in Figure 10.37.

Figure 10.37
Redefine Current Timecode Position dialog box.

3. In the REDEFINE CURRENT TIMECODE POSITION dialog box, enter the time-code number **01:00:00:00** in the DESIRED TIMECODE POSITION field and then click **OK**.

   The picture start in the session has now been offset to the correct time-code number matching the master Pro Tools system.

Configuring the Slave Pro Tools System for 9-Pin Remote Control

To prepare to transfer the audio stem tracks from the master Pro Tools system to the slave Pro Tools system, configure/verify the following:

- Timecode rate is set to 23.976FPS.

- Clock Reference is set to Video Reference SD or HD (based on available clock reference).

- Positional Reference is set to LTC.

Note: The aforementioned Positional Reference setting will automatically switch to Generate once the system is placed in Remote mode using the REM button in the Transport window. You will be instructed to enable Remote mode later in this exercise.

■ Stereo audio stem tracks 1-4 have record inputs set to optical in (ADAT), TDIF, MADI, or AES/EBU inputs 1-8 respectively (from the master Pro Tools system).

■ Setup > Peripherals > Machine Control tab has 9-Pin Remote mode enabled, using Pro Tools machine type (as shown in Figure 10.38).

Figure 10.38
Enabling 9-pin deck emulation for a Windows system (left) and a Mac system (right).

Tip: If you are completing this exercise at an Avid Learning Partner school and you are unsure of which port to enable for 9-pin deck emulation, ask your instructor.

■ Be sure that 9-Pin Remote mode is enabled in the Transport window by clicking the REM button, shown in Figure 10.39.

Note: When working with PAL video, after clicking the Remote button, check the Video Ref Format in the Session Setup window to make sure it is set to PAL.

9-Pin Remote mode enabled

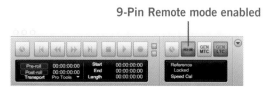

Figure 10.39
Enabling 9-Pin Remote mode in the Transport window.

■ DestructivePunch mode is enabled.

After you have verified all of these settings, the slave Pro Tools system will be ready for remote 9-pin recording.

Note: You must have the slave Pro Tools system set to 9-Pin Remote mode before attempting to enable Machine Control on the master Pro Tools system.

Configuring the Master Pro Tools System for 9-Pin Remote Recording

To prepare to transfer the audio stem tracks from the master Pro Tools system to the slave Pro Tools system, configure/verify the following:

- Timecode rate is set to 23.976FPS

- Clock Reference is set to Video Reference SD or HD (based on available clock reference)

- Stereo audio stem tracks 1-4 have optical (ADAT), TDIF, MADI, or AES/EBU output pairs 1-8 routed to their respective inputs on the slave Pro Tools system

- DestructivePunch mode is enabled.

- Setup > Peripherals > Machine Control tab has 9-Pin Machine Control mode enabled, using the Pro Tools machine type and the correct SYNC Peripheral port. Figure 10.40 is using SYNC HD port 2 for 9-Pin Machine Control.

Figure 10.40
SYNC 9-pin port 2 enabled in the Machine Control tab.

- In the Transport window, ensure that Transport=Machine is enabled and the Transport is Online.

- Choose Window > Machine Track Arming, remote track-arm the first eight tracks on the slave Pro Tools system, and set the record mode to Punch In/Out-Insert (as shown in Figure 10.41).

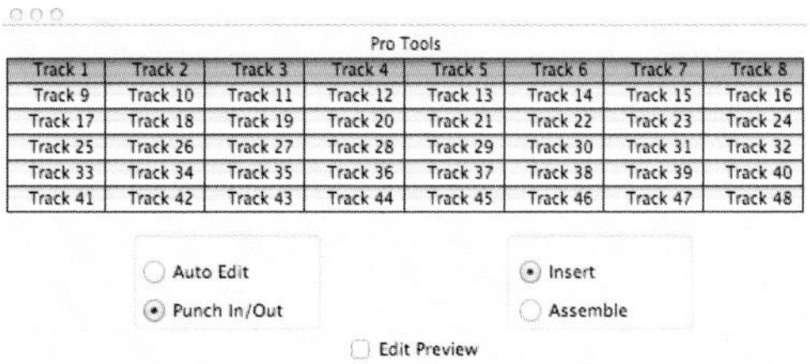

			Pro Tools				
Track 1	Track 2	Track 3	Track 4	Track 5	Track 6	Track 7	Track 8
Track 9	Track 10	Track 11	Track 12	Track 13	Track 14	Track 15	Track 16
Track 17	Track 18	Track 19	Track 20	Track 21	Track 22	Track 23	Track 24
Track 25	Track 26	Track 27	Track 28	Track 29	Track 30	Track 31	Track 32
Track 33	Track 34	Track 35	Track 36	Track 37	Track 38	Track 39	Track 40
Track 41	Track 42	Track 43	Track 44	Track 45	Track 46	Track 47	Track 48

○ Auto Edit   ⦿ Insert
⦿ Punch In/Out   ○ Assemble
        ☐ Edit Preview

Figure 10.41
Audio tracks 1 through 8 enabled in the Machine Track Arming window.

After you have verified all of these settings, the master Pro Tools system will be ready to initiate remote 9-pin recording on the slave Pro Tools system.

Recording (Master Pro Tools System Only)

After the tracks are remote track-armed from the Master Pro Tools system, you are ready to record the stems.

To record the audio to the Master Pro Tools system:

1. Make a selection starting at timecode number **01:00:00:00** and ending at the end of the longest track.

2. Place the Pro Tools transport online and initiate online recording.

   The slave system should start recording at the starting timecode number.

Tip: Since you are using DestructivePunch, you can try punching in/out at different locations.

3. When the recording is complete, save the sessions on both the master and slave Pro Tools systems.

Tip: If time permits and you are working on this exercise with another person, you can switch systems, and start the exercise again, so that each of you gets a chance to configure and run both the master and slave Pro Tools systems.

On Your Own

If there is still remaining time and your equipment setup permits, try printing stem tracks from the master system to the slave system using the Satellite Link option instead of using 9-pin Machine Control.

Tip: The Satellite Link option does not support remote track arming, so you will have to record-enable the tracks manually on the slave system.

Pro Tools HD-Series Audio Interface Calibration

This appendix provides calibration instructions for HD-series audio interfaces, including the HD I/O and 192 I/O systems with mixed HD-series audio interfaces.

Calibrating an HD I/O or 192 I/O

The following procedure describes a method for calibrating both outputs and inputs to the same reference level using either an HD I/O or 192 I/O interface. You will need a VU or dBu meter to perform this procedure, or you can use a multimeter (+4dBu = 1.23Vrms). These steps describe calibrating one channel. Repeat the process to calibrate additional channels.

To calibrate an HD I/O or 192 I/O interface:

1. In Pro Tools, create a new session by choosing FILE > NEW SESSION.

2. Choose SETUP > PREFERENCES and click OPERATIONS.

3. Enter the desired CALIBRATION REFERENCE LEVEL value in dB. A level of either –18DBFS or –20DBFS referencing +4dBu nominal is typical for post production. (It isn't necessary to type a minus sign here.)

Note: Entering a Calibration Reference Level value in the Preferences dialog box only sets the calibration reference mark for Calibration mode, and does not set the reference level of the system.

4. Click DONE.

5. Create a new mono Aux Input track, set its input to NO INPUT, and route its output to the first channel you want to calibrate. This must be a single mono output assignment, because stereo and multi-channel output assignments are attenuated when panned to the center based on the session's current Pan Depth setting.

In the Avid Learning Series

For more information about the Pan Depth setting in Pro Tools, see the *PT 201 Pro Tools Production II* book.

6. Mute the audio monitoring to your speakers before continuing.

7. Insert the Signal Generator DSP plug-in on the track.

8. Set the Signal Generator's output level. This should be the same value you entered for the Calibration Reference level (for example, –20).

9. Set the Signal Generator's frequency to 1000HZ.

10. Set the Signal Generator's signal waveform to SINE.

11. Connect an external VU or dBu meter to the analog output.

12. Adjust the I/O output level trim pot with a small, flathead screwdriver (preferably with a shrouded tip) to align the output to read "0 VU" on the external VU meter.

13. Now connect the output to the first input you want to calibrate.

14. Create another Aux Input track, and set its input to the first channel you want to calibrate. Mute it, so that feedback doesn't occur.

15. Choose OPTIONS > CALIBRATION MODE. The names of all the tracks will begin to flash. In addition, the track volume indicator of the Auxiliary Input track receiving an external input signal will now display the reference level coming from the calibrated output.

16. Adjust the input level trim pot with the same small flathead screwdriver. It is best to calibrate the inputs with the rear of the audio interface facing you and the Pro Tools screen well in sight, or get somebody else to watch the screen. When matched to the calibration level set in preferences, the track name will stop flashing and the peak volume indicator will indicate your headroom value. The Automatch indicator arrows on each track show the direction of adjustment required for alignment:

    • When the incoming level is higher than the reference level, the down arrow will appear lit (blue). In this case, trim the I/O input level down.

    • When the incoming level is lower than the reference level, the up arrow will appear lit (yellow). In this case, trim the I/O input level up.

    • When you have properly aligned the incoming peak signal levels to match the calibration reference level, both Automatch indicator arrows will light: the up arrow will be yellow and the down arrow will be blue.

    • Below the fader in the Mix window is a peak volume indicator. This indicator will show the dB level above and below your chosen reference level. If the peak indicator is showing –21.1, you are –1.1dB below a reference level of –20dB. If the display is showing –16.5, you are +3.5dB above a reference level of –20dB.

Note: Although the HD OMNI interface supports output level calibration, it does not support reference level calibration. The output calibration controls of an HD Omni interface include a combination of Analog Output level and Analog Output Trim functions. These controls are intended for surround sound speaker-level calibration (such as calibration to match Dolby loudness specifications) and not reference level calibration.

Note: An HD I/O can be calibrated just like a 192 I/O. However, the HD I/O has only a single set of trim pots, whereas the 192 I/O interface has two sets of calibration trim pots (labeled A and B) that can be used to switch between two different calibration reference levels (such as −20dBFS and −18dbFS).

Calibrating a System with Mixed HD-Series Audio Interfaces

The 96 I/O is factory set at −14dBFS reference level, and its inputs and outputs are not adjustable. In systems using one or more HD I/O, 192 I/O, or HD OMNI interfaces combined with one or more 96 I/Os, it may make sense to calibrate all I/Os for −14dBFS. This helps ensure that incoming signals will have the same relative levels in Pro Tools regardless of which interface they are connected to.

Caution: When reducing the input and output calibration settings of either an HD I/O or 192 I/O interface in order to match the fixed 14dB headroom of a 96 I/O interface, you are also lowering the available headroom value of the interface. This might pose a problem for professional post production facilities, as the standard maximum signal level for many professional video/audio devices could overload the inputs of the interfaces.

Synchronization Concepts

This appendix is designed to give you a good understanding of synchronization as it relates to Pro Tools, including the basics of using audio and video pull factors for converting between NTSC, PAL HD video, and Film projects. When using a device that sends or receives timecode, such as a videotape recorder, refer to that device's documentation for information on how it generates or receives timecode and how to configure its options.

Synchronization Requirements

It is important for you to research and understand exactly what your synchronization requirements are. For example, if you are using Pro Tools to accomplish audio post production work for video, consult with your production supervisor or video editor to determine what timecode format will be used. Also, there may be additional timecode issues that affect how you use synchronization.

Aspects of Synchronization

Synchronization in a digital audio workstation has two questions that need to be independently considered:

- "Where are we?"—This is called the positional reference.

- "How fast are we going?"—This is called the clock (or speed) reference.

To synchronize Pro Tools to another device (such as a videotape recorder) accurately over an extended period of time, Pro Tools needs to know where the device is and at what speed it is running. Some peripherals can provide only one of these references; for example, a blackburst generator provides only a clock reference. Some peripherals, like Avid's SYNC HD Peripheral, can synchronize using both a clock and a positional reference.

Synchronizing Pro Tools

Pro Tools requires a clock reference, in addition to timecode, to maintain synchronization over time (for example, when slaving to another device).

Video Reference as a Clock Reference

Video reference (also known as video ref, blackburst, and house sync, among other things) is the most commonly used clock reference for standard definition video post production projects (see Figure B.1). Video reference is a composite video signal consisting of all horizontal and vertical synchronization information and color burst. Typically it used as the house reference synchronization signal for all video and audio devices in broadcast facilities. In standard-definition (SD) formats, it can also be known as Bi-Level sync; in high-definition (HD) formats, a variation called Tri-Level sync may be required.

Unlike word clock, which is audio sample-based (that is, 44.1kHz, 48kHz, 96kHz, etc.), video reference is frame-based. Being frame-based makes it perfect for use as a speed reference in video-based editing.

Note: The speed reference is based on the common SMPTE/EBU horizontal line
(or scan) rates that correspond to 25FPS (PAL) or 29.97FPS (NTSC) video:
15.625kHz and 15.734kHz, respectively. For SD video formats, this means
the video reference frequency will be 15.625kHz for PAL or 15.734kHz for
NTSC. Also, PAL-M has a horizontal scan rate of 15.750kHz and a field
frequency of 60Hz across 525 scan lines as opposed to 625.

When fed to all devices, the video reference signal acts as a global clock, controlling and matching the speed of the videotape recorders, AD/DA converters of both
linear and non-linear recording and editing products, and the cameras during a
production shoot. When a video reference is used alongside LTC of the same frame
rate, you can be sure that every synchronized device will be perfectly locked in
terms of both speed and position. If either the LTC or video reference is set to the
wrong frame rate, or only a positional reference is used with no clock reference,
there will be drift between the devices trying to lock together.

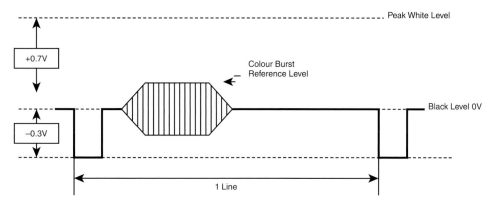

Figure B.1
Standard definition video reference signal.

Both the SD PAL and NTSC video reference signals consist of a blanking pulse
(sync pulse + color burst + "back porch"), and a constant voltage of 0.3 volts of
black color (that is, no picture information is included).

Tri-Level Sync Recap

Tri-Level sync was introduced with the SMPTE 240 analog HDTV standard. Prior
to that, the early HDTV systems used various synchronization waveforms, as provided by their respective equipment manufacturers. The creators of the SMPTE
240 HDTV standard sought to use a standard sync waveform that would ensure
system compatibility with all HDTV systems. Another goal was to provide more
precise synchronization and relative timing of the three component video signals.

HDTV component video has sync present on all three channels: Y, Pb, and Pr. In addition, the sync structure needed to be resilient enough to endure multi-generational recording and other noisy situations. Tri-Level sync meets these requirements.

Tri-Level sync derives its name from the fact that it uses three different voltage levels for each synchronization pulse, as opposed to the two different voltage levels used in standard definition Bi-Level sync signals.

Resolving Pro Tools Using Video Reference and LTC

You can resolve Pro Tools to an external video clock reference while using LTC as its positional reference. For example, you can clock any HD-series audio interface (HD I/O or 192 I/O) to a SYNC Peripheral using the Loop Sync connectors. If the SYNC Peripheral is the loop sync master, clocking itself to video reference, the same clock in turn gets distributed to all other interfaces in the loop sync chain. This resolves the Pro Tools sample clock to house sync, while synchronizing Pro Tools to external timecode. You should do this if you need all your work in Pro Tools to match the speed of other machines in your facility.

About Positional References

Timecode is timing information in the form of a data stream that can be recorded on magnetic tape as an audio or video signal. Timecode can be used as a positional reference, to synchronize the playback and recording of your Pro Tools system with another machine's timecode signal, such as an analog multitrack tape machine or a videotape recorder (VTR).

SMPTE and ISO/EBU Timecode

The "where are we?" question refers to relative position. To describe position, many professional audio, video, and multimedia devices and programs use SMPTE (Society of Motion Picture and Television Engineers) timecode. In Europe, a standard called ISO (International Standards Organization) timecode, formerly called EBU (European Broadcasters Union) timecode, is generally used. These timecode types are almost exactly the same in terms of how they are represented electronically. However, ISO/EBU timecode works at a fixed rate of 25FPS, and SMPTE timecode includes provisions for several different frame rates. For the purposes of explanation, this appendix will generally refer to frame-measured timing information as "SMPTE timecode." This description should be understood to include ISO/EBU and SMPTE timecodes.

SMPTE Timecode Methods

There are two basic techniques used to record SMPTE timecode onto magnetic tape: LTC (linear timecode) and VITC (vertical interval timecode). LTC is recorded or generated on an audio channel or a dedicated timecode track of the audio or video device. VITC is recorded within the video signal in the video "blanking area" of each video frame. VITC cannot be recorded on audio tracks, so it has no application when working with audio tape recorders, but it does offer powerful features for post production professionals who work with video.

There is also a non-SMPTE form of timecode called MIDI timecode (MTC) that some devices use to send positional information.

SMPTE Timecode Units

Timecode describes locations in terms of hours, minutes, seconds, frames, and subframes (1/100th of a frame). The frame is used as a unit of time measurement due to SMPTE timecode's origin in film and video applications. Depending on the timecode frame rate, one frame is equal to 1/24th, 1/25th, 1/29.97th, or 1/30th of a second. For example, a videotape timecode reading of 01:12:27:15 tells you that you are at a position of one hour, 12 minutes, 27 seconds, and 15 frames. However, this timecode address alone does not tell you the frame rate information.

Because timecode stores an absolute positional reference on the tape in the form of timecode, any location on that tape can be precisely located by devices that read timecode. Once the timecode has been recorded or striped onto a tape, it provides a permanent positional reference that allows Pro Tools to link the playback of an event to an exact tape location. For example, with timecode synchronization, a gun shot sound effect can be played at the precise instant that the gun's flash appears on-screen.

LTC (Longitudinal Timecode)

LTC is timecode that is recorded and played back, or generated, in the form of an analog audio signal. LTC is supported by many audio and videotape recorders, and many non-linear devices as well.

LTC Speed Usage

LTC can be read at high tape shuttle speeds, allowing a machine's timecode reader to communicate with synchronizers at rewind or fast forward speeds exceeding 50 times playback speed (provided the tape recorder is able to reproduce the timecode at this speed). However, LTC cannot be read at very slow shuttle speeds (such as when "crawling" the tape frame by frame) or when the machine is paused.

With LTC, the videotape recorder must be running (usually at a minimum speed of about 1/10th normal playback speed) in order to capture and read the SMPTE timecode address.

VITC (Vertical Interval Timecode)

VITC is a type of timecode that is recorded and played as an invisible part of a video signal. VITC is commonly used in professional video editing and audio-for-picture applications. Because VITC is recorded as part of each video frame, it must be recorded at the same time as the video signal—it cannot be added later as LTC can. Because VITC cannot be recorded onto audio tracks, it can never be used to synchronize audio-only recorders. Instead, LTC is most often used in audio-only applications.

VITC Speed Usage

VITC's ability to be read when moving a VTR transport at slow speeds or when the VTR is paused makes it more useful in audio post production environments than LTC.

When VITC is used, Pro Tools can capture the current SMPTE timecode from the VTR when it is paused or in "crawl" mode. However, if you are using additional external transport synchronizers in your setup, most synchronizers cannot read VITC at speeds exceeding approximately 10 times playback speed, preventing slaved machines from maintaining synchronization during rewind and fast forward.

LTC/VITC Auto-Switching

Many synchronizers and devices support automatic switching between LTC and VITC, depending on the speed, to get the best of both worlds. For example, VITC might be used when a VTR is paused or crawling frame-by-frame, while the synchronizer might automatically switch to LTC when fast-forwarding. This requires that both timecode types (LTC and VITC) be present and synchronous.

Tip: The Avid SYNC HD and SYNC I/O both support auto LTC/VITC switching.

Note: Pro Tools can receive and synchronize to a serial version of LTC known as Serial Timecode, sent through a 9-pin (RS-422) cable.

Bi-Phase/Tach Pulses

This electronic pulse stream is used by film projectors, film editing stations, and film mag recorders. You can use this format to synchronize Pro Tools if you have an Avid SYNC Peripheral. Unlike SMPTE timecode, Bi-Phase/Tach doesn't actually contain absolute location information. It simply supplies speed (based upon the frequency of pulses) and direction, and therefore, relative position. Since an Avid SYNC Peripheral can "count" both the speed and direction of the stream of pulses, it can use a Bi-Phase/Tach source to deduce positional information from a starting "address point." The difference between Bi-Phase and Tach formats is that Bi-Phase encodes rate and direction on a pair of signals using a format called phase-quadrature, whereas Tach encodes rate on one signal and direction on the other.

Tip: For more information on Bi-Phase/Tach, see the *Avid SYNC HD Guide*.

Timecode Frame Rates

Seven timecode frame rates exist, and Pro Tools can synchronize to any format with a compatible synchronization peripheral. The supported timecode frame rates are:

■ **23.976FPS**: Used for HD projects that will be edited using NTSC (standard definition) video. It is also used for many film projects that are transferred to video.

■ **24FPS**: International film standard and also used for some HD video and cinema projects.

■ **25FPS**: PAL standard definition audio/video format typically used for video projects (generally used in Europe, Africa, Asia, Australia, and some parts of South America).

■ **29.97FPS (non-drop frame)**: NTSC non-drop frame standard definition audio/video format typically used for film projects that are converted to NTSC video (generally used in North and Central America, and some parts of Asia and South America).

■ **29.97FPS drop**: NTSC drop frame standard definition audio/video format typically used for television NTSC broadcast (generally used in North and Central America, and some parts of Asia and South America).

NTSC color video has an actual frame rate of 29.97FPS, so an hour's worth of frames (108,000) running at 29.97 non-drop frame timecode will take slightly longer than one hour of real time to play. This makes calculating the actual length of a program difficult when using 29.97 non-drop frame timecode. A program that spans one hour of 29.97 non-drop frame timecode addresses (for example, from 1:00:00:00 to 2:00:00:00) is actually 60 minutes, 3 seconds, and 18 frames long.

To make working with 29.97FPS timecode easier for broadcasters, the SMPTE committee created 29.97 drop frame timecode, which runs at exactly the same speed as 29.97 non-drop frame timecode, but compensates for the slower speed by "dropping" (omitting) two frames at the top of each minute, with the exception of every 10th minute. For this reason, the timecode address of 1:01:00:00 does not exist in drop frame timecode because it has been skipped.

Tip: Even though timecode addresses are skipped in drop frame format, actual frames of video material are not dropped.

At the end of a program that spans precisely one hour of drop frame timecode (for example, 1:00:00;00 to 2:00:00;00), exactly one hour of real time has elapsed. Although it sounds complicated, drop frame timecode allows broadcasters to rely on timecode values when calculating the true length of programs, facilitating accurate program scheduling.

- **30FPS**: This is the original SMPTE format developed for monochrome (black and white) video, and is commonly used in audio-only applications. This format is often referred to as 30 non-drop frame format. Some music applications and film referenced audio projects use this frame rate as well.

- **30FPS drop**: This frame rate (which is much less commonly used) is sometimes used for some film projects that will be broadcast on NTSC television.

Note: In addition to the aforementioned frame rates, additional HD frame rates exist, such as 50FPS, 59.94FPS, 60FPS (non-drop), and 60FPS (drop-frame). Although these HD frame rates are not directly supported by the SYNC HD, you can use these frame rates in Pro Tools by selecting a Timecode Rate that is equal to one-half of the HD frame rate. The use of HD frame rates is beyond the scope of this book.

Note: When Auto Match Pull Factors is enabled in the Session Setup window's Timecode Rate menu, Pro Tools adjusts audio playback rates as needed to match any changes to the current session's timecode rate. In some NTSC-Film workflows, QuickTime video can also be pulled up or down 0.1%.

Working with Film-Originated Material

When you do post production work in Pro Tools, you will usually work with video material. However, it is possible that the video you are working on was shot on film.

Film footage and production sound go through separate conversion processes before they reach video and the audio post production stage. The film is transferred to video using a process called *telecine*. Audio can also be pulled down during the transfer, or you might end up working with the original audio that has not been adjusted (production sound).

Typically, during the telecine process, a master digital videotape is created. At the same time, a new audio master may be created by slowing down, or "pulling down" by 0.1%, the production sound to compensate for the change in speed from film to NTSC or HD video, or "pulling up" 4% to compensate for the change in speed from film to PAL video.

Film Telecine to NTSC Using 3:2 Pull Down

A film clip that lasts 1,000 seconds consists of 24,000 film frames (pictures). If you want to transfer that film to 1,000 seconds worth of NTSC color video, you have to "fit" 24,000 film frames into 29,970.02997 video frames.

If you use the black and white NTSC video standard (30FPS) instead of 29.97FPS, the process of converting film frames to video frames is greatly simplified. Now instead of any fractional frames, you have 24,000 film frames going into 30,000 video frames (60,000 video fields). In the telecine process for NTSC color video, each odd film frame is copied to two video fields, and each even film frame is copied to three video fields, creating what is called a *3:2 pull down*. The speed of the film is also "pulled down" to 29.97FPS in order to accommodate the slower speed of NTSC color video compared to NTSC black and white video (29.97FPS compared to 30FPS).

Film Telecine to PAL Using 12:2 Pull Down

When performing a Film telecine to PAL standard definition (SD) video, there are two different methods that are in use.

- **PAL Method 1 telecine**: This method is performing a film speed transfer using a 12:2 pull down telecine process. It involves no speed up, but uses the addition (24->25FPS) or subtraction (25->24FPS) of one frame every second to make up for the 24FPS to 25FPS difference. This method preserves timings but introduces a "jump" in the video every second when the extra frame is added in as a duplication of the previous frame. On talking head shots, this is barely noticeable, but on a wide panning shot it can look bad. A variant on this adds or subtracts one field every half second. This involves more complicated processing to make sure the field ordering remains correct, but produces a much smoother result that is very acceptable. This gives correct speed playback but needs expensive hardware, and can cause odd jitters in the motion. However, it does mean that a non-linear film editing system can edit at 24FPS using a PAL monitor. It also means that the audio is running at the same speed as the picture.

- **PAL Method 2 telecine**: The second PAL telecine process (commonly referred to as a video transfer) simply speeds up the film to 25FPS (a 4.1% speed increase), which gives an accurate frame-to-frame match and an inexpensive way of performing transfers. This is known as a *video transfer*. It is also possible for a film project to actually shoot at 25FPS for television, although using this frame rate is becoming less common because of the increased expense. This method is sometimes known as a 2:2 transfer. Now 4.1% may sound like a lot, but the suggested tolerance for projector playback is actually about 4–5% in the cinema, so this is no big deal. Nearly all DVDs produced in PAL are done this way so again they run 4.1% faster. However, the speed increase can cause problems in the audio realm because the audio must be sped up during the post production editing process to match the video. The audio is 0.7 semitones higher than the original audio.

Film Speed Differs from SD Video Speed

The new SD telecine master videotapes will run at either 29.97FPS (NTSC) or 25FPS (PAL) during post production, so the original field recorder audio (recorded at 24FPS) will be too fast for NTSC (or too slow for PAL), and therefore out of sync with the video. Some adjustment of this audio may be required.

When spotting audio to video that was transferred from film to HD, NTSC, or PAL video, there are two important terms to keep in mind: film speed and video speed.

- **Film speed**: Film speed refers to audio that was recorded and plays back in synchronization with the original film material. This audio often comes from a field recorder, and is usually striped with 24FPS timecode. Film must be pulled down 0.1% when being transferred to 29.97FPS NTSC (SD) video. Film must be pulled up by 4.1% when film is being transferred to 25FPS PAL (SD) video.

■ **Video speed**: Video speed refers to audio that is running at the NTSC color standard of 29.97FPS, PAL color standard of 25FPS, or HD video running at 23.976FPS. HD and NTSC video speed is 0.1% slower than film speed, so audio that is still at film speed will be out of sync with the video. Likewise, PAL video runs 4.1% faster than film, so again audio running at film speed will be out of sync. Usually, you will be working at video speed, although Avid provides several options for film speed (24FPS) workflows as well.

Pull Up and Pull Down

Pull up and *pull down* are terms used to refer to the deliberate recalibration of the audio sample rate clock (speed, or musical pitch) in order to compensate for a speed change. Pro Tools can be used to pull down or pull up audio for use with NTSC, PAL, HD video, or Film.

Pull down allows you to play back film-originated material at HD or NTSC video speed (0.1% down). Pull up allows you to play back HD or NTSC video speed material at film speed (0.1% up), or convert film referenced audio to PAL video speed (4.1% up).

Tip: Using Pro Tools audio sample rate Pull Up/Pull Down modes requires an Avid SYNC HD, SYNC I/O, or other compatible third-party synchronizer.

When to Pull Up or Pull Down

There are many ways to get audio into Pro Tools for post production. Consider your source audio and your final destination format carefully. In some cases, audio will already be pulled down for you. In other cases, audio will have to be temporarily pulled down. In still other cases, you may choose to pull down your audio source file from a field recorder, and then use a D-A-D (digital-to-analog-to-digital) conversion process, or an Avid HD I/O or 192 I/O's Sample Rate Conversion option, to record the audio into Pro Tools at the proper sample rate. Or you may choose only to pull Pro Tools up or down on final delivery of the audio.

Your Final Audio Destination Is Film

If your final audio destination is film, your source audio is at film speed, and your goal is to edit and mix audio in Pro Tools and then export a final file that runs at film speed, you can temporarily pull down the audio by 0.1% in Pro Tools for NTSC video work (or pull up the audio by 4.1% for PAL video work), and then return the audio back to film speed when you're finished (by disengaging the pull settings).

For example, film speed audio from a field audio recorder that is referenced to 24FPS timecode is imported into a Pro Tools session at a sample rate of 48kHz. After all the audio has been imported, and you are locked to a QuickTime video work print (running at HD 23.976FPS video speed), enable 0.1% pull down. If you are using Pro Tools software with or without an Avid SYNC Peripheral, you can select 0.1% Pull Down in the Session Setup window. While the pull down is active, you can work with your reference video and everything will remain synchronized and run at the proper speed (assuming your system is correctly resolved).

Caution: When using sample rate pull up/down in Pro Tools without an Avid SYNC Peripheral, you are limited to NTSC/HD workflows because QuickTime video can only be pulled up or down 0.1%. Also, using sample rate pulls without being resolved to an SD or HD Video Reference clock via an Avid SYNC Peripheral is not a professionally recommended workflow.

Once you are ready to layback your completed project to an audio device running at film speed, enable Auto Match Pull Factors in the Session Setup window. Then change your timecode frame rate in the Pro Tools session back to 24FPS. Once Pull Down has been deselected, the audio played back from Pro Tools will synchronize perfectly with the edited film.

As an alternative, you can either pull down the field recorder source audio during the import into Pro Tools, or after import into Pro Tools, rendering new audio clips running 0.1% slower by using the Time Shift or X-Form AudioSuite plug-ins.

Tip: The Time Shift and X-Form AudioSuite plug-ins have factory presets for NTSC, PAL, HD video, and Film audio format conversions.

Your Final Audio Destination Is Video

If you are working with video that was transferred from film, your audio source is at film speed, and the final layback destination is NTSC, PAL, or HD video, and you want to provide a digital transfer to your clients, you will need to alter the above workflow slightly. Keep in mind that when you are working in Pull Down mode for HD or NTSC video conversion from film, your active sample rate is 47.952kHz (if the audio was recorded at 48kHz) or 44.056kHz (if the audio was recorded at 44.1kHz. For Film to PAL conversion, you need to pull up 4%, so your active sample rate would be 50kHz (if the audio was recorded at 48kHz) or 45.938kHz (if the audio was recorded at 44.1kHz).

- **Pull Down the Audio Source**: Some professional field recorders will let you pull up or down the sample rate as needed. You can then record this audio into Pro Tools using a D-A-D (digital-to-analog-to-digital) process, or Avid's HD I/O or 192 I/O's Sample Rate Conversion option. Then your audio will be at the correct speed for the remainder of the project, since the final destination is NTSC, PAL, or HD video, and no audio pulls are necessary.

- **Note on Sample Rate Conversion**: In many cases, you have to perform a sample rate conversion at some point, either digitally, or by recording in audio using an analog stage (D-A-D). The only situation in which sample rate conversion is not performed is when you are working with film speed audio and your final destination format is film. Then you can simply pull down Pro Tools while you work with the video and deselect the pull down to set the audio back to film speed.

- **Using Digital Input**: If you are working with Pull Up or Pull Down, do not synchronize to any digital inputs that are used as audio sources in Pro Tools. This would override the use of the SYNC HD as the clock reference. Any equipment providing digital audio sources to Pro Tools should be synchronized externally.

The right half of the back panels of the HD I/O, 192 I/O, and the 96 I/O feature a set of non-removable connectors that are mounted permanently to the enclosure. These connectors cannot be used for sample rate conversion. Only the inputs on the digital I/O card on the HD I/O and 192 I/O feature real-time sample rate conversion.

Tip: You also need to select the correct sample rate pull up/down option in the Session Setup window.

Avid ISIS and Pro Tools Workflows

As a supplement to the information presented in the 10 lessons and exercises in this book, this appendix provides information about the Avid networking technologies and workflows that can be used in conjunction with a Pro Tools system. As a Pro Tools post production engineer, you should familiarize yourself with the workflows presented in this appendix.

Avid ISIS 7000

As the high-end enterprise-class solution specifically designed for media production in the Avid networking family, the Avid ISIS 7000 (Infinitely Scalable Intelligent Storage) media network delivers a highly scalable, self-balancing distributed architecture that combines the Avid ISIS 64-bit file system with the intelligent Avid ISIS Engine. Together, they offer support for up to 640TB of raw capacity, or 320TB useable with ISIS mirroring data protection. ISIS 7000 also supports up to 330 real-time clients with simultaneous access to the system, providing facility-wide uninterrupted access to media, powerful yet simple management tools, and an open architecture that supports both Avid and non-Avid clients in a range of mission-ritical environments.

The Avid ISIS Engine is a unique blade-based storage subsystem that features intelligent dual-drive storage blades, integrated Ethernet switching, and redundant power and cooling. Each Avid ISIS Storage Blade is a mini-server including disks, a processor, memory, and networking. The drive blades communicate with one another, constantly load-balancing and, in the case of a configuration change, redistributing data. All processing takes place in parallel to ensure real-time flow and to maintain data resiliency. Administration is straightforward with built-in system-wide health monitoring and remote notification of any critical system events. Avid ISIS Storage Blades can be easily added, removed, or hot-swapped (one at a time if mirrored or two at a time if using RAID 6) while the system is live, allowing work to continue without delay.

Note: ISIS 7000 provides real-time streaming of audio and video for qualified Mac and Windows Pro Tools HD systems running Pro Tools 10.x (or higher) software.

ISIS Components

The main components that make up an Avid ISIS storage system are as follows:

- **Avid ISIS Storage Blade (ISB)**: Intelligent hot-swappable dual-drive storage element (500GB, 1TB, or 2TB per blade) with integrated Linux-based server with dual redundant 1 Gigabit Ethernet ports. See Figure C.1.

Figure C.1
Avid ISIS Storage Blade.

Tip: ISIS v3.5 client software supports up to 2TB storage blades on both Mac and Windows systems.

■ **Avid ISIS Engine**: Chassis that contains 16 ISIS storage blades, which store the actual data, and Power/Cooling Blades and Switch Blades. See Figure C.2.

Figure C.2
Avid ISIS Engine.

■ **Avid ISIS Power/Cooling Blade**: Hot-swappable 600-watt power supply with redundant, 2 + 1 configuration.

■ **ISIS Integrated Switch (ISS)**: Integrated Gigabit Ethernet switch used for direct connections to clients and System Directors. High-speed 10Gb connections are also available for connection to a switch or 10GB Ethernet clients.

■ **ISIS Integrated Expansion Switch (iXS)**: The iXS expansion module is needed only if you are connecting three or more engines. When connecting three or more engines, two iXS modules are installed in one engine, providing high-speed 10Gb interconnects that stack the network switches to create one large virtual switch.

■ **Avid ISIS System Director**: Both the Intel SR2400 and SR2500 servers are mounted in a 2U rack chassis (the newer Intel AS3000 for Avid ISIS 7000 is mounted in a 1U chassis), with dual-mirrored internal drives, redundant power supplies, dual 1 Gigabit Ethernet connections to the blade servers, and dual private system director network connections for communication between two separate System Directors. Two separate System Directors are necessary on an ISIS network, serving as a redundant fail-safe in the case of a System Director failure. The System Directors act as servers to manage the storage and allow clients to access data. The system directors also provide software tools for setup, maintenance, and troubleshooting. Figure C.3 shows the basic Avid ISIS 7000 networking hardware.

Caution: An Avid ISIS 7000 network can be configured with only a single System Director, but the lack of redundancy would then make the network much more vulnerable to a critical system failure.

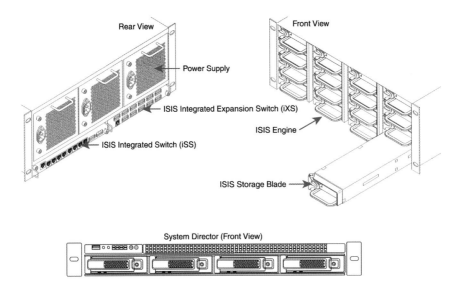

Figure C.3
Avid ISIS 7000 networking hardware.

■ **Clients**: These are individual workstations attached through the Ethernet Switch and administered via the ISIS System Director and the shared storage. The client can be an Avid editing system such as a Media Composer or a Pro Tools system.

■ **Avid ISIS Administration and Client software**: Administration tools for network setup, monitoring, and maintenance as well as client software for accessing and sharing media across the network. Figure C.4 shows the Avid ISIS management and client software.

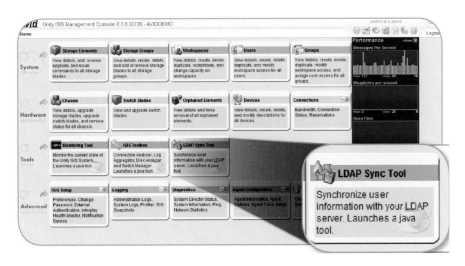

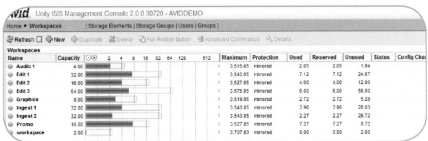

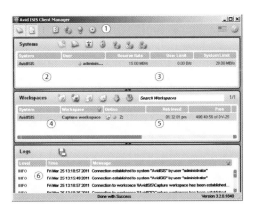

Figure C.4
Avid ISIS 2.0 Management Console (top), Workspace Manager (middle), and client software (bottom).

Avid ISIS 5000

Avid ISIS 5000 is a smaller system than ISIS 7000, designed for facilities that do not need as many client connections and as much available storage as ISIS 7000, priced at a significant cost savings. ISIS 5000 provides up to 90 client connections, 192TB capacity, and the linear performance of ISIS. Figure C.5 shows the Avid ISIS 5000 Storage Engine.

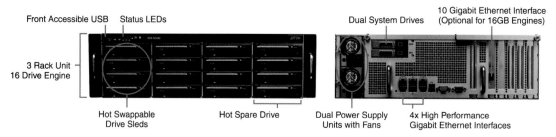

Figure C.5
Avid ISIS 5000 Storage Engine front (left) and rear (right).

Scalability is assured with a capacity range from 16TB to 192TB (24TB to 144TB with RAID) and from 4 to 90 direct client connections. Each ISIS 5000 Storage Engine houses sixteen 2TB disk drives arrayed in three 4+1 RAID5 sets, plus a hot spare drive. A two engine system (or more) is generally recommended to ensure redundancy with fail-safe capabilities between the System Directors in each engine. The ISIS 5000 Engine houses an ISIS System Director CPU that performs system metadata management. The System Director is protected with mirrored, field-replaceable system drives and, if needed, operation can easily shift to the System Director in a different engine. Depending on the model, four 1-Gigabit Ethernet ports or a single 10-Gigabit Ethernet port provide connectivity to one or two external switches, or directly connect to four 1-Gigabit clients.

Tip: ISIS 5000 v3.2 (or higher) client software provides real-time streaming of audio and video for qualified Mac and Windows Pro Tools 10.x (or higher) systems.

Avid Interplay

Avid Interplay is an optional asset-management database providing a uniform user interface to access all media for all users, allowing such things as AAF file transfers through the system, high and low resolution encoding, backup, and archiving.

With the Pro Tools Interplay Option installed, Pro Tools editors can interact directly with the Avid Interplay asset management system to do the following:

- Check out sequences.

- Edit and mix within a Pro Tools session.

- Export the session and any new media back to the sequence on Interplay.

- Use the Interplay Access and Interplay Administrator applications to manage and share files directly with an Avid editor.

Overview of Avid Interplay Components

An Avid Interplay system for use with Pro Tools and Avid video applications is composed of the following components:

- **Avid ISIS storage server**: All the media is stored on the ISIS server

- **Avid Interplay server**: Manages the metadata stored on the storage server.

The following Interplay software applications (which let users interact directly with Interplay):

- Interplay Access

- Interplay Administrator

The following software applications (which let users check in or check out sequences from Interplay):

- Pro Tools HD software with Interplay Option (purchased separately)

- An Interplay-compatible Avid video editing application

The following software options are required when using the Send to Playback feature:

- Avid Interplay Transfer

- Avid Interplay Web Services

- Pro Tools Send to Playback Web service

Pro Tools Avid Interplay System Requirements

Using the Pro Tools Interplay Option requires the following:

- Avid qualified Mac or Windows computer

- Pro Tools HD 10.x software

- Avid DNA video peripheral (recommended)

- Avid editing applications supported by Avid Interplay 1.0.3 and higher

- Direct connection to an Avid ISIS server

- Configured Avid ISIS client

For complete Avid Interplay system requirements, visit the Avid website at www.avid.com.

On the Web

Pro Tools on an Avid ISIS Network

Avid ISIS supports Mac and Windows 7 Pro Tools HD-series 10.x clients. Pro Tools clients are capable of operating as part of mixed ISIS workgroups with Avid Media Composer clients. Incorporating Pro Tools into an ISIS workgroup facilitates shared media (audio and video files) for more collaborative workflows, which means faster and more efficient productions.

Pro Tools HD 10.x systems support real-time streaming of audio and video on an Avid ISIS.

Attaching a Pro Tools client to an Avid ISIS for real-time streaming requires the following:

- Avid qualified Mac or Windows 7 Pro Tools|HD system with an Avid DNA video peripheral (if streaming Avid video is required) and Pro Tools HD 10.x software.

- Avid ISIS: Avid-approved Gigabit Ethernet NIC (Network Interface Card). Only Mac Pro Nahalem and Westmere systems have been qualified using the built-in Gigabit Ethernet connection, otherwise a third party network interface card (NIC) is required.

- Avid ISIS Client software.

Important guidelines must be followed when running a Pro Tools HD system on an Avid ISIS network. To review these guidelines, go to www.avid.com. In the Support & Services tab, check the Avid ISIS compatibility information.

On the Web

Pro Tools and Avid ISIS-Avid Interplay Network Workflows

When working with a Pro Tools HD system on an Avid ISIS network with Avid Interplay, there are a number of useful workflows that can be used.

Media Composer Sequence to Pro Tools from Within Pro Tools via Interplay

You can also import a Media Composer sequence from Avid Interplay into Pro Tools (from within Pro Tools).

To import a Media Composer sequence from Interplay into Pro Tools (from within Pro Tools):

1. Launch Pro Tools (if not already open).

2. If you want to import the sequence into an existing session, open the session.

3. Choose FILE > IMPORT > SEQUENCE FROM AVID INTERPLAY. The Interplay Access window appears.

4. Navigate to the folder containing the sequence you want to import.

5. Right-click the sequence, and choose IMPORT TO PRO TOOLS, and the click OK.

6. If the Name the Session dialog box appears, navigate to the appropriate location either on local storage or on a dedicated workspace on the network, and click SAVE.

Tip: This dialog box does not appear if you are importing a sequence into an existing session.

7. If the Pro Tools Import Session Data dialog box appears, select the appropriate options and then click OK.

Tip: This dialog box does not appear if you configured the Pro Tools Import Settings in the Avid Interplay Administrator. Pro Tools automatically uses those settings to import the sequence.

Media Composer Sequence to Pro Tools from Within Interplay

In this workflow, using Avid Interplay Access, a Pro Tools client is going to locate and import an Avid sequence containing video and audio directly into the Pro Tools system.

To import an Avid sequence from Avid Interplay directly into Pro Tools:

1. Launch Avid Interplay Access.

2. Navigate to the Pro Tools folder containing the sequence you want to import.

3. Right-click the sequence, and then choose IMPORT TO PRO TOOLS. If Pro Tools is not already running, it automatically launches and opens the Avid sequence.

Pro Tools Audio Track Export to Avid Interplay

In this workflow, a Pro Tools client is going to export edited audio tracks back to Avid Interplay.

Tip: It is recommended that you provide completed audio stems rather than audio tracks containing multiple clips and edits.

To export audio tracks from Pro Tools, and then check in audio tracks to Interplay:

1. In Pro Tools, select the tracks that you want to export into the Pro Tools sequence on Interplay.

2. Select FILE > EXPORT > SELECTED TRACKS TO SEQUENCE IN AVID INTERPLAY.

Tip: If a newer version of the sequence you're working on has been checked in by an Avid editor, Pro Tools will display the New Version Exists dialog box. This gives you the option to import the new sequence and update your audio as needed, continue with your export to the current sequence, or export directly to an updated version of the sequence.

3. In the Export Comment dialog box, type a comment and click OK.

4. In the Export Options dialog box (shown in Figure C.6), select one of the following methods for sending edited audio material into the Pro Tools sequence residing on the Interplay server:

- **Replace with Selected Tracks**: Replaces the old audio tracks in the Pro Tools sequence with the edited audio tracks. Select this option if you do not want to preserve the original audio in the sequence.

- **Add Selected Tracks**: Adds the edited audio tracks to the Pro Tools sequence on the Interplay database. Select this option if you want to preserve the original audio in the sequence.

- **Export Stereo, 5.1, and 7.1 Tracks as Multi-Channel**: This option lets you choose the format used when exporting multi-channel audio from Pro Tools to Interplay. Enable the option to export multi-channel tracks as multi-channel tracks, rather than splitting them to mono tracks. Disable the option to export multi-channel tracks as groups of mono tracks, one for each channel.

Tip: **This setting is disabled when exporting exclusively mono audio or when attempting to export an unsupported surround audio format (such as LCRS or 7.1 SDDS).**

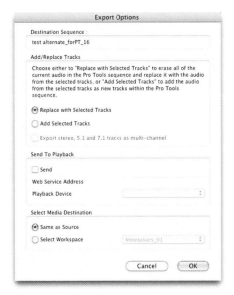

Figure C.6
Interplay Export Options dialog box.

Tip: **You also have the option to send the audio to a playback server, such as an Avid Airspeed Multistream server (if installed in the Interplay environment).**

Tip: When adding selected tracks, ensure that the total number of tracks in the sequence residing on the Interplay server does not exceed 24, which is the total allowed number of tracks for the Avid Media Composer 6.x application.

5. In the SELECT MEDIA DESTINATION section of the Export Options dialog box, choose the destination for your new media from the following choices:

   - **Same as Source**: The default behavior, this option will save the new audio to the same Interplay workspace that houses the first clip on the sequence's timeline.

   - **Select Workspace**: Gives you the choice to save the new audio to the root directory of a different workspace, pending permissions. Click the SELECT WORKSPACE button to open the Select Media Destination dialog box, where the desired workspace can be specified.

6. Click **OK**.

7. If the Pro Tools session start time is different from the start time of the sequence you want to export to, choose one of the following options from the warning dialog box that appears (shown in Figure C.7):

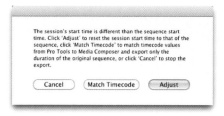

The session's start time is different than the sequence start time. Click 'Adjust' to reset the session start time to that of the sequence, click 'Match Timecode' to match timecode values from Pro Tools to Media Composer and export only the duration of the original sequence, or click 'Cancel' to stop the export.

[Cancel]   [Match Timecode]   (Adjust)

Figure C.7
Session Start Time warning dialog box.

   - **Cancel**: Stops the export operation.

   - **Match Timecode**: Matches timecode values from Pro Tools to Media Composer, and exports only the duration of the original sequence. Any audio outside of the sequence boundaries will be excluded.

   - **Adjust**: Resets the session start time to that of the sequence.

8. In the confirmation dialog box, confirm your selection. The sequence in the Avid Interplay database is now ready to be checked out and imported by the Avid editor.

Transferring Projects Between Local Area Network and Local Storage

Post production facilities that do not have an Avid ISIS network with installed Pro Tools clients transfer projects over a Local Area Network (LAN) to and from local storage devices. Although most non-Avid ISIS Network LANs cannot provide the sustained data rates that are required for real-time playback of multi-channel audio and video, they can allow access to shared transfer storage devices for all editing systems on the LAN, so that projects can be transferred ("pushed-pulled") from a networked storage device to local storage for real-time playback in Pro Tools. In this workflow, all projects that need to be transferred to a different editing system on the network are first uploaded to a storage device that is accessible to all editing systems on the LAN. Once uploaded to the network storage device, the project can then be transferred to local (or Avid ISIS Network) storage for the next editing system to use.

Tip: In the Pro Tools Playback Engine dialog box, enabling the Disk Cache setting might allow real-time playback of audio using other LAN technologies, depending on the amount of RAM available for the Disk Cache and the size of the session. Since video cannot be cached and streamed this way, an Avid ISIS Network can still be a huge benefit.

Although this workflow is obviously not as fast or convenient as having all Pro Tools and Avid editing systems on the same Avid ISIS Network, it still is a viable workflow for smaller post production facilities that cannot afford the costs associated with a real-time, high-speed network such as Avid ISIS.

Figure C.8 shows a network transfer drive in the Workspace browser that can be used to move projects between network and local storage in the background, allowing Pro Tools operators to continue working, even during uploads or downloads to the network.

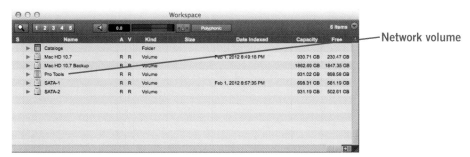

Figure C.8
Workspace browser with network volume for moving projects between network and local storage.

Video Tape Duplication Instructions

Before starting 310P Exercise 3 and 310P Exercise 10 (Part 1), you must first create a separate linear videotape for each exercise that is compatible with your videotape recorder. (See the duplication instructions that follow.)

Caution: If you do not have access to a professional videotape recorder, an Avid SYNC Peripheral (either a SYNC HD or SYNC I/O), and video hardware that can output QuickTime video to your videotape recorder's video inputs, you can skip 310P Exercise 3 and 310P Exercise10 (Part 1).

310P Exercise 3

To complete 310P Exercise 3, you will first need to create a linear videotape with the required Longitudinal Timecode (LTC), picture, and audio for the exercise, matching the tape format of your videotape recorder using one of the following formats:

- Video Tape-NTSC (29.97FPS)

- Video Tape-PAL (25FPS)

- Video Tape-HD (720p–23.976FPS)

For your convenience, three different Pro Tools sessions have been provided that can be used to create a linear videotape with Longitudinal timecode (LTC) in any of the aforementioned video formats. The Pro Tools sessions are located on the book DVD in the following directory: Exercise Media/Video Tape Duplication.

Caution: Before attempting to create a linear videotape using the sessions provided, verify that the session settings are correct for your videotape recorder and make sure that the Pro Tools audio and video outputs are routed to the appropriate inputs of your videotape recorder. You can generate and record LTC by connecting the LTC Out of an Avid SYNC Peripheral to the LTC In of your videotape recorder, and then clicking the GEN LTC button in the Synchronization section of the Transport window. To route the QuickTime video from Pro Tools to the inputs of your videotape recorder, you will need an Avid Video Peripheral (such as Mojo SDI), BlackMagic DeckLink Extreme PCIe card, or other supported video peripheral. Depending on the video format and video output device used, you may need to set a QuickTime video sync offset by choosing Setup > Video Sync Offset.

310P Exercise 10

To complete Part 1 of 310P Exercise 10, you will first need to create a linear video-tape for audio layback with the required Longitudinal Timecode (LTC) for the exercise, matching the tape format of your videotape recorder using one of the following formats:

- NTSC SD Video (29.97FPS)

- PAL SD Video (25FPS)

- HD Video (720p–23.976FPS)

It is not necessary to include video on this tape, although LTC must be recorded onto the videotape using one of the aforementioned frame rates, starting from timecode number 00:59:00:00 running through timecode number 01:05:00:00 (or later).

Tip: Although no session is provided for creating this videotape, you can reuse one of the sessions provided in the Video Tape Duplication folder, with the only difference being that this tape does not require picture or audio, just Longitudinal Timecode (LTC). You can generate and record LTC by connecting the LTC Out of an Avid SYNC Peripheral to the LTC In of your videotape recorder, and then clicking the GEN LTC button in the Synchronization section of the Transport window.

Appendix E

Answers to Review/Discussion Questions

Lesson 1 Answers

1. 512 tracks

2. 256 tracks

3. Four HD-series audio interfaces

4. Eight microphone inputs

5. Higher voice count with two or more HDX cards, DSP plug-ins, higher numbers of I/O

6. HDX TDM cable

7. Audio interface calibration is the process of measuring and setting the analog input and output levels on an HD-series audio interface across all channels to ensure that they are equal and that the operating levels conform to a specific industry or regional standard. Only the HD I/O and previous-generation 192 I/O interfaces support user-adjustable calibration. The HD Omni supports only speaker/monitor output calibration.

8. When using either an Avid Mojo SDI or Avid Mojo video peripheral with Pro Tools to record or play back video

9. Windows: Optimize hard drive performance, turn off User Account Control, configure System Standby Power Management to Always On.

Mac: Turn off auto software updates, turn off energy saver, re-assign con-flicting keyboard shortcuts, disable Spotlight, enable journaling for audio drives.

10. Restrict access to specific computer hard drives and directories, prohibit modifying or altering System settings, prohibit software installs and de-installs.

11. Open the session in Pro Tools and choose File > Save Copy In. In the Save Session Copy-dialog box's Session Format menu, choose Pro Tools 7 –> 9 Session, then click OK.

12. Pro Tools 9 session (.ptf) and Pro Tools 10 session (.ptx)

Exercise 1 Answers

Tip: Since hardware configurations can vary, the answers provided here are not the only correct answers.

Pro Tools System 1: Film/TV Dub Stage Mixing System

Apple Computer Hardware and Peripherals

Apple Macintosh Pro computer with Lion OS (10.7), 16GB RAM, and (Qty 3) 2TB internal SATA hard drives

(Qty 2) Apple 27-inch Cinema Displays

Avid Pro Tools Hardware and Peripherals

(Qty 2) Avid Pro Tools|HDX PCIe cards with Pro Tools HD 10.x software

(Qty 4) Avid HD I/O audio interface 16×16 digital

Avid D-Control ES with 32 faders and Surround Panner option

Avid Pro Tools Software Options

Avid Pro Tools Machine Control

Avid Pro Tools Satellite Link option

Third-Party Hardware and Peripherals

Black Magic Design DeckLink Extreme PCIe card

Bi-level/tri-level sync generator (supporting all standard SD and HD formats)

HD flat panel monitor with HDMI input

Pro Tools System 2: Orchestral Scoring Stage System

Apple Computer Hardware and Peripherals

Apple Macintosh Pro computer with Lion OS (10.7), 16GB RAM, and (Qty 3) 2TB internal SATA hard drives

(Qty 2) Apple 27-inch Cinema Displays

Avid Pro Tools Hardware and Peripherals

(Qty 1) Avid Pro Tools|HDX PCIe cards with Pro Tools HD 10.x software

(Qty 4) Avid HD I/O audio interface 16×16 analog

(Qty 8) Avid PRE (microphone preamp)

Avid D-Control ES with 32 faders

Avid Pro Tools Software Options

Avid Pro Tools Machine control

Avid Pro Tools Satellite Link option

Third-Party Hardware and Peripherals

Black Magic Design DeckLink Extreme PCIe card

Bi-Level/Tri-Level sync generator (supporting all standard SD and HD formats)

HD flat-panel monitor with HDMI input

Lesson 2 Answers

1. Avid Knowledge Base

2. Running hardware diagnostic tests on Pro Tools|HD and Pro Tools|HDX PCIe cards, verifying Pro Tools–installed PCIe cards, providing slot information for Pro Tools–installed PCIe cards, and updating firmware for HD-series audio interfaces and Avid SYNC Peripherals.

3. Avid hardware firmware is upgradeable software embedded in Avid hardware, acting as the device's operating system, providing the feature set and functionality of the device.

4. An Avid D-Control ES's firmware is updated automatically (assuming an update is needed) when connected and enabled in the Pro Tools software, immediately when Pro Tools launches.

5. An Avid SYNC HD's firmware is updated using the DigiTest utility in the SYNC Firmware tab. After choosing the correct port and SYNC type, click Begin Update, and then follow the onscreen instructions.

6. DigiBase Index files are stored in the following directory:

   - Mac: [Mac System Drive]/Library/Application Support/Avid/Pro Tools/ Databases/Unicode/Volumes.

   - Windows: C:\ Program Files\Avid\Pro Tools\Databases\Unicode\Volumes.

   It is sometimes necessary to delete DigiBase index files because they become corrupted, and there is no way to repair the corruption other than deleting them and having Pro Tools rebuild them.

7. 512 total voices

8. Explicit voices are supported on only previous-generation Pro Tools|HD hardware. They allow multiple tracks to share the same voices, which can allow your system to playback more tracks than it has voices, as long as the tracks sharing voices do not have any overlapping audio that plays during the exact same point in the Pro Tools timeline.

9. Allows the session's audio to be pre-loaded into RAM prior to playback, helping to avoid audio playback errors in sessions containing high track counts and audio densities.

10. Allows the session's audio to be pre-loaded into RAM prior to playback helping to avoid audio-playback errors in sessions due to slow or reduced network bandwidth.

11. Pro Tools|HDX systems provide for 1,536 total time slots, while Pro Tools|HD systems have 512 total time slots.

12. When disabled, Pro Tools recalls I/O assignments from the system (rather than the session), with all output bus paths of the session automatically remapping to the system output paths. Disabling this option allows you to overwrite the session's I/O settings and apply your preferred studio I/O assignments, names, and routings, enabling you to maintain your studio output monitoring path assignments for any sessions you open.

13. Audio and video pull options are necessary for converting the audio and video playback speed of a session, allowing format conversion between PAL, NTSC, and film projects.

14. 0.1% up

15. 4% down

Lesson 3 Answers

1. Loop Sync

2. Video Ref

3. Clock reference provides a speed reference, telling the device how fast it should be going. Positional reference provides a location reference (using timecode), telling the device where it should locate for playback or record.

4. LTC stands for *longitudinal timecode* and is used by Pro Tools as a positional reference, telling Pro Tools where to locate for playback or record.

5. VITC stands for *vertical interval timecode* and is embedded into the video signal. Like LTC, it is used as a positional reference, but it has the added benefit of being read accurately at play speeds all the way down to pause or stop.

6. Auto LTC/VITC allows Pro Tools to read the positional reference accurately regardless of the speed of the timecode master device by auto-switching between reading LTC and VITC. At normal play speeds and faster, Pro Tools reads LTC; whenever the timecode master's speed drops below play speed, Pro Tools switches to reading VITC.

7. PAL: 25FPS; NTSC: 29.97FPS; and Film: 24FPS

8. All audio is offset by the difference between the new timecode session start and the original timecode session start.

9. RS-422

10. Command+J or Option+space bar (Mac) or Ctrl+J or Alt+space bar (Windows)

11. 9-pin cable disconnected or 9-pin device not in Remote mode

12. To auto-spot clips to the currently received timecode

13. Edit-locked clips do not allow any edits without first issuing a warning dialog box providing choices to allow or cancel; time-locked clips allow any type of edit that does not alter the timecode location or sync of the clip.

14. Time stamps are timecode numbers that are embedded within audio clips that allow the clip to be synchronized to its original timecode location or an alternate (user time stamp) timecode location.

15. Timecode numbers that are superimposed over a video image that can be used as a timecode sync reference

Lesson 4 Answers

1. Option/Alt generally affects everything or reverses a function, while Option/Alt+Shift affects only the currently selected track nameplates.

2. The parameter or control can be adjusted with a finer resolution.

3. Command-click (Mac) or Ctrl-click (Windows) the Solo button.

4. Edit window: four (including the docked MIDI Editor window); Mix window: one.

5. Command+Option+1 (Mac) or Ctrl+Alt+1 (Windows)

6. Yellow=zoom, display, and numeric time entry; pink=edit functions; blue=transport and navigation functions.

7. Hyphen key

8. D, G, and F.

9. With Link Timeline Edit Selections unlinked, snaps one or more clip's start, sync point, or end to the Timeline cursor.

10. Toggles Insertion Follows Playback on/off

11. Loop Record is Option+L (Mac), Alt+L (Windows), or numeric keypad 5. QuickPunch is Command+Shift+P (Mac), Ctrl+Shift+P (Windows), or numeric keypad 6.

12. Command+Shift+L (Mac), Ctrl+Shift+L (Windows), or numeric keypad 4.

13. A=Trim Start and S=Trim End

14. Shuttle Lock mode can be used when the Numeric Keypad Mode preference is set to either Classic or Transport. Shuttle Lock mode lets you use the numeric keypad to shuttle up to two tracks forward or backward at specific speeds: 5 is normal speed, numbers from 6 to 9 provide increasingly faster speeds, and numbers from 4 to 1 provide progressively slower speeds, with 0 equaling pause. If multiple tracks are selected, only the first two tracks are shuttled. Shuttle mode on a Pro Tools HD and Complete Production Toolkit systems offers an alternative to Shuttle Lock mode. With the Numeric Keypad mode set to Shuttle, playback from the current Edit selection is triggered by pressing and holding the keys on the Numeric Keypad, with playback stopping once the keys are released. Various playback speeds are available in both forward and reverse, and holding the Shift key allows you to make selections while in Shuttle mode.

Exercise 4 Answers

Task 1: Keyboard Editing Shortcuts

1. Press period (.)+numeric keypad 1+period (.).

2. Press Control+Option+Up Arrow (Mac) or Start+Alt+Up Arrow (Windows).

3. Press Command+Option+1 (Mac) or Ctrl+Alt+1 (Windows).

4. Press Control+Tab key (Mac) or Start+Tab key (Windows).

5. Press the numeric keypad minus (–) or comma (,) key (three times)

6. Press Command+L (Mac) or Ctrl+L (Windows).

7. Press the semicolon (;) key (twice).

8. Press Command+Option+Tab (Mac) or Ctrl+Alt+Tab (Windows).

9. Press the Tab key (four times).

10. Press the A key.

Task 2: Keyboard Editing Shortcuts

1. Press period (.)+numeric keypad 2+period (.).

2. Press Command+Option+Tab (Mac) or Ctrl+Alt+Tab (Windows).

3. Press the semicolon (;) key to move the cursor to the MX_01 track, then press the Tab key once.

4. Press Option+Shift+Return (Mac) or Ctrl+Shift+Enter (Windows).

5. Press Shift+semicolon (;).

6. Press Option+H (Mac) or Alt+H (Windows) and then Enter two seconds later in the Shift dialog box.

7. Press the numeric keypad * key and enter timecode number 01:01:09:17.

8. Press Command+comma (Mac) or Ctrl+comma (Windows).

9. Press the numeric keypad plus (+) key or comma (,) key three times.

10. Control+Shift-click (Mac) or Start+Shift-click (Windows) inside the AMXZ Cue_07F clip with the Grabber tool.

Task 3: Keyboard Editing Shortcuts

1. Use the Tab key and Nudge keys to place the cursor at desired fade start, then press D to fade in or G to fade out. As an alternative, you can select the whole clip and press Command+F (Mac) or Ctrl+F (Windows) and apply Batch Fades.

2. Press period (.)+numeric keypad 3+period (.).

3. Press Command+Shift+G (Mac) or Ctrl+Shift+G (Windows).

4. Press the semicolon (;) key to move cursor to FX_02 track, then press Shift+S.

5. Press the T key to zoom in, then press Tab once, then Shift+Tab (three times).

6. Press Command+C (Mac), Ctrl+C (Windows), or the C key (with Commands Focus enabled).

7. Press numeric keypad *, enter timecode number 01:00:32:14, press the Enter or Return key to confirm number, and then press Command+V (Mac), Ctrl+V (Windows), or the V key (with Commands Focus enabled) to paste at the cursor location. Repeat step for timecode number 01:00:34:15.

8. Press Shift+S.

9. Press the P key to move to the FX_01 track, then press numeric keypad *, enter timecode number 01:00:56:21, and press the Enter or Return key to confirm the number.

10. Press Command+Option+numeric keypad plus (+) key (Mac) or Ctrl+Alt+numeric keypad plus (+) key (Windows).

Lesson 5 Answers

1. The Avid PRE communications protocol is an open standard using MIDI.

2. Input source, impedance, phase, high pass filter (HPF), pad, insert, 48-volt phantom power, and gain.

3. 85Hz

4. −18dB

5. 3dB

6. Using an Aux Input track allows you to adjust the record level of the signal with finer increments (0.1dB increments on the Aux Input track instead of PRE's fixed 3dB increments).

7. It allows you to leave an audio track record-enabled while moving and repositioning microphones, without passing on any bumps or other loud sounds to the control room speakers.

8. While Foley artists watch the picture, they use either streamers (also called *wipes*) as a visual cueing system for their recordings or audio beep tones (similar to ADR recording).

9. Audio Foley is always going to be easier to sync to picture, sounding much more natural and more convincing than MIDI Foley, which often requires more editing and mixing to sound acceptable.

10. Sample-based Instrument tracks have an absolute timebase that does not realign clips to the timeline after tempo changes. This allows the recorded MIDI Foley to maintain its sync with the picture, even after tempo changes are applied to other tick-based tracks within the same session.

Lesson 6 Answers

1. Audio conforming is the process of re-editing audio in a Pro Tools session to sync with new picture changes for a film or television project.

2. Third-party sound librarian software offers additional features including Boolean full-text searching, quick searching of massive sound libraries, synonym searches, clip editor with pitch control, multi-user database and network support, support for additional metadata, QuickTime Sync Audition, and a multi-track sequence clip editor.

3. Reverse, Pitch Shift, Time Compression-Expansion (TCE), Digital Delay, Eleven, D-Fi (Lo-Fi, Sci-Fi, Recti-Fi, and Vari-Fi)

4. The Vari-Fi plug-in provides a pitch-change effect similar to a tape deck or record turntable speeding up from or slowing down to a complete stop.

5. Elastic Audio provides the ability to change the speed of the audio with or without changing the pitch, while Elastic Pitch allows you to change the pitch of the audio independently of the speed. Elastic Audio can be used to speed up or slow down ADR (to correct sync), voice-over, music, or sound effects. Elastic Pitch can be used to change the key of music or to pitch a sound effect up/down, creating an all new sound. For example, you could pitch-shift a lion growl down one octave to make it sound like a dinosaur.

6. Monophonic and Varispeed

7. Press Command+Option+numeric keypad plus (+) or minus (–) (Mac) or Ctrl+Alt+numeric keypad plus (+) or minus (–) (Windows).

8. M key (earlier) and the alphanumeric slash (/) key (later)

9. Press Control+numeric keypad plus (+) or minus (–) (Mac) or Start+numeric keypad plus (+) or minus (–) (Windows) to move the material by the current Nudge value.

10. To trim the clip's start point by the current Nudge value, press Option+numeric keypad plus (+) or minus (–) (Mac) or Alt+numeric keypad plus (+) or minus (–) (Windows). To trim the clip's end point by the current Nudge value, press Command+numeric keypad plus (+) or minus (–) (Mac) or Ctrl+numeric keypad plus (+) or minus (–) (Windows).

11. You can create a new playlist on the first selected track by pressing Control+backslash (\) (Mac) or Start+backslash (\) (Windows). You can create a duplicate playlist on the first selected track by pressing Control+Command+backslash (\) (Mac) or Ctrl+Start+backslash (\) (Windows).

Lesson 7 Answers

1. Quantization error is the difference between the original signal's amplitude and the signal described by the measurement scale.

2. Dynamic range is the difference between the quietest signal and the loudest signal a system can reproduce. The theoretical dynamic range of a 24-bit signal is 144dB.

3. Previous-generation Pro Tools|HD hardware uses a 48-bit fixed-point mixer, while Pro Tools|HDX and Pro Tools Native mixers utilize a 64-bit floating-point mixer.

4. Pro Tools|HDX uses 32-bit floating-point DSPs to re-create the 64-bit floating-point mixer, while Pro Tools Native uses the computer's processor to create the mixer. While Native-based systems do not have dedicated DSP chips like Pro Tools|HDX, they utilize the same 64-bit mixer technology, allowing their mixes to run on the dedicated DSPs of Pro Tools HDX and sound nearly identical, while completely off-loading the host-based processor for other tasks (such as processor-intensive virtual instruments). When using AAX-based plug-ins, sessions automatically switch between Native and DSP versions of the plug-ins.

5. Bit depth used for the data pathway on Pro Tools|HD is 24-bit and on Pro Tools|HDX it is 32-bit.

6. Some of the advantages of the Pro Tools|HDX mixer over Pro Tools|HD include the following:

   - HDX uses 32-bit data paths to preserve fidelity and accuracy throughout the mixer.

   - Using floating-point processing allows you to build very large complex mixers using less DSP.

   - Using an FPGA chip to manage voices allows a single card to have more available voices and frees DSP for other processes.

   - The combination of an FPGA chip managing voices, floating-point mixing, and more powerful DSP results in a four to five times increase in processing power versus previous generation Pro Tools|HD Accel cards.

   - 32-bit floating-point processing prevents internal clipping in plug-ins.

   - 64-bit summing allows for an extraordinarily high number of tracks to sum and not clip the inputs of the HD mixer. For example, 512 audio tracks at full code would still not clip the input of a master bus. However, the master bus fader would need to be lowered to –90dB to avoid clipping the outputs.

7. Additional voices are used for routing the plug-ins to the computer's processor and back again.

8. A stereo Auxiliary track would use four additional voices. A stereo audio track would use no more additional voices.

Lesson 8 Answers

1. Choose Setup > I/O Setup > H/W Insert Delay.

2. You will be able to see if stereo bus 5–6 is clipping if you use a Master Fader. The Master Fader's track meters will give you a true reading of the input level of the Aux Submaster channel.

3. Choose Track > Coalesce VCA Master Automation or right-click on the VCA Master's track name and choose Coalesce VCA Master Automation.

4. When Latch Prime is enabled, any parameters that you touch or click in Latch (or Touch/Latch for parameters other than volume) while playback is stopped are "primed" for automation recording. Any track that has primed controls inverts its automation mode indicator from red text on a white background to white text on a red background (just as any automation mode indicator does when writing automation). When you begin playback, the parameters that you have touched or clicked will begin writing.

5. Two families of Write To commands include the following:

    - The Write to All/End/Start/Next/Punch commands (in the Automation window) can be used during playback and stop (if using Write, Latch Prime, or Preview and Capture), writing automation to all parameters that are currently writing or parameters that are isolated in Preview mode.

    - Write to Current and Write to All Enabled (and their variants) only write to parameters on tracks containing an edit selection, and within the current edit selection's time range. The Write to Current and Write to All Enabled commands are considered automation playlist Edit commands, and are unaffected by track automation modes.

6. Auto off disables all of a track's automation parameters for both playback and writing. Preview mode allows you to choose which automation parameters are disabled by simply touching the controls, allowing other automation parameters to play back and write.

7. Command-click (Mac) or Ctrl-click (Windows) the Preview button in the Automation window or Avid worksurface.

8. Capture mode by default captures the settings of any parameters that are currently writing automation, but can also be forced to capture selected or all parameters regardless of their write state. Once captured, these settings can then be written to other locations in the session using Punch Capture. When working with long format post production projects (such as film), you can save time by capturing automation from an earlier point in the project and then applying it to similar audio at a later point in the project.

9. AutoJoin automates the process of resuming automation writing from one pass to the next. With AutoJoin enabled, Pro Tools will remember where playback was stopped and which faders were writing in Latch mode. With that information, if the engineer stops to go back and check or redo part of an automation pass, Pro Tools will resume writing automation for all previously writing controls at the precise position that the previous pass was stopped.

10. The Glide automation commands let you manually create an automation transition (or glide) from an existing automation value to a new one over a selected area. This is useful in post production projects, since it allows controls to smoothly glide (or morph) from one setting to the next, providing smoother and more precise transitions between automated controls (such as plug-ins or volume faders).

Lesson 9 Answers

1. High track count sessions that exceed the processing power or track count of one system, splitting common elements to different systems to allow dual mixers (i.e., a dialogue and music mixer on System 1, with a sound effects mixer on System 2), keeping high-quality HD video on a separate system from the audio playback system because of PCIe bandwidth limitations.

2. 12 total HD systems, or 11 total HD systems with the addition of either a Video Satellite or Video Satellite LE system.

3. Setup > Peripherals > Satellites

4. The Disk Cache setting allows all or most of the audio in a session (depending on available RAM) to be streamed over a network and pre-loaded into a RAM cache before playback starts, so that the network speed and performance are less of an issue.

5. 1

6. Option-click (Mac) or Alt-click (Windows) the Solo button.

7. An AFL-soloed track on a linked system can be muted by a Solo in Place (SIP) on another system. To avoid this, use PFL instead of AFL.

8. All other linked systems stop playback as well.

Lesson 10 Answers

1. Correcting a general sync problem or unintentional offset in a session, all the audio in the session requires a global timecode offset to sync with a videotape master, layback of television commercials starting in the Pro Tools timeline at differing timecode numbers that need to match the correct starting timecode number on a corresponding master videotape.

2. MMC, 9-pin, Sync, and Satellite

3. Command+numeric keypad 6 (Mac) or Ctrl+numeric keypad 6 (Windows)

4. Insert allows you to record only the audio tracks you record arm to the VTR, while Assemble record enables all possible tracks—audio, video, and timecode (or Address track)—on the VTR.

5. Film, NTSC, PAL, and HD video formats do not all run at the same speed, so when converting between any of these formats, a speed change is often necessary to match the video/audio speed of the source and destination format.

6. When Pro Tools is acting as a 9-pin remote device, it can be controlled by other 9-pin devices and also can be used as a printmaster device for creating final deliverables for film and video projects.

7. When using a Windows-based Pro Tools HD hardware system as a remote 9-pin device with a long cable run

8. When Chase LTC is disabled, Pro Tools is in Full Remote mode, responding to all transport commands coming through the serial connection, including bump and crawl commands necessary for a tape machine to locate and cue. When Chase LTC is enabled, Pro Tools can still respond to track arming and record commands. However, Pro Tools will chase incoming LTC instead of serial timecode, behaving as a master or slave device with the machine controller. By slaving Pro Tools to the LTC source instead of slaving the machine to Pro Tools timecode, you can avoid the waiting (and tape wear) that occurs while a machine transport locates and bumps tape to the cue point. Unlike Full Remote mode, Pro Tools waits until it receives only specific transport play, record, and track record commands from the machine (ignoring most other transport commands).

9. DestructivePunch recording allows you to stop in the middle of a printmaster recording to correct a problem in the mix and then pick up where you left off recording, allowing you to append and merge the new resumed recording with the previous to deliver one continuous sound file, saving lots of time.

10. Machine Track Arming Profiles are files that store custom track arming, track naming, and mapping, allowing you to save configurations for different machines. These profiles can then be imported and reused so that you can quickly reconfigure track arming as needed for future projects.

11. This would allow you to sync multiple Pro Tools systems via Satellite Link, while driving other hardware devices connected to a 9-pin synchronizer. Machine Control can be used to operate a 9-pin synchronization device (such as a Soundmaster ATOM or a CB Electronics 9-pin synchronizer), allowing Pro Tools to act as a "timecode-only master" for other systems controlled by the synchronizer while simultaneously syncing with other Pro Tools systems configured in the Satellite Link network.

INDEX

License Agreement/Notice of Limited Warranty

By opening the sealed disc container in this book, you agree to the following terms and conditions. If, upon reading the following license agreement and notice of limited warranty, you cannot agree to the terms and conditions set forth, return the unused book with unopened disc to the place where you purchased it for a refund.

License:

The enclosed software is copyrighted by the copyright holder(s) indicated on the software disc. You are licensed to copy the software onto a single computer for use by a single user and to a backup disc. You may not reproduce, make copies, or distribute copies or rent or lease the software in whole or in part, except with written permission of the copyright holder(s). You may transfer the enclosed disc only together with this license, and only if you destroy all other copies of the software and the transferee agrees to the terms of the license. You may not decompile, reverse assemble, or reverse engineer the software.

Notice of Limited Warranty:

The enclosed disc is warranted by Course Technology to be free of physical defects in materials and workmanship for a period of sixty (60) days from end user's purchase of the book/disc combination. During the sixty-day term of the limited warranty, Course Technology will provide a replacement disc upon the return of a defective disc.

Limited Liability:

THE SOLE REMEDY FOR BREACH OF THIS LIMITED WARRANTY SHALL CONSIST ENTIRELY OF REPLACEMENT OF THE DEFECTIVE DISC. IN NO EVENT SHALL COURSE TECHNOLOGY OR THE AUTHOR BE LIABLE FOR ANY OTHER DAMAGES, INCLUDING LOSS OR CORRUPTION OF DATA, CHANGES IN THE FUNCTIONAL CHARACTERISTICS OF THE HARDWARE OR OPERATING SYSTEM, DELETERIOUS INTERACTION WITH OTHER SOFTWARE, OR ANY OTHER SPECIAL, INCIDENTAL, OR CONSEQUENTIAL DAMAGES THAT MAY ARISE, EVEN IF COURSE TECHNOLOGY AND/OR THE AUTHOR HAS PREVIOUSLY BEEN NOTIFIED THAT THE POSSIBILITY OF SUCH DAMAGES EXISTS.

Disclaimer of Warranties:

COURSE TECHNOLOGY AND THE AUTHOR SPECIFICALLY DISCLAIM ANY AND ALL OTHER WARRANTIES, EITHER EXPRESS OR IMPLIED, INCLUDING WARRANTIES OF MERCHANTABILITY, SUITABILITY TO A PARTICULAR TASK OR PURPOSE, OR FREEDOM FROM ERRORS. SOME STATES DO NOT ALLOW FOR EXCLUSION OF IMPLIED WARRANTIES OR LIMITATION OF INCIDENTAL OR CONSEQUENTIAL DAMAGES, SO THESE LIMITATIONS MIGHT NOT APPLY TO YOU.

Other:

This Agreement is governed by the laws of the State of Massachusetts without regard to choice of law principles. The United Convention of Contracts for the International Sale of Goods is specifically disclaimed. This Agreement constitutes the entire agreement between you and Course Technology regarding use of the software.